JAMES STEWART

Behind the Scenes of a Wonderful Life

JAMES STEWART

Behind the Scenes of a Wonderful Life

LAWRENCE J. QUIRK

APPLAUSE

NEW YORK • LONDON

AN APPLAUSE ORIGINAL
JAMES STEWART Behind the Scenes of a Wonderful Life
© 1997 by Lawrence J. Quirk
ISBN 1-55783-329-X

Library of Congress Cataloging-in-Publication Data

Library of Congress Card Number: 97-80440

British Library Cataloging-in-Publication Data

A catalogue copy of this book is available from the British Library

APPLAUSE BOOKS
211 West 71st Street
New York, NY 10023
Phone (212) 496-7511
Fax: (212) 721-2856

A&C BLACK
Howard Road, Eaton Socon
Huntington, Cambs PE19 3EZ
Phone 0171-242 0946
Fax 0171-831 8478

10   9   8   7   6   5   4   3   2   1

Contents

Acknowledgments . . . . *ix*

1. Introduction 1

2. Daddy's Boy 5

3. Wide-Eyed at Princeton 14

4. Life Upon the Wicked Stage 21

5. Going Hollywood 46

6. Norma, Olivia, Loretta et al. 93

7. Mr. Smith — And Top Stardom 113

8. Off to the Wars 143

9. A Wonderful Renaissance 155

10. A Bridegroom — At 41 186

11. Going West with Macho Mann 196

12. Life on Hitchcock Heights 223

13. Settling In 251

14. Holding His Own 262

15. Tackling TV 295

16. Grand Old Man 307

    The Career of James Stewart:

       Films 322

       Stage Plays 324

       TV 324

    Bibliography 325

    Index 327

Other Titles by Lawrence J. Quirk

Fasten Your Seat Belts: The Passionate Life of Bette Davis

Margaret Sullavan: Child of Fate

Jane Wyman, The Actress & The Woman

Paul Newman

Claudette Colbert

Cher

Lauren Bacall: Her Films & Career

The Kennedys in Hollywood

The Great Romantic Films

Great War Films

The Films of Joan Crawford

The Films of Robert Taylor

The Films of Myrna Loy

The Complete Films of William Powell

The Films of Katharine Hepburn

The Complete Films of Ingrid Bergman

The Films of Warren Beatty

The Films of Ronald Colman

The Films of Frederic March

Dedication

For Don Koll and Bob Dahdah
Two Good and Proven Friends

Acknowledgments

This biography of James Stewart is the result of some thirty years of research and interviews. I am grateful to all those living and dead, those named throughout this book, and others who requested they not be named, all of whom shared memories and impressions of James Stewart with me. Since my career as journalist and biographer began in 1946, on the editorial staff of Hearst's *Boston Record-American*, which led to other newspaper jobs, magazine editing and free-lance writing, and finally, beginning 30 years ago, to authorship of some 30 books, James Stewart was among those special star-favorites of mine on whom I collected all sorts of material, with a view to one day writing his biography. I interviewed, and socialized with, him on a number of occasions over those thirty-odd years, and knew, was friendly with, and interviewed many who had known him personally and had associated with him professionally.

My deep appreciation to my publisher, Glenn Young, my editor Bruce G. Bradley, and my publicist, Kay Radtke, for believing in this book and making it a reality. Thanks also to Paul Sugarman and Jason Ronallo. My thanks also to my colleague William Schoell for his helpful suggestions and input, and to Doug McClelland, who lent some wonderful pictures and clippings and contributed interviews. Also to John Cocchi, who lent fine photographs and was helpful in other ways. Special mention must be made of my old friends Don Koll and Bob Dahdah, to whom this book is dedicated, and who also offered input. And with warm special thanks to my agent, Dimitri Nikolakakos.

Among those who have passed on, I wish to single out the late Billy Grady, Jimmy Stewart's friend and mine, who gave me many wonderful insights into our mutual friend. Also my fond reminiscential appreciation to other old friends, such as the late Ruth Waterbury, the late Adela Rogers St. Johns, the late Helen Ferguson, the late Hedda Hopper, the late Louella and Harriet Parsons; also others now passed on, such as Jim Reid, Mac St. Johns, Jerry Asher, Sonia Wolfson, George Cukor (at age 74 I have, sadly, outlived many, too numerous to mention singly, who helped me with material on Jimmy along the way). And in loving memory of James E. Runyan (1930-1997) a cherished friend and colleague.

Also my warm appreciation to: the late Mike Ritzer (1949-1994) another cherished colleague; Arthur Tower, the late Albert B. Manski (1909–1997), Barbara Barondess MacLean, James Kotsilibas-Davis, Gregory Speck, Douglas Whitney (so generous with pictures on a number of my books), Mary Atwood and Ed Maguire, Lou Valentino, Curtis Roberts, Andy Humm, Mike Snell, John Gallagher, Barry Paris, the late DeWitt Bodeen, Dr. Rose Hayden, John A. Guzman, Jim McGowan, Frank Rowley, the late Howard Otway, and my agent and lawyer's partner in Paris, Dimitri Philopoulos.

Also to the James R. Quirk Memorial Film Symposium and Research Center, New York; Mary Corliss and the Museum of Modern Art's Department of Film; the staff of Margaret Herrick Library of the Academy of Motion Picture Arts and Sciences, Hollywood, and Sam Gill; the British Film Institute, London; Dorothy Swerdlove, Rod Bladel and the current staff of the Billy Rose Collection, New York Public Library at Lincoln Center, New York; Ernest D. Burns and the former Cinemabilia, New York; Ron and Howard Mandelbaum of Photofest, and Jerry Ohlinger's Movie Material Store, New York.

And in fond memory of Henry Hart (1903-1990), Editor of *Films in Review* from 1950 to 1971, and one of my early mentors.

Chapter One

Introduction

James Maitland Stewart always lived in two worlds. In one world he was the conventional solid citizen, war hero, reliable husband and father, hard worker, faithful Republican. In *this* world, he made millions of dollars (money — lots of it — being the legitimate aim of the solid American bourgeois). With the onset of middle age, he became sensible, solid, a paragon of the All-American virtues. He stayed married (after a late start at 41) to one woman, and carefully raised kids who have turned out equally conventional. In advanced old age, he became a pillar of respectability, an icon of the national spirit and aspiration.

And then there was that other James Stewart. Stewart the Artist. The man who plumbed the depths of human complexity and ambivalence in Hitchcock's Vertigo. The man who defied convention as the fey, iconoclastic Elwood P. Dowd in *Harvey*, who, with his friend the invisible rabbit, blithely flouted earthbound manners and mores. And the man who went maniacally angry and destructive in the Anthony Mann Westerns. The artist defied his conventional small-town parents to take up acting, to their distress; the artist eschewed architecture, his Princeton major, for the uncertainties of the New York theatre and its concomitant poverty and insecurity. The artist lived with male roommates almost up to the time of that late marriage. The artist cut a wide romantic swath with numerous lovely ladies until he finally settled down.

The deep ambivalence in James Maitland Stewart has always been apparent.

The Solid Citizen has been paraded in his surface, day-to-day life.

The Artist is to be found, *today*, in his greatest roles, preserved forever on film.

He paid a price for containing those two disparate worlds within himself.

He was the All-American Boy Transcendent, the Super Boy

Scout, the Perfect Image of Decency. He personified Clean-Cut Manliness, Honest Intentions, Lofty Ideals, Noble Aims. The country fell in love with him in *Mr. Smith Goes to Washington* (1939), the archetypical Stewart incarnation: a clean, naïve young Senator who does fierce battle with the forces of political corruption. He wins out in the end because "his strength is as the strength of ten because his heart is pure."

It's a Wonderful Life (1946) showcased another variation on the manly, decent American hero, this time as a small-town businessman who thinks his life has counted for nothing until an angel cues him in on all the terrible things that would have happened, had he never existed.

He was the sweet young soldier who went to France fortified by his love for tough showgirl Margaret Sullavan in *The Shopworn Angel* (1938). Audiences wept *en masse* when he died in battle. When he danced and "sang" with Eleanor Powell, or clowned with Ginger Rogers, or whispered sweet boyish nothings to Katharine Hepburn; when he stood gawky and befuddled before the shattering beauty of Hedy LaMarr; or wept with Carole Lombard, or matched winsome profiles with Jean Arthur, his admirers, out there in the dark, were with him all the way.

A nation gasped — or anyway the fan mag readers did — when in real life, Norma Shearer appropriated a frightened (but game) Jimmy for her very own; and when Joan Crawford — between marriages — attempted to find out what all the shouting was about; and when he awkwardly bumped into Greta Garbo outside her dressing room. They hung breathlessly on stories that he found Jean Harlow "a good kisser" and shyly courted Olivia DeHavilland. They cheered in admiration when he generously declared that Henry Fonda should have won the 1940 Oscar for *The Grapes of Wrath* (Stewart had won it for *The Philadelphia Story* — his consolation prize for *Mr. Smith* the year before).

Everyone knew of his small-town origins, the father he emulated, the All-American mother and sisters he adored; his Triangle Club triumphs at Princeton and his successes on Broadway; and how talent agent Billy Grady discovered him for MGM and how, after a slow start, the Glory Years in Hollywood ensued; and how James Maitland Stewart, sturdy Scots-Irish scion of a sturdy, historically well-rooted, Pennsylvania family, thrived and prospered and bumbled and stumbled into the hearts of his countrymen.

And then there was James Stewart the War Hero, who did his intrepid, patriotic duty as an Air Force pilot flying missions over Germany, with all the resulting decorations and citations and rapidly successive promotions from private to colonel and ultimately to Brigadier–General in the peacetime Air Force Reserve.

Then he enjoyed a triumphant postwar return to Hollywood in the Hitchcock thrillers and the Ford westerns, complemented by his one-and-only, decades-long marriage, and the exemplary paternalism toward his kids, and the sturdy Republicanism and political conservatism. He played Glenn Miller and Monty Stratton and Carbine Williams, all of them, at one time or another, national icons. He revelled in TV successes and a triumphant stage return in *Harvey*. In the fullness of years, he was cited and honored with endless awards, including another (honorary) Oscar, and fêted on his 75th and 80th and 85th birthdays. Larger than life, despite his folksy demeanor, grateful always to an America that had given him "such a wonderful life," he told one interviewer after another that he wanted to be remembered as a hard worker with a love of country, family, community, and God.

Those who tried to get James Maitland Stewart on paper over the sixty-odd years of his career, or those who tried to dig into the truth of the legend about whom "nobody wants to read anything bad" and about whom "nobody should write anything bad," have always been stuck on the horns of a dilemma. If a writer praises him to the skies, recites his triumphs and his feats of character, his solid image as The Ideal American who would have made a better President than Ronald Reagan himself; and tells how he was the Perfect Lindbergh, and the Perfect Reforming Senator, and the Perfect Image of Virtuous, Hardy Small Town Americana — that writer stands accused of being a glorified publicity flack. Worse, of being a cravenly adulatory fan.

On the other hand, should a writer attempt to present James Maitland Stewart in rounded human terms, examining in equal parts his yang and his yin, his strengths and his weaknesses, how his shortcomings ran neck and neck with his virtues; if a writer dared suggest that his penis erected and his armpits broke out in sweat, and that he occasionally stumbled from the path of rectitude and gave in to selfish or lustful impulses and was, if only for a time, "fallen from the Grace of God," he would — this hapless, reckless, iconoclast — be promptly and savagely pilloried by critics, and

smeared by all the Stewart faithful as a scandal-dispensing, charac-
ter-assassinating, money-grubbing, lowlife fit only for the hellish
outer darkness of the *National Enquirer*, *The Star* and other "terrible
tabloids."

So, faced with a damned if you do, damned if you don't
dilemma, what does a writer who honestly and sincerely seeks the
middle road do? What if such a writer wants to show a man as he is,
allowing for the long-proven fact that no human being can ever
really know another completely and fully?

The philosopher George Santayana has asked: if we knew another human being thoroughly and unsparingly would we love them
more or would we love them *less*? And Santayana has his answer right
to hand: We should love that person *more*—*far* more—for we
would understand all the conditionings and myriad influences that
had come together to make that individual the fully human and
complex entity that he or she is.

Over fifty years ago, in the darkness of the Capitol Theater in
the small Massachusetts city of Lynn, I hero-worshipped and sought
to emulate, as much as any right-minded, amiably-dispositioned kid
of sixteen could, the heroic figure of Jimmy Stewart doing battle in
Mr. Smith Goes to Washington. He slew the dragons of human frailty
and evil, and emerged, with his pure, strong heart, the victor. For
me, the actor and the man were one.

The patterns of our surface lives over the decades were to be
very different, Jimmy Stewart's and mine. For years I did not consider myself "*his* kind of man," but now, in my 70s, I have come to
realize that while we seemed outwardly at variance, there were
many *inward* similarities. He has won a far greater fame, he has
made much more money, but I empathize with the inner Jimmy
Stewart. I may not understand perfectly, for we all have our own re-
alities and inner schematics and mystiques, and we are all, in the
final analysis, deep mysteries to one another. But I see him clearly
and I see him whole, as Santayana would have wished for me.

What I hope to reveal in these pages is not directed by the un-
questioning adulation of a fan, nor the unbridled cynicism of a
tabloid iconoclast. It is an honest, humble, objective attempt to
share with you the understanding I have acquired of the complex,
gifted, colorful and yet poignant human being known to the world
as James Maitland Stewart.

Chapter Two

Daddy's Boy

Jimmy Stewart was born on May 20, 1908, a Wednesday, in Indiana, Pennsylvania, a small town with a population of about 7000 in the foothills of the Allegheny Mountains. About fifty miles to the east of Pittsburgh, Indiana was the county seat set smack in the middle of a rural area, and the farmers came in on weekends to shop. One of the busiest and most prominent stores was a hardware establishment called J. M. Stewart and Company. It had been founded by Stewart's grandfather, James Maitland Stewart, for whom he was named. The Stewarts had been in the location for sixty years, their ancestry being Scots-Irish. The original James Maitland Stewart had founded the hardware store in 1853, fifty-five years before his grandson's birth, and later had gone off to fight for the Union Army in the Civil War. When he came back in 1865, he married. His son, Alexander Stewart, went to Princeton, Class of 1898, did service in the Spanish-American War later that same year, then married Miss Elizabeth Jackson, whose father, S. M. Jackson, had been a noted general. The names of Stewart and Jackson went back to the 18th century in American history, and when Alexander and Elizabeth's first and only son was born in that spring of 1908, he was the seventh generation in America. In 1912, Jimmy's sister Mary was born, and in 1914 his sister Virginia.

In his later performances, James Stewart was to evoke small-town life so ably and truly because he was steeped in its manners, mores and values for his first fifteen years, until he went away to school. His father was a hearty, exuberant man, an inch taller than Stewart was to become in his own manhood. "My father was a profound influence on me," Stewart later said. "I spent some of every day with him in the store, and he told me stories about his war experiences and gave me the kind of advice and attention every boy wants from his father and not all get. He was always there for me, and I wanted to be as much like him as possible. My solid values, my ideals, I got from my father and mother. They have served me well."

A hard worker and a prosperous businessman, respected by the whole town, Alexander Stewart nevertheless had his quixotic side. He would accept goods, food and other instruments of barter from the more impoverished farmers and townsmen, in place of cash. "I'll take this chicken for now," he'd say, "and when you have some loose cash you can pay me with that later." Later never came, or if it did, Alex Stewart was more likely than not to say, "Keep it, save it, pay me in cash next time!" As Stewart recalled, "And then *that* next time, it would be the same thing all over again!" Nonetheless the older Stewart was a shrewd businessman. He got his just due from the more prosperous people of the town, "the people who can afford to pay, and should, and don't miss it," and the Stewart family circumstances were comfortable. The hardware store became a prime meeting place for the citizens and neighboring farmers. Alex Stewart was often urged to go into politics, but scorned the notion, saying business was complicated enough "without playing the games and bartering the favors necessary in politics."

Alex's only concession to "that damned political nonsense" was serving as a member of the volunteer fire brigade. His wife Elizabeth played the organ in the Presbyterian Church and ran sewing circles and socials, and was actively involved in benefits for the poor. It was all solid and conventional and straight-arrow. Stewart later recalled that his parents drilled his sisters and himself in the Golden Rule tenets of treating others as one wished to be treated, of being honest and square, of keeping oneself decent and respected.

Bright and lively, young Jim early exhibited an introverted streak, and enjoyed being by himself. His shyness was accentuated by the glasses he had to wear for some years. "He had great inner resources," his sister Virginia later recalled. "The other boys and girls we knew always had to be together, feeding off each other; if they were alone for two minutes, they were lonesome. But Jim was the self-sufficient kind. I wouldn't say he was a loner — other children always liked him, and he could joke and clown with the best — but he could spend a lot of time absolutely alone, his own best company, and never mind it."

One of Jimmy's earliest childhood memories was his father jumping out of bed and clumping down the stairs with his firefighter's equipment and heavy boots, all primed to follow wherever the noisy fire alarm led. Often he followed his father to the fire, and he wound up a pet of the volunteer firemen. One Christmas, to his delight, they presented him with a uniform. He performed chemistry experiments in the basement, once causing a minor explosion. Years later, in Hollywood, one of his characters had to conduct inflammatory experiments in a basement (the film was *You Can't Take It With You* [1938]). Stewart drew on his early experiences to serve as a kind of informal technical advisor. As he recalled it, his mother had a bridge club to the house one day a week, and one of his "flare-ups" from the basement sent all the ladies rushing out of the house, scared out of their wits. Later one of his mother's friends tactfully suggested that the bridge club meetings be held down the street from then on.

On occasion he raided the mammoth stockroom of the hardware store to get the materials for building his own model airplane, an interest that was to become an adult passion. He got a model "aeroplane," as it was called circa-1914, as a Christmas present, and, at age 9, made a larger version from wood and canvas that he drove around pretending it was about to take off. "Then, on a dare, he took it up onto a roof and nearly broke his neck trying to fly off on it," as one writer who had spoken to his sisters, reported it.

Like chemistry, radio would later become one of his passions and his father helped him build little crystal sets. He was a good and conscientious Boy Scout, well liked by the other boys. Magic tricks became another obsession.

His father encouraged him in every pursuit he showed interest in, but he was also strict. Gruff but essentially kind, Alexander Stewart applied discipline and affection in equal parts, as did his mother. "My mother was a quiet, reserved little lady," Stewart later recalled, "while my father was big and boisterous and loud and tended to be domineering. But she always knew how to handle him, with her patience and persistence, and she got her own way more often than not."

Anticipating a passion he was to indulge in late middle age, Stewart, at 12, was intent on going on an African safari of the kind popularized by Teddy Roosevelt. His father encouraged him in this, too, but managed to drag out the "preparations" so long that his son, already distracted by another enthusiasm, postponed the African trip "until I'm really ready."

Stewart's memories of that early period were mellow and positive. He remembered that at the age of eight, in 1916, his father moved the family to a larger house in the Indiana suburb of Vinegar Hill. He was to recall it as "a rambling house of no particular architecture but with a large front porch loaded with wicker furniture. The living room, high-ceilinged and trimmed with dark woodwork, held a grand piano, around which we gathered for family sings."

His sister Virginia played piano, his other sister, Mary, the violin. His father taught him to play the accordion, a skill which was to come in handy when his acting career began. "I was never all that good at it, but I got by," he was to say later. He remembers that during their soirées his father "sang very softly — compared to the bellowing he did in Church — so as not to cover up Mother's clear, sweet voice."

When young Jimmy was nine, the United States entered into World War I. His father, always a gung-ho patriot, as had been his grandfather, went off to fight for the second time. Though now in his forties, he told the family and his friends in Indiana that he felt it his duty, and he was soon a captain in the Ordnance Corps, based at Camp Dodge in Iowa. "You are the man of the house for now," his father told Jimmy when he left, "so act accordingly. I shall hold you responsible until I return."

While making sure that his mother and sisters were "protected and cared for," as he wrote his father, young Jimmy was working up a lot of patriotic steam on his own. He started writing and performing plays, which he showed to local children in the basement. They had titles like *To Hell With the Kaiser* and *The Slacker*, described by him as "a no-good who redeems himself and goes off to war and makes a man of himself." In 1918, when his army captain father was home on a visit, an enthusiastic Jimmy put on *To Hell With the Kaiser* for him and the family upstairs in the drawing room. He later recalled his father being red-faced and spluttering through some of the performance. "He was too kind to tell me he could hardly keep from laughing."

His sister Virginia was to recall, "Jim was terribly intense about his plays, just as he is about everything he gets interested in. There are no halfway measures with him." The theatrical performances ceased as of 1919 when his father returned and was again master of the store and the house. "He sensed that his father didn't care for actors and show business, thought them foppish, shifty types of people, so he played that down for a while," Mary recalled.

Throughout these years Stewart did odd jobs in his father's store, ran errands and made deliveries on his bicycle. By 1920 one of his main interests was again aviation. He hero-worshipped the retired aviators from the war who went through Pennsylvania towns starring in stunt shows and offering rides in dangerously rickety aircraft. His mother was nervous about this new enthusiasm and begged 14-year-old Jimmy not to "go up in one of those hellish, dangerous contraptions." His father overruled her, saying "the boy is not to cultivate fear — if we forbid him, he will start getting fear thoughts about a lot of things." So Jimmy rode in one of the aircraft, with his mother watching nervously, and his father proudly, from the ground. The cost, as he recalled, was fifteen dollars for fifteen minutes, "a dollar a minute," his father warned. "You'll have to do extra work in the store if you want me to advance *that*!" Alex later told Billy Grady, "I liked his spunk and his fearlessness, so I advanced him the money. He paid it back to me, too — every damned cent, though it took him several months."

Jimmy Stewart was later to say of his childhood and adolescence: "I can't recall anything unpleasant. Those things I remember best were getting my first long trousers when I was halfway through high school, vacationing in Atlantic City during the summer, and not particularly liking school because I was only a fair student."

Jimmy, with his father's amused encouragement, continued perfecting his accordion skills. As he later recalled it, his father got an accordion as a barter object and at first gave it to Virginia, hoping she'd take it up. But she thought it too cumbersome, so it went to Jim. Jim joined the Boy Scout Band and was soon playing it rather skillfully, as his father admitted, in their weekly concerts.

Alexander Stewart believed in cultivating the habits of work, sobriety, self-discipline and general steadiness. Jim was told he would have to work after school and on Saturdays at fixed hours, not only in the Stewart store but via any handyman work he could find among the neighbors and other shopkeepers. "My love for hard work came from those years," he said later. "My father always said, 'Be steady, be persistent, be respected, do your part, hold up your end at all times!' I guess those early lessons stuck."

By age 15, Jimmy Stewart was an impressionable but balanced

adolescent coping with his new physical urges as best he could, and keeping busy with exercise, jobs, and social life. He learned to dance at the socials, and taught his sisters, then 9 and 11 respectively, the new steps. "We looked up to him, worshipped him," Mary later said. "He was always there for us, never pulled his age-rank, always spoke to us on our own age-level but was nonetheless protective."

That year, 1923, when he turned 15, he always recalled as the year of President Harding's death. The President had died on August 2 in San Francisco, while on a trans-national tour. The funeral cortege, via train, was scheduled to pass through Pennsylvania on its way East, but at a point twenty miles away. As Stewart later recalled it, "I wanted desperately to go and see this train, but Mother pointed out that it passed at 3:30 in the morning of a school day. And that ended the discussion. At 2:30 that morning, however, I was awakened by Dad's hand on my shoulder. He said, in a voice as near to a whisper as his nature would allow: 'Jim boy, get up! It's time to go and see the funeral train!' We drove the twenty miles through the night without talking much, but bound together by the comradeship of disobedience."

Virginia and his mother both agreed later that Stewart wanted to be as much like his father as possible. "That was the best compliment you could pay him," his mother recalled. "He positively glowed when you told him he was 'just like your dad.'"

But Myron McCormick, who was to room with him years later when they were starving young actors together, recalled him talking of those years with a mingling of affection and regret. "I worshipped my parents and felt protective toward my sisters; I knew I had to please the folks and set Virginia and Mary an example," he told him. "But in some ways I was lonely then—*damned* lonely!" He told Myron that there were things "you just couldn't talk to Dad about—like playing with yourself and what to do about girls or about other people" (here, McCormick recalled, he didn't specify) "who would approach me in a funny way in the woods or at the toilet in the town hall." When Jimmy would try to broach these subjects, Alexander Stewart would redden and bluster and say, "These are things you'll find out for yourself in time; they're not fit to talk about! Just keep clean and decent and self-respecting, and other people will treat you the way *you* want to be treated!"

The household, he later recalled, was female-ruled; his father saved all-out rule for the store. So it was from his mother and sisters he learned respect for women. "Treat every girl you meet as you would your mother and sisters," Elizabeth Jackson Stewart would tell him. "If you hurt or dishonor a girl, you are hurting and dishonoring yourself as well as her. You must never have anything like that on your conscience, or staining your soul." From other boys, teachers, and in one session with the Presbyterian minister (which Stewart was to recall as "more embarrassing than anything else"), he got a general idea that there were "girls who went bad, and infected men" and that there were "bad places where bad men bought girls and took them to bed." Jokes were made about the town hall men's toilet where "sick, bad men" stalked young boys and men. Oddly, it was his mother who broached, albeit gingerly, the subject of sex. "Keep your body pure and clean — save it for the girl you one day marry," she would say to him, in her best Presbyterian manner. "Your body is the temple of the Holy Spirit and it must never be defiled!"

Jim shied away, as he later told McCormick, from the coarser pursuits of the youngsters about him ("I doubt he even attended a circle-jerk," Henry Fonda was later to laugh, "though I'm sure that, alone, he did what all of us did — if he didn't, he was either an adolescent saint or a eunuch"). Always conscious of his "sacred duty" to the parents he loved and "the necessity of setting a good example" to his impressionable younger sisters, the adolescent James Stewart seems to have suffered a great deal of frustration and emotional displacement. Nevertheless, to fan-mag biographers and writers he persisted in talking of those years as "happy and uncomplicated and wholesome."

One of his great comforts and amusements was his grandfather, the original James Maitland Stewart, who lived to a very great age and was around into the 1930s. "Grandfather was very down-to-earth and sensible, quite alert for his advanced years," Jim told John Swope, another roommate, years later. "Once I tried to talk about love and girls, and even sex, to him, and he gave me the best answer I ever remember at the time. 'Things have a way of sorting themselves out,' he said. 'Make do with each day's problems and challenges and handle them the way that makes you feel easiest, and don't get too worked up if you make mistakes or do things you feel you need to. It's not a crime to be human — make allowances for yourself. There are no saints or heroes around here, or anywhere else. Just ordinary people making do their own way.'"

And that was how James Stewart, as he turned 15, came to conceive of himself: as an ordinary guy making do the best he could, trying always to be his best self, but not unduly depressed if he occasionally "fell from the grace of God" as the minister put it. "But I think he did try to be the best boy in all the world," John Swope said later, recalling the all-night "bull sessions" he and Stewart had as roommates in Hollywood, when they discussed their childhood and formative influences. "And I think he paid a heavy price for it later. That 'Super-ego-Id' thing — it gave him a *hell* of a lot of trouble!"

This, then, was the Jimmy Stewart who went to Mercersburg Academy in the fall of 1923. Alexander Stewart, Princeton '98, was determined that his son should follow in his footsteps, and Mercersburg offered one of the best college preparatory curriculums that could be found at the time. Comfortable but not rich, Stewart the Elder vowed to give all three of his children solid educations. "A good education is like a rubber tire," he used to say. "It carries you through the bumps of later life. Nothing can be accomplished without it." Jimmy's classmates at Mercersburg, from 1923-28, found him a shy but humorous boy who treated girls (whenever they showed up for dances or socials) "like a gentleman." He went out for the sports he felt himself best suited for, notably track and football. "He said he was too light for football and never should have attempted it," McCormick later recalled," but at track he was fleet and swift and did rather well at it." As a high hurdler and high jumper he was to excel, and even in the football sphere he forced himself into the captaincy of the "lightweight team."

Alex and Elizabeth were pleased when Jimmy wrote home that he had been accepted by the choir and the glee club. Just before matriculating at Mercersburg he had met a young magician named Bill Neff. They worked up an amateur act featuring magic and accordion playing, which they later toured professionally to raise money during lean periods. Bill Neff, according to Swope, "was Jim's first real friend. He always spoke of Bill Neff with special affection, though there *was* an element of reserve when he spoke of him." In Swope's opinion, "Bill opened up Jim emotionally, led him to new horizons, fed the artist in him. This he never could get from his father. His father's attitude, even after Jim became famous as an actor, was that show people, or artists or whatever, were suspect: shifty, morally shaky." According to Myron McCormick, who was also to hear about the young magician, "Neff was the one who gave him the courage to be himself, in the end; to strike out, to explore 'beyond the horizon' of conventional small town manners and mores."

"My long legs were a help in track," Stewart was later to say of the Mercersburg years, "but I never overcame a certain awkwardness, and I resorted to clowning to cover up my self-consciousness. I shot up in height, to my *father's* height, and when I'd come back from school summers, I'd get a kick out of his surprise. 'You've put on two more inches, boy!' he'd invariably say in greeting. 'When's it going to stop!'"

According to McCormick, it was Bill Neff who encouraged Jimmy, at 16, to take up drawing and painting, and he became, at 17, art director of the yearbook. Singing in the choir and the glee club, and playing the accordion in the Mercersburg school orchestra, led Jimmy to amateur dramatics. In his senior year, 1927-28, he went after, and won, a role in a school play called *The Wolves*. In the summers between 1923 and 1928, Jim invariably went back to Indiana, where he did hard physical labor to build himself up, such as pouring highway cement and working for a construction company as a brick placer.

He was later to say that he had no girlfriends from age 15 to age 20, the years he was at Mercersburg. "He said he was inhibited around them," Swope recalled. "He had the classic variation, even in those tender years, of the Madonna-Whore complex. *Good* girls were to be respected, *bad* girls avoided . . . . His mother's well-meant injunctions had sunk in *too* well — more than she had intended, perhaps."

Chapter Three

Wide-Eyed at Princeton

Princeton had actually been Stewart's second choice—after the United States Naval Academy at Annapolis. "I had some romantic idea at the time—I was 20—that the career of a Naval Officer would be fulfilling," he reminisced. "Snappy uniforms, adventures on the high seas, that kind of thing!"

His father, back in Indiana that summer, soon talked him out of that. 1928 was Alex Stewart's thirtieth anniversary of his own graduation from Princeton, and nothing would do but for Jim to carry on the family tradition there. While he did hard physical labor on the highway that June, Stewart decided that Princeton would be it.

The bashful, gangling young man who showed up at the glamorous college in the handsome little New Jersey town that fall wasn't quite sure what to do with himself. He was, he reasoned sourly, only the son of a modest Pennsylvania hardware-store proprietor. He didn't think himself handsome. He had none of the airs and graces, the snappy suits and stiff, angular posturings of the boys from the top families who belonged to the best clubs. His father, to be sure, had provided generously for his first year, but the young Jim tormented himself with what his mother, in her letters, called his "false guilt." "Father wants you at his alma mater; a good education from a top school will serve you well all your life. Just take solid, sensible courses and get decent grades. That is where your responsibility lies." From these words she had written him, he tried to take heart and plan just such a sensible course.

The curriculum represented an embarrassment of riches, as he recalled, or was it only an embarrassment? Wrong moves could be fatal. Time marched on and, at 20, he was several years older than the average freshman. He must not let the folks at home down.

Lonely, masturbatory, fretful, he had not yet formed any real friendships on the eminent campus. At first he elected for courses in electrical engineering, but his grades in mathematics were too weak to sustain these, and he shifted to political science. Bored by this course, he went on to geometry, a descriptive, introductory kind that guided the student into making model houses and bridges. Since this reflected a pursuit he had enjoyed in earlier years, he finally hunkered down to studies leading to a degree in architecture.

Alexander and Elizabeth at home were glad to learn that he was finally "main-lining" in something that interested him. He didn't disillusion them by telling them that his interest was only relative. For the next four years, he was to doggedly pursue the architectural studies that led him to a 1932 degree, at 24. His father called this major "good, solid, with a future," adding: "Good money can be made in that field! And at Princeton you may make the connections that will lead to your first architectural job."

Unfortunately, young Jim had not wormed himself into the "top" clubs where he would have made the contacts with the architectural movers-and-shakers' sons — one of whom, in Alex's hopeful schemes, would one day take him home to meet Dad — and then it would be off to the races!

That fall, however, Jimmy met a man who was to change the course of his life.

Joshua Logan, born October 5, 1908, in Texarkana, Texas, had spent his childhood in Mansfield, Louisiana. He was four-and-a-half months' Stewart's junior, but was a school year ahead of him, in the Princeton Class of '31. Mercurial, high-strung, living constantly in his emotions, Logan had had a childhood and adolescence very different from Stewart's. His lumberjack father had died when he was three; much later he learned that the deceased had been mentally ill and a suicide. Always on the edge, stretching his nerves to the limit, Josh Logan was to have several mental breakdowns during the course of a brilliant career as a director and playwright. Neurotic, bisexual, oversexed, passionate, and overwhelmingly charismatic, he was a ruggedly handsome man in 1928. His mother had remarried to an Army officer who taught at Culver Military Academy, where Josh had matriculated, and where he had headed a boxing team. Called a "sissy" throughout his boyhood, he had been toughened up by his stepfather, and at 20 was wobbling wildly between his macho posturings and his artistic aspirations. He was busily (some said maniacally) acting out his dichotomy in the Triangle Club, Princeton's famous theatrical group, and at Theatre Intime, a drama group.

In his autobiography, Josh Logan tells of his first encounter, as a Junior, with that "lanky, drawling sophomore, Jimmy Stewart." Logan immediately sensed the warmth and the sensitivity beneath the reserve, the wounded self-image, the uncertainty. As a Big Man on Campus, and the elected President of the Triangle Club, Logan was gathering an organization about him that would later blossom into the University Players, which he helped found with his friend, Charlie Leatherbee. He later toured Russia, winning a scholarship to the Moscow Arts Theatre, where he met Stanislavsky and came back with fresh, exciting theories he would shortly be applying in the American theatre.

As Logan recalled it, he was determined to write something to showcase Stewart. He had learned that Jimmy played the accordion, and he drew out of the diffident, stammering young man that he had acted in amateur theatricals at Mercersburg. Logan perceived the inner glow under the shyness; he decided to fan it into a flame. So he prepared a Triangle Show — to star James Stewart. As he remembered it:

"My show was called *The Tiger Smiles*, and the juvenile lead was written for [Jimmy] with his droll Pennsylvania drawl in mind. He spoke in a stately pavane even then. He still felt he was an architect. This stage 'monkey business' was just fun. But he was so good I knew deep down he loved acting but was too embarrassed to admit it. *The Tiger Smiles* opened at the McCarter Theatre and was well-received. [Jim] was gangling and hilarious singing and dancing 'On a Sunday Evening,' which I had written for him. He winced as he sang my corny rhymes."

As Jimmy opened up more and more to Josh and his troupe, he began to sing old songs from his earlier years, while they drank and kibitzed until four in the morning. Josh later remembered the names of a few of those songs: "Itsy and Boo-Boo," "Flamin' Mamie," "Fat Phoebe and Ruth." Years later, Josh Logan was to say of Stewart, "Get a few drinks in Jim and all that shyness and awkwardness would disappear as if by magic. The personality buried deep down was exciting, dramatic, intense!"

Josh had written some lines and songs into *The Tiger Smiles* for himself. There is an interesting extant picture of Jimmy and Josh singing together, with Jimmy in a high collar and fancy vest with a wide lapel and a funny gray hat; Josh is in a visor cap and athletic sweater with a beer mug in his hand. They look alive and excited and glowing: the interaction between them is clear to any beholder.

Among other productions that Stewart appeared in for the Princeton Triangle Club and Theatre Intime was *The Golden Dog*, in which he played the accordion in a snappy, amusing number entitled "Blue Hell." The Triangle Club Musical, which toured nationally at Christmas and on other occasions, found him conspicuously cast as actor and musician. Decades later, Josh Logan was to say that his favorite rendition of Stewart's in the Princeton period was an accordion solo, "So Beats My Heart for You."

Kent Smith and Myron McCormick remembered that they felt that the Logan-Stewart juxtaposition was (in Smith's words) "like a love affair. They got completely wrapped up in each other." Josh's hitherto "best friend," the Harvard boy Charlie Leatherbee, later married Josh's sister, and died young. Stewart and Logan became inseparable around the campus during the day and far into the night in each other's rooms.

"It was the 'opposites-attract' principle," Myron McCormick said. "Jimmy, so shy and introverted and gangling and unsure of himself (*except* when he was on stage performing), and Josh so egoistic, pushy, ambitious, and strongly masculine. There was a mutual pull there — a strong one."

If Stewart at 20 did fall in love with Logan, as a number of people have indicated, it must have been the first, and greatest, romance of his life. Now he was able to externalize all those yearnings and needs that in darker, more private moments, at home in Indiana and later at Mercersburg, he had only partially acknowledged to himself. With Josh he was spiritually galvanized; he came truly alive. From all he has written and said, and from all who have talked about the relationship, Josh Logan apparently reciprocated what Jimmy felt, and drew sustenance from it. The strong character and the steady decency that Stewart's background had made so rock-solid, became a kind of comfort and anchor for Logan's own inner confusion, his inability to handle his odd blend of macho physicality and artistic explosiveness. Stewart, stable and dependable, governed his feelings and impulses in a way that the impetuous, highly manic Logan could only envy and never quite emulate. In later years, Logan would speak of Stewart only in the warmest, most respectful terms.

For the years that would immediately follow, their relationship would be one of utmost intimacy, in varying settings.

Then along came a young woman with whom both men fell in love. While both seem to have made a conscious effort to keep their attraction to women (or bisexuality, to use later parlance) alive, in the case of Margaret Sullavan it didn't take any effort. All came naturally with her. But while Logan felt a deep attraction, for Stewart it was love at first sight, and was to remain love for all the years that followed.

In 1932, Stewart's senior year, Margaret Sullavan was invited to be the Triangle Club's guest in the Princeton commencement play. (She had Joined Logan's University Players in West Falmouth, Mass., in 1929.) For some time, and by popular demand, Logan, who graduated in 1931, had boosted her. As Josh told it, Sullavan had been on tour with Preston Sturges' hot comedy, *Strictly Dishonorable*, and was already a Broadway veteran. In 1931, she had made a hit in New York in a slight comedy called *A Modern Virgin*. Stewart in Princeton found himself the stage manager for Sullavan's Triangle debut, *The Artist and the Lady*, and they met for the first time on the set.

Logan described the impression Margaret Sullavan made on all comers: "She had a pulsing and husky voice which could suddenly switch, in emotional moments to a high choirboy soprano. Her beauty was not obvious or even standard. It showed as she tilted her head, as she walked, as she laughed, and she was breathtakingly beautiful as she ran!"

Born in 1909 in Norfolk, Virginia, Sullavan had studied dance and drama from childhood, and had become an actress at 19; nothing else in the world would do for her. A year after Stewart met her she would go to Hollywood and win immediate stardom in *Only Yesterday* (1933) for Universal, where she was under contract. She was then to go on to become one of the great screen legends, in films like *Three Comrades* (1938), *Back Street* (1941), and *The Shop Around the Corner* (1940). But in 1932 she had just ended a short-lived marriage to a sensitive, gangling young actor named Henry Fonda, whose heart she had so thoroughly broken that his career was temporarily short-circuited. Sullavan, in short, was a classic *femme fatale* who had a strong nymphomaniacal streak which led her into numerous promiscuous affairs. The devastating effect that she had on the vulnerable Fonda during their marriage was described by him later in his autobiography, when he found her cheating on him in their Greenwich Village apartment with producer Jed Harris (who was as much a satyr as Sullavan was a nymphomaniac).

Fonda described his marriage to Sullavan as "like living with lightning. Her tantrums struck at any hour and on any subject. Scenes are what actors play best, and Sullavan created them about everything, the weather, the food they ate, the clothes she wore… time after time that slender girl's words stung me like a wasp." He went on: "It got to the point where we didn't live on love. We were at each other constantly, screaming, arguing, fighting." She ridiculed the nervous and humiliated Fonda's premature ejaculations, hinted at his bisexuality, and when her career soared as his foundered, she gloated over him mercilessly, before finally deserting him. Later in Hollywood, when his screen career caught up with hers, they would resume as friends, even make a movie together (*The Moon's Our Home*, 1936). But the memories of what they had gone through would never be completely laid to rest.

At the time he met her, Stewart had heard of her tempestuous year-long marriage to Fonda, her restless pursuit of any man who took her fancy, and her stinging, sharp tongue. His cautious nature recoiled from her freewheeling lifestyle, yet he was in love, too. Barbara O'Neil, who was a member of the University Players (along with Kent Smith, McCormick, Fonda, Logan and others), felt that his caution won out over his infatuation with her. But the deciding factor in the transmutation of his love into a lasting friendship was Sullavan's motherly-sisterly protectiveness toward him. "He was a lost lamb in the jungle," Sullavan told O'Neil. "He would have broken like the finest china if we had ever had an intimate relationship. I couldn't do that to him. He was too sweet and nice then." Then as O'Neil recalled it, she added: "The kid isn't my type anyway; he's too shy and nervous; it would be Fonda all over again. Only *worse!*"

Fonda and Stewart had met earlier, but their friendship did not really get on the rails until 1932. Devastated by the Sullavan fiasco, unsure of his sexual identity, Fonda was tottering uncertainly. Reputedly he had succumbed to the attentions of older men in a position to help him, or at least keep him from starving. As Logan later recalled, "Hank's masculinity had been so wounded by Maggie that it's a wonder he hadn't gone permanently impotent!"

This man, who was to emerge as one of Hollywood's greatest stars, had been born in 1905 in Nebraska. In 1925, after two years at the University of Minnesota, he joined the Omaha Community Playhouse (at the behest of Marlon Brando's mother!) where he learned his craft as an actor for three years. The year 1928, age 23, found him playing in summer stock in New England, where he met up with Logan, Mildred Natwick, Myron McCormick and the other University Players. Invited to enlist in their group, he soon found himself acting opposite Sullavan, who joined them whenever her schedule permitted. Their acting, as Josh Logan later recalled, "burned up the stage. Those love scenes were something; they were in a world of their own."

But in 1932 this was all behind him, and a discouraged Fonda had tried his luck (mostly bad) in New York, while the Players made plans for the summer season.

The University Players had attracted the interest of a Broadway producer named Arthur Beckhard, who used them to try out road companies and trial appearances for his actors and plays. His wife, Esther Dale, later the popular Hollywood character actress, had starred in a play, called *Carry Nation* (spelled Carry not Carr*ie*), which Beckhard was anxious to preview with Broadway in mind. Described by Logan as "ten years our senior, owlish, seemingly benign, with a soup-strainer black moustache and puckish ways," Beckhard had, in Logan's words, "convinced us to try out two or three plays for him [the summer of 1932]. We were flattered; a real Broadway success was interested in collaborating with us. Before we knew it, he was swallowing our company." Beckhard had two plays in mind for a fall 1932 production on Broadway: *Carry Nation* with his wife, and *Goodbye Again*, a new play by Allan Scott and George Haight. Howard Lindsay starred in it that summer, but the role was taken over on Broadway by Osgood Perkins (father of Anthony).

Graduating that June of 1932 with a B.S. in Architecture, Stewart was worried about his future. It was the bottom of the Depression, and very little building was going on; in fact most architects — and other specialists — were tramping the streets looking for jobs. He tentatively applied for a scholarship for a Masters in Architecture at Princeton, and debated whether he should go back to Indiana, Pennsylvania for the summer, and work in the hardware store.

Chapter Four

Life Upon the Wicked Stage

But Stewart was still very much under Logan's spell. When the latter indicated that an accordion player would be welcome to entertain the guests at the tea-room attached to the West Falmouth theatre, Jimmy snapped at it. For added bait, Stewart was offered occasional bits on stage. As he remembered, "I was a terrible accordion player. The guests ran at sight of me, and I was switched pronto to the theatre!"

After fooling around awkwardly with props and doing go-fer duty, Stewart was suddenly catapulted into a role in the University Players' opening production that June of 1932. It was a revival of *Magnolia*, Booth Tarkington's sardonic Southern comedy that had been on Broadway in 1923. Logan directed Stewart with special care, with felicitous results, and later recalled that he "was howlingly funny in it as a lanky Southern slob." Next Logan directed him in a play called *It's a Wise Child* by Laurence E. Johnston. His performance in this was so striking that Logan decided once and for all that his friend was "a fine actor — honest and talented." With Fonda gone and Sullavan otherwise occupied, Logan felt that "Perhaps [Jimmy] could carry us all on his shoulders — as Fonda and Sullavan could have done."

Stewart continued on successfully with the University Players, showing an amazing range and adaptability in whatever parts Logan could find for him. But by August 1932 he found that decision time was looming. Princeton had awarded him the scholarship for graduate study in architecture. "I thought it all over very carefully," he later recalled. "My sisters Mary and Virginia were growing up right behind me. Mary was scheduled for an art course at Carnegie Tech, Virginia was going to Vassar. If I went back to Princeton my tuition would cost nothing, but I would need money for food and clothes. I'd be an added expense. Dad didn't seem to worry about it, but I did. Money at home wasn't limitless. I knew that and I felt I had had my share. I wrote the trustees expressing my appreciation for the scholarship and I wrote Dad telling him what I had done!"

Later, on a brief visit home to Pennsylvania, Stewart sat the family down and told them that acting was his first love, that nothing else in the world would do, that he had to face his own individual needs and aspirations, and was prepared to take his chances. His father and mother both told him that it was "a vagabondish, uncertain, pathetic life," and that his chances of ever making a real living were minuscule. He countered that there was no work to be had in architecture, or anywhere else for that matter, that he couldn't see himself settling down in the hardware store. "Find a nice girl back here, and get married, and carry on the family business; you'll be safe and secure, among the people who care about you," his father argued. But Stewart remained adamant, and returned to New York with a tiny stake from his father that was soon gone.

Meanwhile Arthur Beckhard, to Logan's annoyance, had moved in on the University Players, and eventually took it over. The players did a brief season in Baltimore that September of 1932, but their trust turned to disillusionment and, finally, anger when Beckhard took them all to New York to open *Carry Nation*, on October 28, 1932. The Players at that time were Mildred Natwick, Logan, McCormick, Bretaigne "Windy" Windust, later a famed director, Stewart, Cynthia Rogers, Kent Smith, Barbara O'Neil and Norris Houghton. Beckhard got most of them involved with *Carry Nation*.

Esther Dale had been a talented concert lieder singer, but acting was new to her. Logan and the others were mightily surprised when Mrs. Arthur Beckhard proved herself a fine stage actress. But the play was thoroughly panned by the critics, and in his first Broadway role, as one Constable Cane, hardly more than a bit, Stewart found himself utterly ignored. *Carry Nation*, of course, had been a maniacally cartoonish crusader against liquor, tobacco and just about anything else that came to mind, and Esther Dale played her broadly and raucously under the direction of Blanche Yurka, which, as Logan later recalled, "was the only way she could possibly have been played." Stubborn, bigoted, offensive, Carry Nation was not an appealing figure, certainly not to Depression audiences, and the run was short-lived. Stewart later counted, as the only plus, the satisfaction that he and his friends felt at finally hitting Broadway. He also enjoyed the clever and astute direction of Blanche Yurka, the noted actress, whom he would later support in another play.

But Beckhard had another card up his sleeve with *Goodbye Again*. On December 28, 1932, Beckhard opened it with Osgood Perkins starring, and it was an immediate hit, running for a total of 200 performances. Stewart had gotten some laughs with a walk-on part in the Falmouth tryout, and Beckhard took him on for the Broadway run. The plot has to do with a temperamental and authoritative author (Perkins) who goes on a lecture tour where he meets an old flame. She tries to resume with him, but is foiled by the author's secretary, who is secretly in love with him and wins her man in the end. *Goodbye Again* won Stewart his first good notice in the Broadway theatre. He had just two lines as the chauffeur. He brought a book into the author's living room and gave it to the butler. In the first line, he said: "Mrs. Belle Irving would sure appreciate it if she could have this book autographed." The second line came when the author relayed his refusal through the butler: "Mrs. Belle Irving is going to be sore as hell!" That latter line brought down the Broadway house as it had the one in Falmouth. As actor Myron McCormick remembered it, "Jimmy said it with such a drawling, almost snarling comic outrage that the audience broke up!"

Nor were the critics, this time around, impervious to the 24-year-old actor's attractions. The *New York Sun* critic pronounced, "It seems apropos to say a few words about James Stewart, a player in this mad piece, who is on the stage for exactly three minutes and speaks no more than two lines. Yet before this gentleman exits, he makes a definite impression on audiences because he makes them laugh so hard."

Stewart was to cite the star, Osgood Perkins (father of Anthony), as one of his first influences in the theatre. Perkins, who died prematurely in 1937 at the age of 45, was a seasoned professional of both stage and screen. Long of face, saturnine, brooding, with a small, well-cut moustache, Perkins was one of the great technicians of his time, and while waiting to get his one laugh, Stewart enjoyed standing in the wings watching him go through his high-comedy paces. "He was a wonderful listener and reactor," Stewart remembered, "and he had grace and flawless timing. He was one of my original acting models—just to watch him, night after night, was an education in acting." Stewart added that he felt sorry when Perkins died in 1937, "with so much he might yet have accomplished. I felt sorry that Tony Perkins, who was five when he died, never knew this wonderful man who was his father." (Stewart was to express great satisfaction when Tony Perkins later named one of his own sons Osgood.)

Meanwhile, offstage, Josh Logan, who had been serving as company manager and in the box office, proposed that he, Stewart and Myron McCormick move in together to save money. As he later recalled it: "With Jimmy now making thirty-five dollars [weekly] and Myron thirty, we took a small, smelly apartment on West Sixty-Third Street just off Central Park West. It consisted of a soot-colored bedroom with twin beds, a living room with two spring studio couches, a bathroom with a mildewed shower, and a huge kitchen stove out in the hall." A totally broke and starving Fonda, embittered by Sullavan's mistreatment, his room rent on his West 40th Street fleabag overdue, soon joined them, declaring that as soon as he landed something he'd pay his share of the expenses. Gangster Legs Diamond lived (and died violently) nearby at the Majestic. The apartment house swarmed with prostitutes, their pimps and their johns. Odd people showed up in the hall, and even invaded the premises; Josh and Jimmy would steer them to the prostitutes across the hall. "We drank, laughed, listened to good jazz, rotated our sleeping arrangements so as to leave the living-room couches to those who had dates," Logan later remembered. Often Logan and Fonda would go over to the YMCA across West 63rd Street to work out and swim.

Josh noted that Stewart, despite the ups and downs of their existence, had developed by that time an all-consuming passion for the theatre. He and McCormick, who was to do well in radio, had little trouble in finding jobs as compared to Fonda, who "had the worst luck at that time," as McCormick remembered. "It was very humiliating for him, and it was Jimmy who kept his spirits up, lent him money, fed him."

Everything comes in threes, as the saying goes. As Logan and Sullavan had profoundly affected him, now Fonda became the passion of Stewart's life. They found that they had much in common. Both were lanky, both were shy, both had known rejection and defeat, and both shared a deep feeling for Sullavan, whose success had hitherto far surpassed theirs. Fonda's memories of her were bittersweet: he said that she had taken part of his manhood with her when she left him. Stewart still saw her through the eyes of a suitor who had found her unattainable, as someone he had deeply loved but whose destructiveness he feared. Slowly they grew close to one another, the wounded 28-year-old from Nebraska and the introverted 25-year-old from Pennsylvania. By the time 1933 arrived, they had forged a deep friendship, indeed a profound love, that was to last them a lifetime.

In later years there were to be many rumors, not only about Stewart and Sullavan but about Stewart and Logan, and Stewart and Fonda, all three the great romantic triumvirate of his youthful beginnings. Billy Grady once said to me that Sullavan had loved Stewart but had not been *in* love with him, and backed off because she knew she would only harm him; that Logan and Stewart had known reciprocal love; but that Fonda had felt more than Stewart had when they had been through their worst times together. "Hank looked up to Jimmy; he felt he was stronger, wiser, that his character was better, that he was less neurotic, more steady. He always referred to Jimmy in hero-worshipping terms, said he had kept him literally alive when he was really down in New York back then," Billy said.

Despite his love for acting, Stewart found the long waits, the rejections, hard. In moments of despair he would say, "Acting is no job for a man. You work two hours a night *when you work*, and you sleep all morning and maybe all day because you have nothing else to do." But as Barbara O'Neil later said, "The passion remained, and grew, and he developed patience, and learned to wait out his fate."

Years later, when an interviewer told Jimmy that Henry Fonda had said that everything came easier to him than to the others, that he had "fallen into things" along the way, Stewart declared, "Hank was always telling that to people — about how hard he'd worked and how I just fell into things. But the fact is that once we'd decided on the theatre, those of us at Princeton and Hank and the others, well, we all worked hard and we all starved a lot!"

But 1933, with the closing of *Goodbye Again* in the late spring, seemed less than promising. Stewart finally landed a job as stage manager for Jane Cowl, who was appearing in Boston in *Camille*. A flamboyant actress of great talent and considerable fame, Cowl had made her mark in the theatre years ago by capitalizing on the dramatic highlights in her scenes. Stewart recalled standing timidly and uncertainly "at duty" in the wings while Cowl worked herself up to the famous death-scene dénouement of the classic Dumas *fils* play. The audience was silently enthralled one night as Cowl, with her Armand in sobbing attendance, was coughing away her life. Stewart was supposed to ring down the curtain at the proper moment, but was suddenly distracted by thudding noises. He deserted his post to come upon a drunken tramp who was busily throwing stones on the theatre roof.

Having dispatched the inebriate, Stewart feared that he had missed his cue, and, zealously, rushed back and rang down the curtain. He realised, to his horror, that Cowl had not breathed her last and he had ruined her climactic moment. He never forgot La Cowl's wrath as she rushed from her "deathbed" and gave him the tongue-lashing of his life. "Do you know what you've done?" she screeched. "You've ruined my performance! Ruined it *completely!*" In short order, a disheartened young stage manager found himself on the train back to New York.

In that early fall of 1933, fresh from the debacle with Jane Cowl in Boston, Stewart's spirits couldn't have been lower. With a limited budget, he couldn't eat properly, and thought back wistfully on the "Steak and Beer Parties" he and his roommates would throw one night a week. He, Fonda, the others and their respective girlfriends would gather at a speakeasy on West 41st Street, with the proprietor offering them all they could eat for one buck apiece (a buck went a long way in 1933). In the basement, where they were assigned, were long trestle tables, rickety chairs and even an out-of-tune piano. One of their former University Players cohorts, Johnny Morris, initiated them in the preparation of "Hobo Steaks." These were, as Henry Fonda recalled, "huge thick slabs of beef with sides of salt on top of them. [Johnny Morris] would slide the steak into an iron grille and then he'd take them out and lift off the salt like a hunk of plaster." Fonda would then take over the operation, slicing the steaks, applying lots of butter, then putting the meat — prepared to individual preference — on chunks of bread. It all went down famously with generous drafts of beer. "It sure gave us something to look forward to every night, that Spring of '33," Stewart recalled. "And we had some great visitors. Benny Goodman would come over with other guys from his orchestra at NBC where he was musician for the house at the time; they'd eat and drink their fill, then give us music for hours and hours!" The Steak and Beer Club unfortunately petered out when the basement got too hot as summer approached. "I hate to think of how many people went back to bread, rice, and water after that!" Stewart bemoaned.

He was rescued from his own variation of that unappetizing diet when Fonda suggested they rent a couple of rooms at the Madison Square Hotel, down in the Twenties. This time, and for some months, they were to be alone, and their intimacy continued to deepen. "Each other's company was plenty for us at the time," Fonda recalled. Margaret Sullavan's ex-husband was in the dumps that September, for while he was taking whatever odd job he could find, Sullavan had capped her stage triumphs with a brand new Universal Pictures contract, and was off in Hollywood making her first starring film, *Only Yesterday*. "A star in the movies her first time out — and me without a pot to piss in!" Fonda mourned. Stewart consoled him as best he could; he too had foundered on "Sullavan Rock," though not as drastically as Fonda, who was still smarting at the tart-tongued Peggy's aspersions on his manhood. "That early 1933 fall was a low point for us both," Stewart recalled. "We were out of jobs for the umpteenth time and — well, things were grim!" Fonda dug up what passed for food and cooked it on a gas heater at the Madison Square while he reminisced to Stewart about his summer job painting and constructing sets for actor-director-writer Day Tuttle at the Mount Kisco Playhouse, in Westchester. Stewart remembered that he tried hard not to look too closely at the concoctions Fonda dreamed up for their meals: "I couldn't tell how they really smelled because he had salt and pepper and garlic all over the lumps he put in front of me — and I couldn't tell how they looked because he had mustard here and ketchup there, and I always got the cramps afterwards and — oh well. . . ." When they got tired at looking at their drab surroundings (the Madison Square Hotel rooms were, as Fonda later recalled, "a sitting room and a bedroom, furnished in early East Lynne, faded ruby and permanent gray") they went out for long walks "all over Manhattan." Both recalled getting drunk on whatever cheap beer they could rustle up for clean-up work at a nearby speakeasy. At last they'd crawl into the big double bed with the holes in the mattress and cry themselves to sleep in each other's arms. "I thought it would go on forever that time around — a really bummer time," Stewart remembered.

Stewart was the first to get a job — not much of a job, but it was a step back in the right direction. Arthur Beckhard, "who worried over me like a fussy uncle," hired Stewart (at the urging of Esther Dale) as stage manager and bit-part performer for a play starring Blanche Yurka. *Spring in Autumn* opened at the Henry Miller Theatre on October 24, 1933, and Stewart even got to play his accordion as background for the Spanish-style music the piece required. Yurka portrayed a Spanish opera singer who in one scene, to great audience amusement, managed to sing a Puccini aria while literally standing on her head. The slight plot, concocted by one G. Martinez Sierras, adapted by Nene Belmonti, and directed by Stewart's old Triangle and University colleague Bretaigne Windust, had the flamboyant Yurka character returning to her old town and her ex-husband to lend some cachet and respectability to her daughter's imminent marriage. She decides she still loves her husband (Richard Hale) and the daughter decides *she* loves someone other than her would-be bridegroom. Stewart's and Fonda's old pals Esther Dale and Mildred Natwick all but stole the show as sassy comic servants. Stewart's part was too brief to win him any critical notice, but "it was fun playing the accordion. But I was always embarrassed at curtain time to be out there taking a bow with the rest of the cast when nobody in the audience knew who the hell I was, or gave a damn either!"

Spring in Autumn closed after forty-one performances, but Stewart and Fonda lucked out in November when they found themselves cast together in *All Good Americans*, one of satirist S.J. Perelman's inspired collaborations with his wife, Laura. Directed by Arthur Sircom, with imaginative Parisian settings by Mordecai Gorelik, Stewart was one of a group of expatriate Americans who play "snob games" with more newly-arrived Yankees. They "get into a tangle of romantic mixups and false identities and what-not," as one critic described the goings-on. During the course of the play which, as one writer noted, "made fun, for the umpteenth time, of Americans on the loose in Paris," Stewart again played the accordion briefly. He balked, however, when the action required him to throw the accordion out of a window, so Sircom effected a compromise: his precious instrument was left sacrosanct, and a banjo went out the window.

The role paid him $50 a week, and ran thirty-nine performances, into the New Year, 1934. It was made into a movie later in the same year and retitled, with typical Hollywood inventiveness, *Paris Interlude*. Neither Stewart nor any of the other cast members were invited to do the movie. "We didn't mind — the thing didn't amount to much," Stewart remembered. Fred Keating, Mary Phillips (one of the Mrs. Humphrey Bogarts) and Hope Williams were also in the stage cast. Jimmy was somewhat lost in the crowd here, but one critic, John Mason Brown of The New York *Post*, got him into print thus: "James Stewart and Janet McLeary contribute amply to the intermittent amusement of the evening."

Stewart was always to remember the closing night party for *Spring in Autumn*, at which he played his accordion for hours "to help the cast commiserate themselves into some passing fun." That night, dumpy Esther Dale, who had been flooring the audience with her comic feistiness as the servant, sang in a beautiful, clear voice some of the lieder that had helped make her an outstanding concert singer. "She had made them laugh for over a month; that night she made them cry; how they loved her!" Mildred Natwick recollected warmly.

Hating to go home to the grim two-roomer on Madison Square, Stewart and Fonda were among the last to leave. They had gotten themselves pleasantly drunk, and as they crossed Times Square for the subway that would take them down to the East Twenties, Fonda dared Stewart to play the accordion loud and funny to draw a crowd. "That is, *if* you can," Fonda scoffed. Taking up the dare, Stewart began playing vigorously some of his standards, including "Ragtime Cowboy Joe," "Dinah," sections of Gershwin's "Rhapsody in Blue" and "Wait 'Til the Sun Shines, Nellie."

As Stewart remembered it after some forty years: "Four or five people appeared and stood around listening. I played another number and some more people came up. What made the 'recital' such a triumph was that one of the poor souls requested a particular song, 'Shanty Town.' I could play the hell out of that song. Then some of the others started giving requests and I was playing up a storm and singing too. The next thing I knew Fonda was passing around the hat. Our take: thirty-six cents."

Stewart and Fonda always differed on what exactly happened next. According to Fonda, a garishly caparisoned lady-of-the-evening came along and told Stewart he was "cute" and he could come with her for free. In Stewart's version, a cop came up—it was by then going on 5 a.m.—and hit him hard on the back of the leg. "I was furious. I didn't think I was 'disturbing the peace' or anything like it, but that's what he almost arrested me for. He finally let me off with the angry remark, 'It takes me three or four hours to get all these drunks off the streets and asleep in doorways and you come along and start that noise!'"

By February 1934, as Fonda recalled it, "We were broke again and Jimmy was getting so sick from the 'meals' I 'created' out of—well, that's *my* secret—that I got the steak and beer parties going at the speakeasy joint again. Every Thursday we guaranteed ourselves a good meal. Trouble was, we didn't always have the dollar the Irish proprietor wanted from each of us, so Mildred Natwick paid for us for four weeks in a row!"

Stewart and Fonda both recalled that on the way home one night they almost got in trouble with the law again. As Fonda told it: "On that particular night, we did a helluva lot more drinking than eating. We drank beer by the pitcher instead of the mug. There had been a snowstorm during the evening, and it had already been shoveled into high banks along the curbs and against the buildings. We caught a subway train and we were sitting there and I said to Jimmy, 'I can't straighten up. My bladder's so tight from beer.'" Stewart confessed he felt the same way. When they got off the subway, they had four blocks to go to make the Madison Square Hotel. Stewart, according to Fonda, said, "Hank, I don't think I can make it to the hotel. There's no place open and there's no people on the street, let's do it here." Fonda agreed and suggested a contest to see who could piss the longest continuous line in the snowdrift. If a car passed, they'd pretend they were walking along, admiring the snow. Stewart consented, but then Fonda had the better idea of writing their names with piss in the snow. "We must have been pretty pie-eyed, because he agreed," Fonda remembered. "Now I walked two blocks going real slow, and Jimmy walked about three blocks. He complained later that my name was shorter than his, but I had broken the rules anyhow. I had 'piss-printed' my *initials*. Jimmy wrote *his whole name* in those drifts. Come to think of it, he must have had a helluva lot more to drink that night than I did!"

Fonda revealingly said of that roller-coaster period when he lived with Stewart under feast-and-famine conditions: "There is no intimacy like going through the worst things with a roommate, helping each other, comforting each other, laughing and crying together. It beats any other intimacy, including man and wife, or brother and sister, or father and child, cards and spades!"

Early in 1934, Stewart did his first film work, in two Vitaphone shorts. The first was called *Art Trouble*, the second *Important News*. "They had no plots that made any sense and that anyone could remember a minute later, but they were *lively* and they *moved*, and some wonderful comedians were in them," Stewart remembered. "Working with people like Harry Gribbon and Shemp Howard [later one of the famed Stooges] and Eddie Quillan was sheer undiluted pleasure. Everything moved so fast there was no opportunity to learn what they call 'film technique.' We just got up there in front of the camera with our learned lines, what there were of them, and played it all by ear. I did it because I didn't believe they actually paid $50 a day; there were damned *few* days, but $50 per was $50 per!"

In segments of *Art Trouble* that have been shown in retrospective tributes to Stewart, it is obvious that, at 25, he has it all together. All the boyish charm, the comic verve, the ease and personality are very much on display. Seeing him in these shorts makes it eminently understandable what was to happen next. He was, in the course of his next play, to win the love of one of the most important figures on Broadway. Guthrie McClintic, the famed director and husband of Katharine Cornell, fell deeply in love with him.

The play was *Yellow Jack*, by the distinguished Sidney Howard, and it opened on March 6, 1934, at the Martin Beck Theatre. It dealt with the terrible yellow fever scourge in turn-of-the-century Cuba. It was a somber, stately, and quite moving depiction of the efforts to find a cure, and of the heroic human guinea pigs who tested for that cure, some of whom lost their lives. It ran for two hours without intermission, in order to keep the mood and ambience uninterrupted. A critical smash, it failed to impress a 1934 public that, at one of the Depression's low points, was going through equally solemn experiences. "Though it only lasted 79 performances, into May 1934," as Myron McComick remembered, "oh, what a lovely light it gave on Broadway while it lasted!" Stewart played Private O'Hara, a marine who volunteers as a test subject. His was one of the more notable performances, and it finally put him up in lights on Broadway. Stewart was to recall that "I tried out for the part of the Irish soldier but was told my brogue was too poor. So I got in touch with an old Abbey player, Frank Cullinan, and rehearsed with him in the lobby of the old Lincoln Hotel. When the actor who got the part fell ill, I was able to step into it."

For his moving and eloquent interpretation of Sergeant O'Hara, Stewart got his best notices yet in the theatre. Brooks Atkinson of *The New York Times* called his portrayal "excellent" and of all the critics, Robert Garland of *The New York World-Telegram* came closest to the mark in hailing a fresh, wonderful new Broadway talent when he wrote: "Especially do I admire the Private O'Hara of James Stewart, a performance that is simple, sensitive and true and replete with a poetic undercurrent." This, too, was the performance so admired by casting scout Billy Grady.

It was producer-director Guthrie McClintic who made it all possible, and Stewart was always to remember this. "I think that was the turning point of my work on the stage," he said years later, and he told of how thrilled he had been to work with the famed director. McClintic, in one writer's words, "made Stewart appreciate that the theater was a sensitive craft and that it was as worthwhile a task to move audiences as to design buildings."

Stewart found himself working with a first-rate cast in *Yellow Jack*, including Geoffrey Kerr, Sam Levine, Myron McCormick, Robert Keith and Eduardo Ciannelli, several of whom were to know later fame as Hollywood character actors. The play itself was to make it to Hollywood as a 1938 MGM film with Robert Montgomery and Lewis Stone.

Yellow Jack made James Stewart the most discussed young actor on Broadway. Still only 25, he was bewildered by the sudden requests for interviews and photo sessions. Admiration from both sexes poured over him via numerous stage door autograph requests, many letters, and invitations to parties on Park and Fifth Avenues.

"It was Guthrie McClintic who made him a star — Guthrie and no one else," fellow actor Robert Keith recalled. "Guthrie gave him special attention all through the rehearsal period, worked with him through all hours, kept up his morale, calmed his nervousness, even stood in the wings to cheer him on. I remember him looking over to Guthrie at times, out of the corner of his eye, as if for moral support, as if to a father . . . ."

But the frequently foppish and fussy McClintic's feelings were hardly fatherly. He had first noticed Stewart in *Goodbye Again* two years before, and later went back several times to see him in *All Good Americans*. He had wanted to be sure — very sure — that Stewart was ready for the poignant, powerful and complex role of the idealistic, self-sacrificing O'Hara. At first, another actor had the part, while Stewart sought instruction to master the muted brogue that, McClintic insisted to him, was mandatory for full credibility. When Stewart found he had the part at last, "he snapped at it hungrily, brought it home with him, lived it day and night," as his roommate Hank Fonda later recalled. "The part had met the man and he was positively obsessed!" Luckily for Fonda, *he* had found a good spot in a Leonard Sillman review, which kept him happily occupied. But he always recalled the effect Stewart produced on him — and myriad others — when he finally stopped by the Martin Beck to watch his friend from a second row "comp" seat. "He was so electric in the role [of O'Hara], he tore your heart out," Fonda marveled. Sam Levine concurred. "We all knew he was going to be great, that this was just the beginning."

And through it all there was Guthrie McClintic, watching, counseling, worrying. Myron McCormick was to recall Guthrie standing in the wings, dressed to the nines, a handsome coat thrown carelessly over the shoulders of his $500 suit. "This was a man who was sophisticated and tough-minded in the extreme, a man many thought cold and clinical and detached, and he was crying — crying his eyes out at Jimmy's climaxes. Jimmy would complete the scene and go backstage and when he saw what he did to Guthrie as O'Hara, he would cry too." Stewart told one interviewer for *The New York Sun*, regarding McClintic: "That so great a man should have taken an interest in me still leaves me wobbly. He has opened the doors to a new life for me!"

An interviewer described McClintic's directorial method: "He maps out and completely 'routines,' in advance, the action of the play. By the time he is rehearsing on the stage, every solitary bit of the given act is ready, mapped thoroughly in his mind. No business is too small to be neglected — the tip of a head, the swing of an arm." McClintic waxed anatomical in that same 1934 interview:

"There is a moment when the director must put his fingers on the spine of the play, find a dislocation, and snap it into place, like a chiropractor. When that happens, the play that limped gets up and walks."

McClintic and Katharine "Kit" Cornell had been married since 1921. Together they were to do many of Broadway's most distinguished plays, including the much admired *The Barretts of Wimpole Street*, *Saint Joan*, and *Romeo and Juliet*. Their first great hit was the 1921 *A Bill of Divorcement*, which nine years later was to make a film star of Katharine Hepburn her first time out. "I try to find the best available actors," McClintic told another interviewer in 1927, "and then get these actors to return to me what the play gave me when I read it. A good director must have a strong visual sense; he must see it all, from beginning to end, in his mind's eye, before a word has been said." He told the reporter that he insisted on an eight-day preliminary rehearsals period, with the actors seated around a table. "If I can get an actor to read right during rehearsal, the rest of his job will come naturally when he is on his feet." This was the method he had used in turning Katharine Cornell into the most respected theatre star of her time. "She was putty in his hands; he was truly her Svengali," Jane Cowl said. "What David Belasco did decades before for Mrs. Leslie Garter, he did for her."

An extrovert to her introvert, Guthrie went out on his own to all the parties and events because, Jane Cowl recalled, "Kit shrinks from them with a shyness left over from her ugly-duckling childhood."

Broadway's Svengali and his Trilby lived in a beautiful, tastefully-appointed townhouse at 21 Beekman Place in Manhattan through all the years of their marriage. Judith Anderson, who with Helen Mencken was to soar to stellar heights when McClintic directed them in the 1935 theatre version of *The Old Maid* (a Pulitzer Prize Winner which later gave Bette Davis her finest movie in 1939), was always fascinated by the McClintics. Theirs was "a marriage of convenience. They both went their own way; there was no sex in their marriage. They even lived several floors removed from each other. They were wonderful friends, good partners, respected and revered each other, yet love was, somehow, absent," said Anderson. "I was not in love with Kit," McClintic told another interviewer of 1932 with surprising frankness, "but nonetheless I had a deep and perfectly natural conviction that she and I would one day be married." The couple rotated between Beekman Place and their summer places at Martha's Vineyard and Sneden's Landing, where they played golf together ("Kit always beat me," he related).

McClintic had been born in Seattle, Washington, in 1893. The product of a cold, unloving family of a distinctly philistine bent, he escaped their oppressive influence at the earliest opportunity, and from age 17 on, lived by his wits. The theatre was his only goal, so he tried acting first and graduated in 1913 from The American Academy of Dramatic Arts in New York City. Proud, isolated, skittish, a loner who stepped from the beginning to his own unique drummer, he later found his true calling in directing and producing because, he said, "I want the grand overall view, the final concept, in my grasp at all times."

At a precocious 24, he married the winsomely eccentric actress Estelle Winwood, who was to live to age 100. Her weirdly individualistic personality was not limited to the stage: She was ten years older than he, and the marriage fell apart in 1919 when he learned she had not divorced her previous husband. He encountered the 21-year-old Katharine Cornell at the Washington Square Players that same year, and a friendship-magic was born. She married him for the same reason he married her; she knew they would be perfect life partners, mutually supportive in their respective careers.

But partnership was all Guthrie McClintic had to offer his wife — which she found quite sufficient — for he was a tormented, promiscuous homosexual all his life. Men were an obsession, "and he knew a lot of hurt and humiliation and disillusion with one after another," as Helen Mencken, a good friend, later said. Through the years he would find himself threatened, blackmailed, abused and deserted; a chronic love-letter writer, his letters "could have been scattered in the wind and carried all over the United States, Canada, the Arctic and points East and West, there were so many of them," as George S. Kaufman scathingly observed. Yet only in his ardent outpourings to assorted handsome young men, many of them actors, did his writing gift, such as it was, find expression.

McClintic, as Moss Hart readily confessed, had been the inspiration for the character of Carlton Fitzgerald, the egomaniacal, flamboyant, slightly effeminate director in Moss's 1948 play, *Light Up the Sky*. Some ten years after his encounter with James Stewart, he would figure in another actor's life. Kirk Douglas, in his memoir

The Ragman's Son, made no bones about McClintic's attempts to seduce him on a quiet afternoon at Beekman Place, while the servants
were out and Kit away at Martha's Vineyard. According to Douglas,
then a humble beginner and stage manager for a McClintic play, he
had gotten up quickly and rushed out in fear when McClintic had
made his move. Douglas intimated that his rejection of the auto-
cratic director had, for a time, short-circuited his theatrical hopes,
at least in that production.

The Stewart-McClintic encounter, however, if Fonda, Mc-
Cormick and Josh Logan are to be believed, was quite another matter. For one thing, Stewart in 1934, at 25, was a more compassionate
young man than Douglas would be ten years later. He had spent
some six years or so struggling with his own bisexual impulses, and
the great loves of his life to that point, emotionally and spiritually,
if not necessarily physically, had been Margaret Sullavan, Josh
Logan and Henry Fonda. Stewart had heard all the whispered stories about McClintic, the cruel jokes, the tittered warnings never to
get alone with him. He had listened to other young actors in assorted "bull sessions" rapping unkindly on McClintic.

Henry Fonda, who was struggling with his own sexual-identity
problems, shared Stewart's distaste for bigotry against homosexuals,
as did, surprisingly, Margaret Sullavan. In my 1986 book, *Margaret
Sullavan: Child of Fate*, I tell of her disdain for her then-husband Leland Hayward's anti-gay sallies. She once brushed aside Hayward's
remark about "what a compulsive queer" Noël Coward was and
how "no man was safe around him" by asking her suddenly embarrassed spouse what he would have done had he found *himself*
"queer." "With your evident attraction to pleasure and fun and sen-
suality, if your bent went that way, would you deny yourself?" she
grilled him. "You damned well better bet you wouldn't! So shut up
about it!" Stewart and Fonda were later to nervously ponder her
opinion of *them*. Had her brief marriage to him failed because she
suspected him of *that*, Fonda once wondered to Stewart? And on
Stewart's end, he could not help wondering if he had gotten Sullavan "all motherly and sisterly" but not predatory, as was her wont,
because she had wondered about *him*? Neither would ever find out:
she was too loving and tactful with Stewart to tell him, and too remote with Fonda to enlighten *him*. Fonda was to have a notoriously
checkered marital history (his second wife wound up a suicide) and

went through five wives before he was done. Stewart married only once, but it took him to age 41 to do it.

So if any two young actors understood and sensitively appreciated Guthrie McClintic, Stewart and Fonda did. "Guthrie always made me feel sad," Fonda later said, "I don't think he has *ever* been happy, not *really*!"

When Stewart met him for *Yellow Jack*, McClintic was 40. A chain smoker, he was constantly in motion, tense, electric, paranoically watchful, ever-fearful of being hurt, yet doggedly aggressive. Many thought McClintic handsome, with his piercing dark eyes, sensual mouth, strong patrician nose. He was to live to 1961, aged 68, and one of his last visitors, Gladys Cooper, the brilliant English actress and noted Hollywood character player, remembered that he had asked "How is Jimmy? Is he still the same nice person he always was?"

Only McClintic and Stewart really know what transpired between them during Stewart's frequent visits to Beekman Place, where they spent countless hours on *Yellow Jack*, followed by drinks and long philosophical discussions. Henry Fonda, then his roommate and intimate, doubtless knew, as did others now past telling. What *is* known is that Jimmy Stewart with his sincerity, tact and kindly empathy, managed to become one of the great loves of the tormented McClintic's life. With so many others it had been merely sexual curiosity, the joy of the conquest. With Stewart it had not been mere adventure: McClintic had fallen in love. Because he knew the unreciprocated love was doomed, for the one time in his life he withdrew with grace, while continuing the friendship.

McClintic was disappointed when *Yellow Jack* failed to win from the public the warm response the critics had accorded it. He told a reporter from *The New York Times* the day after the show closed: "It was fine drama; it was absorbingly interesting. Even on the closing night I told myself, 'This is so good that I wonder if I really did it.'"

Knowing that Stewart planned a summer with a theatre troupe at Locust Valley, Long Island, McClintic began looking for a play in which to showcase him that fall of 1934. He soon found it.

Stewart's high-water mark as a Broadway actor came with *Divided by Three*, which starred the redoubtable Judith Anderson, and opened on October 2, 1934. A play in three acts by Margaret Leech

(Mrs. Ralph Pulitzer) and Beatrice (Mrs. George) Kaufman, it concerned a harried, romantically-driven lady (Miss Anderson), who was confused between her love for her husband, her lover, and her son. Stewart is Teddy Parrish, the son, playing a role of a 21-year-old boy who adores his mother. As described by Brooks Atkinson in *The New York Times*, "The son is a wholesome lad, alive with admiration for his mother and faith in the rectitude of mankind." But his mother is forced to financially support her socially prominent but indigent husband. She has opened an art gallery, and is being kept by a lover, but is a woman of honest expediency doing what she thinks necessary to survive and prosper. Anderson, wrote Atkinson, played her "with deep compassion."

The strongest scene in the play came when Stewart, who is to marry a young Ivy Leaguer as strait-laced and honorable as himself, confronted his mother with her adultery. He made graphic his pain and disenchantment, and completely won over the audience, exiting with the line, "This house stinks!" So powerful was his acting that he stood up to one of the theatre's first ladies and almost took the scene away from her.

It was a great break for a young actor to play with Judith Anderson, aged only 36 but already remarkably distinguished and versatile. Born in 1898 in Australia, she had made her stage debut at age 17 in Sydney, and first appeared in New York in 1918. She was to go on to solid parts during the 1920s on Broadway, culminating in her role of Lavinia Mannion in *Mourning Becomes Electra* in 1932. She was later to be Gertrude to John Gielgud's *Hamlet* (1936), essayed Lady Macbeth to great acclaim in 1937 and 1941, and hit her peak in *Medea* in 1947. In 1960 she was to be named by Queen Elizabeth II a Dame Commander of the British Empire for her outstanding contribution to world theatre.

Offstage, Anderson, while often tart and imperious, was a charming and affable person, and in her own objective, disciplined way was encouraging toward young actors she knew had talent. She proved an invaluable mentor to Stewart during *Divided by Three*, which won considerable critical esteem, though it lasted only thirty-one performances. Anderson had completed her first movie the year before. It was called *Blood Money* (1933), directed by Rowland V. Lee, with George Bancroft and Frances Dee. In it, underworld bail-bondsman Bancroft fell in love with socialite Dee, to the consternation of his associate, Anderson, described by one critic as "gutsy and amorous." The picture was only fair, but the somewhat miscast Anderson had given all the signs of becoming a major Hollywood character actress. Seven years later she was to achieve her pinnacle in Alfred Hitchcock's *Rebecca* (1940), as the evil housekeeper, Mrs. Danvers.

Since her *Blood Money* experience in Hollywood, Anderson had found herself in a position to advise young performers with no film experience about the hazards and trials of moviemaking. During and after rehearsals, Anderson told the inquisitive Stewart about life on the set: the endless waits, the bits and snips of dialogue necessitated by camera shiftings, etc. She confirmed his earlier impression, from the shorts he had made that spring, that the stage was better for him. In this surmise he was to be proven wrong; ironically, one of his first screen tests was a scene from *Divided by Three*.

Hedda Hopper, who later found fame as a Hollywood columnist, was a supporting player in *Divided by Three*, and was deeply impressed with the young Stewart's performance. Later she was to claim that when she went back to Hollywood in early 1935 she strongly advised MGM people to put him under contract.

Stewart owed much of the effectiveness of his impassioned performance to the careful direction and offstage coaching of Guthrie McClintic, who continued to be deeply in love with him. Awed by Anderson and his night-after-night juxtaposition to one of the theatre's great actresses, and eager to live up to the devoted McClintic's hopes for him, Stewart socked home a powerhouse performance that won him solid critical huzzahs. Opening night was a resounding triumph for him, which further reinforced the impression he had made in *Yellow Jack*. Later he was to say to Fonda and Myron McCormick that he found tears in his eyes not only from the audience's wild applause but from the joyful expression on Judith Anderson's face and the ecstatic happiness in Guthrie's eyes. "That night, at that moment, they were the two people whose approval counted most," he later said.

Many of the critics were kind to Stewart personally, with Brooks Atkinson of the *Times* calling his acting "responsive," and Percy Hammond of the *Herald-Tribune*, one of the leading theater critics of the day, rhapsodizing, "What impressed me. . . . as much as anything in the drama was the playing of James Stewart as the harried lad who struck his mother [in the climactic scene Stewart had not only whacked Judith in the face but called her a whore]. He was refreshing in his untricked method and acted the role without a single stagy affectation." Hammond called the play "smart, smooth and oily."

Burns Mantle of the *New York Daily News*, another critical doyen, called Stewart "splendid — a quietly forceful actor completely free of affectations or the cheaper tricks of his profession." John Anderson of *The Evening Journal* joined in the chorus of praise, writing, "As Teddy, James Stewart is excellent, bringing to the performance much intensity and veracity."

Later, at the party for the play, Stewart basked in the admiration of McClintic, Anderson (who had collected her share of fine notices), Hedda Hopper, Hunter Gardner, who had played his weak father, and James Rennie, cast as Anderson's lover.

Henry Fonda, whose fortunes had yet to compare with Stewart's, recalled going backstage to see Stewart during the *Divided by Three* run, and asking himself, "Where did this come from? How the hell did he get to be so good?"

Fonda added, "I guess by this time it dawned upon Jim himself that he was pretty good at what he was doing, so he decided to stay in the business and go on from there. But it ruffled my feathers a little. Here I was busting my shoe leather trying to make it in the theatre and this lackadaisical fellow Stewart just stumbled into it!"

In 1964 Hedda Hopper told me, "Oh, we all knew he was going to be a film star — and a big one! I remember watching him from across the stage in *Divided by Three* and telling myself, 'If he can pack such a wallop for a live audience, boy, what he'll get across with closeups and long and medium shots out in movies, especially with the right director!' I went to Al Altman of MGM's New York office and told him, 'There's a kid acting with me in the play I'm doing, and if you don't get your duff over there before its closing, you'll miss out on a future movie great!' When I went back to Hollywood, I pushed for him again! Billy Grady, of course, did the most for him, as everybody knows, but I am proud I did my bit, for what it was worth!"

Billy Grady, in New York during the run of *Divided by Three*, dropped by to see Stewart in the play, and in his notebook wrote:

"This kid has finally arrived. Unaffected and sincere in everything he does!"

When *Divided by Three* closed, Stewart went right into *Page Miss Glory* at the Mansfield Theatre. In this he had the good luck to be directed by George Abbott, who educated him in some subtle tricks of comic timing. He played a smalltime promoter, one step above a con man; a demon with the lens, he craftily composed a photograph comprised of all the salient features of major film actresses. The picture wins a top beauty contest, but then he has to come up with the woman who matches the composite! John Mason Brown led the contingent of critics singling Stewart out for praise, saying, "James Stewart [and others] all give it the twist and inflection of scatterbrained comedy." Warner Bros. bought the play (which lasted 63 performances, into early 1935) as a Marion Davies vehicle, with Pat O'Brien playing Stewart's role. Stewart later credited Abbott with the sharpness of his own performance: "He was a tough director but an actor-oriented one."

In 1931 my old friend Billy Grady, who was one of my early mentors in Hollywood and New York, had been engaged by Louis B. Mayer and Irving Thalberg as a talent representative. He roamed the country in search of promising fodder for the MGM personality-mills. Our families had been close friends in our hometown of Lynn, Massachusetts, and Billy was always a kind and a helpful source of intimate anecdotes on Hollywood people. He was the real discoverer of James Stewart, with whom he later became the closest of friends and was best man when Stewart eventually married. Billy had begun his career in show business as an artist's representative in New York, and from 1917 to 1929 his roster featured many prominent theatre stars, including W.C. Fields and Al Jolson. He subsequently joined the Charles Dillingham organization (Dillingham was a major Broadway producer of the 1920s and 1930s) and rose to be Dillingham's general manager.

After Billy wound up in California as associate to Benny Thau, the MGM executive in charge of talent and casting, he became advisor and confidante to many of Metro's top personalities. Besides Stewart, he discovered such luminaries as Eleanor Parker, Rock Hudson, Joan Blondell and Van Johnson. A gruff, but kindly and sentimental Irishman, he was full of stories of his early days in Lynn and elsewhere. What he didn't know about the "inside" worlds of Broadway and Hollywood was not worth repeating.

Billy remembered his first meeting with Stewart, in 1932, thus: "My friend George M. Cohan had invited me to attend the opening of his new play in Atlantic City. Driving down, I stopped at Princeton for lunch. While waiting to be served, I telephoned my office in New York and was informed that the Cohan play, due to a production difficulty, had been postponed one day. In order not to waste the day, I decided to attend the annual Princeton University Triangle Show opening that evening. Princeton shows were always interesting; this one was no exception. It got off to a good start with a line of thirty-two male undergraduates in female chorus garb, trying to emulate Broadway showgirl ensemble routines. They were a motley group, and like all amateurs, accentuated their ridiculous appearance with excessive mugging and gestures. All but the skinny guy on the end. He was six-foot-four, towered over the others, and looked uncomfortable as hell. While the others hammed it up, the thin one played it straight and was a standout."

Billy recalled that "later in the show the thin one did a specialty, singing a song to his own accompaniment on an accordion. He could not seem to coordinate the lyrics and the instrument. First the accordion was a bar ahead, then the lyrics would be behind the instrument. The audience thought it a comedy routine and rewarded with loud applause. I noted that the singer had an ingratiating personality, an asset in my scheme of things theatrical."

Billy sought out the young man for a talk backstage. He discovered that Stewart had no plans for a show business career, and intended to become an architect. Nonetheless, Billy from then on kept running notes on him in his reference book.

Billy saw Stewart several times between 1932 and 1934. In his notes for *Yellow Jack*, he wrote: "Jim played an Irish soldier, and though I couldn't give him much for his brogue, he did a very creditable job."

Yellow Jack had opened on Broadway in March 1934, but by the summer of 1934 Stewart was reduced to working with a stock company, the Red Barn Theatre, at Locust Valley, Long Island. As Billy remembered it: "There was a tryout of *All Paris Knows* at the Red Barn; the troupe was quite a favorite in Locust Valley. I liked to see plays there. Next door was a wonderful restaurant, the Stagecoach

Inn. Good food and a drink specialty called a stirrup cup, brandy with other good things. Three stirrup cups," Billy recalled, "and you wanted to marry a horse!" Billy remembered that the Red Barn Theatre was just over the fence from the Long Island Railroad tracks. "Coal-burning locomotives hauling freight and passenger trains noisily rushed through during every performance. If, at rehearsal, it was discovered that an important scene would be in progress as the 9:12 freight passed, the starting time of the play would be changed. It made no difference with inconsequential scenes."

Billy delightedly recalled that Stewart had a big love scene that had been slated to start *after* the 9:12 went through, but on the auspicious night he saw the play the 9:12 was overdue. Unfortunately, it came clanging by just as Stewart went into a clinch with the leading lady. "Undaunted by the noise, Jim held the kiss and ninety cars of freight passing helped make history. It was the longest kiss in the history of the American theater!" That night Billy noted in his little book, "Heh — my man is sexy! A good type!"

Stewart received very little remuneration for his 1934 summer at the Red Barn Theatre, and counted his pennies, expecting yet another lean season in New York. The girls of the troupe found him cordial but reticent. As he later recalled it, "I was humiliated because I had so little money to spend, and I had to keep social engagements — if that is what they were — limited. Very limited." One young actress, who found the 26-year-old Stewart "cute," brazenly took the initiative and asked him to take her out. When he asked her to pay for it, feeling that would put her off, she cattily accused him of preferring the actors' company to the actresses.' "If I do, it's for a very simple reason," he smarted. "Guys go dutch. Girls want to be paid for."

It was duly noted that Stewart preferred to clown and socialize with the men of the troupe, and ignored the ladies all summer. "I can relax with the guys — they don't expect extra attention and they can be casual and companionable with each other," he wrote Fonda. "Girls put me off — they are demanding and expensive, and they're not as indispensable as they imagine they are!"

In February 1935, Stewart found himself back on the street again. Despite the best efforts of Grady and Hopper, nothing had yet happened with the MGM test he had made. As Stewart later recalled: "It was only because I was down to my last bean that I went into *A Journey by Night*. It was vile. But it paid me one hundred good American dollars a week. I spent seventy on a suit I had to wear in it. I could use that suit—and how! And thirty dollars in my pocket was a darn sight more reassuring than only one had been!"

According to Myron McCormick, Stewart had not wanted further subsidies from the folks in Indiana, feeling that he should be pulling his own oar by that point. Nor did he want to take any money from Guthrie McClintic, feeling that he had imposed on Guthrie's affection for him long enough. According to Arthur Goodrich, who adapted Stewart's new play, *A Journey by Night* from the German of Leo Perutz, McClintic was still a guiding force. Unbeknownst to Stewart, he had persuaded director Robert Sinclair and the Shuberts, who were producing, to cast Stewart in the part of a Viennese bank clerk who falls in love with a shady lady and winds up a murderer and an embezzler. As one commentator later put it, "He was about as Viennese as a hamburger," though Stewart later reported that he had harried anyone he could find who was of German or Austrian origin, in an effort to perfect his dialect. The play opened on April 16, 1935, and demonstrated painfully that he need not have bothered.

John Anderson of the *Evening Journal* wrote: "James Stewart appeared somewhat more or less than Austrian, which would be about the same degree, let us say, as would have been expressed by Will Rogers. He is a young actor of fine potentialities but he is as American as a doughnut." The play closed after seven performances. It was to be his last Broadway performance for many years, for he went to Hollywood for further screen tests. He returned to New York "scared and worried," as he recalled, but was promptly summoned back to California by a cable from Billy Grady: "Report to Hollywood—part available with three months' option on your services."

Fonda, at age 29, was not to spend much time feeling wistful over Stewart's break in *Divided by Three*. A month later he was to get, at last, his own big Broadway break. The play, which opened late in 1934, was *The Farmer Takes a Wife*, and it was about life in the 19th Century on the Erie Canal. Marc Connelly and Frank B. Elser had adapted it from a novel by Walter D. Edmonds, *Rome Haul*. The tryout in Washington went extremely well, and the raves for Fonda, June Walker his co-star, and the play were all-out when it opened in New York. Marc Connelly admiringly expressed as well as anyone the effect that Fonda, in a starring part which finally showed his true mettle, unleashed that opening night: "He had that gee-gosh, foot-dragging quality about him that Gary Cooper and a few others have always had. But likeable, very American, and very good." Stewart was to note that Fonda, as described by Connelly and by enthusiastic reviewers, sounded amazingly like himself. "Slats, we have rubbed off on each other more than we reckoned!" Fonda chuckled.

Fonda's success now equalled Stewart's, though they continued to mark time at the Madison Square Hotel, and their close relationship remained unchanged. They got going on a new project: model airplane building. As Fonda recalled later: "We wouldn't allow any of the hotel maids into our rooms. It was ankle deep in balsa shavings and we were afraid if they came in to clean they'd wreck our plane, which, if I remember, was a replica of a United States Army Air Corps Martin bomber. We finished the framework and covered it with silk, but I had to leave the painting to Jimmy because I got a call from Hollywood." Leland Hayward, Fonda's agent, had fixed it for him to make the movie version of *Farmer Takes a Wife*, opposite Janet Gaynor, a big Fox star. Stewart was still waiting impatiently for Billy Grady's efforts to take hold. Fonda exacted two promises: "Let me know when you can join me in Hollywood and we'll bunk in together — I'll find the place — and paint this damn plane and apply the finishing touches. Then bring it with you!" Stewart agreed to both stipulations and in March of 1935 took Fonda to the train station. It was to be a briefer separation than they could have imagined.

Chapter Five

Going Hollywood

Billy Grady, MGM's casting director, later gave his own version of Stewart's 1935 advent in films:

"The New York office [of MGM] finalized a contract with Stewart while I returned to the studio in California after seeing plays in New York. It was my intention to start Jim in a William Powell-Myrna Loy *Thin Man* picture, but the next one was at least four months away. I promised to look for a picture for him to fill the interim.

"At the studio was a script that needed casting. It was called *Murder Man* and was to star Spencer Tracy and Virginia Bruce. The producer of *Murder Man* was Harry Rapf, a close friend of L.B. Mayer. In the script was the part of a police reporter called Shorty, for obvious reasons. I thought it would be a good part for our new contract player, though he was far from being a Shorty physically. I had a talk with Rapf, made my pitch but got nowhere. He insisted he wanted a jockey-sized actor, nothing else would do. I was accused of trying to rewrite his script. Our talk wound up with a loud and definite 'NO' on Stewart."

Billy continued. "Tim Whelan, a friend of mine who was the director of *Murder Man*, had started shooting on Stage 18. I went to see him and told him all about Stewart. Whelan and I always did see eye-to-eye on talent. Tim's answer was 'Bring on your man, the hell with Rapf, I'll start Stewart and say nothing to Rapf.'

"A phone call to Jim at Vinegar Hill (he had gone home to see the folks) found him mowing the lawn. He let out a whoop and dropped the mower, and a few days later was at the studio. The next day he was Shorty and did a helluva job. Whelan was delighted, as was Spencer. I now had Rapf to contend with. When he saw the film with Jim and not a jockey-sized reporter, he raised hell and went immediately to L.B. Mayer's office. Though I knew Rapf back in New York in his struggling days, he insisted to Mayer that I be fired for disobeying orders."

Billy reported that this didn't bother him in the least because he had just signed a new five-year contract. But Mayer summoned him to his office. As Billy then recalled it: "I received the first of the many bawling-outs I was to get from Mayer over the years. I waited for him to finish and asked that he withhold judgment until he had seen the film. The three of us [Billy, Mayer and the still-outraged Rapf] went to the projection room and reviewed Stewart's first day-of-shooting rushes. At the end, Mayer turned to Rapf and bawled the hell out of *him*! I got a pat on the back and was complimented by Mayer. My man Stewart was on his way!"

Murder Man (1935) was Spencer Tracy's first film under contract at MGM, though he had worked there the year before on a one-picture loanout from Fox. He felt that his roles at Fox were unworthy of his talents and, with the exception of *The Power and the Glory* (1933), Tracy had been wasted in one potboiler after another. MGM executives knew he could be emotionally unstable, was not faithful to his wife, and tended to drink excessively, but the feeling at the studio was that Tracy could be built into a major star. (Within three years he would win two Academy Awards in a row.)

Stewart found Tracy and his lovely co-star, Virginia Bruce, in a mellow, friendly mood. Tim Whelan recalled that Tracy was delighted to be free of what he called "The Fox Chain Gang." He joyfully embarked on what he had been assured would be just a warm-up to his co-starrer with Jean Harlow (*Riff-Raff*, 1936) and other choice items which were being scripted with him in mind.

The plot of *Murder Man* was standard melodrama of the more forgettable B-picture kind. Tracy is a crack reporter who avenges the death of a relative by framing one of the two men responsible for the victim's failure in business. The other miscreant is killed by Tracy himself and he blames it on the murdered man's partner. There is a trial, but before the innocent man meets death, Tracy suffers an attack of conscience and admits to the crime.

Murder Man was the first of two MGM films Stewart was to do with Tracy (the other, fifteen years later, was to feature them as equal co-stars.) Cast incongruously, but humorously, as the aforementioned Shorty, Stewart found Tracy wonderful to play with. Tracy, himself a veteran of the stage who instinctively played "big brother" to New York theatre people gone Hollywood, gave Stewart a piece of advice he never forgot: "Just forget the camera is there and be yourself."

Stewart, as the eager-beaver news hound, did not have many scenes, but when the picture was shown he remembered being thoroughly shocked at what he considered his all-arms-and-legs awkwardnesses. As he remembered it, "I would barge into a scene from left and almost barge myself off the right frame before anyone was fully aware I was there!" Director Tim Whelan recalled telling Stewart: "Stay in the god-damned frame! Stay the hell on those marks!" He confided to Grady and others, however, that Stewart had a graphic, vital presence onscreen. "He is one of a kind. There just isn't anyone around like him, and that is always a good start for a kid." Whelan added: "An original — no matter what kind of original — always has a good running start in a medium where being distinctive is all-important!"

Stewart admitted to a man-sized crush on beautiful, blonde Virginia Bruce. She had just weathered a brief unhappy marriage to tormented ex-MGM star John Gilbert which had produced a daughter, Susan. Gilbert was in despair at the loss of his once-great career, a casualty of his alcoholism, bad temper (he once socked Mayer and the latter never forgave him), and his diminished talkie impact (he had been in his heyday in the silents). In *Murder Man*, Bruce played a girl reporter who is struck on Tracy and tries to help him find himself. Now that she was legally free, Virginia had a train of male admirers. She found Stewart "cute and sweet" and played along with him for a while, but she did not reciprocate the steam that he was projecting toward her. Stewart was to fondly recall Virginia as "very lovely, and very sure of herself. She had a self-contained steadiness that marked her as a survivor." Virginia had embarked on a promising leading-lady career at MGM that later fizzled into B-movie status. By 1937 many regarded her as the inspiration for the Janet Gaynor role in the original *A Star Is Born*: she had married a great star in decline and had then struck out on her own career. The principal difference was that Virginia never attained the stellar heights that Gaynor's Vicki Lester did in the film.

Murder Man boasted a cast of fine character actors including William Collier Sr., William Demarest, Lionel Atwill and Robert Warwick, several of whom took the fledgling Stewart under their wing and educated him on camera tricks.

William Demarest later said: "Frankly, when I worked with Jimmy in that picture I didn't think he had that much potential as a film actor. He was terribly awkward and tall, and thin as a beanpole, and that speech hesitancy seemed to me a handicap for an actor. Was I to be fooled later on! I kicked myself for my lack of judgment, for within three or four years the very qualities I thought were handicaps turned Jimmy into the most uniquely distinctive film actor of his kind — and it all came from just being himself!"

The *New York Herald-Tribune* critic took note of Stewart, recalling his work on Broadway thus: "That admirable stage juvenile, James Stewart, who was so fine in *Yellow Jack*, is wasted in a bit that he handles with characteristically engaging skill." A Chicago critic commented on Stewart's "unique naturalness. He's not Hollywood-Handsome — he's far from the standard type they go wild for out among the palms and oranges, but he can act, and he's not like anyone else." Critical verdicts like these consoled Stewart when the publicity department passed them on to him.

Henry Fonda had met him at the train when Stewart first arrived in Hollywood, and soon they were ensconced in a Mexican-style farmhouse in Brentwood. An affable elderly couple was always on hand to look after their basic needs. Fonda and Stewart both loved cats, and took in more than a few strays. Soon the house was overrun with them, and the noise they made, especially during their mating hours, was fearsome.

Stewart was beside himself when Fonda informed him that their next-door neighbor was none other than Miss Greta Garbo! She was making *Anna Karenina* (1935) at the time, and never did she want to be alone more than during this period. She was at the studio from early morning to early evening, rushing home for a quick dinner, script study and then bed. The Stewart-Fonda feline menagerie became the bane of her existence. They never saw her in the flesh, but a servant would come over and say, "Miss Garbo would like to know if you plan to do anything about all those cat noises." "It's the cats or Garbo, and we don't want to lose Garbo!" Hank Fonda declared. But neither did they have the heart to put out the cats, which had become like family.

Luckily for them, Garbo didn't move, and for a while — a short while — the boys had it both ways.

Stewart had seen all Garbo's movies in New York in the

1932–34 period. He could even recite lines from her movies, verbatim, much to the annoyance of his exasperated housemate. Fonda recalled, "He'd go around the house reciting them under his breath — it made our servants very nervous. The way they looked at him, I was scared they would pack and leave any time!"

Garbo continued to remain elusive. Stewart adopted all kinds of stratagems to get a glimpse of her, but to no avail. They learned that her solution to the cat problem was to put up an eight-foot wall around her property, so the boys devised a scheme to tunnel under the wall into her front yard. "We'd pick a time when she was maybe sun-bathing on a Sunday," Fonda recalled. "And then — eureka! — we'd jump out of the other hole after a rigorous dig and pretend to be surprised to see her." Stewart rehearsed what they would say at the crucial moment: "Oh, Miss Garbo, forgive us this intrusion, but this is so unexpected, and a real pleasure!" The tunneling operation, Stewart recalled, proved abortive when they busted a water main. "The water was flying down on us, the cats jumping all around in terror, and from across the wall we heard some servant yell to us: 'Stop that noise! Miss Garbo is trying to rest!'"

But Stewart remained steadfast in his See-Garbo mania. Even at the studio, he recalled ruefully years later, he couldn't get a glimpse of her. Her set was firmly closed to all — even Louis B. Mayer was treated like an intruder. Finally, in 1936, while Garbo was making her masterpiece, *Camille* (Stewart's later-declared favorite of all her movies), Stewart made a more ambitious attempt to confront The Great One.

As he remembered it: "Her dressing room might as well have been Fort Knox. A big closed limousine would deliver her at the set door the first thing in the morning, then pick her up again and whisk her away at the end of the day. I got very discouraged about ever being able to see her. But I had a friend who was a boom operator, and one day he called me and told me he was working on her set."

The pal told Stewart he would have to stay close to a phone on his own set; then when he got the word he'd have to move, fast! "I was practically glued to that phone," Jimmy laughed. "And sure enough, he called the very next day. 'She's just finished shooting,' he whispered. 'She's getting ready to leave right now.' And he even told me, which was supposed to be a very great secret, which door she was going to leave by!" Stewart recalls he "ran like the Devil and must have knocked ten or more people off balance. And when I got over to her set I was just tearing." But just as Stewart raced up to the door she was scheduled to exit, she opened it from the inside. "I was still going full speed, and I not only bumped right into her, I knocked her down! I sure tried to help her up, but I couldn't think of one damn thing to say. All I could do was just stand there and think that here I'd finally met Garbo and all I'd done was knock her down!"

Stewart reminisced in a later interview about his reaction to Hollywood as he found it in 1935:

"The Hollywood I came out to in the 1930s was the Hollywood of the Big Studio. It's all gone now, and there'll never be anything like it again. In some ways, that's too bad, because it was by far the best way to make movies — and I mean from the point of view of pictures and the actors. If you were an actor, it made it possible for you to learn your craft not by having someone talk to you about it, or by sitting in a classroom, but by doing it. You started out with little parts in little pictures, and then you went on to big parts in little pictures, and finally to big parts in big pictures. It gave you a home base, and you worked every day — six days a week. If you didn't like a part and wanted another one, you'd do it anyway. The studio heads would tell you 'Just do this one, and we'll see if we can get you something you like better later on.'"

Stewart added: "The people who ran those studios were a tough crowd — Mayer, Goldwyn, the brothers Warner, Harry Cohn and the rest of them. Hell, they were in the boxing ring with each other half the time. But they had one redeeming feature: They loved the movies, and they all had incredible judgment about what the public wanted."

Stewart started at MGM at $350 a week, working a six-day week, fifty-two weeks a year. A new contract player was required to do just about everything under the sun: make screen tests with even newer players; even work out in the studio gym; go on junkets to promote studio pictures that featured everyone but oneself. As Stewart recalled it: "You didn't pick your movies. You did what you were told. Your studio could trade you around like ball players."

At one point in 1936 he found himself working in five pictures at the same time. Each morning he had to make a check on what lot or set he would go to and *who* he was supposed to be in *what* picture for the next day's shooting. "It was damned confusing, usually hectic, but oh! the excitement in the air, the constant excitement I felt!" he remembered.

Stewart was to recall the life he and Fonda knew together in Brentwood in 1935-1936 as "equal parts work and play," and they loved both. A young photographer from Harvard, Johnny Swope, joined them shortly, and the threesome struck out to enjoy the movie capital. The year 1935 brought days of unremitting work. Fonda had started right off with three consecutive leads: *Farmer Takes a Wife*, *Way Down East*, and *I Dream Too Much*, this last as Lily Pons' leading man. His career had accelerated faster than Stewart's, who teetered from supporting parts to a lead with Margaret Sullavan in *Next Time We Love* (1936) and back to supports. "I was playing a character one could call Elmer for a while there—he was always the guy who lost the girl to the star—I was glad to get out of *that* rut—oh boy *was* I!" Stewart said later.

The wide-eyed trio were soon sampling the Hollywood nightlife. Fonda remembered: "We'd go over to the Trocadero or the Cocoanut Grove. They were wonderful sorts of nightclubs. We didn't get very good tables because the maître d's didn't know who we were."

Ringside tables, he recalled, were for studio owners, major stars, favored relatives or top producers. Stars on the wane, feature-players and directors made up the middle of the room. Starlets, mere contract players, and of course the lowly writers, received only indifferent service, and were kept behind the ropes, or banished to seats near the exits. Waiters hoping to be "discovered" for films catered obsequiously only to the famous.

Stewart remembered: "They stayed open all night, those nightclubs, and the most famous people just got up and performed. Mary and Jack Benny, George Burns and Gracie Allen, Red Skelton, and I remember one night Judy Garland's mother brought her. Judy wore pigtails and bobby sox and she sang for an hour. Absolutely terrific! I don't know why people had, and have, the impression that Hollywood is a cold, unfriendly place. Hank and Johnny and I had great times!"

And then there were women. Stewart and Fonda led off with double dates—with Ginger Rogers and Lucille Ball, respectively.

Ginger Rogers was already a star in 1936; her films with Fred Astaire had made her one of the most celebrated dancer-actresses in America. Ball, also an RKO player, was on her way up. Rogers had just come off her second marriage — to Lew Ayres — and had had enough of serious relationships for a time. Ayres had been "too quiet and scholarly and intellectual" for her, she told Stewart. Lew seemed to prefer the company of his close pal Billy Bakewell, who had appeared with him six years earlier in *All Quiet on the Western Front* (1930). He also had his fair share of fleeting involvements with women. Based on the Erich Maria Remarque novel, *All Quiet* is one of the great movie war pictures, uncharacteristically portraying a sympathetic view of the German side of WWI. Many of the actors formed strong friendships (what today would be called supermale-bonding) and Lew, Billy, Russell Gleason, Ben Alexander and others were always to be spiritually close. The film had imbued the sensitive Lew with such a hatred of war that he became a conscientious objector in World War II, but ironically became a war hero for nursing soldiers as a medic on the battlefields.

Ginger admired Lew and wished him well, she told Stewart, but he was too staid for her taste. Soon it appeared that she found Stewart himself a little slow for her speed, and she let him know it. They continued to date as friends and later co-starred in *Vivacious Lady* (1938), as did Fonda and Ball in *The Big Street* (1942). The Fonda-Ball pairing generated slightly more heat than did the other; as Lucille later put it: "Hank and I got along fine, but we did not fall in love with each other — the chemistry wasn't there — and while we enjoyed the necking and petting (as they called these things then) we wound up just pals."

Meanwhile the foursome spent a lot of time together, and the fan mag mavens and the gossip columnists had a field day. "Let them think whatever the hell they want, and print it too," Howard Strickling, MGM's publicity head, told Stewart. "We've got to make you big with the girls; the fans like it. What they don't know won't hurt 'em. Anyway, they like to use their imaginations."

Lucille was to recall pleasant evenings at Hank and Jim's. Hank would whip up what she called "tasty" meals for them (his cooking had obviously improved since the Madison Square days). They'd turn up the radio and Ginger would perfect their dancing skills, teaching them fancy turns like the Carioca, which was a rage on the ballroom floors at the time and which she and Astaire had introduced in one of their films. Then they went dancing at the Cocoanut Grove.

This pleasant quartet, with wistful Johnny Swope hoping to break in somewhere along the line, continued for some months. Soon the 10-cent-variety fan magazines were having a field day with stories titled: HAS JIMMY HELPED GINGER FORGET LEW? and CAN GINGER CHOOSE BETWEEN FONDA AND STEWART? and GINGER'S TRAIL OF HEARTBREAK—CAN SHY, SWEET JIMMY STEWART BE THE ANSWER TO HER PRAYERS? Ginger's favorite was: GINGER ROGERS CONFESSES TO HER FANS: I NEED A MAN! (*Is Jimmy Stewart Home Port for Her?*)

Fonda fondly recalled: "We'd all laugh over those fan magazine stories, and once we decided to play a gag. We had three lady fan-mag writers over to Brentwood for dinner and put on the act of the century. We pretended that Jim and I had become a triangle for Lucille and were fighting over her, and that Ginger was jealous because Jim was allegedly neglecting her for Lucille, and Johnny Swope played along with it by pretending he was busily out to break up Jim and Lucille, and then Ginger confessed that she had tried cooking and had made a special cake for Johnny and this put Jim's and Hank's noses out of joint, and so on and so on. We got all that packed into three damned evening hours, and darn, the lady fan-maggers ate it all up, pulling out notebooks during the dessert and frantically scribbling away!"

Stewart recalled, laughingly: "I don't know what in tarnation would have happened if Hank hadn't blabbed to a Fox publicity man about his 'joke,' and Fox notified Strickling and MGM publicity, and it took a lot of wining and dining to brainwash and beguile the ladies out of printing any of it!" Meanwhile, back at the hardware store in Indiana, Pennsylvania, Alexander Stewart was sternly writing his son to the effect that he was 27 years old and ought to be getting married and not letting those "racy, loose" Hollywood women take him up the wrong path. "There's nothing like a good, long-lasting relationship such as your mother and I have had to make a real man of you," he admonished in one letter. Phone calls along the same lines followed, and finally Stewart sat down and wrote his father that he couldn't conceive of marrying until he was really, truly, permanently in love. Since this blessing had not yet come, he was having fun and enjoying being young while he was young. He concluded that everything would come in due course.

Stewart's mother was equally concerned, and in one letter cut innocently and unconsciously close to the bone. She made him wince with an observation that "you've been living with men too much, and that's not real domestic living." Stewart didn't argue that one — he let it pass.

Soon the senior Stewarts' neighbors were leaving fan magazines at the hardware store, with clips and folded corners pointing to articles that had Jim madly in love with Ginger Rogers and in a triangle with Fonda for Lucille Ball (the sly Strickling had obviously let the fan-mag mavens have their head after all, "and after pretending indignation, too!" Jimmy spluttered to Hank). The Stewarts' opinion of Rogers and Ball were wary and reserved, along the lines of "Wasn't *she* married?" "Isn't *she* divorced?" and "*She* seems on the loose side." Then the column items really went to town: Jimmy had a yen for Janet Gaynor, found Jean Harlow a wonderful kisser, adored Eleanor Powell, still had a crush on Margaret Sullavan (a lady the Stewarts of Pennsylvania considered *particularly* racy and unsuitable), was "that way" about Wendy Barrie, longed with every fiber of his being for Jeanette MacDonald, and so on *ad nauseam*. All of these ladies, of course, were appearing with Jim in various movies during 1936, and the MGM publicity department was working overtime. Unaccustomed to the recondite ways of Hollywood and its "press relations," the Stewarts worked up considerable fright over Jimmy. He began to get letters about "the danger of catching social diseases from loose women" and how there might be safety in numbers but there was cheapness, too, and how the Stewarts' neighbors were kidding them about these titillating headlines. Stewart sighed and gave up rejoinders home, confining his letters to reports on his acting work.

In his second film, some months after his initial stint, Stewart found himself supporting Jeanette MacDonald and Nelson Eddy. The powerhouse singing stars were cashing in on the success of their debut pairing in *Naughty Marietta* (1935) with yet another hit, *Rose Marie* (1936). In this Stewart plays John Flower, criminal younger brother of opera star Marie De Flor (MacDonald). She learns, while singing in Montreal, that Stewart has fled to the wilds

James Stewart and Nelson Eddy, *Rose Marie*, MGM, 1936

of western Canada after killing a policeman. She determines to find him, and after her guide deserts her, she is taken in by Mountie Eddy. He accompanies her in full knowledge (unknown to her) that she is looking for the brother he is pledged to apprehend. When Eddy and MacDonald fall in love, he sets his duty first and arrests her brother, leaving her heartbroken. Later, she suffers a nervous breakdown and takes a sabbatical from her operatic career, but the Mountie finds her and they are joyfully reunited.

All of this is set forth in lavish musical terms, with MacDonald and Eddy giving their all to music and songs by Rudolf Friml and MGM's musical director Herbert Stothart, who even tried his hand at a song or two for MacDonald.

It is to the 27-year-old Stewart's credit that he is neither cowed nor drowned-out by the stars' singing feats. He gives a credible and sympathetic performance as the young murderer who is deeply saddened by his sister's grief over him, and even touched by the love between her and the Mountie.

Stewart remembered that MacDonald showed him every kindness during the shooting: "It was only my second picture, and Jeanette couldn't have been nicer from start to finish. She knew I was green and she kept my spirits up in ways great and small. She even asked Woody Van Dyke [the director] to show me to advantage in some of the shots." Eddy, too, he found down-to-earth and kindly. "Nelson was always a solid, no-nonsense guy — he was no male prima donna. He knew he could sing but always considered himself a lousy actor. He was in many ways a humble person, and I think," Stewart added, "that he preferred the stage and nightclubs to films because he was in control as a singer and not pushed this way and that, as is inevitable in films."

A number of fans and critics sat up and took notice of Stewart in *Rose Marie*. He was particularly proud of the fan letters he got from his home town in Pennsylvania — even from people who had worked with him in New York. Billy Grady was particularly pleased with the impression he had made, and told him, "You've got all it takes for the camera. It's just a matter of time."

Frances Goodrich wrote the screenplay for *Rose Marie* with her husband Albert Hackett, adapting it from the musical play by Otto Harbach and Oscar Hammerstein. She told me in 1981, regarding Stewart: "Word had gotten around the studio that the boy was good, and we added some dialogue to build up his scenes. We had seen him in the Judith Anderson play in New York a while before, and Albert and I both agreed that he was a comer."

There was no burgeoning romance of any kind between Stewart and MacDonald. Aside from the fact that they weren't each other's "type," she was seven years his senior. The healthy chemistry between them had to do with maternal concern on her part and respectful awe on his. But he didn't allow this to mar his honest spontaneous approach to the brother-sister intimacy their parts called for. Even at this early date in films, Stewart was completely natural and unassuming.

One critic noted: "Newcomer James Stewart who, we understand, has done himself credit on the Broadway stage, is completely winning as MacDonald's young brother who runs afoul of the law. While his role is brief and strictly subordinate, he gets himself across in fine style. It is said that all supporting players dread to be in a MacDonald-Eddy film because no matter how good they are or how well-written their parts, they find themselves overshadowed by the stars' singing pyrotechnics. Young Stewart weathers this right nicely."

It was Margaret Sullavan who accelerated Stewart's rise to film stardom. She had come a long way from their University Players days four years before. Now she was a major star, as big a woman on the Universal lot as Katharine Hepburn, her professional and romantic rival, was at RKO. Sullavan's 1933 movie debut, in *Only Yesterday*, had made as big a splash as Hepburn's in the 1932 *A Bill of Divorcement*. They had also been, and would continue to be, love rivals for Broadway producer Jed Harris and famed agent Leland Hayward, with Sullavan emerging the victor in both tournaments.

Since *Only Yesterday*, Sullavan had solidified her position with film audiences and critics in such films as *Little Man, What Now?* (1934) and *The Good Fairy* (1935). Her direct, no-nonsense style and affecting, emotional underplaying had won her a loyal legion of admirers. In 1935, with her first marriage, to Henry Fonda, firmly in the past, Sullavan embarked on an epic marital mismatch with brilliant director William Wyler. Unfortunately, they had associated themselves, as star and director, with *The Good Fairy*, and while the final result added to both their laurels, their temperamental clashes on the set had become the stuff of legend.

Sullavan had taken note of Stewart's flounderings at MGM. She was touched by his abiding love for her, and because she sincerely wanted to help, she maneuvered Universal into borrowing him as her leading man for her upcoming film, *Next Time We Love* (1936). Based on Ursula Parrott's novel, it was scripted by Melville Baker under the title *Next Time We Live* (the original title had been *Say Goodbye Again*) with Sullavan urging that "Love" be substituted for "Live."

She wasn't wild about the script, but felt something might be made of it with sincere, expert acting, and she knew that Stewart was ideal for the co-starring role. She had some difficulty in getting the Universal powers-that-be interested in borrowing a young MGM contract player who had appeared only fleetingly in two recent films. "But who the hell is *he*?" they asked her. After citing his solid experience in Broadway plays, she did a selling job, making his roles in *Murder Man* and *Rose Marie* seem weightier than they actually were (she gambled that no one at Universal had seen either).

She told them that this new man, all of 27 years old, had a totally unique persona that audiences would instantly respond to if he were properly presented. "But what if we should build up an MGM contractee on loanout and send him back a star — wouldn't MGM get the best of it on that?" they asked. The feisty Sullavan's patience began to wear thin at that. "Well, you boys don't think he's worth anything now," she rejoindered, "so if you are worried about *that* possibility, well, then, you must secretly think as highly of him as I do!"

Confronted with the adamant Sullavan's stellar clout, they agreed to borrow Stewart. Ray Milland was assigned to the other leading role, and Edward H. Griffith, a lackluster but efficient director, was put on the picture.

The story of *Next Time We Love* dealt with fledgling newspaperman Stewart and budding actress Sullavan who fall in love while they are struggling in New York. He goes on to success as a correspondent in Europe after their marriage, and she, over the course of

James Stewart and Margaret Sullavan, *Next Time We Love*, Universal, 1936

the next ten years, achieves Broadway stardom. Their respective careers keep them apart most of the time, though they never lose their love for each other. They have one child, a son. Milland plays a producer who has long loved Sullavan, but who knows when he's licked in a tournament of amour.

But while visiting Stewart in Europe, Sullavan learns that he is dying of a disease he contracted while on a stint in China, and promises that she will stay with him for what time remains. She makes the rueful observation that if they ever have another life to live, they will find the requisite time for each other that they didn't manage the first time around.

Judged as cinematic art, *Next Time We Love* is no great shakes, much of it being soapy and contrived, but the fine, sincere playing of Sullavan and Stewart more than compensates for the inherent deficiencies of the script.

During the shooting, Sullavan carefully analyzed Stewart's persona — there was that boyish awkwardness, the hesitancy in the mannerisms, the drawling speech patterns, yes. But under the proper stimulus of the situations called for by the script, these endearingly quirky traits could suddenly change into an intensity and authority that were surprising. Stewart, confronted with his first major film role, was understandably nervous, nor did he find much approval from director Griffith, who thought him inexperienced before the camera, and that he tended to fall back on stage projections. Soon Griffith was bullying him, reducing him, on occasion, almost to tears. Griffith went to Sullavan with his complaints that their boy was wet behind the ears, that his stage career had only been brief, that he was going to mess up the picture.

Sullavan insisted that Griffith was wrong, that the picture was going to take Stewart a giant step toward film stardom. Soon she was coaching him herself, evening after evening, helping him to scale down his mannerisms. They went over the script together line by line. Patient, understanding, indeed maternal, she kept him going on lots of coffee, heard all his complaints about Griffith, held his hand — figuratively if not literally.

Soon Griffith and the Universal executives were surprised at what they saw in the rushes. Admitting at last that this new Stewart boy could really act, Griffith put out his hand in reconciliation to his male star, and after that matters proceeded smoothly to the end of shooting. In later years, Griffith would say, again and again, "It was Maggie Sullavan who made Jimmy Stewart a star!"

Billy Grady told me: "That boy came back from Universal so changed I hardly recognized him. In his next few pictures at MGM [during 1936] [Jimmy] showed a confidence, a command of film technique, that was startling. [Sullavan] had taught him to march to his own drummer, to be himself, completely — and in doing that she had unleashed the unique and distinctive qualities that made Jim Stewart one of the greatest of film stars."

Of course, Jimmy Stewart's ongoing love for Maggie Sullavan (whom he was always to call Peggy) was one of the cardinal factors in their wonderful onscreen interplay. He showed, especially in his love scenes, a warmth and tenderness and utter sincerity that he was never to approximate quite so fully with any other actress. This, no doubt, was the factor that was to influence MGM to cast him in three more pictures with Sullavan when she too went under contract to them.

In *Next Time We Love*, Stewart had grabbed the chance to express toward Sullavan, via the coincidental felicities of the script, emotions he had long been harboring but had been too fearful to express. As of late 1935, when the film was shot, Stewart had not yet embarked on his career as Hollywood Stud-Around-Town Supreme, and was still projecting these virginal qualities that many found endearing.

There was some protracted debate among Hollywood insiders in the 1936-40 period (when they made four films together) as to whether Sullavan and Stewart had ever slept together. Billy Grady didn't think they did. He felt that playing around with other men's wives had never been Jimmy's style. During that same period Sullavan went through two more husbands. As for Sullavan, she loved him, but it was not the physical, lecherous love other men had aroused in her. "He got her all motherly and sisterly" one friend said, "and those aren't very sexy emotions."

Was Stewart disappointed over Sullavan's attitude? Many friends felt he was, but he didn't do much talking about it, even to John Swope and Henry Fonda. In fact he was quite reticent about his exact feelings for Sullavan. Howard Strickling, the MGM publicity man, felt that this was not only in deference to her married status, but to protect his pride. His public pronouncements on

Margaret Sullavan usually ran along such lines as "I owe so much to her professionally. She made me a star with that role in *Next Time We Love*. And she has been such a good friend." And so forth and so on.

When rumors persisted that Stewart did not marry until age 41 (in 1949) because he was carrying a year-in-year-out torch for Sullavan, he did nothing to dispel them. But Jerry Asher and George Cukor, among others, felt that Sullavan, who knew men very well, had possibly wondered about his sexual predilections. She had heard the gossip about his prominently-placed older male admirers while he was a young actor on Broadway, and while always a firm defender of gay fellow performers, she wasn't chancing it in a more intimate context. As the years went on without his marrying, sinister rumors of this kind kept cropping up. Jerry Asher mused: "Just because he was able to bluff along with the other guys at that whorehouse MGM set up to keep their actors out of trouble didn't mean all that much. Perhaps Jimmy was a better actor than he was given credit for — offscreen, I mean."

For a while in 1936 some glamour of a sort was added to the Stewart legend when rumors abounded that temperamental director Willy Wyler had blamed him for the breakup of his marriage to Sullavan that year, though he in reality had had nothing to do with it.

"Willy resented all the time Sullavan was giving Jimmy on *Next Time We Love*," Ruth Waterbury told me. "He was building it into a romance, though he was wrong. Maggie made the mistake of taking Willy to a screening of the picture, and he boiled over when he saw how intensely and sincerely Jimmy was playing the love scenes." The critics picked up on the screen teaming, with the *New York Herald-Tribune* finding Sullavan "honest and beautiful" and Stewart "admirable." "Promising," "individual," "a welcome addition to the roster of leading men" were other kudos he relished.

Back at MGM again after the Universal outing, Stewart found himself playing second — or was it third? — romantic fiddle to superstars Clark Gable and Robert Taylor. Gable was already long-established, and Taylor was the hottest new male actor since his hit with Irene Dunne in Universal's *Magnificent Obsession* (1935).

In *Wife Versus Secretary* (1936), with Gable, who plays a publisher, Stewart is the also-ran boyfriend of Gable's secretary, Jean

Harlow. He gets in a few scenes with her along the way, but Gable grabs the lion's share of Harlow's attention. Also on hand is Myrna Loy, who stands in danger of becoming the also-ran wife of Gable, what with Gable and Harlow spending so much time together, and working late and all that. When Myrna calls her husband while he is on a Havana business trip and secretary Harlow answers the phone (yes, they've been working late) the Perfect Wife suspects the worst. She almost leaves her husband, but self-sacrificing Harlow, who certainly has a yen for Gable, tells her to stay with him and not be a fool, for nothing has been going on.

Production Code strictures were rampant in 1936, so it is, retrospectively, a pity that nothing did follow those tentatively hot-eye-exchanges Gable and Harlow indulge in during those Havana hotel room scenes. Having done the right thing by giving Gable back to Loy, Harlow belatedly — but not too belatedly — decides that Stewart is more promising hubby material than she had thought.

Harlow and Gable in 1936 were approaching the zenith of their careers. Harlow had done a number of pictures with Gable over the previous four years, but in 1937 would tragically die in the middle of yet another Gable co-starrer, *Saratoga*. Gable, of course, went on to scale the heights in *Gone With the Wind* (1939). As of 1936, the Harlow-Gable-Loy combination was a hot one, with Loy, who had also appeared often with Gable, supplying the balance in their respective chemistries that made for stellar fission.

Stewart was strictly along for the ride against these power-houses, but he makes his few scenes with Harlow count. Many years later Stewart described Harlow as "all woman. When she kissed, she really kissed. Some actresses fake it. Not Jean. I did quite a love scene with her — long before it became the thing to do on screen. I remember it to this day — we did it six times. And that dress! Yes, she was braless and she didn't seem to wear anything under the dress." He added, "Well, I forgot my lines. That's what I did!"

Harlow was, at least histrionically, overwhelmed by Gable's manly charms, and in early 1936 was pursuing a passionate, largely-unrequited love affair with yet another sometime co-star, William Powell. The *Thin Man* star wouldn't offer her marriage, however, because he had (for a time) soured on the institution after his debacle with Carole Lombard. Harlow, always an experienced "man-

izer" (the term editor Jimmy Quirk of *Photoplay* magazine had once coined to describe a woman who knew her way around men and then some) had meantime taken full note of Jimmy Stewart's boyish reservoirs of passion. For reasons known to her alone, she left them untapped, much to Stewart's great disappointment. He later admitted that he would have liked very much to have added her to his roster of conquests offscreen, but it was not to be. In retrospect Stewart blamed William Powell, who seemed to have siphoned off all of Harlow's deeper emotions, but she was, after all, engaged to the man.

Harlow did confide to Stewart, and any other cast members who would listen, her desperation over not being able to talk Powell into marriage. "He's through with it for good," she lamented. "Twice burned, permanently warned, I guess." The irony in this is that when Powell finally did marry, three years after Harlow's death, he stayed married for forty-four years to starlet Diana Lewis, until his death in 1984.

Myrna Loy always had relatively little to say of Stewart, especially since in later years their politics differed, she being a liberal Democrat, Stewart a conservative Republican. They had no scenes in *Wife Versus Secretary*, in fact were never to officially co-star together, but she did say that everyone thought in 1936 that he was a very striking and promising individual. Neither of them, then or at any other time, was ever accused of even the faintest romantic interest in the other.

Robert Taylor was the other MGM star that Stewart found himself playing second banana to in *Small Town Girl* (1936), which co-starred Janet Gaynor. Janet, at 31, was on loan from 20th Century-Fox, having passed her zenith as a star. She felt keenly her neglect at the hands of the new Zanuck-led henchmen at Fox, and she was to make only a few more films before retiring in 1938 and marrying MGM designer Gilbert Adrian. She made one final cinematic appearance, in *Bernardine* (1957).

Romantic yearning and girlish dreaminess were Janet's specialty, so she was co-starred with the six-years-younger Taylor in a flimsy romance, scripted by John Lee Mahin from a Ben Ames Williams novel. It concerned a socially prominent young doctor who picks up a — what else? — small town girl, gets drunk with her, and winds up next morning her husband. Taylor's snooty family, to save their so-

cial reputation, suggest they stay as man and wife for six months, live together, take vacations together, and so on. Of course Gaynor realizes she is permanently in love, and the dashing, but initially confused Taylor finally reaches the same conclusion. He ditches his social-climbing fiancée (Binnie Barnes) in favor of his wife.

But the path of true love never runs smooth. Before the happy ending, Gaynor, temporarily in despair, returns to the small town and, it would seem, her hayseed boyfriend Elmer. This thankless role was essayed by a hapless Stewart.

Stewart had a time of it making Elmer at all interesting. He is written as earnest but boring, intelligent enough but hopelessly literal-minded. As it turns out he has little chance to bore Gaynor for long, as Taylor sees the light and comes, forthwith, to reclaim her.

Despite his difficulties with a role that gave him only a few trivial scenes with which to establish a characterization, and despite the unsympathetic William A. Wellman, who felt as alien to directing this kind of romantic hogwash as Stewart did to acting it, Jimmy did manage to garner a set of decent reviews. A Baltimore critic commented that "James Stewart does what he can with a boring yokel and even succeeds in making him minimally sympathetic at times." Another critic was less kind, stating: "Whether it is his intrinsic personality that is to blame, or the deadly dullness of his role, Mr. James Stewart cannot seem to get Janet Gaynor's castoff boyfriend beyond the starting post."

Stewart later admitted that playing the also-ran to the stellar likes of Gable and Taylor got him mightily down at times, but, as always, the supportive Billy Grady tided him over the rough spots. "Your turn is coming, kid, and it's coming big when it does!" Grady told him more than once.

There has been much rumor and speculation about Stewart's relationship with Janet Gaynor. She was between husbands at the time, and she succumbed, as many a woman before and since, to Stewart's boyish charisma. Eddie Mannix told me he had watched them "commune" during the shooting of *Small Town Girl*, and he was convinced that it was more on her side than on his. "Jimmy was never the man to say no to any halfway-attractive woman who indicated an interest," Eddie told me. "Not because he was so generous with himself, but because he enjoyed feeling attractive." Eddie added, "And it wasn't narcissism or a power complex or any of that

other Freudian bunk. I think it had more to do with some fundamental insecurity in Jimmy. He needed to feel attractive!"

The Gaynor-Stewart involvement, such as it was, did not last
long. Gaynor was only at Metro on loanout, and she soon went elsewhere. With an embarrassment of riches among the MGM contract
list to choose from, to say nothing of other available ladies from the
outside, Stewart did not keep Gaynor in his thoughts for long. "Out
of sight out of mind," was Eddie Mannix's dismissive verdict on the
Gaynor-Stewart "thing," whatever it was or might have been.

After suffering through Elmer in *Small Town Girl*, Stewart, to
his delight, found himself co-starring with Eleanor Powell in the
charming musical, *Born to Dance* (1936), which holds up well even
after all these years, thanks to the sprightly direction of Roy Del
Ruth and the songs by Cole Porter. Writers Jack McGowan, Sid Silvers and B.G. DeSylva concocted a lively confection of a plot and
cameraman Ray June made Powell and Stewart look attractive indeed.

Stewart owed his co-starring stint in this latest project to the gay
songwriting genius Cole Porter, who had fallen in love with him
and made no bones about it. Porter had first developed a yen for
Stewart from first-row seats at *Yellow Jack* and *Divided by Three* in
New York. Reportedly he had been introduced to Stewart by the
unlikely, but in this case mightily accommodating, Judith Anderson.

Stewart was to get the role of Ted Barker, the submarine crew-
man, who with his buddies Sid Silvers and Buddy Ebsen, meets
Eleanor Powell at the aptly-named Lonely Hearts Club. He proceeds to sing and dance with her such snappy Porter compositions
as "Hey, Baby, Hey." Later he was required to sing one of Porter's
most inspired love songs, "Easy to Love," in an intimate tête-à-tête
with Powell.

But there was one drawback: Stewart didn't sing well. That did
not deter the smitten Porter, who had all MGM gossiping with his
vociferous determination to get Stewart the starring-singing-danc-
ing role of Teddy. One writer has quoted Cole Porter's diary for
April 24, 1936, which tells of how Porter "lured" (if that is the word)
27-year-old Stewart over to his house for an "audition." According
to the diary, "[Jimmy] came over to the house and I heard him sing.
He sings far from well, although he has some nice notes in his voice
[sic], but he could play the part perfectly."

Billy Grady and Eddie Mannix later told me of Porter's man-sized crush on Stewart. "Louella Parsons knew all about it," Billy told me, "and we could have drawn and quartered her for her sly, mean innuendoes about it in her column. Oh, nothing the uninitiated world would have caught on to that easily, but it was an embarrassment, and I know it embarrassed Jimmy."

Mannix opined that "Jimmy loved admiration no matter where it came from. If Cole was sweet on him, he felt, that was Cole's problem, but he wanted that part—it was not only a lead, but it widened his range. I tried to tell him he couldn't sing or dance for shit, but he said he could bluff it and could even make it entertaining by buffooning it up a bit."

Word of all this got to studio head Louis B. Mayer, who considered Porter a musical genius and had even allowed him a production say, much to producer Jack Cummings's annoyance. But Mayer took precautions. "It's Porter's kind of material, but keep him at his piano, writing at home and off the set as much as possible. And for God's sake, don't let Jimmy Stewart go over to his house again! If he wants to see Jimmy he'll have to come to the studio—and he is *not* to see him alone!"

How man-mad Cole Porter reacted to all those strictures and precautions is not recorded for posterity—some twenty pages of his diary for April and May 1936 were mysteriously excised, whether by him or someone else is not known. But the picture was a bright enough musical, with Eleanor Powell, some seven years before her marriage to Glenn Ford—following up well on her tap dancing success in *Broadway Melody of 1936*. Her terpsichorean proficiency, as always, was exemplary; her acting, as always, was negligible.

The frantic MGM publicity department, whose insiders were alerted to Porter's alarming passion for Jimmy Stewart, began pouring out pages of drivel on the new Powell-Stewart "romance." In actuality that came to nothing, for both were too much alike to find each other appealing. Eleanor Powell has been called, perhaps unkindly, a "female Jimmy Stewart." She shared his penchant for awkward gaucheries and gawky stances, which, in Jimmy's case, proved assets. But in her case these were liabilities that the studio covered up by keeping her splendid legs on fitting display along with her magical taps. Virginia Bruce was briefly on hand as Eleanor's on-screen love rival for Jimmy. One reviewer wrote, "Thanks to Cole

Porter's romantic inspirations [sic], the Powell girl and the Stewart boy make a charming twosome."

It was Billy Grady, on the watch as always for Stewart's best interests, who talked the MGM executives into casting Stewart in his first MGM lead. True, the vehicle selected, *Speed* (1936), was designed strictly for the bottom half of a double bill, but to Grady it spelled progress for Pal Jimmy. Billy told me years later:

"I told L.B. and the other boys that this kid had made a splash over at Universal with Maggie Sullavan in *Next Time We Love*, and for that matter he was no kid, being a ripe 28 years old, and why the hell was he playing third-fiddle bits in Jean Harlow and Janet Gaynor pictures when he had all the earmarks of a star! I'm glad to say the boys went for my selling point."

Edwin L. Marin, who as a director was distinctly one of MGM's also-rans, was assigned to get the Michael Fessier-Milton Krims-Larry Bachman story on film. The result ran only 65 minutes, but Stewart had pretty Wendy Barrie opposite him, and such strong supports as Ted Healy, Una Merkel and Ralph Morgan on hand. The story was fast-paced trivia about a race car mechanic-test driver who invents a carburetor that gets tested on the Indianapolis Speedway. Wendy works for Stewart's auto company boss, and she and Stewart begin a three-cornered romance with handsome Weldon Heyburn, an engineer who is Stewart's rival, of a sort. After some false starts, Stewart's idea is proven sound, and he gets the credit — and the girl.

With his eye constantly on the lookout for fresh feminine charms, Stewart cottoned mightily to Wendy Barrie, who led him on for a while but soon made it clear she was occupied elsewhere. "He was a bit on the intense side for me," Barrie later said, "but the boyish charm that guy had! I think part of his aggressiveness with women, and he *was* agressive, was due to his feeling that he was not handsome — he had this image of himself as a tall, gawky loon — and I felt that Weldon Heyburn, a Henry Wilcoxon type who was the conventionally handsome type, made him uneasy. Of course the irony here was that Weldon, for all his masculine come-hither and good looks, was to fall by the wayside while Jimmy ended up the big star!"

Others at the time felt that Stewart was just as well out of it with Wendy, who had a penchant — or possibly just the bad luck — for taking up with shady underworld characters, one of whom established a lifelong romantic monopoly on her. Stewart might just have found one or both of his long legs broken had his timing been wrong.

Stewart later told one of his biographers, Tony Thomas, that his only solid memory of *Speed* was the sound advice Ted Healy gave him: "He told me to think of the audience not simply as watchers but as collaborators, as sort of partners in the project. He was right, and that helped me in my attitude toward the business."

Shot quickly on a limited budget typical for a "B," *Speed* used up plenty of MGM stock footage, including an automobile factory and the Indianapolis Speedway. But the *Los Angeles Examiner*, while passing quickly over what was obviously a minor MGM programmer, commented: "Young Mr. Stewart shows his mettle to some advantage here. He has vitality and screen presence. We predict he will go places."

Eager to find out what Maggie Sullavan thought of the film, Stewart dragged her to a projection-room screening. With her usual directness, his benefactress from Universal told him that *Speed* was processed dog food, and added that while she had put in such effort to raise his stock in her picture, why the hell was his home studio throwing him away?

Stewart tried to interject that it was at least a starring part, but she snorted contemptuously. She told him that it was better to get two or three minutes in a Harlow or Gaynor movie than the lead in "hogwash no one is going to look at — or not much — while they're waiting for the big picture they really came to see!" She added, "At least when they're all eyes for the big female star you're in a scene with, they can't help looking at you, too!"

In his next picture, he got more than three minutes, but he was lost in a swarm of king bees buzzing around yet another major female MGM star.

The Gorgeous Hussy (1936) was the first of two pictures Stewart made with the flamboyant and egoistically self-conscious Joan Crawford. And this time Joan had four — count 'em, four! — leading men. Stewart, naturally, was the least of them. As a character incongruously named Rowdy Dow, he didn't even get to make love to her; he merely postured around in 1830s costumes and long sideburns making what passed for snappy retorts that screenwriters Ainsworth Morgan and Stephen Morehouse Avery, revamping from a Samuel Hopkins Adams historical novel, considered proper to the period. Even so, due to the Production Code strictures, Crawford could not be as blatant a hussy as the situations seemed to imply.

The period is the 1829-1837 Presidency of Lionel Barrymore's Andrew Jackson. Crawford is the innkeeper's daughter who becomes the scandal of Washington due to her many romantic liaisons, advanced views on women's suffrage, and other distaff issues. She is even rumored to be involved with the President, thus qualifying the august Barrymore, then a ripe 58, as her fifth leading man. Of course Lionel is in love with his wife, the pipe-smoking Rachel (Beulah Bondi) and it's an outrageous canard, worthy of dueling, suh! But there are no duels to speak of, only a succession of marriages and love affairs, with Stewart losing out in both categories. First, Crawford's Peggy, during her upward climb on a ladder of men, gets rejected by a senator (Melvyn Douglas). Then she marries handsome naval officer Robert Taylor who gets killed in short order after an in-and-out (no pun intended) appearance. Then — let's see — there's Crawford's real-life husband at the time, Franchot Tone, a cabinet minister who marries her and takes her to the uppermost heights of Washington society — for a time. Soon she is the victim of political and social opprobrium for her "manizings" and liberal stances. Result: the President orders an inquiry, she is completely exonerated, but chooses to leave Washington so as not to further embarrass the Adminstration. While happiness for her and her husband are implicitly presaged, her character as limned would seem to have become mightily bored without challenges to struggle against — a fitting description of the real-life Crawford, incidentally.

Stewart gets horribly lost in the shuffle, but the Stewart personality, at least, seems to fit the historical ambience more authentically than do some of the more modern players, most notoriously La Crawford herself. This was Crawford's first costume role, and since she had always been so garishly and emphatically contemporary, she seemed as out of place as a cat swimming in a fish tank.

The 28-year-old Stewart's manly charms were not lost on Crawford, but (happily for him) she was in the first year of her marriage to Franchot Tone, and when Joan was in love (or thought she was) she tended to give her all to one man at a time. Tone's acting talent (he never got his just due in Hollywood, which embittered him profoundly) and his intellectual and cultural prowess awed and impressed Joan mightily. They got involved in amateur theatricals and went on other cultural binges, with the erudite Cornell-graduate-Tone as master, and former chorus girl opportunist Crawford as pupil. The marriage was to come apart within three years, with Tone beating his wife (her facial bruises used to horrify the makeup department) and jealously brooding over her greater filmic success. Her miscarriages were an added problem, as both desperately wanted children.

But in mid-1936 all this was in the future. Joan Crawford had demanded of Louis B. Mayer that she—the third of the celebrated Garbo-Shearer-Crawford Trinity of the Lion Studio—be allowed to sashay through a historical film in the most lavish period costumes Adrian could devise. Always jealous of Shearer, who had appeared that same year in *Romeo and Juliet,* and awed by Garbo, who had done such costumers as *Anna Karenina* (1935) and would do *Camille* (1937) in the same period, Little Joanie felt that *The Gorgeous Hussy* would complete her ascent—indeed crown it—from kitchen-slavey to chorus-girl to shopgirl-on-the-rise to adventuress-about-town—all of which incarnations had taken her to top stellar fame from 1925 to 1936.

It is significant that Crawford avoided period films from the time of *The Gorgeous Hussy* on. Not only was her heroine-deluxe role of Peggy Eaton watered down by the Production Code, she tried too hard. She was too self-important, overawed by the wonder of her flouncing costumes, the horses and coaches, and other furbelows of the 1830s. As a result she came on as unconvincing and false, and more than one major reviewer came right out and said so. Sullenly she henceforth surrendered the "costume stuff," as she called it, to Garbo and Shearer.

Writer-publicist Jerry Asher spent a great deal of time on the *Gorgeous Hussy* set, as he told me many years later. A close friend of both Crawford and Tone, he was often a guest at their Brentwood home, and he was the recipient of Crawford's confidences in her dressing room throughout the shooting. "She knew she had made a strategic blunder, and Joan was never easy to be around when she was behind the game," he told me. "She kept all the men on edge too, because they knew how unhappy she was, and she blew her lines so often that she had them fluffing, too. Clarence Brown, the director, who had started with high hopes, was feeling low most of the time, exasperated as he was trying to make 1936-style Joan make like 1836."

Jerry also remembered the young Jimmy Stewart: "He was giving one of the best performances in the picture, second only to Lionel Barrymore, who had done many costumers and knew instinctively what was required to make a year like 1836 come alive on an MGM sound stage." Jerry added, "There was a wonderful adaptability to Jimmy. His lines were somewhat false and stilted at times, but he gave them an edge of reality and down-to-earth force and credibility. It was obvious he was going places, and in this film was only marking time."

Nor did reviewers fail to notice him. One wrote: "Lionel Barrymore and James Stewart seem at ease in the period — which is more than can be said for the star."

In his final MGM picture of 1936, Stewart found himself supporting the redoubtable William Powell and Myrna Loy in the second of their *Thin Man* films, this one titled *After the Thin Man*. MGM probably felt it was doing the increasingly noticeable Stewart a major favor by casting him in a film with the surefire box office team. But if they hoped to cash in on the Powell-Loy fan following, it didn't really do that much for Stewart, primarily because he was sadly miscast as the murderer, a neurotic young society man who has become deranged and embittered by rejection in love.

Some critics have claimed that Stewart was in a role beyond his depth, which is not really true. At 28 years old, he was by then seasoned by three years on the stage and eight prior films in the 1935-36 period. The real problem lay in the fact that the fans cross-country had come to visualize Stewart as a nice guy, a gangling variation on the ultimate boy scout, and they found it difficult to accept their clean-cut hero as obsessive and murderous.

Miscasting aside, Stewart is professional enough, indeed effective, in the scene where he is discovered, pulls a gun, struggles and is overcome. He even injected some manic stances and expressions which should have alerted more objective observers to his potential for a variety of characterizations. But the public at large wanted their Jimmy uncomplicated, wholesome, and eminently likeable.

Stewart was always unduly modest about his depiction in *After the Thin Man*, stating that he was "ridiculous in a role over my head at the time," and while he gets points for modesty, he loses them for objective veracity about his potential.

The plot was standard Powell-Loy *Thin Man* fare. Loy gets Powell to investigate her cousin's (Elissa Landi) tangled marital situation. It seems her missing husband (Alan Marshall) is involved with a singer, and the Stewart character, Robert, has offered him $25,000 to go off with her because he himself is in love with Landi and wants the coast clear for a divorce so he can marry her. Landi, who has homicidal designs on the husband she has come to hate, finds to her surprise that quite a few other people would like him permanently out of the way, but eventually Nick's shrewd sleuthing unmasks Stewart's Robert as the killer.

William Powell was one of those, like Spencer Tracy, who held Stewart's talents in high regard, and they came to know each other well during the making of *After the Thin Man*. Stewart not only had a healthy respect for Powell's formidable acting resources but also wistfully envied his emotional hold on Jean Harlow. Her bra-less love sessions with Jimmy during the making of *Wife Versus Secretary* continued to keep him in something of a reminiscent dither. It was well known around the studio that Stewart was hoping against hope to be made her leading man in one of her upcoming pictures. He couldn't resist bringing the subject around to Harlow during their talks between camera setups but he found the reticent Powell to be the consummate gentleman: no teller of romantic tales after school was he.

Stewart also knew that Powell had been married to Carole Lombard from 1931 to 1933. That year she had co-starred with Powell over at Universal in the well-received *My Man Godfrey* (1936), but the unflappable Powell proved equally tight-lipped regarding Lombard, saying only that he was delighted at her rise to stardom and that her talents amply warranted it. (Stewart was, in 1939, to be given the opportunity to study Lombard at close quarters when he was assigned to *Made for Each Other* with her.)

In 1936 Powell was 44 years old, sixteen years Stewart's senior. He was a film veteran since 1920, and he gave Stewart some valuable tips. He reminded Stewart that the screen was primarily a medium for highlighting star personality, and that acting, though essential, was secondary. He assured Stewart that he had an inimitable, unique quality that would take him far in films and that it was obvious the camera loved him.

Stewart later recalled that he had less contact with Myrna Loy, who was not as forthcoming as Powell. They were never to head each other's Mutual Admiration Society, but they were always studiedly polite toward each other. Over at 20th Century-Fox, the redoubtable Darryl Zanuck, who was just getting into high gear with a slew of formidable pictures, having effected the amalgamation of his 20th Century Productions with the old Fox organization, had been watching Stewart's slow but sure progress at MGM, and he asked that Stewart be loaned for a remake of the old Fox classic *Seventh Heaven*. In 1927 arch-romantic Frank Borzage's film had swept Janet Gaynor and Charles Farrell to stardom, winning Janet a Best Actress Oscar. A silent with a musical scoring and a theme song, "Diane," that sold well as sheet music, the old film was, in Zanuck's view, due for reworking. This was a rare instance of Zanuck's miscalculating. The 1937 version lacked credibility, and seemed old hat and falsely arch, despite fine direction by the veteran Henry King and apt photography by Merrit Gerstad.

Stewart gave a sincere, and at times even moving performance as Chico, the pre–World War I Parisian sewer worker who has been hurt by love and lost his religion. Cynical and swaggering, Chico takes into his seventh-floor garret, his "Seventh Heaven," a prostitute waif played by Simone Simon, Fox's French *femme fatale*. Their attachment gradually grows into love, but Chico is off to war before they can marry. She waits for him four years; when he returns he is blind, but the faithful, loving Diane is ready for him in their Seventh Heaven, and the resolution is happy.

Much too American in looks and manner for the role of a French sewer worker, Stewart's sincerity and expert playing could not counter the obvious miscasting. His co-star, Simone, at 26 was a veteran of five years in French films, and the previous year, 1936, had made something of a splash in her debut films at 20th Century, *Girls' Dormitory* and *Ladies in Love*. Added interest was brought to the movie's release via reports that the two co-stars had fallen in love in real life. This was primarily a concoction of the studio publicity department but some credence was due: Stewart was reportedly bemused, for the run of the shoot at least, by his attraction to the fetchingly French and saucy Simone.

Though well-cast and obviously as Gallic as they come, Simone had problems with her accent. She gave a winning interpretation of Diane, but it didn't do for her what it had done for Gaynor. She later gave out some publicity to the effect that Stewart had helped her a great deal with making her heavy French accent, as adapted to the relentlessly English sentences, more understandable to audiences.

Certainly Zanuck and Company went all-out to give it a lavish and relatively expensive production, and with a 102-minute running time (quite long for 1937) it was given the top treatment in theatres, but to no avail. Even more regrettably, a fine roster of character players, including Gale Sondergaard, Jean Hersholt, Gregory Ratoff, John Qualen and Mady Christians, found their collective efforts wasted, though they gave it their best shots.

In 1956 Gregory Ratoff told me that he didn't think the picture was as bad as reviewers at the time made out, and that there was a lot of authentic sincerity and romanticism in it. Stewart's attitude toward the film, as per his statements in later years, has always been rather mixed.

"It certainly was a starring part," he said, "one of the earliest ones I got, and I felt Henry King got nice performances out of everyone, even me, American as I was in a French role." King had told Stewart that, like Borzage, he felt that the universal values implicit in the love story of two damaged and disillusioned people who find and restore each other, transcended national origins. But the 1937 public, and the majority of the critics, did not agree, with one Washington reviewer declaring:

"A lot of work and good acting has gone into this remake of the 1927 Gaynor-Farrell smash, and since this is 1937 it must have been timed as some kind of tenth anniversary tribute or something of the kind, but James Stewart, comer that he is, is no rational person's idea of a French sewer worker and Miss Simon's accent, while appropriate to the ambience, is a shade too thick and unintelligible for American audiences. Director Henry King and all hands aboard meant well, to be sure, but this is distinctly a miss."

After completing *Seventh Heaven* on loanout, Stewart returned to MGM and found that, for a full six months, he was not given a picture assignment. There was talk of his appearing in the Luise Rainer-Paul Muni starrer, *The Good Earth* (1937). Set in China, it was to win Rainer her second Oscar in a row. All the characters were Chinese, and when Stewart was made up and dressed for his projected role, Paul Muni volunteered the observation that *that* was the tallest, weirdest-looking Chinaman he had ever seen! Accoutred with slanted eyes, pasty facial makeup and with his hair covered by an artificial "bald" rubber, he so horrified the casting people that he was promptly yanked out, "to my everlasting gratitude," as Stewart later reported.

Network radio programming was now a big thing with the Hollywood people, and if offered an excellent additional outlet for the talents of actors, directors and technicians of all kinds. MGM execs had decided that since Stewart had one of the most individual and expressive voices in Hollywood, he would begin hosting the *Good News* show. Under the joint sponsorship of MGM and Maxwell House Coffee, it consisted of an hour's worth of interviews, music, talk, and the ubiquitous commercials. *The Silver Theatre*, a popular radio dramatic series, also showcased Stewart, and on June 14, 1937 he played opposite Ann Harding in *Madame X* for Lux Radio Theatre, a top series hosted by Cecil B. DeMille. Stewart cannot remember the total number of radio shows he did "but there were many of them. I always regarded radio as great for voices because you had to concentrate harder in that area to make up for the lack of the visual element." There was some wonderment that MGM had not cast Stewart in the film remake of *Madame X* that was released in 1937 with John Beal in the role Stewart played on radio. Gladys George co-starred in the film version. The up-and-coming Beal gave an excellent performance as the son who defends a woman, whom he does not know is his long-lost mother, in a murder trial. The picture did not suffer for lack of Stewart, though he admitted he would have liked the role: "That courtroom scene; I could have gone to town with that!"

Billy Grady, who was always working on Stewart's behalf, recalled that on the film end, Stewart was up against tremendous competition. The better starring assignments were apportioned among the likes of Clark Gable, William Powell, Robert Taylor, Spencer Tracy, Robert Young, Melvyn Douglas, Franchot Tone and

Robert Montgomery. Stewart was, Billy recalled, a distinctive, individual type, and for a while he was regarded as difficult to cast. Yet, looking back on that period, Stewart's memories were cordial and his deference to other actors of the time generous. "The big studios," he said, "were much more than the huge factories they are today. They were big families of contract players and technicians where actors could learn their business in the best possible way — by experience." He added: "The executives, as I knew them, were not power-drunk tyrants. Producers and directors and writers had freedom and were treated very well [Grady and others were to disagree with his sanguine observations here], and actors were well-treated. You worked all the time, fifty-two weeks a year. And they took you under their wing. They protected you if you got into a scrape. They fixed your teeth and gave you voice lessons and took care of your publicity."

But nonetheless he ran into problems. Portrait photographer Ted Allan, who worked at MGM in 1937, told John Kobal: "Two years after Stewart had been with the studio, we still didn't know what the hell to do with him. Was he a comedian, or a romantic leading man? We tried photographing him outside, leaning over fences, working with a shovel, with a tennis racket — but while that worked with Robert Taylor in making him more athletic, it didn't work with Stewart. There was no problem with making him look handsome — he had great eyes and a generous mouth, but in the time I worked with him, I wouldn't have guessed he'd become a star."

According to Billy Grady, "I was the guy who told Mayer and Mannix to send him over to 20th for *Seventh Heaven* after Ty Power backed out of the part. I regretted it later, because Ty had had a good instinct for self-preservation and the picture did nothing for Slats. But at the time it seemed to me to be another loanout "star-builder" of a role like *Next Time We Love* had been for him at Universal a year earlier. That time I miscalculated."

It was Billy Grady who enlightened me on another "special project" Mayer and his minions had initiated — a deluxe whorehouse for the studio actors just a short distance down the street from the front gate.

"Mayer was always piss-worried about the guys going off the reservation and getting into sex scrapes. Gable, Tracy, Franchot

Tone were always womanizing, and they were married, too! Howard
Strickling was in on it, even selected the girls and the decor. 'This
is no job for a set designer,' he said. Then there was Bob Taylor, in
1937 still unmarried, and stories going around that he was a sissy
and possibly queer. We solved that by putting Bob into tough-guy
roles — or maybe partially solved it is more accurate. And then
there was Jim. He blushed and stammered up a storm when I told
him that Mayer had passed along the word that the guys were to get
their rocks off strictly with the whores, and leave the starlets and
publicity dates strictly alone. It wouldn't do to get starlets and other
young actresses pregnant; bad for business."

According to Billy: "The whores were hand-picked; starlets who
had given up on their careers; cast-off girlfriends of well-placed men
who wanted to make a buck; some were imported from Mexico for
the guys who liked them Spanish. Mayer's boys got them thoroughly tested for venereal disease; *that* the MGM actors needed like
holes-in-the-head. Every effort was made to suit the girl to the actor
— if we could find Gable's or Tone's type, so much the better. They
were a horny bunch and most of them thought of it as a convenience. We hired a guy from back East who had run a prostitution
ring on Park Avenue — very high class, too! He brought some of his
girls with him; they were educated, ladylike, well-dressed — and
knew how to make guys happy. Running that joint was no job for a
Franklin Pangborn type — he had to be cool and alert at all times.
Of course, the cops were paid off — some of them even patronized
the joint!"

Mayer, Billy said, had yet another reason for justifying such an
establishment. He had been driven out of his mind by the homosexual scandals that Ramon Novarro and William Haines had gotten into, and had let both boys go by 1935, the year Stewart arrived
at MGM. Gay actors, it seemed (though Billy used the word
"queer"), were a public relations headache to Howard Strickling
and his flacks, and the straighter, or at least the more discreet the
actor, the easier the going was with the press and the fan mags. But
Billy worried that Jimmy Stewart, still unmarried and pushing
thirty, was arousing Mayer's suspicions and putting his future in
jeopardy when he flatly refused to join Gable, Tracy and Taylor over
at the cathouse.

"I had to lay down the law to him," Billy declared. "I had to tell him: Jim, if you don't go over there and give a manly account of yourself at least a few times, Mannix and Mayer and the others will start lumping you in with Novarro and Haines, and you need *that* like a hole in the head. It will undermine all the casting efforts I'm making for you. So get your ass over there and get those rocks off with at least two of those broads. Christ, they're hand-picked and clean and healthy; you're not gonna *catch* anything!"

Stewart finally gave in to Grady's pleading and paid several visits to the deluxe MGM bordello. "He insisted," Billy laughed, "that I go with him each time. I was happily married to my Margaret and was pushing 50, and my whoring days were in the past but I took one lady into a room and sat and chatted with her, and Jim, satisfied, I guess, that he had a 'partner-in-sin,' went into the next room. The walls were rather thin (on purpose, I always thought; guys liked to hear each other perform, I guess) and when I heard a long, slow groan followed by some grunts, I figured Jim had done his duty. When he came out, he looked a little tired. 'Did you enjoy it, Slats?' I asked. 'Wa-a-al, Billy,' Jim replied slowly, 'that lovely lady was either a very good actress or she really liked me or maybe both. She asked me to come back.'

"And he did, too, several times," Billy added. "But I never felt he was at ease with such situations. He called them mechanical and forced, however physically releasing, said he'd rather be in love when he did it. 'Be glad you're not in love,' I told him. 'It's love that causes the troubles of life far more than sex. What about all those divorces and unhappy marriages around you?' 'That's what worries me,' Jim said. 'And it's one of the reasons I stay single.'"

Billy Grady was not the only one to tell me about that MGM cathouse. Adela St. Johns and Ruth Waterbury mentioned it to me, and even Helen Ferguson, once a silent actress, later a leading press agent, laughed about it. The consensus of opinion from all three ladies: it kept those guys out of trouble. There were hilarious stories about Clark Gable forgetting to put his false teeth back in when he visited his favorite lady; how Robert Taylor, even after he married feisty, strong-minded Barbara Stanwyck, used to visit it. Barbara, Adela told me, was too rough on Bob's ego, always putting him down, calling him a lousy actor, casting aspersions on his manhood.

It seems Taylor had a hunting buddy named Bob Cousy, and he spent more time out in the woods hunting with Bob than he did at home with Barbara. Stanwyck got fed up with this, and one time when Bob Cousy called asking for Taylor, Stanwyck held up the phone to him and yelled, "Hey, Bob, your wife's on the phone!"

It was, of course, known to insiders that there was a house-of-prostitution of quite a different stripe, not exactly sponsored by MGM and the other studios, but tolerated, and patronized by some of their personnel. This was a gay brothel made up of failed young actors, body builders, physical education instructors, and even some down-on-their-luck writers and sound technicians. Some of them were married to women, as was a goodly percentage of their clientele. "A number of married actors had beards," Jerry Asher told me. (A "beard" was a convenient wife for publicity purposes.) "When Ross Alexander's wife, Aleta Friele, killed herself in December 1935 because she found out Ross was gay after she caught him with a guy, he almost went out of his mind with grief and guilt." Jerry added, "Fonda and Stewart were great to Ross — they had known him in New York, and they even took him in for a while — he couldn't stand to be alone. Of course Warners was so scared that they let out the word to the press that it had been a gal Ross was caught with. Anyway, when Ross began disappearing all night, and then brought some sinister-looking young guys home a few times, Stewart and Fonda put him out. That kind of thing wasn't their style. Whatever they did, they did it with discretion and class." (Ross killed himself in 1937.)

For his second 1937 film, Stewart found himself back at MGM supporting Edward G. Robinson, on loan from Warners, in *The Last Gangster*. Robinson was an actor Stewart much admired, and he delighted in telling the great star of his sessions in various movie houses of the early 1930s studying his technique in films like *Little Caesar* (1930). Even in 1930, unsure of his own future career course, Stewart at 22 had responded to the galvanic performances of great actors on film and stage, never dreaming that he would one day join them. Robinson, a cultivated man and a patron of the arts, usually found himself playing gangsters and thugs. He warmed to the younger actor's expressed enthusiasm and they had many conversations between takes.

Though written by the talented John Lee Mahin, based on a

story by William A. Wellman (moonlighting fleetingly from directing) and Robert Carson, and expertly photographed by William Daniels (usually assigned to more weighty "A" fare), *The Last Gangster*, at 81 minutes, was no great shakes. Briefly, it concerned a racketeer (Robinson) who, upon release from prison, tries to find his immigrant wife (Rose Stradner) and son (Douglas Scott). They have disappeared because Stradner did not want her son to grow up in the notorious shadow of his father. Stewart is the newspaperman she marries, and they are put under siege in a town outside Boston when the enraged ex-convict tracks them down. But after a session with his son, Robinson realizes the boy is better off where he is, kills some rival thugs who threaten to reveal his son's identity, and is himself killed. So much for the plot.

Susceptible as always to whatever feminine charms presented themselves along the pike, Stewart formed a good friendship (some called it a burgeoning romance) with the lovely Viennese émigré Rose Stradner. Nothing came of it though, and Stradner went back to Europe after American audiences failed to respond to her. Her thick accent and rather quiet personality were not Hollywood assets either, but Stewart always recalled her as kind, gentle and womanly. "They should have kept her on, and given her roles more suited to her," he later said of Stradner. Stewart is effective in his role, stands up to Robinson very well in their limited footage together, and even sports a moustache — an adornment he rarely sported — in the later scenes.

It was now "uniform" time for Stewart, this time at Annapolis, with his third 1937 film, *Navy Blue and Gold*. He acquitted himself well as an earnest cadet with a problematic family background and a football-playing skill which, of course, wins the big game for Navy.

Robert Young co-starred as an ambitious cadet with a talent for intrigue, and pretty Florence Rice was on hand for romantic interest, though the cadets are kept pretty busy with naval activities and football practice. Also appearing is Lionel Barrymore as an old-timer Navy man who is idolized at the Academy, and supporting ably were such as Tom Brown, Billie Burke, Samuel S. Hinds, Paul Kelly, and Frank Albertson.

One of Stewart's better reviews for this effort came from the critic of the *New York Herald-Tribune*, who wrote: "If *Navy Blue and*

Robert Young, Florence Rice, and James Stewart, *Navy Blue and Gold*, MGM, 1937

Gold is not the most beguiling service-college picture yet filmed, it is not Mr. Stewart's fault...Although he has been denied Robert Young's beauty and has been endowed with none of the strong, silent intensity of Gary Cooper, he breathes life into his character to hold a formulized theme to a strict pattern. It is due to his expert rendition of a rather preposterous part that a rather preposterous show becomes generally exciting."

The *Herald-Tribune* was not alone in its admiration for Stewart in this film. He collected from cross-country a host of encomiums ranging from "charming and agreeable" to "more of a romantic lead than has been supposed" to "sensitive and entirely unique in his projection."

After this film invidious comparisons to other players who were supposedly more comely and more charismatic practically disappeared from reviews. It became increasingly recognized that Stewart was a prime individual with his own unassailable brand of masculine charm and appeal. Always rendered self-conscious by references to his alleged lack of handsomeness, Stewart came increasingly to realize that a host of women, on and offscreen, considered him exactly that: handsome. Leading lady Florence Rice, who reportedly had quite a crush on Stewart all through the shooting of *Navy Blue and Gold*, once told an interviewer, shortly after the film's release, that Stewart "had height, and that is one of the nicest things a man can have — girls like to look up — way up; it makes them feel feminine and somehow secure. Also Jimmy has wonderful eyes and a wonderful expression — for my money he's one of the best-looking men in films!"

Whether studio publicity department-inspired or generated by a woman's admiration, references such as these, when they made the public prints, confirmed Stewart's growing suspicion that women found him as appealing as any of the more touted romantic leads.

The story of *Navy Blue and Gold* is as negligible as most service-film plots of the period were — something to do with Stewart's being the son of a man who was once dishonorably discharged from the Academy, this unfortunate instance giving Stewart added incentive to shine and win football games and become one of the Big Men on the Parade Ground. When one of the motivations for winning the Big Game is to pay a special tribute to patriarch Barrymore, Stewart's Cadet Truck Cross has all the grist he needs to turn matters positive on all fronts.

Lionel Barrymore, who had already appeared with Stewart in *The Gorgeous Hussy* and who would figure significantly in future Stewart films, was another of his great inspirations. The formidable Lionel tended to wax impatient with Stewart's boyishly sincere, but somewhat repetitious adoration and honest amazement at finding himself appearing with him after having so long admired him from movie house balconies. But Barrymore saw what other discerning actors like Tracy and Powell saw: a great star in the making. "You've got something special going for you, Stewart, and it's going to blossom, you'll see," he told the enthralled 29-year-old. "Just keep in there pitching, and it will happen."

To her regret, Florence Rice and her crush went the way of all womanly flesh upon the picture's completion. Stewart had new words — and women — to conquer. "He was suffering, if anything, from an embarrassment of feminine riches at the time," Billy Grady remembered.

Of Human Hearts (1938) was one of director Clarence Brown's pet projects — he had always longed to film the Honore Morrow book, *Benefits Forgot*, but MGM tended to shy away from Civil War-era fare, feeling it was box office poison. This was a year before the smash success *Gone With The Wind* proved everyone wrong, but Brown finally got permission to make his dream come true. In it, James Stewart proved most touching as a man who leaves a mean, bigoted Ohio town where his impoverished minister father and forebearing mother (Walter Huston and Beulah Bondi) are taken for granted by the niggardly parishioners. Father and son have long fought over their different views, and Bondi scrapes to finance her son's medical studies in Baltimore, where he hopes to find a better life than his parents have known.

Stewart, oblivious that his father has died and that his mother is living in poverty, becomes an Army surgeon. In one of the more unlikely scenes, President Lincoln calls Stewart to the White House after receiving a letter from his mother inquiring as to his whereabouts. There Stewart receives a lecture on his crass filial ingratitude and is given leave to visit his mother.

These are the bare bones of the plot, but the fine acting and sensitive direction of Brown turn it into a moving and arresting period film, with Huston, Bondi, and Stewart perfectly in character and thoroughly believable.

Particularly genuine was the admirable Beulah Bondi. When she reminisced about this film, among others, with me years later, I told her that I had been deeply moved as a boy of 15 in Lynn, Massachusetts, by a scene in which, reduced to abject poverty, she gazes wistfully at a pair of warm mittens in a store on a cold winter's day. Played almost entirely in pantomime, it was utterly authentic. I remember running home to my aunt and saying "Poor Beulah couldn't buy the mittens for her cold hands, and I cried," to which my aunt replied, "It's only a movie and she's only acting." Miss Bondi seemed most affected by this anecdote, and said, "That is the power of the movies — to think I could reach all those thousands of unknowns all over the country with a little scene like that." Then she confided, with a sly wink, that this was one of *her* favorite scenes in the movie!

Of Stewart she said: "He was about thirty then, and approaching the height of his powers. I felt that the picture showcased something warm and real in him that within a year was to move the whole nation [Beulah was referring to *Mr. Smith Goes to Washington*, in which, again, she played his mother]. And Jimmy was very suitable for period parts — he could be wonderfully convincing in modern roles of course, but his was a talent that transcended eras; he was absolutely convincing at all times."

Another associate on *Of Human Hearts*, director Clarence Brown, agreed with her. "The role of Jason Wilkins couldn't have been better played," he told me years later. "Jimmy had it all there in that film, all the sincerity and integrity that was to so distinguish him later. And he was such an easy actor to direct! Always responsive, and at times even ahead of me, adding nuances I hadn't conceived of — the art that conceals art — that was Jimmy, a natural actor, in the sense that Garbo was natural — it had nothing to do with technique; it all came from instinct, pure instinct, with of course a hell of a lot of seasoned professionalism thrown in!"

Walter Huston was the nominal lead in *Of Human Hearts*. He was indeed powerfully effective as the put-upon minister who persists in his religion to the bitter end, an attitude that costs him the love of his son. "Walter and Jimmy played off each other superbly," Brown told me. "Their chemistries meshed — Walter and Beulah and Jimmy gave as fine an example of ensemble playing as you'll find anywhere in movies, in that film." Brown added, "I wasn't in the least surprised when Jimmy became a major star a year or so later — you never could hide that light under any bushel, not for long!"

Friends joked that Jimmy's one problem with *Of Human Hearts* was that he had no leading lady to fall in love with, unless one counts Ann Rutherford, who, Stewart was first to admit, did not spark him up particularly. (She was infinitely more suited to Mickey Rooney's Andy Hardy.) Another pleasant surprise was John Carradine — of all people — acquitting himself ably and convincingly as Abraham Lincoln.

On loan to RKO later that same year, Stewart had himself a delightful part and a wonderful director, George Stevens, for *Vivacious Lady* (1938). And the biggest bonus of all was his co-star, Ginger Rogers, who had proven her dramatic talent and her comedy skills conclusively after the well-received *Stage Door* in 1937. Reportedly Rogers had asked for Stewart for *Vivacious Lady*, as she was curious to know if he had "grown up a little more" since 1936. Rumor had it that his prowess as lover had kept up with his rise in the cinema firmament, but for Ginger, practical as always, seeing was believing, or rather, *feeling* was believing. She was determined to get "the feel" of Stewart this time around. In 1936 she had been freshly separated from introvert-husband Lew Ayres and was in no mood for introvert-boyfriends like Stewart. (She would finally get around to divorcing Ayres in 1940.) But, friends assured her, the Stewart of 1938 was not the Stewart of 1936.

Stewart still felt a residue of humiliation because Ginger had not previously found him man enough for her. When the love scenes came up, he gave out with the famous "sexy, insinuating vocal tones," and kept his lovemaking proportioned as 10 percent boy-scout-ardent and 90 percent get-down-to-business. Rogers was not to be blamed, according to Ruth Waterbury, if she began to wonder if Stewart, so "grown up," as she told Waterbury, could repeat his onscreen lovemaking on the same kilowatt level privately in the sack.

Just how far the "new Jimmy Stewart" got with the "prove-it-to-me, Buster" Miss Rogers remains a secret to this day. "I wasn't under the damn bed," Ruth Waterbury told me in 1965, "but I have a feeling they did okay together."

Whatever sparks flew between them showed up excitingly and amusingly in *Vivacious Lady*, with director Stevens giving I.A.R. Wylie's story an intelligent, wistful, sly charm that was well-received by critics and public alike. The story, in brief, has to do with shy botany professor Stewart whose domineering daddy (Charles Coburn, who else?) is President of the College where he teaches and whose Monster Mom (Beulah Bondi in a departure from sweetness-and-light mothers) manipulates him via a fake heart condition. When he brings brash showgirl Rogers back to the college, he must run afoul of parental disapproval, and at first he cannot bring himself to acknowledge her to them as his wife. After the male students take a shine to glamorous Rogers, with ensuing complications, Shy-Guy Stewart finally takes the bull by the horns and informs his parents that he is a big boy now and he loves her and she's his wife and — well, they better accept it or else!

George Stevens always believed in Stewart's potential for comedy. "His comic sense is far more sophisticated than people give him credit for," Stevens told an interviewer. "I am sure it is all instinct with him — he is an instinctual rather than a trained actor, but he has a wonderful knack for paradox and surprise and character-trans-

Ginger Rogers, James Stewart, *Vivacious Lady*, RKO, 1938

formation, and in *Vivacious Lady* he rang all the changes!" Modestly disclaiming that he had served as any variety of Svengali in that instance, Stevens said, "Jimmy is a self-starter. As soon as he grasps a basic situation he goes right to town with it. Many trained seasoned performers I have known don't have that knack, or anyway don't have it as fully developed as Jimmy does. He's the kind of guy who can be easily underestimated — then he pulls the rug out from under you with crackerjack delivery!"

The critics were all kind to Stewart's performance in *Vivacious Lady*, with that overworked term "the art that conceals art" being applied more than once. One reviewer even raised Jimmy's eyebrow — and flattered him to the nines at the same time — by comparing him to the Great Garbo (with whom, to Stewart's everlasting and lifelong regret, he was never to appear). "He may not be a master of technique in the way that many seasoned actors are; his art is purely instinctual and springs from the wellsprings of his unique personality," as one critic put it. "In this he bears a similarity to Greta Garbo, whose magical effects never came from technique but from pure instinct."

"Something magical happens to Mr. Stewart when he is up against (literally and figuratively) a new co-star, in this case Miss Ginger Rogers," another reviewer noted. "It's as if every new on-screen encounter with an opposite-sex co-star is something freshly felt and observed by him — and it plays — oh how it plays!" Certainly Miss Ginger Rogers, on her end, could not have agreed more.

Stewart, in the spring of 1938, was to find himself reunited with Margaret Sullavan for their second picture — this time at MGM, where Sullavan was now under contract. She was to win acting honors that year for her performance in *Three Comrades*, the film version of Erich Maria Remarque's novel. The two met on more equal terms on this occasion, for Stewart had learned his film craft thoroughly, and though sometimes miscast, had made a fine impression with fans and critics.

The new Sullavan-Stewart picture, *The Shopworn Angel*, had a rather shopworn history by 1938. It was originally a 1918 *Saturday Evening Post* story by Dana Burnett called "Private Pettigrew's Girl." In 1919 it became a silent film with Monte Blue and Ethel Clayton. Ten years later, in 1929, it was a part-talkie starring Nancy Carroll and Gary Cooper. But Louis B. Mayer, who loved schmaltzy stories, felt that Sullavan and Stewart, whose teaming in *Next Time We Love* had stayed fresh in his memory, would lend extra conviction to another remake. They were soon before the cameras, via a screenplay by Waldo Salt and with H.C. Potter directing.

The story dealt with a simple farm boy from Texas in 1917 who gets drafted into the army. Naïve and idealistic, he finds himself in a camp just outside New York as his unit is preparing to embark for France, where the fighting has turned fierce. He "meets cute" with a hardened, cynical Broadway actress-singer (Sullavan) who is the mistress of man-about-town Walter Pidgeon. At first she finds his boyish simplicities and honest purity of spirit entertaining; he in turn puts her on a pedestal and falls in love with her. But she comes to like him, and just before he sails for France, she gratifies his wish that they marry, so that he can carry her picture into battle and write to her. He is, of course, killed in France, and the affecting final scene shows her singing "Pack Up Your Troubles" in a nightclub while Pidgeon, who has understood and has stood patiently by, opens a letter from the War Department and a small package containing his pitiful effects. The camera zooms in on the stricken Sullavan's face as she sings the last words of the song, "smile — smile — smile . . . ." In the end she has come to realize that the unaffected, decent soldier from Texas has enriched her life and given it new direction. She is now free to pursue her relationship with Pidgeon with newfound maturity.

Louis B. Mayer and Sullavan did not always agree on projects, or anything else. On one occasion, a film she had insisted upon making had brought in good returns. She and L.B. met outside a sound stage one day, and when he congratulated her she had said, "Stick with me and you'll never go wrong." An irritated Mayer had later told one of his aides, "That dame has gall to spare!" But this time they did agree that *The Shopworn Angel* was indeed the right vehicle for her and Stewart.

Walter Pidgeon later discussed the Sullavan-Stewart teaming in *The Shopworn Angel* with me at length. Since he was the third actor on it and was with them all the time, his observations are worth repeating: "I really felt like the odd-man-out in that one. It was really all Jimmy and Maggie, and that was the way it should have been. It was so obvious he was in love with her. He came absolutely alive in his scenes with her, playing with a conviction and a deep sincerity I never knew him to summon away from her. Of course, Jimmy was a wonderful actor in any and all situations and with anyone he played with, but with Maggie he really surpassed himself.

"Of course, they both kept up the front that they were old friends, and that their mutual affection was purely platonic. For her it may have been, though sometimes I felt she was more emotionally involved, off-screen, with Jimmy than she consciously was aware she was. Or maybe, being the flirtatious Southern belle she was, in most situations, she got some ego-kick out of his adoration of her, but Hank Potter [the director] and I both commented to each other, out of their hearing, that their scenes together carried strong conviction over and beyond good acting, or even friendship."

Pidgeon also felt that the amorous sentiment was more on Jimmy Stewart's side than Sullavan's, and that Sullavan was "in love with love, and she loved Jimmy's being in love with her; it enhanced her feelings about herself." Walter Pidgeon added that he thought having men at her feet gave Sullavan a sense of power. Mayer's evaluation was that he didn't know what it was but it sure jumped off the screen, and it was to be Mayer who pushed the idea of their teaming for MGM twice more.

Leland Hayward, who in 1938 had been Sullavan's third husband for two years, and with whom she had had a daughter, Brooke, reportedly got as nervous about what he saw on set and on screen as Willy Wyler had two years earlier. No one knew better than Hayward his wife's track record with men and her numerous, often compulsive love affairs. It also annoyed Hayward that Stewart and John Swope, later the husband of Dorothy McGuire, had set up bachelor quarters together very near the Hayward-Sullavan homestead. Stewart and Swope spent a lot of time there when Hayward was in the East on business, though they were less in evidence when the paterfamilias was in residence.

Sullavan, who liked to keep her husbands, and her men in general, on edge, took her husband to a sneak preview of *The Shopworn Angel*, and according to another cast member, Sam Levene, positively enjoyed watching Leland squirm at the realistically-played love interludes. "I was there and I know," Sam told me. "I was sitting right behind them and she spent as much time sneaking looks at Hayward as she did watching herself and Jimmy on the screen." Levene also noted that Hayward looked positively livid as he and his wife went up the aisle later.

Hayward, of course, had heard all the stories about the young Stewart and his middle-aged male admirers in the Broadway days. He expressed his annoyance over Stewart and Swope living uncomfortably nearby, by snidely inferring that the attractive young Mr. Swope was "the latest of Jimmy's roommate-lovers."

Hayward's cracks about anyone he suspected of being gay were, in Sullavan's view, reflections of his least attractive qualities. Once, in 1936 in New York, shortly after she and Hayward were married, she had called him on it. Now she was to do it again. Though Hayward was to be good friends with Fonda and Stewart always, and represented them both at times, he seemed to have a predilection for homosexual humor concerning them. When Stewart had warned Fonda off a second romance with Sullavan in 1936, when the duo had done *The Moon's Our Home* (she was married to Willie Wyler at the time), Hayward had offended Fonda by remarking that the first time around, four years before, he "hadn't been man enough for her" so why did he think he was going to do any better this time around? Stewart's warning to Fonda had been couched in more tactful terms: "You may be starring equals now, but don't take more chances in bed! Nothing may really have changed, at least for her, there." Nothing came of the prospective Sullavan-Fonda re-teaming, at least off-screen. But when Hayward made a crack about Fonda being another of "Stewart's roomie-lovers," Sullavan lost patience a second time. "You yap about guy-guy love so much, I'm wondering if you're the kind who is repressing some queer impulses in himself!" she castigated Hayward, which seems to have shut him up for good, at least on that subject.

The *New York Herald-Tribune* critic wrote, upon the release of *The Shopworn Angel*, "James Stewart brings the Texan private to glowing life and keeps the characterization solid and appealing even when the script gives him little aid. Unless I am mistaken [the film] boasts two of the finest actors appearing on the screen today."

The New York Times critic was more waspish, writing, "There really ought to be a Margaret Sullavan Act to prevent the charming and gifted lady of that name from wasting her talents on such frivolously tragic productions, from having to speak such forced, insincere lines, from growing finally to look almost spooky herself because of the maudlin unreality of the character she is trying to portray." The *New York Daily Mirror* unflatteringly assailed Stewart's performance: "[He] interprets the role by giving an imitation of Stan Laurel."

But around the country, reviewers, for the most part, waxed ecstatic over the second Stewart-Sullavan alliance, lavishing on them such phrases as "the most affecting screen interplay in a long, long time," followed by "they act out their scenes with such heartfelt sincerity, with such affecting warmth as to give rise to suspicions that offscreen, while possibly not all the way in love with each other, they are certainly heavily in *like* with each other."

Billy Grady and Eddie Mannix always felt that Stewart began to acquire a heavy reputation as a Stud Around Town from 1936 on because he was trying to work Sullavan out of his system — or possibly he wanted to find someone, unattached and responsive, of course, whose appeal to him equalled hers. Or maybe he still hoped to catch Sullavan between marriages. But her union with Hayward was to endure longer than usual, producing two more children, Bridget in 1939 and Bill in 1941. There also is the possibility that having surveyed Sullavan's track record with husbands and lovers both, Stewart had a deep inner conviction that her feelings would never match his, at least not over the long haul.

The Shopworn Angel holds up very well in revival a half century later. I have seen many modern women, who are supposed to be so much more independent and hip about men and love, crying outright at screenings of the picture. Certainly *The Shopworn Angel* is far more than a mere "woman's" picture. It is an honest study of true love and simple sincerity winning out over worldly cynicism, and is as relevant today as the year it was made.

It was ridiculous to pigeonhole certain romantic dramas as woman's pictures since men had had so much to do with the directing, producing, writing, photographing and lighting of them. Moreover, pictures that appealed to half the human race had to have some humanistic integrity. The fear of too many American males that they would be called "sissies" if they indulged, and developed, whatever creative bents they had, was responsible for a scandalous loss of male artistic talent in this country. Certainly Stewart could never be accused of holding back with the finer emotions. His silky, insinuating voice, his limpid expressions, his unabashed masculine tenderness, were never on more dazzling display than in his four pictures with Margaret Sullavan.

Chapter Six

Norma, Olivia, Loretta et al.

In the spring of 1938 Norma Shearer discovered Jimmy Stewart. She had been the lonely widow of the great producer Irving Thalberg for a year and a half, and was romantically disoriented and love-hungry to an extreme degree. During the making of her "come-back" picture, *Marie Antoinette* (1938), an elaborate costume masterpiece, she had fallen passionately in love with Tyrone Power. Shearer played the unfortunate French queen who scintillated for years at her 18th-century court in Versailles and then lost her head in 1793 on the guillotine, the most famous casualty of the French Revolution. She had insisted that Power be borrowed from 20th Century-Fox to play Count Axel Fersen, the Swedish nobleman who gave the ill-fated monarch romantic surcease. At the time, she was fourteen years Power's senior (37 to his 23), and he was involved with the woman he later married, Annabella. A promiscuous bisexual, Ty Power was the original "can't-say-no" boy and his affairs with men as well as women (he had started off in New York as the lover of Diana Barrymore's half-brother, Robin Thomas, who killed himself with pills and booze) were well known in Hollywood gossip circles. Always sexually and emotionally stimulated by impassioned admiration, Power was flattered by Shearer's obvious desire for him, but when Norma finally realized that her ardor was unreciprocated she went looking elsewhere for the fulfillment she craved.

Genius that he was, Irving Thalberg had been a physically delicate man. He managed to father two children by Norma, but his sexual energies were pallid compared to hers, and she had indulged in discreet affairs during and after the marriage, which terminated in Irving's death in 1936 from pneumonia.

Shearer's ego and feelings were dented by the incomplete forward-pass directed at Power, and she derived little satisfaction from the popular perception (albeit true) that she had sent him away because she knew it wouldn't work. Norma was, indeed, ripe for something more physically intense and directly reciprocated.

Marion Davies gave another of her famous come-as-whoever costume parties. Norma was still smarting because Hearst papers had spurned her for three years, ever since she had usurped the role of Elizabeth Barrett Browning in *The Barretts of Wimpole Street* from Marion. She determined to come in the elaborate ballroom costume from *Marie Antoinette* that had been Adrian's *pièce-de-résistance*. Hearst had been obsessed for years with the idea that his mistress, Davies, should play heavy drama and costume, though her real talent lay in comedy, in which she could be delightful, as her many excursions into that genre attest. Davies, always a fair, generous person, had agreed in 1934 that Norma had been far more suitable to play the languishing poetess redeemed by her love for Robert Browning, but Hearst had been affronted and had huffily withdrawn Marion and her entourage from MGM to Warners.

Now here was Norma, sailing into the costume party in a gown that, forced all kinds of adjustments to the decor, the doors, the furniture, so wide and extensive were its folds and flounces. George Cukor told me she had angered Hearst that night because his papers were arguing with the French over political and trade matters, and now, here's Norma "in the costume of a French queen forcing the Hearst minions to take the hinges off doors and move tables around to accommodate [Shearer's] costume. And what did Marion think of it? She thought it was a laugh riot!"

Always the civil host, Hearst received Shearer courteously and even appeared with her and Marion in a "friendly" picture. But inwardly he seethed while Norma preened. Flushed with her triumph, fussed over and fawned upon by all the guests, Norma was feeling thoroughly in command of her situation, but as Cukor put it, "That night, as on all nights, Norma's eyes were roaming, looking for that something special, for that male person who would cooperate with her in igniting a new 'great romance.'"

Then across her path lurched, a tall, graceless, stuttering young man dressed in a cowboy outfit, slightly drunk and a little bleary-eyed, who awkwardly crashed into her hoop-skirt. It was 30-year-old James Stewart, who had been at MGM for three years, a male rose blushing unseen among the contractee thorns. Hitherto he had gone unheeded by the Queen of the Lot, but this time she noticed him — really noticed him.

Josh Logan told what happened next in his autobiography, *Josh*:

"In a moment of alcoholic gallantry [Jimmy] told Shearer with blazing eyes, that she was the most gorgeous creature he had ever seen. Jimmy's remark hit her like a thunderbolt, which was more than he reckoned on. Since then she had taken royal possession of him. She transported him about town openly in her yellow limousine, even though he slumped down in the back seat hoping his friends would not recognize him in his thralldom."

Josh continued: "As proof of her ownership she gave him a gold cigarette case sprinkled with diamonds, so that she could ask for a cigarette in front of others, hoping her gift would advertise the giver. But Jimmy, not wanting to see sly looks, would fumble in every pocket until he came up with a crumpled pack of Lucky Strikes — his badge as a free man." To Josh, Jimmy at this point in time was still "the long, shy, former architecture student shuffling and stuttering his way through the gaudy glamour of movie city."

Shearer and Stewart undoubtedly needed each other, but for widely varying reasons. She needed the sexual excitement of a harmless romantic union with a decent, virginal-appearing "tall-doll" who was obviously not trying to use her. The fact that he was eight years her junior gave her renewed assurance that, with her 38th birthday looming, she could still attract men in their full bloom of virility. He, meanwhile, derived added self-assurance and self-approbation from the conviction that the greatest lady in filmdom, who had romanced many men on screen and off, found him *the* man. Like Power, Stewart revelled in the conceited kick of giving pleasure, of seeing whatever allure he had being mirrored admiringly in the eager eyes of the most feminine of women. Even William Haines, cashiered from MGM circa 1934 for his shamelessly open homosexuality, had found Norma to be a narcissistic ego-enhancer, and had given a four-star performance in bed with her.

The Shearer-Stewart affair did not last beyond several months, nor was it not intended by either that it should. He gave her sexual and romantic urges the necessary lift, and she left him just a little more sophisticated and self-confident than she had found him. Compassionate and understanding with women, Stewart always referred to her, in later years, with his habitual respect and admiration. Indeed, late in the affair, he was proud to get off the floor of the limousine and have himself photographed openly with her at various events. In one such shot, taken on a double date at the Ice Follies with Douglas Fairbanks Jr. and Merle Oberon, Norma Shearer looks glowing and radiantly fulfilled; and the wide-eyed Mr. Stewart looks fervently admiring, if somewhat bewildered.

Henry Fonda later said that this was the pattern Stewart followed with many of the movie queens he had escorted and romanced and, on occasion, slept with in the 1935-1941 period. They were amused by his gentlemanly compassion; they were enthralled and sexually stimulated by his wide-eyed, velvety-voiced approach. "And there was no softer, coo-ier male voice in all of damned Hollywood," Hedda Hopper later told me, laughing raucously. "Look for it in the romantic scenes of his movies. It drove the ladies crazy! He lowered his voice to a kind of crooning tremolo as he whispered sweet nothings in their ears. Oh, how that lowered, muted damned voice of his cooed away. The girls couldn't get enough of it!"

Billy Grady claimed that the heavy fan mail that Stewart got after his love scenes with the likes of Carole Lombard, Jean Arthur, and Ginger Rogers, embarrassed him. "I don't wanna read those love letters; I feel damned sorry for the poor frustrated girls who write them!" he told Grady. "Gable, for God's sake, is sexier, Taylor handsomer, Montgomery suaver. Why me?" "If you don't know by now, I'm not gonna waste time spelling it out for you," Grady replied.

Then there was the James Stewart-Olivia DeHavilland involvement. Nobody in Hollywood could figure out if their romance had progressed to the giving-their-all-in-bed stage, but it certainly filled a lot of column space. Their affair garnered the kind of romance publicity that, Howard Strickling once said, "you couldn't buy for love or money."

The nearest either one of them came to letting it all hang out was almost a decade later. DeHavilland told *Photoplay*, in March of 1947, that, "It's true I was in love with Jimmy Stewart — crazy about him. But, believe me, we were more like a matured high school romance. We had fun. We had dates. We went to parties, to the movies and held hands and we loved to dance. But never at any time was there any thought or talk of marriage between us." Others, like Jerry Asher, disagreed. "I think they got closer to the altar than was known at the time," he said, "but they 'scaredy-catted' out of it. They were a lot alike, Livvy and Jim. Prim, well brought-up, decent, considerate, but as romantic and sexy as any guy or gal around. Livvy always came on like such a lady (especially as Melanie in *Gone With the Wind*) and the girls around the country who wrote Jimmy all those mash notes fantasized him as Virginal Mr. Smith in Naughty Washington, but they had other sides to them, believe you me!"

Jack Holland, the fan magazine writer, told in *Motion Picture's* October 1941 issue that he had introduced Jimmy and Livvy to each other in early 1938. The affair, or whatever it was, was now over, but Jack was still stirring up some smouldering ashes. "Why did it go *pfft?*" he asked readers, rhetorically. "Are they secretly married? Does the flame still burn? Are they as cold as yesterday's headlines?" At the time Jack was writing this, Olivia had gone on to other romances and Jimmy was in the service, revelling in the platonic haze of Barrack Buddyhood.

Reminiscing, Jack Holland continued, "I'm not hanging myself out on a limb by saying that if Livvy and Jimmy had started to go together a few days after that luncheon when I introduced the two, three and a half years ago, they'd probably have been hitched rather securely by now. At the time, Livvy (then 21) was nervous as a cat about meeting Jimmy (who was 29). When he and I arrived at the studio for our visit with her, we found her poking a typewriter with a spasmodic case of jitters that would have been a credit to the champion of nervous breakdowns. As for Jimmy, he wasn't saying much but he was plenty excited."

As matchmaker Holland related it, the couple didn't get together until months after that first meeting, and then it went great guns — for a while. Jack Holland, after much cogitation, arrived at this conclusion:

"I'm not going to be authoritative and say I know why they stopped seeing eye to eye. Nobody in Hollywood but Jimmy and Livvy can honestly say what happened, and they aren't talking — yet. It's only my hunch, knowing them both quite well, that Livvy wasn't sure she was — or is — ready for a step as serious as marriage."

By the time of DeHavilland's 1947 *Photoplay* confession about the Stewart involvement, she had been married to writer Marcus Goodrich for a year. Like Stewart she had taken a long time to walk down the aisle, being the ripe age, for a woman, of thirty when she took the plunge. "I think Livvy was sort of glad she had waited so long," Helen Ferguson later said, "because she was to plunge into a lot of marital headaches, a nasty divorce, children problems and all the rest of it. Joan Fontaine, DeHavilland's sister, who was also to have a (professional) encounter with Jimmy in a later picture [*You Gotta Stay Happy* (1948)], angered her by saying of her first husband, 'I think he's had five wives and only one book,' so Livvy snubbed Joan at her Oscar-winning ceremonies in 1947 when she copped the Award for *To Each His Own* — an apropos movie title, under the circumstances."

Both Olivia DeHavilland and Norma Shearer later told interviewers that they keenly regretted never having done a film with Jimmy Stewart. "Norma probably wanted to put on filmic record her private experiences with Jimmy, so she could look at them and remember, any time she wanted," Jerry Asher later commented, "and Livvy probably would have liked to find out in somewhat more detail what she missed out on."

In the spring of 1938, James Stewart and Frank Capra teamed up for their first movie together. *You Can't Take It With You* marked the birth of a historic collaboration which was to carry them through three unforgettable films. Capra had already made a considerable mark as the Oscar-winning director of *It Happened One Night* (1934) and the creator of such blockbusters for Columbia as *Mr. Deeds Goes to Town* (1936) and *Lost Horizon* (1937). Earlier he had made Barbara Stanwyck a star in *Ladies of Leisure* (1930). He became a goldmine and attracted considerable prestige for gruff Harry Cohn, Columbia's shrewd head honcho. Cohn came to dote on Capra, and paid the then-phenomenal price of $200,000 for the film rights to the George S. Kaufman-Moss Hart Broadway hit of 1936, *You Can't Take It With You.*

Up until 1938, Gary Cooper was Capra's perfect concept of the hero. In the hit *Mr. Deeds Goes to Town*, Cooper, to the life, was what one film observer called "an idealistic individual, an improbable hero bucking all odds and thwarting the antisocial schemes of materialistic cynics." One night in 1937, at a preview, Capra found yet another actor who fit like a glove his utopian notion. The film was *Navy Blue and Gold*. Capra later described the impression Stewart made on him: "I sensed the character and rock-ribbed honesty of a Gary Cooper, plus the breeding and intelligence of an Ivy League idealist." He was determined to borrow Stewart from MGM, which was making small fortunes loaning out its stars for various projects while the performers continued to subsist on their weekly contractual salaries. But it was already becoming apparent that Stewart was profiting, too. His loanout roles gave him strong material to cut his teeth on, and invariably sent him back to MGM a more pronounced personality than when he had left. "Sure, I would have liked more dough at the time, Stewart later said, "but the loanout breaks, and indeed some of the home-studio films, were building me up step by step — on balance I had no beef."

Frank Capra has eloquently explained his own approach in words no writer could improve upon. "I would sing," he wrote, "the songs of the working stiffs, of the short-changed Joes, the born poor, the afflicted. I would gamble with the long-shot players who light candles in the wind, and deplore others being pushed-around because of race or birth. Above all, I would fight for their causes on the screens of the world. Oh, not as a bleeding-heart with an Olympian call to 'free' the masses. Masses is a herd term — unacceptable, insulting, degrading. When I see a crowd, I see a collection of free individuals; each a unique person; each a king or a queen; each a story that would fill a book; each an island of human dignity."

Capra recalled that, when in New York for the opening of *Lost Horizon* at Radio City Music Hall, he had slipped into the rear of Broadway's Booth Theater to see *You Can't Take It With You.* "Its witchery was so entrancing," he recalled, "that wild horses couldn't have dragged me away before the final curtain." The play fit perfectly the concept Capra had come to cherish in his films.

With Robert Riskin, his proven associate, again on hand to write the screenplay, and with Joseph Walker to photograph and Dimitri Tiomkin to score, Capra went about picking the character stars he thought most ideal: Lionel Barrymore, Edward Arnold, Mischa Auer, Ann Miller, Spring Byington, and Samuel S. Hinds. Capra and Riskin made some changes to accommodate the play for film, and Donald Meek was written in as a hilarious maker of original toys.

The story deals with the wacky and highly eccentric Vanderhof family, who take their cue for living from Grandpa, well-played by Lionel Barrymore. Grandpa is a retired businessman whose philosophy is that you should live life joyfully and individualistically, regardless of material or social consequences. Byington, his daughter, accordingly writes plays; her husband, Hinds, makes fireworks in the basement; his granddaughter, Miller, does endless ballet turns around the house coached by Russian choreographer Mischa Auer. The only (relatively) practical person of the household is Jean Arthur, who works as secretary to rich boy Stewart. Stewart's father is a tycoon (Edward Arnold) who has designs to buy the Vanderhof property to further a real estate development. Arnold is the antithesis of Barrymore; he is predatory, materialistic, and money-mad. The rest of the story deals with the star-crossed courtship of Arthur and Stewart and the gradual conversion of Arnold from material to spiritual orientations.

The film is replete with hilarious situations. When Arnold and his wife come to the house to meet their future in-laws, they arrive on the wrong night and are horrified to observe the bizarre antics of the household. After the police arrest everyone in the house because of fireworks explosions in the basement, there is a highly amusing courtroom scene with Arnold trying to bluster his way out of trouble, while Barrymore looks on with objective serenity. Eventually the Stewart character elects for the Vanderhofs over his own family and his chastened father, realizing he is losing his son, takes a fresh new look at Barrymore's values — and his own.

You Can't Take It With You went on to win the 1938 Best Picture Oscar, as well as one for Capra's direction. It went a long way to solidify Stewart's highly distinctive and original cinematic image. Typical of his rave reviews was this from the critic of *The New Statesman*: "No actor on the screen today manages to appear more unconscious of script, camera and director than Mr. Stewart." This was Stewart's first pairing with Jean Arthur, and their chemistries meshed so wonderfully that within a year they would be co-starring in an even more memorable Capra film.

Stewart has said of working with Capra: "He brings out the best in an actor. He doesn't *demand* effects; he *coaxes* them out of you; I wouldn't call his direction subtle so much as evocative, gently guiding. You fall in with his spirit, and before you know it you are acting in accordance with it, naturally, effortlessly. I think his approach is a unique one among directors. Certainly it worked magically for me."

Stewart was billed third among the four stars — after Arthur and Barrymore, but before Edward Arnold (wonderfully right as the tycoon who reforms). He is given some amusing moments by Capra and Riskin. In a nightclub scene, for example, he does a fantastic Big Apple, then demonstrates how to work up a gradual scream; later he coaxes Arthur into screaming so loudly that she's seen a rat that she empties the nightclub.

In a retrospective notice for *Quirk's Reviews*, film critic William Schoell wrote: "This adaptation of the hilarious Kaufman and Hart stage play is somewhat undermined by being tailored for the needs of Frank Capra and Jimmy Stewart. New sequences 'open up' the play, and show Stewart at work or dating Jean Arthur, etc., but these scenes slow down the action, and only one of them (a funny sequence of mishaps in a restaurant) adds to the madcap atmosphere. In the play, Stewart's character was essentially a supporting one; now he's the lead, and the film is another 'common man' Capra picture that says absolutely nothing Capra hasn't said before (or after)."

Schoell added, "It's one of those films that (inadvertently?) assures the poor that they should not worry — rich people are really miserable, after all. The best and funniest scenes are taken directly from the play; attempts to add grim drama (a business rival of Edward Arnold's commits suicide) don't really come off so well, and Arnold's change of character at the conclusion is unbelievable and abrupt. On the less literal stage, it was all more acceptable; here in a film, it seems contrivance of the most condescending sort. The gags are still great, however, and there are many fine performances and humorous sequences. Jimmy Stewart is as charming and capable as ever."

Lionel Barrymore always enjoyed working with Capra, whom he deemed "a fine artist with a magical way with the camera. I played two diametrically opposite characters for him, and with his guidance I made both of them convincing. In *You Can't Take It With You*, I was a benign man who scorned materialism, and in *It's a Wonderful Life* I was a mean old scrooge who cared only for money. Frank borrowed me from MGM for both roles, and they were ornaments to my career, especially as they gave me sharply contrasting characters to play — and as anyone knows, nothing pleases more an actor who wants to be well-rounded." Lionel's one regret was that his brother John never got to play under Capra's directorial guidance: "Now *that* would have been a combination to reckon with!" Of Stewart Lionel said: "Jim is one of my favorite actors — and favorite people!"

Also in 1938, Stewart briefly dated the lovely Hungarian actress-singer Ilona Massey, who would win stardom at MGM as Nelson Eddy's co-star in *Balalaika* (1939), and go on to do other well-received films. According to her son, the noted film and stage producer Curtis Roberts, Ilona's dates with Stewart were the inspiration of the studio's ever-busy publicity department, but a genuine friendship developed, and Ilona Massey always spoke of Stewart with respect and admiration. One reason the friendship did not catch romantic fire at the time was that Ilona was the girlfriend of the somewhat older, but highly ardent and possessive film executive Sam Katz. Katz permitted Massey's dates with Stewart only because Mayer impressed on him that it helped her public image, but she jilted Katz in 1941 to marry the handsome MGM actor Alan Curtis.

Curtis Roberts has perpetuated his mother's friendship and admiration for Stewart (Ilona Massey died in 1974.) "I have the greatest respect for him, both personally and professionally," Curtis said in an interview. "He began his film career as a juvenile but played everything well, including heavies, which most people may forget. He has always been a great credit to the industry, and to this very day personifies what true film stardom represents. As a Brigadier-General [in the Air Force Reserve] he served his country well, and he certainly utilized his small-town Pennsylvania All-American qualities, that were an integral part of his education and upbringing, in the development of his career. No matter how sophisticated the role he always managed to bring an effective homily to each characterization."

Curtis continued: "[Stewart] has lived a Horatio Alger type of life, it seems to me, and I would strongly recommend — no, urge! — all fledgling actors to carefully study the nuances and the progression of his work, and his lifetime pattern as well. As a movie star, and as a human being, he accepted acclaim with a disarming sense of modesty and makes everything he does appear to be very simple and natural. It is this combination of talent, class and growth, as a performer and as an individual, that has made and kept him an international star for many, many years."

To close friends, Stewart often expressed his impatience with having to escort various starlets (and stars, for that matter) on "publicity jaunts," as he termed them. Henry Fonda recalled him saying that "It's a chore when you don't have much to say to each other, and the chemistry isn't there, even for an innocent night out at a premiere or screening-with-dinner. But I know it's important to keep in the public eye."

His friend Johnny Swope would kid him that it was sure a great way to meet people of the opposite sex, and since they were usually from the same studio, one thing could lead to another, so to speak. "He didn't seem to find this particularly funny," Johnny once recalled. "I do know there were people he was seen with for publicity purposes, such as Eleanor Powell and Ilona Massey, whom he genuinely liked and whose company he enjoyed. He used to talk about Eleanor's down-to-earth common sense and Ilona's kindness and humor, but I will spare you the things he used to spout off about some of the others!"

To Johnny Swope, who later married Dorothy McGuire in a 1943 union that was to last a lifetime, "Jimmy never lost a certain shyness and nervousness. I know it was part of his charm, and it all came off well on-camera, but I always felt it was a deterrent to him psychologically, a subtle handicap." Johnny took many photographs of Stewart in informal settings and attitudes "and even when he was relaxed or reasonably happy the pictures reflected a certain tension and unease. He was very blunt about the photos I did. 'If they saw these at MGM I'd be fired and on my way back to New York on the next train!' he once laughed. I thought the stuff I did on him was quite good, and I wanted to show it to the boys at the publicity department but Jim said no. My work was 'fine, sensitive and professional' (as he kindly volunteered) but they were somehow, he felt 'too psychologically revealing.' I don't know what he meant by that—I still don't!"

The 1939 gossip mills were grinding fiercely over the lovely star Loretta Young's "obsessive passion" for Jimmy Stewart. Loretta had been married briefly in her teens to actor Grant Withers, but since her 1930 divorce had been footloose and fancy-free, and had acquired a formidable reputation as a "super-manizer." Loretta made no secret of her affection for the male sex, though many felt she carried her romantic roamings a bit far. After appearing with Spencer

Tracy in *A Man's Castle* (1933), she busily tried to break up his marriage. But Tracy was a Catholic and refused to leave his wife, Louise, and his deaf son, John, to whom Louise was devoted. (She later started a clinic for the deaf in the son's name.) A combination of guilt and concern for his family (he also had a daughter, Susie) kept Tracy legally unavailable. This did not stop him from carousing, however, and he and Loretta weathered a stormy, albeit brief, affair. On the rebound from Tracy, Loretta made *Call of the Wild* (1935) with Clark Gable. The picture was certainly aptly named because endless persistent rumors claimed that Loretta's daughter Judy (whom she claimed was adopted) was Gable's. Judy, now in her early 60s, made no bones about being Gable's daughter, and after a career as a soap opera actress, wrote an autobiography revealing all.

William Wellman, director of *Call of the Wild*, was once asked if the rumor of the Loretta-Clark baby was true. "All I know," he laughed, "is that Loretta and Clark Gable were very friendly during the picture, and it was very cold up there. When the filming was finished, she disappeared for a while and later showed up with a daughter with the biggest ears I ever saw except on an elephant!" Later, Judy underwent plastic surgery on the ears, and when Loretta finally married Tom Lewis, an advertising executive, in 1940, Lewis adopted Judy.

George Eells once listed, with the injunction "to name only a few," the many boyfriends of Loretta Young in the 1933-1940 period. They included, besides Married-Man Gable and Married-Man Tracy, such Studs Around Town, as George Brent, Gilbert Roland, Ricardo Cortez, Wayne Morris, Herbert Somborn (the second Mr. Gloria Swanson); directors Eddie Sutherland, Joe Mankiewicz and Gregory Ratoff; writers Robert Riskin and John McClain; tennis star Fred Perry; socialite Jock Whitney; playboy Willis Buckner; frequent co-star Tyrone Power; Cesar Romero, David Niven — and Jimmy Stewart.

Stewart seems to have been her biggest squeeze of the time. "Loretta carried a big, big torch for him, chased him shamelessly, and made a god damned fool of herself," Adela St. Johns reported to me later, "She scared him off, she was that intense."

Nor did Loretta herself make any secret of her attraction, either then or later. Forty-odd years after the event, she told Peter Swet of *Parade Magazine* (January 28, 1990): "I prayed like mad that Jimmy

Stewart would ask me to marry him! And he didn't! Jimmy took me out many times, but he just wasn't sending out the same signals I was! I realize now that it wouldn't have worked between us, because we were both actors, so God had something better in mind for him than me. And Jimmy got exactly the right woman!"

Loretta had Swet busy with the pen and paper, as she regaled *Parade*'s readers with details of her love life: "I've been in and out of love many times in my life. I often wonder if I've ever really been in love. I used to pray about it." Asked about the Gable baby rumors she was oddly elusive. "It was a rumor *then*, and a rumor *now*. I guess it will *always* be a rumor." But Jimmy Stewart doubtless felt that all those rumors hardly qualified Loretta as a wife.

Margaret Ettinger, Louella Parsons' cousin, a public relations executive and an old friend of mine, said she thought the much-vaunted virginal male element in Jimmy excited the somewhat nymphomaniacal Loretta more than usual. "She liked them elusive — some of them were married — and otherwise unattainable. Loretta had more than a little of the masochist to her." Eddie Mannix, the MGM executive, said that Stewart made no bones of the fact that he had always masturbated excessively. "He said *that* was what calmed him down when his father kept telling him to get married when he was very young, and his mother repeated over and over to 'save your clean manly body for the right woman — bring it to her as an undefiled, unpolluted temple.'"

Burgess Meredith, Stewart's roommate circa 1940–41, revealed that the word "pollute" always meant "masturbate" to Jimmy. Instead of using terms like jerking off, whacking off, or beating the meat, Jimmy, in jest ("the truth is expressed in jest") would come in from a date and say that such-and-such had gotten him so aroused that the urge to "pollute himself" had overwhelmed him.

Certainly the shyness and somewhat removed tone of his addresses to her excited Loretta. "I'm positive his parents fucked up his sex life with their conventionalities and admonitions," Jerry Asher recalled. "He may have gone to bed with some of the people he was linked with, but most of them were publicity and escort things." Benny Thau, MGM executive, recalled Stewart confiding, after a few drinks at a party, that he distrusted his male friends' boasts about how they made out "with the fuck of the century," as one put it. "They probably did what a lot of us do," Stewart drawled. "Penetrate, then use our hand to get down the home stretch."

Stewart, Henry Fonda recalled, was particularly sympathetic when he told him of how Margaret Sullavan used to ridicule him when they were married because of his premature ejaculations. Actor Kent Smith, a close friend of both, told me that the two big problems in the Sullavan-Fonda marriage had been sexual and professional: "Due to the constant tension he felt when they made love, Fonda was given to premature ejaculations. She called him an adolescent, asked him if he was a chronic masturbator, told him here he was 26 years old and he still didn't know how to love a woman properly. She added that if [Fonda] couldn't satisfy her, she could always find some man who would. She wasn't going to be left high and dry by his boyish inexperience and his inability to control his orgasms until he had satisfied her the way 'any sophisticated and experienced gentleman would be able to do.'" Doubtless these accounts of marriage-bed horror stories kept Stewart and his right hand best friends right up to age 41. "Oh, he got sexually involved with all kinds of people," Mannix told me "but in his head he stayed 'virginal' for a hell of a long time."

Stewart's curiosity about the fiery and mercurial Carole Lombard was to be somewhat gratified in 1939. Stewart, this time on loan to David O. Selznick, found himself playing opposite her in *Made for Each Other*, a rather turgid soap opera about the marital travails of a young New York lawyer and his wife.

Lombard had grown impatient with extollings of her comic prowess in films like *My Man Godfrey* (1936) and *Nothing Sacred* (1937) so David Selznick gave her the chance to be thoroughly dramatic and she went to town on it. Stewart once again displayed his standard, but highly compelling filmic persona: the diffident and inwardly-sterling young man who breaks through to succeed in a positive denouement.

Among the couple's starting liabilities: a tyrannical judge boss in Stewart's firm (Charles Coburn, who else?), and Lombard's domineering mother (in this case Lucile Watson) who lives with them. Lombard eggs Stewart on to become more aggressive about advancement at the law office, but he is content to bumble along as usual. A baby adds to the complications when it gets sick and needs

James Stewart, Carole Lombard, *Made for Each Other*, MGM, 1939

a lifesaving serum. Coburn and Watson get off their high horses and show they are human and accessible after all, and Stewart fights his way to a partnership and — well, you can fill in the rest.

The talented director John Cromwell worked extremely well with Lombard and Stewart, smoothing out the more unlikely turns of the Jo Swerling script. Photographer Leon Shamroy made both Stewart and Lombard look mighty pretty, though the love scenes, such as they were, play a distinct second fiddle to the domestic melodrama.

The film did not do well in its first previews. Selznick, who was always given to heavy tinkering in an obtrusive bid to harness audience interest, hiked up the ending with the serum subplot. But while it provided some suspense, it stimulated only a moderate rush of adrenaline. The picture was decidedly on the quiet side, considering the potential for excitement its magnetic stars could generate.

Stewart, ever curious about each new female co-star, found that his romantic timing with Lombard was all wrong. Lombard was utterly wrapped up in Clark Gable, whom she would marry shortly after *Made for Each Other*'s release. Stewart got lost in the shuffle, but he shrugged it off philosophically, later telling Henry Fonda that Lombard was too brittle and unpredictable, not exactly his type anyway.

Lombard was also very concerned that Gable was currently

working with the recently widowed Norma Shearer in *Idiot's Delight* (1939) at MGM. She recalled the hot chemistry Shearer and Gable had generated in *A Free Soul* (1931), and was concerned what sparks a prowling Shearer might ignite with Clark. So preoccupied was Lombard with the possible extracurricular activities between Gable and Shearer that she never thought to ask, or possibly didn't recall, that Stewart was an expert on Shearer. He may actually have reassured her, since Gable and Shearer were destined not to make it. In any event, any potential romance between Lombard and Stewart off-set was scotched. One critic, observing the lack of any real on-screen chemistry, remarked that it was probably just as well that the lovemaking was limited to celluloid: they just weren't likely candidates for each other.

Made for Each Other got mediocre reviews, but Stewart came out well in most of them, even though some reviewers commented that he was doing yet another variation on his standard *shtick*.

Stewart found himself in a second picture with Joan Crawford, *Ice Follies of 1939*. He was her bona fide leading man this time, though this was scant consolation given the hackneyed story and silly situations. *Ice Follies* so enraged Crawford, who had done the picture most reluctantly, that she went to Mayer and demanded something worthwhile be given her before her professional morale collapsed irretrievably. The result was *The Women*, which restored her status considerably later that year.

Ice Follies was produced by Harry Rapf, who usually did B-movie throwaways, and directed by the negligibly talented Reinhold Schunzel, of whom not too much was heard thereafter. The story, a sort of ice extravaganza-musical-drama hybrid, concerns ambitious actress Crawford and would-be producer Stewart who bankrolls ice shows with associate Lew Ayres (a talented actor, haplessly along for the bumpy ride). Crawford gets a movie offer and leaves Stewart behind, though they have recently married, to take off for Hollywood. Just as it seems that they are permanently to lose each other, producer Lewis Stone reunites the couple in Hollywood, and Joan acts while Jimmy produces movie ice extravaganzas. So much for that.

The three leads, Crawford, Stewart and Ayres, were shown on ice skates in many of the publicity shots, but the actual ice performances were (mercifully) left to top professionals who performed gracefully in striking Technicolor.

One reviewer minced no words: "This represents the nadir of

the bad assignments Miss Crawford has gotten from Metro-Gold-wyn-Mayer and if she stages a cataclysmic rebellion after this, no one can blame her. The story is banal, the situations brazenly and unbelievably contrived, and even good actors like James Stewart and Lew Ayres seem to be straining in their attempts to inject some vitality and situational relevancy into the arch and foolish proceedings. The only one who emerges with any dignity intact is the unassailably dignified Lewis Stone, who rises above all — in part because he is not called upon to put on skates!"

Offscreen — and on the set — Crawford seemed far more impressed with Stewart than she had been three years before in *The Gorgeous Hussy*. He was not just another face in the crowd of Crawford cronies this time around. Competitive as always, Crawford had heard of Stewart's amorous prowess with such as Norma Shearer. She was, moreover, a divorcee for the second time, Franchot Tone having been dispatched to wherever outworn former hubbies go. Lonely, restless, and hungry for a new romance, or at least a dalliance, Crawford set her cap for Jimmy. Jerry Asher, who was on hand, as usual, as Joan's close confidante, felt it was one of her "default" encounters, meaning that Jimmy Stewart would not have been her first choice: he was merely the most convenient and accessible. Of course, there was handsome Lew Ayres, but he was not really Crawford's cup of tea. She regarded him as the "gentle, introspective and retiring" type, an evaluation such former red-hot Ayres brides as Ginger Rogers and Lola Lane might have confirmed.

Always easily aroused sexually, and as susceptible as the next man to a legend as flamboyant and glamorously sexy as Crawford, the curious Stewart went along with her — for a time. But as Billy Grady said later, "Joan was far down on the list of Jimmy's involvements, for the simple reason that she wasn't really his type. She was, for his tastes, too aggressive and self-consciously arch, and overly theatrical in her manner — he liked some semblance of sincerity in his women, and he felt Crawford acted offscreen as much as she did on — maybe even more so."

I asked Billy if Crawford and Stewart had "hit the sack," one of Billy's favorite terms for sexual dalliance. He said he was sure they did, but it didn't "go beyond a few bouts." Why not? According to Billy, "Jimmy liked to do the chasing — he didn't like *it* to come after *him*, it threw him offstride, and he told me once that Crawford was more like a man than a woman when she pursued the object of her affections and 'a guy likes to be in control.'"

Stewart was rushed into a would-be screwball comedy called *It's a Wonderful World* (1939) which co-starred, for less than felicitous results, Claudette Colbert. Both stars gave earnest, proficient accounts of themselves, they couldn't save the mediocre mishmash concocted by writers Ben Hecht and Herman J. Mankiewicz, and directed practically overnight by Woody (One-Take) Van Dyke.

The plot is outlandish, convoluted silliness about a detective (Stewart) tracking a poetess (Colbert) whose car he appropriates after escaping from a train where he is on his way to prison for conspiracy. The bad rap was occasioned by his efforts to protect framed murderer Ernest Truex. Now he is out to find the real murderer, and while on the lam and on the prowl Stewart and poetess Colbert masquerade as a couple to avoid detection. She naturally starts to fall in love with him. He is something of a cynical misogynist (Stewart fans did not approve of these aspects of his role) and at one point even socks her. But love wins out in the end. There is much hurrying and scurrying and hiding out, with all the peregrinations associated with the late-era Screwball School which, by 1939, was already running dry.

There was no romance between Stewart and Colbert, only a mutually respectful professional association. It was her first MGM

Doug McClelland Collection

Claudette Colbert, James Stewart, *It's a Wonderful World*, MGM, 1939

film, made during her yearly loan-out deal from Paramount, her home base. She was probably attracted by the script, a cross between her Oscar-winner *It Happened One Night* (1934) and the British hit *The Thirty-Nine Steps* (1935). But it looked a lot better on paper than it did on the screen. This was not one of Colbert's favorite films, as she told me emphatically in 1981. She did not feel that Woody Van Dyke was the right director for her, though she knew Louis B. Mayer liked him because he rushed films through in a minimum of time via his one-take technique. At Paramount Colbert was accustomed to directors who took their time and to cameramen who photographed her with care (she had a thing about getting only her left profile shot; she felt her right was defective). All the hurly-burly disconcerted her, though she managed a thoroughly convincing performance. "I didn't like the treatment I was getting on that film," she told me, "but I had too much professional pride not to give it my best shot anyway." She spoke well of Stewart, said he had a natural talent, replete with excellent timing, and that he had played back to her ably.

It was obvious, however, when I talked to Stewart, that neither was the other's romantic type. Colbert had been, in any case, happily married to Dr. Joel Pressman for four years and, moreover, was a good five years Stewart's senior. When I interviewed Stewart in 1957, he spoke well of Colbert, calling her "a real pro" and "a considerate and sensitive co-worker." He shrugged off the picture, however, saying, "Speedy Van Dyke, as he was known, had shot the thing in something like two weeks and it looked it, too!"

The picture has had little exposure since its original release, did poorly at the box office, to both the stars' annoyance at the time, and is something they, and their fans, preferred to forget. When it was revived at Frank Rowley's Regency theatre in 1984, I called it "sketchy, dull and only intermittently funny."

It was roundly dismissed by most 1939 critics, one intoning: "Mr. Stewart and Miss Colbert doubtless thought they had, based on their reading of the script, a peregrinative comedy riot in the making, but despite their best efforts the final result is more leaden than laughable. This kind of peregrinative screwball plot has to be executed with care and nuance, and neither are present here on the part of director or writers. Mr. Van Dyke, Mr. Hecht and Mr. Mankiewicz — go to the back of the class!"

James Stewart , Mr. Smith Goes to Washington, , Columbia, 1939

Chapter Seven

Mr. Smith — And Top Stardom

In his second picture with Capra, again on loanout to Columbia, Stewart solidified his stardom for all time with one of his greatest and most fondly remembered roles, as Jefferson Smith in *Mr. Smith Goes to Washington* (1939). Portraying the idealistic young senator who fights almost overwhelming political interests, Stewart showed a combination of awkward, well-intentioned aspiration and fierce determination when cornered that registered strongly. He garnered his best reviews to date, with *Newsweek* congratulating him on "the most persuasive characterization of his career as a one-man crusade against political corruption." But most typical of his fine notices was that of *The Nation*, whose critic wrote: "James Stewart as Jefferson Smith takes first place among Hollywood actors.... Now he is mature, and gives a difficult part, with many nuances, moments of tragi-comic impact, and he is able to do more than play isolated scenes effectively. He shows the growth of a character through experience...in the end, he is so forceful that his victory is thoroughly credible." The critic continued, "One can only hope that after this success, Mr. Stewart in Hollywood will remain as uncorruptible as Mr. Smith in Washington."

The story has become legend. In a Western state, Jefferson Smith (Stewart) runs the Boy Rangers, an organization of boys' clubs. He is a clean-cut believer in the Golden Rule who seems a perfect blind for the corrupt state machine, which sends him to Washington when a U.S. Senator dies. There he worships the senior senator, Claude Rains, who had known his father, but he is soon disillusioned when he finds Rains is an unscrupulous man of expediencies who advises Stewart to compromise his simplistic ideals. In order to get any good done, Rains advises, one must play along with political hacks and their cynical agendas. When the Washington press corps ridicules Stewart's innocence of senatorial politics, he is, for a time, discouraged. Sitting at the Lincoln Memorial, he admits defeat to himself, but is rallied by his secretary, Jean

Arthur, a hardboiled political insider who has come to believe in Stewart's decency.

One of the most salient scenes in *Mr. Smith Goes to Washington* is an affectingly quiet one in Stewart's senatorial office. Arthur is trying to help him prepare a bill for a boys' camp, which the cynical Rains has assigned to him in a bid to stop him from nosing into his state machine's malfeasance. Arthur has hitherto been tolerantly contemptuous of Stewart's bumblings, impatient with his flounderings, but as they discuss how the bill is to emerge, Stewart makes a simple, eloquent speech, part of which goes: "Liberty is too precious a thing to be buried in books . . . Men should hold it up in front of them every single day of their lives and say 'I'm free, to think and to speak.' My ancestors couldn't. I can, and my children will."

That fine and sensitive actress Jean Arthur is fifty percent of this scene, for Capra keeps the camera on her much of the time. As she reacts to what this bumpkin with the noble heart is saying, we realize, through her changing expressions that she has perceived the heart of this man, and that she is falling in love with him.

The fly plops messily in the ointment when Stewart proposes to

James Stewart, Astrid Allwyn, *Mr. Smith Goes to Washington*, Columbia, 1939

place his boys' camp on land that the special interests back home, headed by Edward Arnold, plan to use for less admirable purposes. When they try to lay down the law to him, and apprise him of their underlying schemes, he goes to the Senate to expose them, but is outwitted by Rains, who tries to reverse the situation by accusing *him* of corruption.

All of which leads to the famous filibuster scene. Stewart holds the entire Senate at bay for twenty-three hours, speechifying, quoting from books, making points, supported only by Arthur in the gallery and their journalist friend (Thomas Mitchell) who has been won over to his cause. Later, when the going gets rough, Harry Carey's vice-president flashes him surreptitious looks of encouragement. Stewart is in his prime in this scene: boyishly impassioned, righteously indignant, refusing to be cowed by baskets of hate mail. Even his homestate populace, brainwashed by the entrenched interests' control of the press, condemns him. He gradually tires, his voice grows hoarse, but still he is unrelenting, determined to do or die. His fellow senators, many of whom had retired to the cloakrooms in disgust, come back to listen to him, warmed by his sincerity and conviction, and motivated by wonderment as to how long he can last. Eventually he triumphs, though he must collapse from sheer exhaustion before that happens. Rains, overcome with guilt and remorse, and deeply impressed by Stewart's game persistence, rushes to the front of the chamber declaring that every word the junior senator says is true.

Frank Capra let Stewart have his head in *Mr. Smith Goes to Washington*. He said later that Stewart's inner schematic and that of the fictional Jefferson Smith were so close that sheer instinct kept Stewart superbly on track. "He played it with his whole heart and his whole mind, and that is what made it so real, so true," Capra said. He laughingly recalled that when some technical problems went beyond even Stewart's ability with the character, Capra was there with the right solutions. Stewart had to simulate convincing hoarseness late in the filibuster scene. Capra, in his autobiography, told of the method applied: "Twice a day Jimmy's throat was swabbed with vile mercury solution that swelled and irritated his vocal chords. The result was astonishing. No amount of acting could possibly simulate Jimmy's intense pathetic efforts to speak through real swollen chords." Capra cited this as a prime example

of Stewart's willingness to take physical chances, even of a hazardous kind, to assure authenticity in his characterization.

Many at the time had wondered why Capra hadn't chosen Gary
Cooper to play Jefferson Smith, since Cooper had made an earlier
success in Capra's *Mr. Deeds Goes to Town* in a somewhat similar role.
Capra later related that, at 38, Cooper seemed too old to project the
necessary boyish naïveté. As Capra put it, "This boy had to get
across that his strength was as the strength of ten because his heart
was pure, or a sure and solid variation on that beloved old cliché, but
Cooper at that point was too experienced and sophisticated, for all
his honesty and directness, to get it across." Stewart, Capra recalled,
was quite another story; he was young enough for the part — after
all, a senator had to be age 30 to serve and Stewart had just passed
that milestone — but he could come across with honest, unabashed
emotion. Above all, given Stewart's private sensitive nature, he
could completely lose himself in the part.

Stewart, that golden year of 1939, went on to win the New York
Film Critics' Award for Best Actor. He was nominated for an Academy Award, but lost to Robert Donat's touching, though hardly
blockbusting, portrayal of the title character in *Goodbye Mr. Chips*
(one of the mysteries of the Academy's history). Informed opinion
at the time had it that Stewart and Clark Gable (for *Gone With the
Wind*) had cancelled each other out in the voting, with Donat sneaking in through the back door.

Two actors who worked with Stewart in *Mr. Smith Goes to Washington* had fond memories of him years later. On tour in Boston in
the fall of 1947 with *An Inspector Calls*, Thomas Mitchell gave me
several hours in the Ritz-Carlton bar. Not only did he talk at length
about Stewart and the other actors in *Mr. Smith*; he had been with
Stewart only months before in the recent Capra blockbuster, *It's a
Wonderful Life*. "He was the most naturally gifted actor I ever
worked with," Mitchell told me. "It was all instinct, all emotion; I
don't think it came from training or technique — I don't think he
ever took an acting lesson — it came from forces deep within him;
there was an authentic passion in that man, and he made you feel
that he meant everything he was supposed to be feeling and saying
— meant it all, deep deep down. As a result, Frank [Capra] just had
to turn the camera on him and let him go. The result was magical!"
Claude Rains told me some ten years after *Mr. Smith*, "Jim was such

a responsive, pliable actor — and he was a wonderful listener and re-actor — he listened with the same wonderfully natural simplicity with which he spoke. That is *great* acting."

Hard on the heels of his successful Columbia loanout for *Mr. Smith Goes to Washington*, Stewart went over to Universal for *Destry Rides Again* (1939), directed by George Marshall. He had always wanted to essay a Western, and this was to be his first. Later, he marveled to friends that he had even landed it, but he could thank producer Joe Pasternak for his good fortune. Pasternak thought it would be a refreshing change of pace for Stewart, but he had to buck the Universal executives whose consensus opinion was that he was "this weak, skinny kid with the soft face. What kind of stalwart Western hero would *he* make?" But Pasternak prevailed.

Pasternak huddled with the writers, Felix Jackson, Gertrude Purcell and Henry Myers, who were trying to do a fresh retread on the old novel by Max Brand and the 1932 Universal movie with cowboy hero Tom Mix. Pasternak urged the writers to use their sources only as takeoff points while they came up with a completely new concept, shrewdly tailored to the evolving Stewart persona.

In the new *Destry*, Stewart is the son of a famed marshal who once employed Bottle Neck's sheriff, Charles Winninger. Winninger is a hopeless drunk, put in his post by bad-guy saloon owner Brian Donlevy so that he can run the town as he chooses. When the Stewart character arrives in town, he is taken for a mollycoddled wimp, because the townspeople's first sight of him is as he emerges from a stagecoach with a parasol and a birdcage in his hands. He is only trying to help the lady who owns them, but it is an unfortunate first impression. The bad guys' concerns are further alleviated when Stewart informs one and all that he is pacifistically inclined and hates to carry firearms. When Donlevy challenges him, he backs off with the words, "You see, if I had carried a gun, one of us might have got hurt — and it might have been me." This incurs the disdain of Donlevy and his gang and they promptly write him off. Even the saloon gal, Marlene Dietrich, contemptuously hands him a broom, saying that *this* is the only form of cleanup *he* is likely to effect! But matters shift when Winninger is killed by Donlevy's henchmen. Stewart, the town's new marshal, shows his true colors by strapping on his holster and guns and going after the bad guys. He leads the townspeople in a law-and-order march on the saloon, and it turns out he is a crack shot. Dietrich, who has now fallen in love with him, or at any rate with his new incarnation, takes a bullet meant for him, and dies in his arms.

Such was the plot, but it was the inventive conceptions of the screenwriters, George Marshall's well-paced direction, and the solid acting of the principals and supporting players, which turned *Destry Rides Again* into one of 1939's top hits.

The success could not have come too soon for Marlene Dietrich, who had not made a movie for two years. In 1937, the flops *Knight Without Armor* and *Angel* resulted in her being named one of Hollywood's "Box Office Poison" stars. She had beat a retreat to Europe where she was, in the summer of 1939, contemplating doing a French film. Meanwhile, she was relaxing on the Riviera with her husband, Rudi Sieber, director Josef Von Sternberg, novelist Erich Maria Remarque, one of her many rumored involvements, and Joe and Jack Kennedy. In her memoirs she talks warmly of the Kennedys, but says nothing of the rumors that Joe Kennedy had tried, despite the presence of her husband and Remarque, to add her to his female-star trophy wall. (She actually speaks more highly of young Jack, then 22, than she does of his father.) She was convinced that she was washed up in Hollywood, so when Joe Pasternak called and said he had a great part for her, she laughed ironically, especially when she was told it would be in a Western. But Joe talked her into it, and after she read the script she showed it to Von Sternberg, who advised her that it would be an excellent career move for her.

Certainly Dietrich makes a smash comeback in *Destry Rides Again*. Unlike the pallid personas forced upon her in recent films, her "Frenchie" was a fully-fledged saloon queen, feisty and exciting, with a few Mae West-ian overtones. Pasternak told the press that he had always known Marlene was a red-blooded gal and that this film would prove it once and for all, which it did. And when Frederick Hollander wrote two show-stopping songs for her to sing, "You've Got That Look That Leaves Me Weak," and the even more combustible Frank Loesser-penned "The Boys in the Back Room," Dietrich was home free. Her performance in *Destry Rides Again* is every bit as strong as Stewart's. Her famous fight scene with rival Una Merkel in which they knock each other around a bar, pulling hair and kicking, is stopped only by Stewart throwing a bucket of water on them. It was a knockout with audiences.

According to Charles Higham and other biographers, as well as Joe Pasternak, it was a case of lust-at-first-sight when Dietrich beheld Stewart. He, however, seems to have been frightened of her. When she heard that he loved Flash Gordon comics, she had the studio art department make him a lifesize Flash Gordon doll. Accounts vary as to whether Stewart gave in to Dietrich all the way, though it was not for lack of her trying. According to Una Merkel, Dietrich used every ploy under the sun to get him alone in her dressing room. Stewart was not too keen on married women, though he had heard that Dietrich's longtime marriage to Rudi Sieber, by whom she had had a child, Maria, was an open one. He had also heard of all the romances, and didn't fancy being the latest notch on her headboard. He was, however, in the full flood of his satyr phase, so it is possible he did acquiesce to her on at least one occasion. At some point along the way, though, he must have rebuffed or offended her, for Dietrich's references to Stewart in later years were mostly derogatory.

In her autobiography, Dietrich goes out of her way to put Stewart down, even denigrating what she refers to as the "what's-happened-to-my-other-shoe?" style of acting, adding, "James Stewart was the inventor of this original style. Even when he visibly made an effort to play a love scene, he always gave the impression he was wearing only one shoe and looking for the other while he slowly droned his lines." Dietrich doesn't stop there. She continues: "One day I told [Stewart] about these ruminations of mine, and he answered, 'How's that?' Obviously his sense of humor was poorly developed. He performed this way throughout his life, and became very rich and very famous. Now he no longer had to look for his other shoe." Miss Dietrich, than whom Hell truly had no greater fury, continued to reinforce the impression that she was somehow a woman scorned. Her scathing reference to Hollywood actors who had a peanut for a brain leaves little doubt that she was referring to Stewart. One paragraph later she is calling Spencer Tracy "the only really admirable actor with whom I worked," but other references to Tracy make it obvious that she wasn't physically attracted to him, which may account for her benign attitude toward him.

In his subsequent references to Dietrich, at least as they have appeared in print, Stewart has been politely affirmative but somehow distant, even a little patronizing: "*Destry* did good things for both of us: it showed I could handle a Western — it was my first — and it put Marlene back on top of the Hollywood heap after two bad years in which she didn't work and got that box-office-poison label." Certainly *Destry Rides Again* was a solid hit, and launched Dietrich into a successful run of Hollywood pictures over the next few years before she took time out to entertain American troops in World War II.

The critics were kind to the film, commenting on its fresh approach as written and directed, and remarking that the Dietrich-Stewart teaming, on first thought one of the most highly unlikely in cinematic history, had turned out to be one of Joe Pasternak's happiest inspirations. In Pasternak's view, "the chemistry was so right between them because her European exoticism and sophistication, and in that role her brazen aggressiveness, contrasted excitingly with his homespun Boy Scout All-American aura." The *New York Times'* Bosley Crowther, one of my early guides and mentors, nailed down the essence of Stewart's hit performance, commenting: "It was a masterpiece of underplaying in a deliberately sardonic vein — the freshest, most offbeat characterization that this popular actor ever played."

The Shop Around the Corner, shot in late 1939 and released in January 1940, is one of James Stewart's and Margaret Sullavan's more affecting pairings. There were complaints from the critics that Stewart's role was the stronger and more active, while Sullavan was forced to be passive and peripheral to the proceedings. Nevertheless, it is one of their best-liked appearances and they are gently charming as a pair who work together while carrying on a pen-pal relationship without knowing that each is the object of the other's addressals.

The admirable Frank Morgan has one of his best character outings as Matuschek, the proprietor of a Budapest notions shop. He suspects his wife (unseen on screen) of infidelity with his chief employee, Stewart. He fires Stewart, but later learns through a detective that the culprit is actually silky, treacherous fellow-employee Joseph Schildkraut (who plays an unpleasant, sleazy character with brilliant unpleasantness and sleaze). After being rescued by office-boy William Tracy from suicide, Morgan puts the restored Stewart in charge of the shop, and he galvanizes the employees to make it the best Christmas shopping season ever for Matuschek and Company.

Stewart's dealings with Sullavan, their inability to get along as co-workers, and their ignorance of each other's true identity, are charmingly detailed under the gossamer direction of Ernest Lubitsch, who in *The Shop Around the Corner* seems to have eschewed his usual ironic cynicism and subtle leg-pulling in favor of a frothily touching romantic approach.

An excellent cast of players, including fellow shop employees Sara Haden, Felix Bressart, Inez Courtney and Charles Smith, conveys the wistful, gently humanistic ambience Lubitsch is out to achieve. The serenity of pre-war Budapest is depicted with a fidelity that is all the more commendable, given that the entire proceedings were shot on an MGM sound stage with added scenes on the back lot.

Samson Raphaelson, the scenarist, wittily translated the graceful nuances of Nikolaus Laszlo's Hungarian play, *Parfumerie*, and there are many gently amusing and touching scenes. Sullavan and Stewart are certainly not Hungarian types, by any stretch of the imagination, yet the miracle here is that they definitely suggest a Continental sensibility that somehow transcends national boundaries. Nonetheless, they are completely authentic in spiritual and emotional terms. And never has their ensemble acting been more quietly expert, more fully attuned, which probably accounts for the fact that, of the four films they made together, if modern audience response is to be given credence, *The Shop Around the Corner* is the enduring favorite.

Considering that he had just come off the ironic but sparkling *Ninotchka* (1939), with Greta Garbo as the lady communist who finds love in Paris with dilettante nobleman Melvyn Douglas, Lubitsch reveals a surprising amount of tenderness here, doubtless influenced by the mystique and chemistry of the matchless Sullavan-Stewart duo.

Joseph Schildkraut, who had one of his more colorful roles as the villain of the piece, spoke in glowing terms of the Sullavan-Stewart interplay when I interviewed him some years later. "I won't resort to a cliché phrase like 'the art that conceals art,' but I am tempted to use it when describing Jimmy's and Maggie's acting in that. They made it seem so spontaneous, so natural, so deeply felt."

Schildkraut told of having seen the final print with a preview audience, "and that pair held the audience spellbound! You could feel the affection that wafted up to them, the liking, the empathy, the admiration."

When I mentioned to Joseph Schildkraut that Stewart's off-screen love for Sullavan had been a source of speculation for years in Hollywood, he smiled and said, "Whatever went on between them, it was extremely effective on the screen. They were a lucky pair, too, in that the camera had an ongoing love affair with them. I have seen stage actors who were really wonderful technicians, flawless artists before a live audience who seemed like zombies, dead things, when seen on the screen." He added: "The camera is a peculiar instrument — it likes you or it doesn't like you, and it makes its preferences known, sometimes cruelly, but always effectively. Jimmy Stewart and Maggie Sullavan were *born* for the camera, and it always showed!"

Frank Borzage told me, "Jimmy and Maggie, whatever their off-screen relationship, were in the great romantic tradition of screen duos. Something magical happened between them; it was indefinable, but so potent, so touching." Borzage cited a scene in *The Shop Around the Corner* when Stewart comes to visit the ill Sullavan, who still does not know that he is her pen-pal and paramour: "The tenderness he showed toward her, the protectiveness, the sincerity and the sensitivity, and her half-bewildered, half-fascinated response to it — magic moments like that are what have enriched the screen." Modestly, Borzage disclaimed credit for producing similar effects in their scenes: "They had such a spontaneous interplay that all you had to do was tell the cameraman to let it roll, and they were 'on'!" Borzage also noted that "they never, ever blew a line when they did a scene together, a rarity in intimate scenes."

Brooke Hayward, Sullavan's daughter by third husband Leland Hayward, once interviewed Stewart about her mother for her book, *Haywire*, and what he says is of great interest:

"Humor. She had great humor. It wasn't mechanical with her. It was a part of her. This was one of the things that made her great. When you'd play a scene with her, you were never quite sure, although she was always letter perfect in her lines, what was going to happen. She had you just a little bit off guard, and also the director. I've always called what she would do planned improvisation — she could do just moments that would hit you, maybe a look or a line or two, but they would hit like flashes, or earthquakes; everybody'd sort of feel it at the same time. It's a rare thing."

Stewart also remembered that Sullavan hated too much dialogue in a scene and that she would say "we don't need all this talk." Like Sullavan, Stewart tended to simplify, to get to the core of the scene, separating the essential from the inessential. In 1957, Stewart told me that what made his teaming with Sullavan so great, so real was "the simplicity. The true classic simplicity of our mutual approach. So natural. So spontaneous. So effortless."

The critics were not slow to pick up on the magical quality of the Sullavan-Stewart onscreen pairing. Of *The Shop Around the Corner*, the critic for the *New York Herald-Tribune* wrote:

"The plot.... does not make much of a claim on one's photoplay memories, but the characters and the incidents have been so brilliantly treated that the film becomes disarming and beguiling comedy.... Mr. Stewart [brings] all of his great gift for shy understatement [to the film]... once more [Miss Sullavan] shows that she has few colleagues who can match her for crowding a line or scene with emotional intensity, even when it is a minor situation." And from the *New York Daily Mirror*: "It is gay and light and beautiful and as sparkling as the foam atop a glass of Pilsener."

The Shop Around the Corner was made a few months after Stewart's great triumph in *Mr. Smith Goes to Washington*, and he seems to have attained an extra degree of confidence and force in his projection. Later critics would express surprise at Stewart's capacity for pure, unadulterated, forceful anger, but it is very much on display here when he fires the perfidious Joseph Schildkraut for betraying employer Frank Morgan with his wife. First, he assaults Schildkraut with cutting words, then he physically attacks him. Sara Haden later said something oddly penetrating about Stewart: "There must have been things, occasions, struggles, problems in his early life that aroused a lingering anger, for I am sure he used them in scenes that called for such emotional explosions; he reached far back into the past."

Haden was more perceptive than even she knew.

In early 1940, *The Mortal Storm*, presented a serious problem for Stewart. In a role that cried out for an authentic German, he neither looked, talked, nor felt remotely Teutonic. A trenchant study of anti-Nazi Germans in the 1933 advent of Hitler's regime, it was based on a well-received 1938 novel by Phyllis Bottome.

Many have wondered why Stewart was cast in this role. As a German farmer, he competes for the love of Margaret Sullavan with Robert Young. When Young becomes a fanatical Nazi, Sullavan loses interest in him and turns to Stewart. Frank Morgan, as Sullavan's professor father, gives one of the best performances of his distinguished career as a man who scorns Aryan racial purity. His most celebrated line in the film is, "I've never prized safety, either for myself or my children. I've prized courage." When his hitherto idolatrous students turn on him, Morgan is arrested and later dies in a concentration camp. Sullavan and her mother attempt to escape to Austria, but when a seditious (translated: anti-Nazi) manuscript of her father's is found in her luggage, she is turned back at the border. Stewart, who has moved to Austria after falling into disfavor for befriending a liberal professor, returns to rescue her; she is shot as they cross the border into Switzerland, and dies in his arms.

So much for the plot of *The Mortal Storm*. Sullavan, Young, and director Frank Borzage had been that way in 1938. *Three Comrades*, was set in post–World War I Germany, and they had acquitted themselves admirably in it. But this was Stewart's first foray into areas Teutonic and he came on more glaringly apple pie than apple strudel.

Billy Grady felt that there was a paucity of German or Dutch actors around who could guarantee the box office so Stewart had won, as he put it, "sort of by default." Frank Borzage told me that he felt Stewart's "manly affirmation and decency" had resulted in the casting. Eddie Mannix put it more tersely: "He was just a damned good actor and the role needed strength and fundamental positivism."

In this fourth, and last, of their films together, Margaret Sullavan complements Stewart as capably as always. She has many poignant moments, though her character seems to react to events rather than bring them about. This kind of passivity (as in *The Shop Around the Corner*) did not sit well with her, nor did it showcase her to maximum advantage. Nevertheless, Frank Borzage, always a firm Sullavan admirer, maintained that she sacrificed her own role for the benefit of the picture more often than she was credited for doing. "They accuse Maggie of star temperament," Borzage said, "but I often found her putting the good of the picture ahead of her own interests, in the several films I did with her."

Stewart does redeem his miscasting with an intense sincerity, to be sure, and his moral strength and righteous anger are major ornaments to *The Mortal Storm*. Robert Stack, who played a young German in the film, was to recall, at the age of 70, how impressed he was with Stewart in the picture. He referred to him as a "tower of strength" and called attention to his unassuming but well-conceived technique. At the time Stack appeared with him he was just 21 (he had made his film debut the year before with Universal's *First Love*, in which he had given the 17-year-old Deanna Durbin her first on-screen kiss). *The Mortal Storm* was much sterner stuff, and Stack was awed with the way Stewart and Sullavan lost themselves in their roles. "Bill Orr [another young actor] and I studied them closely, wondering how they did it — on the surface they were so unassuming, but they sort of lit up from within when the strong scenes came. We were deeply impressed."

The Mortal Storm was released in June 1940, right on the jack-booted heels of the German triumphs over France and the Lowlands. Although it was slightly behind the news, so to speak, the film made a telling impact, and was later credited with accelerating American involvement in the War, as well as heightening American awareness of the Nazi threat to human rights everywhere.

Claudine West, who had co-written the screenplay with Anderson Ellis and George Froeschel, told me in later years that the film had dramatically and poignantly highlighted the most disastrous aspect of Nazi tyranny: "its invasion of privacy, its interference with individual lives — and loves — and hopes — and dreams."

Sullavan and Stewart act the script with the sincerity and emotional commitment that one expects of them. The mutually compelling qualities that make them one of the finest co-starring duos the screen was ever to know are on sterling display here, as the critics did not fail to note. There was to be much regret in later years that they did not come up with further pairings, as the Hepburn-Tracy and Powell-Loy teams had. Claudine West told me she had always hoped they would appear together on the stage. "It would have been wonderful," she said, "to see how their respective chemistries — and they were magical — interrelated in the flesh before a live audience. Oh, the electricity those two would have generated!" Though both eventually returned to the theatre, it was never together.

Howard Barnes of the *New York Herald-Tribune* echoed the opinion of many: "[Stewart] is scarcely the type for a German farmer, but he acts with such intense sincerity that the personal tragedy which is the core of the piece is the most sustaining note in the proceedings." The critic of the English paper *The Spectator*, with odd dichotomy but with an underlying note of approval, wrote that "Margaret Sullavan and James Stewart act with a kind of unwilling [sic] intensity which is extremely effective."

It is true that there is a cardboard aspect to the characterizations, with everyone either all black or all white. Some grayish ambivalences might have lent more reality to the proceedings, but on its own terms, and in its time period, *The Mortal Storm* was most effective and powerful.

On loan to Warners in mid-1940, Stewart found himself paired, for the one and only time, with Rosalind Russell, an actress who could equal him in comic nuance and high style. Their conjunction in *No Time for Comedy* (1940) is highly felicitous, and thanks to their joint efforts it still registers as a bright, clever and ironic film. Directed by William Keighley, who understood this material and guided it accordingly, and well-written by Julius J. and Philip G. Epstein, the film became one of the more creditable items in the Stewart pantheon.

S. N. Behrman's play had been a hit on Broadway, with Katharine Cornell and Laurence Olivier in the lead. *No Time for Comedy* was a biting, thoughtful study of the ups and downs of Broadway success, but producer Hal Wallis, urged on by watchful Jack Warner, made sure that Keighley and the Epsteins "Hollywoodized" the story to emphasize romance. On Broadway the script had favored Cornell, but the leads were given equal footing on film, which was a wise decision as two superb comedy players gave an evenly matched account of themselves.

The story has hayseed newcomer Stewart making a comedy hit as the writer of a vehicle for star Russell. He then repeats his initial success several times over, thus winning a permanent niche as a comedy playwright. Genevieve Tobin, a flirtatious busybody and the wife of philosophical Charlie Ruggles, brainwashes Stewart into

Allyn Joslyn, Rosalind Russell, James Stewart, *No Time for Comedy*, Warner Bros., 1940

believing he can also be a great dramatist. This causes an estrangement between wife Russell and himself, so she takes up with Ruggles for a while as he, in turn, gets involved with Tobin. The Great American Drama he essays, of course, flops miserably. Stewart contritely returns to his wife, with future comedy successes presaged if he stays in his own creative backyard henceforth.

The film is full of shrewd observations about the theatre and its creative process, and the bright comedy talents of Russell and Stewart are a joy to watch as they play off each other with consummate timing and verve.

Stewart collected his fair share of fine reviews, that of Bosley Crowther in *The New York Times* being typical:

"As usual, Mr. Stewart is the best thing in the show—a completely ingratiating character who ranges from the charming clumsiness of a country playwright to the temperamental distraction of an established writer with complete and natural assurance."

Russell also garnered her warranted share of raves, and years later she told me during an interview that Stewart was one of the co-stars she remembered with particular affection and esteem: "There was no romance between us — we just weren't right for each other, not that there were any regrets, and anyway we were, if I recall in his case as well as mine, otherwise 'involved' at the time. But oh, the respect I had for that man's timing! He was a joy to play off of because he just never let you down — he was there for you, at all times, which is a lot more than I could say for other actors I have worked with. It's always depressing when you have to drag someone along with you either because he is insecure in his role or just lazy or preoccupied, but Jimmy never — he is as professional as they come, and he understands teamwork."

William Keighley also praised Stewart's work to me in a later interview. "There was a natural talent," he said. "A true natural. You never had to give him directions — he was a jump ahead of you. I never saw such wonderful instinct — a natural gift — and it came to him spontaneously, without any effort, nor did he seem to have to think things out in advance. A real joy to direct — and one of the nicest people I ever knew, incidentally."

Stewart, in an interview published just after the release of *No Time for Comedy*, said that he did not mind at all being loaned out. "I've been to Selznick, Universal, Columbia, you name it, and it was wonderful to study the different studio approaches. All the studios have their own distinctive personalities and approaches — it was like a round-the-world tour of different styles, and it was a real education. I wouldn't have missed it for the world!"

There were those who felt that, in his final film for 1940, James Stewart was a small fish in a big pond. *The Philadelphia Story* was supposed to be the star turn of Katharine Hepburn, reprising her phenomenal stage success of 1939. There was also the charm and authority of Cary Grant, who demanded and got top billing, and there were on hand the assorted talents of John Howard, Roland Young, John Halliday, Mary Nash, Henry Daniell and Virginia Weidler. Yet it was for this film that Stewart copped his one and only Academy Award for acting.

It was the common opinion at the 1941 ceremonies that here was a consolation prize for his performance the previous year in *Mr. Smith Goes to Washington*. This was not unprecedented: Bette Davis had won the 1935 Oscar for a much weaker film, *Dangerous*, than the explosive 1934 (*Of Human Bondage*) performance for which many had boosted her. Claudette Colbert had swept the 1934 Oscars for *It Happened One Night*, along with her co-star Clark Gable and director Frank Capra. The next year, Davis had been "consoled."

It is true that in *The Philadelphia Story*, Stewart does not have the hefty overall footage that an Oscar-winning star turn usually commands, but he made the most of his role of a newspaper reporter who falls in love with the bride-to-be (Hepburn) at a society wedding. They have one night of laughter and lovemaking, but Hepburn finally decides to ditch her stuffy fiancé (John Howard) and take up yet again with her ex-husband (Grant), who has been maneuvering all along to win her back.

After a brilliant six-year run in Hollywood (1932-1938), during which she had won an Oscar (for the 1933 *Morning Glory*) and critical admiration for such films as *Alice Adams* (1935) and *Little Women* (1933), Hepburn had run into a snag, and in 1938 had been labeled box office poison by a film trade paper. The fact that she suffered a putdown in the good company of Marlene Dietrich, Joan Crawford

James Stewart, Katharine Hepburn, John Howard, Mary Nash,
The Philadelphia Story, MGM, 1940

and Kay Francis did not lessen the blow for her. She bought out of her RKO contract, and after a fine performance in *Holiday* at Columbia in 1938, Hepburn went back East to hibernate and renew her energies. Playwright Philip Barry felt Hepburn should tackle the stage again, so he brought her the outline of what became *The Philadelphia Story*, which greatly intrigued her. He completed the play, and she and Barry put up half the capital for it to be produced (the Theatre Guild took up the rest of the tab). They opened on March 29, 1939, for a smash-hit run that lasted over 400 performances on Broadway.

Having been several times burned and more than a few times warned by her prior Hollywood experiences, Hepburn was determined to stay on top of any movie deal, and she obtained, in advance, the rights to the play. When the studios put up bids, they learned that not only did Hepburn control the movie rights, but she insisted that she should star in the film incarnation of Tracy Lord. MGM made the best offer, and took Hepburn along with the vehicle. Louis B. Mayer admired Hepburn ("Her hard Yankee mind understood him only too well," as one writer put it) and she was to last at MGM for the next dozen years, going on to a historical onscreen and offscreen pairing with Spencer Tracy.

But even though he was in Hepburn's corner, cheering on her startling renaissance, Mayer still questioned whether her box office clout was strong enough to carry such an expensive production. Hepburn, as much the realist as he, went along with Mayer's suggestion that she be complemented by two strong male stars. She had already done three films with Cary Grant – *Sylvia Scarlett* (1936), *Bringing Up Baby* (1938), and *Holiday* (1938) – and they worked extremely well together, so Grant was approached. Since he was a freelancer who commanded high fees and took what he fancied, he demanded that he get top billing. Hepburn and the studio capitulated, knowing that his box office clout counted more than her vanity, and contractee Stewart was drafted in for the third starring part. Though he stood third in the billing, after Grant and Hepburn, Stewart knew instinctively that there were fine opportunities in the role, and gave it his best efforts.

Seasoned director George Cukor, who had guided Hepburn through her first film, *A Bill of Divorcement* (1932), and through three subsequent films (*Little Women, Sylvia Scarlett* and *Holiday*), was an ideal choice to transcribe her hit from stage to screen. His pre-Hollywood theatrical background was extensive, and Mayer knew that he could make Hepburn sparkle and simmer with star-power as few directors could.

James Stewart, Katharine Hepburn, *The Philadelphia Story*, MGM, 1940

Katharine Hepburn and James Stewart had never done a film together before, and knew each other only through mutual friends. They shared a background of good family and Ivy league schooling (Bryn Mawr, Hepburn's alma mater, was the Princeton of women's colleges), and they got along in relaxed style. But, as George Cukor told me, no one realized how seamlessly and smoothly they would play together until they were actually before the cameras. "While offscreen the mutual chemistry for any kind of romance was completely lacking," Cukor recalled. "Onscreen, the camera did wonders for both of them in juxtaposition. They were really magical together!"

Cukor was also to make no bones about what he felt was his just credit for guiding Stewart to an Oscar-winning performance. "I wanted him to be his natural self, only I wanted him to highlight and underline his boyishness, his spontaneity, his stunned wonder when love hits him during the scene when he and Hepburn take a midnight swim together. He followed along with my ideas, and never regretted it," Cukor said.

Stewart was reportedly ill-at-ease with Cukor, a well-known homosexual though highly closeted, and he resented the jokes about George having a crush on him. That certainly explained to the gossips and set busybodies why Cukor seemed to take more time with Stewart than the star. He even guided him through the love scenes, substituting himself for Hepburn in the rehearsals to get his points across. Something about Cukor reminded Stewart of the predatory gays he had known as a young actor in New York, but Cukor kept the relationship professional and made nary a private pass. "Jimmy was a darling," Cukor told me years later. "So sensitive and boyish and sweet; and it was his unleashed ardor that made his love scenes with Kate so believable!" Cukor even made the statement to me that he felt he had gotten the best performance ever out of Stewart, and that *The Philadelphia Story* had *not* been a consolation prize for what Capra had done with Stewart in *Mr. Smith Goes to Washington*. There was never any real love lost between emphatically heterosexual Capra and secretively gay Cukor, especially when Cukor heard about the fag jokes Capra had made about him. To hear Cukor tell it, the fact that *he* "was the one who got the Oscar performance out of our boy Jimmy" was a source of considerable annoyance to Capra.

Stewart did have the prescience to realize that Cukor was highlighting his best aspects in the film, and later he was to make polite, albeit restrained, complimentary references to his directorial guidance. Significantly, they never made another film together. Cukor made snide references to "all that overmasculine [translated: macho] posturing Jimmy insisted on with those Westerns Tony Mann put out," as if to imply that Stewart had sacrificed his true artistic instincts to what he thought was the necessary "image."

Katharine Hepburn has always been protective toward Cukor, of whom she was extremely fond. She was, of course, aware of his predilections, but she preferred not to face them head on. "Kate saw only what she wanted to see," Ruth Waterbury said later. "I always found that business about Spencer Tracy having to cue her in about gays laughable; why, she had been up to her ears in them for many years on stage and screen! Who was kidding whom?" Also, constant lesbian gossip about Hepburn and the women she associated with intimately ("Kate and her Giddy Girlfriends," as sharp-tongued Margaret Sullavan termed them) hardly gave her license to look down her nose at others. Since Sullavan was solidly in Stewart's camp, and had married agent Leland Hayward, with whom Hepburn had professed to be in love, it should have created strains between Hepburn and Stewart, yet somehow it didn't. "Their work together sang along like a dream," as Cukor, somewhat oddly, phrased it.

The story of the Grant-Hepburn-Stewart hit is ordinary enough in the telling, and it hardly seems the basis for a phenomenally successful play and movie. But Philip Barry's amusing dialogue coupled with the vivacity of the lead performances, aided by solid supporting stints, made all the difference.

The plot deals with one Tracy Lord (Hepburn), an apparently superficial and spoiled Philadelphia society girl, who has discarded one husband and is about to marry another. Rakish publisher C.K. "Dexter" Haven (Grant) pressures the family into allowing reporter Stewart and his girl friday, Ruth Hussey, to cover the story, under pain of exposing the romantic indiscretions of the playboy father (John Halliday) whom Hepburn finds an embarrassment. ("You lack an understanding heart," is one of Halliday's reproaches to his daughter.) During the course of events, Hepburn and Stewart kindle romantically, but she returns to the man who has always loved her in spite of her faults (Grant) and leaves stuffy fiancé John Howard to fend for himself. Through her experiences, Hepburn has learned humility and her latent femininity has emerged, which sounds like pretentious folderol, yet the dexterity of Cukor's direction, and Donald Ogden Stewart's excellent adaptation, produce a deliciously sincere result.

Joseph Ruttenberg photographed the proceedings, laid in a handsome Philadelphia mansion, with creative élan, and Franz Waxman's music, while discreet, enhanced all the apposite moods.

Cary Grant, surprisingly, told me in 1957 that he felt Stewart had had the best written part and that his own insistence on top billing had done him little good. Grant was bisexual, and his earlier affair with handsome Randolph Scott had been one of Hollywood's most gossiped-about relationships. He had developed an unreciprocated crush on Stewart, according to Cukor, and did not take well the rebuff that was shortly forthcoming. So his annoyance over Stewart getting the most sympathetic role and winning an Oscar for it might have had a sour-grapes taste. "Jimmy owed his hit in that to Cukor — Cukor pounded it out of him," was one of Grant's unflattering comments on the subject.

Katharine Hepburn has had little to say about Stewart over the years. There seems to have been some antipathy between them, and Billy Grady felt Hepburn had been annoyed that Stewart copped the Oscar for "her" picture. In 1990, when their protracted love scene in *The Philadelphia Story* was the *pièce de résistance* film clip shown during the Film Society of Lincoln Center tribute to Stewart, everyone expected Hepburn to come out at the end (other Stewart co-stars had appeared earlier.) But though she had recently made several public appearances, there was nary a sign of her that night, which came as something of an anticlimax.

The reviewers were very kind to *The Philadelphia Story*, and Grant, Hepburn and Stewart seem, overall, to share equally in the plaudits. "What a salutory occasion," one critic gushed, "to see Miss Hepburn, Mr. Grant and Mr. Stewart shining like the true stars they are!" William Boehnel of the *New York World-Telegram* commented, "George Cukor has directed it with tonic imagination, the acting of every member of the cast is flawless, the lines sparkle and bubble...." And from Eileen Creelman of the *New York Sun*: "Cary Grant plays the ex-husband with dignity and a sharp humor, making an excellent contrast to James Stewart's slow, easygoing comedy [sic]. Miss Hepburn, more natural than she has ever been on screen or stage, misses neither the fun nor the tender qualities of [her] character." Though failing to get an Oscar for her efforts, Hepburn consoled herself with a New York Film Critics' Award.

One of Stewart's more terse retrospective evaluations: "It was a high point for me."

Somebody at MGM got the (supposedly) inspired idea of pairing James Stewart with Hedy Lamarr in a Patterson McNutt story, produced and directed by the famed Clarence Brown. Then someone else came up with the racy title, *Come Live With Me*, a borderline notion indeed for the prissy Production Code to stomach, yet, for some reason, stomach it they did. The net result, despite solid character players like Ian Hunter, Verree Teasdale and Donald Meek pitching away, was fluffy, forgettable stuff. Worse, the chemistry between Stewart and Lamarr failed to ignite as hoped.

A Louis B. Mayer discovery (he dubbed her The Most Beautiful Woman in the World) Hedy had made a rather vulgar splash in a 1931 Czech film, *Ecstasy*, in which she appeared nude. Born Hedwig Kiesler in Vienna in 1913, she came to America in 1938, and made something of a hit with Charles Boyer in *Algiers* that same year, though *he* had to do all the acting. Hedy managed to get away with *re*-acting, thanks to Boyer's professionalism, but the truth was, Miss Lamarr at the time was a regrettably bad actress. The camera,

Hedy Lamarr, James Stewart, *Come Live With Me*, MGM, 1941

though, had a love affair with her, and her roles were tailored to disguise her limitations. Strong male co-stars like Clark Gable, Robert Taylor, and Walter Pidgeon, managed to carry her along, after a fashion.

Up against Stewart's natural and spontaneous effervescence in *Come Live With Me* (1941), Hedy paled considerably, nor were the two stars overly enamoured of each other during the shooting. Clarence Brown later told me that Stewart had opined to him that "Hedy has the face, yes, but no body to go with it." His disparaging remarks about her tiny breasts and lack of voluptuous curviness got back to Lamarr in the middle of shooting and "the frost on hand more than made up for the pre-air-conditioning era mugginess under those hot lights," as Eddie Mannix later chuckled.

The highly-forgettable story has Stewart as an impoverished writer hired by Lamarr (an alien, and the mistress of a millionaire publisher), to marry her so that she won't be deported back to Austria. The plot line rang something of a private bell with the Jewish Lamarr, who dreaded Nazi-dominated Austria. As is predictable from reel one with such plots, Lamarr and Stewart fall in love, though they have a marriage in name only, maintaining separate establishments. Stewart tries to use the situation as a story, but after the publisher-lover (Ian Hunter) gets a divorce and is ready to marry Lamarr, she must divorce Stewart. Misunderstandings ensue, which are straightened out, and boy and girl are ultimately in each other's arms — and legally, too, according to the Production Code.

Among the interesting character performers in *Come Live With Me* was the redoubtable Adeline DeWalt Reynolds. A phenomenal woman, she had graduated from college at 68 and had taken up acting at 70. This was her first film, made when she was 78, and it launched her on a nice career (she was nearly a hundred when she died in 1961). In the film she plays Stewart's understanding grandmother, and it is at her country place that the visiting couple discovers the depths of their love for each other. Both Stewart and Lamarr have recalled Reynolds with great affection as a fountainhead of wisdom and sage humor. Once, she asked Stewart why he had waited till age 32 to marry, and he said he had to be sure before taking such an important step. Amazingly she predicted that he would marry around 40 "because it will probably take you that long to be *really* sure!" (Stewart married at 41!)

Hedy was divorced from munitions king Fritz Mandl and was, at the time of shooting, ending a marriage with ladies-man writer-producer Gene Markey, who was to number Joan Bennett and Myrna Loy among his wives. The mismatched Lamarr-Markey alliance lasted only a year or so, and Reynolds told Hedy "to think not only twice but many times before you leap again." Hedy failed to take her advice, and there were to be four more marital mishaps along the line for The World's Most Beautiful Woman.

Typical reviewer reaction to *Come Live With Me* was that of a Baltimore critic: "In this Hedy acts too little and Jimmy acts too much, and this trifle of a picture gives neither much to do, in her case mercifully, in his case regrettably."

The musical *Pot O' Gold*, for which Stewart was loaned out to United Artists, was a disappointing early-1941 entry to follow in the footsteps of his Oscar-winner *The Philadelphia Story*. There were certain ironies surrounding the film, for James Roosevelt, son of then-President Franklin D., was the producer — a staunch Democrat in charge of a film starring Mr. Republican himself. Jimmy Roosevelt, in his first and only film production effort, was eager to have

James Stewart, Paulette Goddard, Horace Heidt's Musical Knights, *Pot O' Gold*, UA, 1941

a hit, and pulled many strings to persuade Louis B. Mayer to lend him his sure-fire star. Mayer was also a Republican, but saw the need to keep the Roosevelts happy, as they made a useful connection, and he agreed. Jimmy Stewart was not overly anxious to appear in the amateur production effort of the other Jimmy, but after Roosevelt the Younger applied his famous charm in a pre-production meeting, Stewart went along with Mayer's decision.

James Roosevelt was a tragic man who was doomed to live in his father's giant shadow. He failed in a number of career pursuits, including politics, and found that film-making, too, involved a number of variable and unpredictable factors necessary for a successful result. In the case of *Pot O' Gold* they just didn't materialize.

In his first musical since *Born to Dance*, Stewart is lithe, clever, and reasonably adept with the harmonica. He seems to be trying hard (perhaps too hard) to bring vitality and verve to a rather limp, if convoluted story line. Vivacious Paulette Goddard is paired with him, and United Artists publicity flacks, probably at the apprehensive Roosevelt's urging, did their best to make a hot offscreen team out of her and Stewart. Goddard, of course, had been involved with

Charles Chaplin, then Burgess Meredith, and later the novelist Erich Maria Remarque. In 1941, she let it be known that Stewart was a bit too much the boyish hayseed for her, even though, at age 33 he had acquired a Lothario reputation to rank with the best. Stewart wasn't that crazy about Paulette, either. He told Henry Fonda, among others, that her acting talent was limited and that she had to fall back on wisecracking levity to get by—an unfair assessment, some felt. In any event, the flacks came a cropper in their efforts to generate any publicity steam over these two.

Like many fluffy films, *Pot O' Gold* had an unwarrantedly complex plot line, concocted by writer Walter De Leon, based on a trivial Monte Brice story. It had originally been inspired by radio's NBC giveaway program series, a Tums-sponsored running hit featuring Horace Heidt and his Orchestra. Handsome though he might have been, Horace was a simply terrible actor, wooden and self-conscious. Stewart, Goddard, and character veterans Charles Winninger and Mary Gordon, had a mostly unsuccessful time of it covering up for him.

The story has Stewart working in a music shop; he is obsessed with music, though his wealthy and tyrannical uncle, Winninger, wants him in the food-manufacturing business. Stewart runs across Heidt and his boys practicing at a boardinghouse run by feisty, fussy Gordon. There he meets Gordon's pretty daughter, Goddard, who is also a music freak. Of course, they all convince Winninger that his products can best be promoted on radio via the Heidt Orchestra, combined with audience participation, prizes, and what not. After 86 minutes of the usual vicissitudes, it all works out to a cheerful conclusion.

Along the way, Stewart not only works the harmonica but sings, and despite some charitable reviews, he proves conclusively that singing was not one of his fortes. Goddard is amusing and vital, but her love duet with Stewart strikes a false note, as their mutual chemistry, on screen as off, fizzles. They were never to be paired again, which doubtless proved a relief to both.

One Boston reviewer, blunt and forthright but dead on target, declared: "This picture, if nothing else, proves that Jimmy Roosevelt can't produce, Jimmy Stewart can't sing and Horace Heidt can't act. George Marshall *can* direct, and keeps the pace lively, but this gifted director, with his finely tuned comic sense in other films, was wasting his time here. And MGM ought to be ashamed of itself, throwing its recent Oscar winner to the dogs in this throwaway. Come on, Mayer and Co., is that the way to build a star? Maybe Jimmy Stewart should rebel!"

Fresh from the tawdriness of *Pot O' Gold*, Stewart found himself back at Metro-Goldwyn-Mayer for his last film before going into the service — and it was yet another musical! However, in the lavish, 131-minute *Ziegfeld Girl* (1941), Stewart's role is a straight romantic one, and not too much footage is devoted to it, which must have seemed to him like adding insult to the *Pot O' Gold* injury.

Grandly produced by Pandro Berman, still flush from his recent RKO musical triumphs with Astaire and Rogers, and directed with élan by the veteran Robert Z. Leonard, the Marguerite Roberts-Sonya Levien screenplay, based on a William Anthony McGuire story, is lovingly photographed by the gifted Ray June. Herbert Stothart, MGM's highly talented answer to Warners' Steiner and Korngold, gives it his best musical inspirations.

Stewart gets top billing, inexplicably so, since he is almost invisible in this overblown recital of the sorrows, loves, triumphs and tragedies of three showgirls. Judy Garland is one of them, and she steals the show in a hot number called "Minnie from Trinidad." Then there's Hedy Lamarr who, mercifully, is required to do little more than pose and strut with statuesque éclat as one of Ziegfeld's loveliest showgirls. Lana Turner goes from elevator girl to Ziegfeld showgirl with dizzying speed, leaving behind truckdriver boyfriend Stewart, who takes to bootlegging to keep up with her financially, but ends up in the clink. Meanwhile, Turner is encouraging the attentions of millionaire socialite, and stage-door-Johnny, Ian Hunter. Out of jail, Stewart tries to persuade Turner to marry him, but the fast life has overwhelmed her and alcohol has become her nemesis. It all winds up with Turner, a pathetic has-been, doing a famous scene in which she walks down a flight of lobby stairs, collapses and dies. She has had her last moment of moments in the style to which she had grown accustomed.

The other plot lines have Lamarr caught between her violinist husband, Philip Dorn, and lead singer Tony Martin — Dorn (predictably) wins. Garland is the daughter of vaudevillian Charles Winninger, who winds up equalling his daughter's success onstage by reuniting with his old partner, Al Shean (on hand as himself).

With everyone ending up happily, except for Turner, and Stewart, the trend of *Ziegfeld Girl* is basically upbeat, and the finale, built around the famed song "You Stepped Out of a Dream," benefits from the choreographic inspirations of Warner refugee Busby Berkeley. It's all very garish and at times rather vacuous, but Robert Z. Leonard keeps it moving at a brisk pace and it is not without its engaging passages, especially when Judy Garland is giving her all.

Some publicity efforts were applied to exploit the allegedly explosive pairing of Turner and Stewart, but her acting, while appealing, is uncertain, and he seems impatient with the necessity of carrying her through her scenes. Certainly *Ziegfeld Girl* was the breakthrough film for Lana Turner, who went on to co-star with the likes of Spencer Tracy, Clark Gable and Robert Taylor within a year. Certainly her last walk down that flight of stairs has gone down as the first of her career milestones.

Stewart told friends that he couldn't help feeling some resentment that his name was being used to assure box office success for such unworthy efforts. He considered his part badly written, psychologically unmotivated, and, in retrospect, that it was essentially unplayable. Seen today, it is obvious that while he is his usual professionally conscientious self, there is a dourness and a deadness in Stewart's part that belies even his sincerest efforts. Stewart also regretted leaving for the service on such a downbeat note: 1941 had produced three films that are among his least memorable. As for Lana Turner, though badly in need of any publicity she could get at the time, she went out of her way to inform Louella Parsons that an item stating she had a crush on Stewart was totally wrong. "I admire him greatly as an actor," she sniffed to Louella. "But personally he's not my type — not *that* way!"

James Stewart always felt guilty over the Oscar he won for *The Philadelphia Story*. His speech on the night of February 27, 1941, at the Biltmore Hotel in Los Angeles was brief and humble. He told Alfred Lunt, who presented the statuette, that the honor was all the greater because this premier actor of the Broadway theatre had handed it to him. He told friends later that he wished it had been Guthrie McClintic instead of Alfred Lunt, because "he should have been the Broadway figure to give it to me — he helped make it come true years before!"

His guilt was compounded by the fact that his friend, Henry

Fonda, had been nominated for *The Grapes of Wrath*, along with Raymond Massey for *Abe Lincoln in Illinois*, Laurence Olivier for *Rebecca*, and Charles Chaplin for *The Great Dictator*. Stewart told reporters, with becoming modesty, that he felt all these actors had given better performances in 1940, especially Fonda, whose Tom Joad in *The Grapes of Wrath*, based on the John Steinbeck novel about the Okies who fled West to find a new life during the Depression, had been widely and justly acclaimed for its gritty realism.

Stewart knew as well as anyone that he had been caught in the consolation prize cycle, and he even voiced to the press what he perceived as the unfairness to other actors that such a tainted award entailed.

Generously, he gave the credit for his fine performance in *The Philadelphia Story* to his co-stars, Katharine Hepburn and Cary Grant. He felt they should have gotten an Oscar along with him. This did not sit well with Ginger Rogers, his former date, who had won Best Actress Oscar for *Kitty Foyle*. "He ought to keep his damned mouth shut!" Ginger reportedly yelled the next day on an RKO set. Grant had not even been nominated, but Hepburn had, along with George Cukor and Ruth Hussey, who also lost. *The Philadelphia Story* was passed over as Best Picture when *Rebecca* copped the prize, but the other Stewart, Donald Ogden, won for Best Screenplay for *The Philadelphia Story*.

James Stewart during WWII

Chapter Eight

Off to the Wars

From the time World War II broke out, in September 1939, Stewart knew that the United States would eventually be drawn into it. For a year or so before that, he had taken intensive, professional flying lessons, and in 1938 had bought a two-seater Stinson 105. In this plane he indulged his long-standing passion for flying with a vengeance, and by the time he joined the Air Force, he had already clocked up over 400 hours of flying time.

As 1940 came in, his resolve to serve in the Armed Forces continued to grow. He was determined to do his father's and grandfather's military traditions proud, and often thought back on the stories both had told him of their Civil War, Spanish-American, and World War I service. But he had a problem: his weight had hovered for years at about 130 pounds, and with his lanky figure he continued to look strikingly skinny. Conscience continued to smite him late in 1940 when he and Hank Fonda volunteered to sing, dance and do a magician act at the training camps where the draftees, many of them unwilling conscripts, languished. They were greeted courteously, but Stewart could see in their envious faces that they scorned these movie stars who went back to their glamorous life while the grunts alternated between KP and the rifle range.

In November 1940, he went to an Air Corps recruiting office. By then he had hit 140 pounds but was told he was still ten pounds too light. He fattened up on all the high-calorie foods he could stuff in, and when he was called up for the draft in January 1941, he made it — barely. He was always to remember his "308" draft number, and his pride in making it into the military far outmatched the drop in his salary from thousands per week to a mere $24 a month. On March 22, 1941, he became a private in the Army Air Corps. According to Billy Grady, Mayer had wanted to pull strings to get him deferred, but Stewart would have none of it. Soon Clark Cable, Robert Taylor, and Robert Montgomery had made it abundantly plain to MGM that the satisfaction of serving their country far outweighed any perks of stardom; moreover, they did not want their War service used in any way for publicity purposes. "It was Jim, who beat the others in by a whole year, who set the tone for *that*," Billy Grady said.

Billy remembered going with Stewart and his roommate Burgess Meredith down to the induction center. As it turned out, Meredith and Billy had to drive in Grady's car while Jimmy got into the vehicle that transported the other inductees: "I'm one of 'em from the start," he declared. Meredith would later recall Stewart rushing out of the medic's office in his shorts crying out with boyish glee, "I'm in — I'm in!" Stewart went first to Fort MacArthur for basic training, then to Moffet Field, an Air Force training base in Northern California. Soon he had won his corporal's stripes, but ran into problems when the starstruck officer's wives and local civilians kept lionizing him and inviting him to parties. When one over-enthusiastic young lady told him he looked "adorable" in his uniform, he realized something would have to be done. When he complained to a superior officer, he was rebuffed and told he might function best in morale or special service units.

Brooke Hayward recalled what happened then. Stewart had come back to Hollywood on leave and was attending a party at the Haywards: "He said everybody up there [at the post] was leery of him, didn't know what to do with him, and wanted to make him a morale officer [he had just won his lieutenant's stripes after intensive officer-level training]. And *that* made him sick to his stomach. He kept on bitching about it to Father [Leland Hayward, his agent and close friend] and Father bitched to Ken McNaughton, an Air Force general. From then on, Jimmy was on his way." In a relatively few months he had gone from peeling KP spuds to serving as an aircraft mechanic to officer duty.

Then had come the assignment of his dreams. He went to New Mexico's Kirkland Field, where he applied his flying skills to the intricacies of piloting four-engine bombers. He was later to tell a writer, "When I was transferred to heavy bombers I had to work pretty hard at subjects I'd forgotten and was never any good at anyway. Math, for instance. Most of the fellows were quite ten years younger than I and they'd work out in a few minutes the navigational problems that I'd have to mull over for an hour or more." Asked how he got along with the other enlisted men, he replied, "I

S/Sgt. Ralph W. McClure, S/Sgt. Angelo Fermo, S/Sgt. James R. Kelley, Brig Gen. Edward J. Timberlake, Lt. Col Ramsay Potts and Maj. James Stewart, USAF, 1944

got the usual razzing at first — that 'movie-star-thinks-he's-slumming' bit. But I think I won them over when they realized I just thought of myself as one of them, that I was just a guy trying to do a job, as they were." And when the word quietly got around that Stewart had passed up the deferment MGM had tried to maneuver for him, and that he had made sincere efforts to volunteer for service, they began to warm to him. Soon the warmth turned to admiration and then, in many cases, to hero worship. One of his commanding officers said later: "He was so simple, so unaffected, so down-to-earth. The guys would go to the post movie house and see other guys like Gable and Power up there starring in movies with beautiful girls, and here with them was a guy who had just won an Oscar a month before he got into the service; yet here he was, one of them, and glad of it!"

Hollywood was not to see him again until early in 1942. On February 26, almost a year to the day after he had won his Oscar, he presented Gary Cooper with *his* award for *Sergeant York*. Later, on July 20, 1942, he went on radio with Cary Grant and Katharine Hepburn to do a version of *The Philadelphia Story*. In it he was billed as Lieutenant James Stewart; he had made this concession only because it was billed as a U.S. Government Victory Show. He also narrated, but did not appear in, two shorts that year. The first was about the Army Air Corps, their way of life, their training, their aims, and it was called *Winning Your Wings*. The second dealt with the Pearl Harbor attack by the Japanese on December 7, 1941, and it was called *Fellow Americans*. "I had some attacks of conscience about doing even these things," he said years later, "even though I knew they were for a good cause. Actually I felt much better when all that stopped and I was assigned as an instructor to pilots flying those heavy bombers known as Flying Fortresses."

Stewart, on July 4, 1943 — "imagine, Independence Day!" he wrote to his watchful and concerned parents — was promoted to the rank of Captain. In November, he flew a B-24 Liberator as a final training jaunt. This took him from Florida to Brazil, then on to North Africa. From there he was posted to Tibenham, in Norfolk, England, where he joined the 445th Bombing Group. That became his permanent base, and he immediately adapted himself to the service life there and to the constant training operations.

"One problem I had — a major one," he later recalled, "was the British press. Movie cameras, photographers, reporters were everywhere, checking up on me endlessly. I found that infinitely more nerve-racking than the actual duties I undertook on the bombers. I used every trick in the book to escape them, I had a very kind and understanding senior officer who kept me in the air so much that those intruders came to seem like tiny specks down there on land." To one reporter, who persisted until he got a few grudging words from the star turned Air Force Captain, he said, "It's not good for me or for the other fellows — I'm nothing special as I am now — never was, for that matter. Just please leave me alone and let me do my job." This elicited a headline in a London newspaper, STEWART 'JUST WANTS TO DO HIS JOB' that was picked up by New York and Boston papers. A wave of sympathetic support came his way from both the British and American public, who besieged the papers with thousands of letters encouraging them to *let* him do his job! Leave the guy alone!

Stewart commanded a B-24 Liberator as part of the Second Air Division of the Eighth Air Command. He flew deep into Europe from his English base for over twenty combat missions, both at night and in broad and vulnerable daylight. "I didn't care what time of night or day — I just wanted to pitch in and get the job done," he wrote his father. In December, 1943, his group raided the German city of Bremen with devastating results, and throughout 1944 he and his group flew straight to Berlin, more than once. After being promoted to the rank of Major, he conducted a spectacular, and much-publicized raid, on the Brunswick aircraft plants. This brought him the Air Medal with Oak Leaf Cluster, and later the Distinguished Flying Cross.

Stewart always tried to be reticent about his war experiences, and later had it written into his movie contracts that they were never to be the subjects of publicity stories or other promotional ideas. Regarding the daring February 20, 1944, raid on Brunswick, he would only say: "All of us pitched in to do that job; all of us shared the responsibility and any credit due. My contribution was a small part of it." He later rose to Squadron Commander, with several hundred pilots serving under him. After another successful eleven missions (by then he was a lieutenant-colonel), he was promoted to Chief-of-Staff of the Second Combat Wing of the Eighth Army Air Corps. When his service ended in 1945 he was a full colonel with a war record far surpassing any other actor's who had gone into service.

Reporters continued to find him a tough interview on details of the war. "I saw too much suffering. It's certainly not something to talk about — or celebrate. Sherman said 'War is Hell' — how right he was: how truly he spoke!" Stewart conceded that he had had a lot of close calls; indeed, had often feared for his very life.

One reporter who seemed to sufficiently gain his confidence was Leslie Salisbury of the publication *TV Times*. He told Salisbury, "There were, oh, lots and lots of times when I must have wondered whether I was going to get back after a mission, but I didn't think of it at the time. There just wasn't the time. Afterwards, well, you thought for a few seconds, then before you knew it you were up there again."

He told Herbert Kretzmer, another newsman he liked and trusted, "When I was piloting bombers over here I was always afraid I'd make a mistake at the controls, make a wrong decision. A lot of guys depend on you when you're in charge of a Flying Fortress. Fear of a mistake was stronger than fear for my safety." He elaborated: "Our group had suffered heavy casualties during the day, and the next morning at dawn I would have to lead my squadron out again, deep into enemy territory. Imagination can be a soldier's worst enemy. Fear is an insidious and deadly thing; it can warp judgment, freeze reflexes, breed mistakes. Worse, it's contagious. I knew my own fear, if not checked, could infect my crew members, and I could feel it growing in me. I remembered talking to my father when I was a boy and asking him about his experiences in World War One and the Spanish-American War. I had asked him if he'd been afraid. He said, 'Every man is, son, but just remember you can't handle fear all by yourself. Give it to God. He'll carry it for you.' I re-read the 91st Psalm that my father had given me when I left and I felt comforted, felt that I had done all I could."

Years later I asked Jimmy Stewart how he had survived the contrast between the celebrated existence of a movie star in Hollywood and the privations of a rough and brutal service life. Didn't he miss the parties, the innocent fun, the dates, the lovely women? "I had known worse times," he replied, "when I was starving with Hank in New York. When we weren't sure what would happen to us from day to day, didn't know if another stage job would even show up. And I was not married or a father at that time. I had lived in the company of men most of my life, at Mercersburg and Princeton and in rooms in Manhattan. I felt no loss of privacy in the service, as some guys did; I had had little enough privacy in my civilian past. I was living in a house with other guys in Hollywood right up to entering the service."

And, he added, "I have always *enjoyed* the company of men. I like the feeling of all of us getting caught up in something bigger than ourselves, working together toward a common goal. I felt that way in school, as a young actor in New York. And I certainly felt it in the service."

His expression became animated. "Why," he reminisced with a glow in his eyes, "I met the most wonderful assortment of guys you'd ever want to know during those four years in the service. I came to know what went on in their minds and hearts, I shared their hopes and fears and privations as an enlisted man, and I tried with all my might to lead and protect them when I became an officer. I lost a few men — all my efforts, all my prayers couldn't stand between them and their fates, and I grieved over them, blamed myself at times, even. But my father said something wonderful to me when I came home after the War. He said 'Shed all blame, shed all guilt, Jim. You know you did your very best, and God and Fate, both of which are beyond any human being's efforts, took care of the rest....'"

And then he confessed, "Gosh, I was, in many ways, far happier in the service than I ever was at any time in my life. Closeness and camaraderie with all those wonderful guys. Feeling I was part of a whole, of a divine scheme, with an obligation to do my very best. I wasn't play-acting life then; I was living it! And I know that I came out of the service more fully-rounded, and a better, more truthful actor because of all my experiences."

He was discharged from the service in September 1945. Billy Grady remembered: "Jim's family and myself were in New York to welcome him home. Alex, with his World War I button signifying he was a captain, looked a bit envious of Jim's eagles denoting the rank of colonel. It was a happy group, proud of the soldier who went from draftee to colonel in three years, a soldier who earned every award the hard way."

Billy had been assigned by Mayer to persuade Stewart to re-sign with MGM. Technically, Stewart still had three years on his old contract, but Mayer had waived any stipulations in that regard with the approval of MGM's President, Nick Schenck, in New York. Through Billy, Mayer told Stewart that he could have a new contract, as of 1945, but it would have to be a regular studio deal; Nick Schenck would have no part of the "New Order of Things."

However, Stewart's agent, the ever watchful and protective Leland Hayward, had forewarned him what that new order of things consisted of. Stars were now working independently, and for a star of Stewart's calibre, this meant a minimum of $750,000 for every picture. Salaries often soared skyward into the million dollar class, which was very good money by 1945 standards. Under MGM he would have gotten a meagre $125,000 for two or three pictures. Like any other salaried actor he would be denied participation of any kind in the profits. Schenck, often apoplectic on the subject, insisted that profit-sharing was "out of the question, fantastic, impossible!"

The new order of things had been greatly facilitated by, of all people, Olivia DeHavilland. She took Warners to court during the

War in a bid to prove that an artist could not be held beyond the stipulated length of a contract merely because of absences or suspensions. The court agreed and her historic victory was hailed as the DeHavilland Rule. As a result, the outside limit on a studio player's contract was set at seven years, including periods of suspension. For a time it had made Olivia unpopular at some studios but she prevailed. By 1949 she had won two Oscars, for *To Each His Own* (1946) and *The Heiress* (1949), both made at Paramount.

Stewart elected to henceforth go with Hayward on the percentage deal. Mayer (surprisingly) took it in good part. Billy Grady was always to remember L.B.'s obliging magnanimity as this toughest and most merciless of studio moguls told him: "This man gave distinguished service to his country; he went over there and risked his life. He is entitled to all that any of us here in the America he fought for can give him, and if those new terms as a freelancer are what he wants, good luck to him, and God bless him!" Mayer proved as good as his word; Stewart independently made several films for MGM.

Before returning to Hollywood, Stewart was prevailed upon to visit his hometown. He went back to Indiana, Pennsylvania, for "a quiet visit" with the mother and sisters and town friends he had not seen for years, but he ran into a hero's welcome. There was a parade down the main street of the town, many speeches, and much lionizing, from which, he admitted, he cringed.

Life magazine had sent a reporter and crew to cover it all. Henry Fonda recalled that the *Life* photographer wanted some "atmosphere." Unaware that Stewart knew absolutely nothing about fishing, he suggested that they get out on the water and do it. According to Fonda:

"Jimmy wanted to be accommodating to the people from *Life* and the photographer [Peter Stackpole], and he felt too sheepish to say he couldn't fish. So he had a pal of his run over to the hardware store and pick up some tackle. They wound up in a rented boat in a small lake near town. Jim's in the middle of this boat, his friend is at one end, and the photographer is at the other end ready to take pictures. But Jim doesn't know how the hell to fish. He's staring at the hooks and the line and he finally thinks, 'Well, what can I lose? I'll try it.'"

Fonda went on: "Stackpole starts snapping the pictures and Jim whips up the rod, there's a backlash, and the next thing he knows, he's caught Peter Stackpole, famous *Life* photographer, and hooked him right under the eyebrow! And I don't have to tell you, Stewart's reactions aren't too fast. He just sat and looked."

Stackpole returned to New York after his ordeal, replete with a bandaged left eye. The managing editor asked if it hadn't been "thrilling and exciting to be with Jimmy Stewart while his home town lionized him!" "It was okay," Stackpole grimly replied, "but not worth losing—or almost losing—an eye for!" Years later Stackpole was to do yet another assignment with Stewart, in Hollywood. "We'll go golfing, Peter, and you can snap your shots on the course," Stewart said. Rubbing the slight scar below his eyebrow, Stackpole rejoindered, "Anyplace, Jim, so long as it's not fishing!"

On the Superchief back to Hollywood, with Billy Grady in tow, Stewart solemnly averred that he would never fly again. He even laid a wager with Billy that he never would go aloft, but within a year Billy had won the bet; Stewart just couldn't keep out of a cockpit. The bet was made during a gin rummy game. "From Chicago to Pasadena, Slats didn't win a game. I wound up," Billy later related, "with a million matches."

Back in Hollywood that September of 1945, Stewart had occasion to wonder if Leland Hayward had steered him right in suggesting an independent course. Other MGM stars, like Clark Gable and Robert Taylor, were soon back at the studio under their old salaried-contract arrangements. Offers weren't coming for Stewart, who had been away from films for four years, and he began to worry.

It was Hank Fonda who cheered him up. Fonda had been away in the Navy for three years, and the offers weren't breaking down his door, either. Slack times, were an old, familiar story, so the buddies resumed where they had left off. Fonda was now married, with two young children, Jane and Peter. His wife, Frances, was a fussy, unpredictable woman obsessed with her looks, who spent a lot of time in bed with lotions and curlers. Stewart had rented the Fonda house while Hank was away, and the lease permitted the current holders to stay on for a while. So Frances and Hank put Stewart in the playhouse (as they called it) behind their house, pending other arrangements. Fonda recalled that it was a "large, 'adult' type of playhouse, with a living room with a couch convertible to a comfortable bed, a kitchen, bathroom, nice shower, all the comforts of home — sort of."

John Swope, who had married Dorothy McGuire in 1943, joined them for fun and games, with Frances and Dorothy trailing behind at the many parties they went to that year. Fonda was to remember an especially riotous wingding at Marion Davies' beachhouse. Marion had told the Fondas on the phone: Come as your favorite American Revolutionary figure. They decided to do a Marx Brothers variation on the Spirit of '76, with Stewart as Chico with a bandaged head, Swope with a Harpo wig, and Fonda with a big cigar and a fierce Groucho moustache. They were the hits of the evening.

Fonda warmly recalled that fall of 1945: "Frances and Jim and I'd come home from these parties and Frances would go to bed and Jim and I would sit in the playhouse and listen to our collection of records. We would spend hours scouring the music shops for oldies. Johnny Mercer, Hoagie Carmichael and Nat 'King' Cole used to come over and listen with us. There was no work. Only parties and pleasure." Then Hank and Jimmy took up the good old boyish pastime of kite-building. One night, Stewart came home to a frantic Frances. She begged him to rescue Fonda who was flying off the earth on the tail of the biggest kite they had ever concocted. Stewart successfully hauled him back to terra firma, and later related the incident thus: "I took full credit for saving Fonda. Y'see, that kite was ten feet by ten feet, and if I hadn't arrived in the nick of time, well, Fonda would've made Nebraska by morning."

Billy Grady later recalled how Frances began to get irritated with the constant Fonda-Stewart togetherness out in the playhouse. "They're big boys now," she complained to Billy. "Why, Hank just passed forty and Jimmy is thirty-seven; haven't they grown up *yet?*" "All I could think of to reply," Billy laughed, "was, 'boys will be boys, Frances!' I knew there'd eventually be a divorce when Frances snapped back, 'Not on *my* time they won't be!'" Peter Fonda, then about five, was always to recall his mother "preoccupied with her beauty to the point that she would wear those funny little things on her face to keep lines from forming — little triangular pieces of adhesive tape. I guess she was very concerned about aging."

During the music-and-kite sessions Fonda would unburden himself about Frances, what a drag she could be, how the kids seemed like strangers after his three years away. Stewart, losing patience one time, according to Swope, snarled, "Hank you've wallowed through two marriages and I haven't had one yet, but you sure are no advertisement for the married state!"

Billy Grady always enjoyed Stewart's father, Alex, who continued to keep his son's Oscar on prominent display in the hardware store. It was usually in the front window, surrounded by mint-glossy stills from his movies, all neatly captioned. Also exhibited was a stuffed cobra and other odd items which Alex Stewart kept on hand for the amusement of his visitors. Grady and Alex Stewart became good friends, and Grady, whenever he passed near Pittsburgh on the way to or from New York, made a point to detour in Alex's direction. Grady loved to tell of a local tramp that Alex had befriended, a refugee from the town almshouse who did odd jobs around the store. He wasn't a very prepossessing figure, in his hand-me-down clothes, scraggly beard, and matted, dirty hair. He seldom bathed, and his teeth were bad. After he finished mopping up the store, he'd go to sleep behind the pot-bellied stove, snoring up a storm.

The Oscar and the pictures would lure the curious into the Stewart hardware store, and, when informed that young Mr. Stewart was busy in Hollywood making movies, they'd ask if they could meet his father. Looking portentously sad, Alex would say, "Ah, but it's all very sad!" and point to the tramp snoring away by the stove. "That is the elder Mr. Stewart," he'd whisper, wickedly adding: "He likes a nip, you know."

Billy Grady always thought this story a hoot, but, as he recalled it, "Slats thought the story very unfunny; his mother and sisters were mortified, but then what do you expect of Scots; they have no Irish sense of humor."

When he returned to Hollywood from his scouting tours, Billy would note Stewart's and Fonda's restless unhappiness; idleness, despite the fun and games, was beginning to pall. Then Fonda landed the starring part of Wyatt Earp in John Ford's *My Darling Clementine* (1946). It was a smashing critical and box office success and an impressive postwar film debut for him. Stewart was left alone with the kites, the music records, the playhouse — and an increasingly irritated and remote Frances Fonda.

Then one day, Frank Capra called Stewart. "I've got an idea for a movie that I feel you'd be great in," he told him. "I've only got it on a page or two, and I haven't completely formulated it in mind, but here goes: it's about a guy who thinks his life is worthless, that he's never amounted to anything. He's about to jump in the river, see? And along comes an angel who tells him he can go back as if he'd never been born and see what his hometown would have been like without him...."

Stewart asked him where he had found his inspiration. Capra said a Christmas card verse had struck him hard when he read it, something about everyone being here for a reason.

"If there's an angel in it, I'm interested," Stewart recalled telling him. "We need more angels. Don't say any more. I'm your man."

"But don't you want to know more about the story?" Frank asked. "Anything *you* think is worth doing, I think is worth doing, Frank," Stewart replied. "I've never gone wrong following your lead yet, have I?"

Capra told him that he had formed Liberty Films with (among others) Willie Wyler and George Stevens. Like Stewart, Capra wanted the independence to make the films that really enthused him. "Life isn't worth living if you can't do what you enjoy and work on things that fire you up," Capra told him.

Stewart remembers inviting him to come inside the playhouse and talk about it. The kites and music records went untouched. It turned out, as Capra expounded on his idea, that it had been rooted in his subconscious since Christmas 1939, when Philip Van Doren had sent out a short story with a similar theme. RKO had gotten fired up about it in the early 1940s, and Cary Grant had been mentioned for the lead. But no viable script had been developed, despite the earnest ministrations of several contract writers, and the project had fizzled. Capra opined that Cary Grant didn't seem right for what he visualized: "He's too sophisticated, too knowing."

"Stop right there, Frank," Stewart remembers saying. "I've got a feeling about this. I'm your man!"

Chapter Nine

A Wonderful Renaissance

It's a Wonderful Life (1946) brought us Stewart, at age 38, to the apogee of his charm and charisma. The philanthropic George Bailey was one of his great, definitive roles. Along with Capra's *Mr. Smith Goes to Washington* and Hitchcock's *Vertigo*, it must be ranked among his greatest films. The Stewart persona was on magnificently irresistible display here, as a decent man in a small town who undergoes a great trial of soul. *Mr. Smith* may have called for more resources of passion and *Vertigo* may have demanded a display of his darker, more complex aspects, but he is as affectingly human and charismatically forceful in *It's a Wonderful Life* as he would ever be.

It's a Wonderful Life is the picture that is most associated with Stewart in the public memory. This was the first film he did after the war, and it was poetic justice that Frank Capra should be the man to present the war-seasoned but still decent and affirmative Stewart to a jaded and cynical world. The post-war mood gave rise to *film noir*, in which unpleasant people invited disaster on themselves and others, and this, unfortunately, worked against *It's a Wonderful Life* on its release. It just seemed too apple-pie, too all-American, too ingenuously simplistic to a world that had suffered through six years of human nature at its most terrible. After being drowned in Man's inhumanity to Man in a thousand subtle and overt atrocities, the disillusioned public simply couldn't summon any empathy with the message Capra and Stewart were trying to convey. It seemed a little ludicrous to assert that people were basically good and that small-town values held eternal validity in the aftermath of global destruction. Capra, too, felt disappointment when the poor box office returns and mixed critical reaction seemed to indicate that in 1946 *It's a Wonderful Life* was already old hat.

Yet this film was to know, over the years, a marvelous renaissance. As more wars and trials were visited on humankind, adding layers of both disillusionment and sophistication to the collective psyche, *It's a Wonderful Life* began to assume mythic proportions. It

Thomas Mitchell, James Stewart, *It's a Wonderful Life*, RKO, 1946

seemed to hark back to a time when simple honesty and plain decency were not old-fashioned values, but pointed to the eventual betterment of the human spirit.

And the miracle is that today, in the worldly-wise 1990s, where — often in the worst sense of the phrase — nothing human is alien, *It's a Wonderful Life* is the most frequently revived film of its time; and it sells with vigorous steadiness on videocassette to whole generations unborn at the time of its cinematic release.

It's a Wonderful Life is today a popular Christmas-time tradition. Stewart was to object mightily when *It's a Wonderful Life* was subjected to colorization, but somehow, despite the loss of the nuances of the black-and-white version, color seems appropriate for this particular picture. Its holiday spirit, its enthronement of noble values and selflessness over cynicism and expediency are clearly emphasized by the addition of Christmassy tones.

It's a Wonderful Life even has a Scrooge figure. The town banker, Lionel Barrymore, is crippled in body and mind, though, unlike Scrooge, he remains unrepentantly gnarled to the end. It is he who refuses to lend the money after Stewart's building and loan business is about to go under when his bumbling uncle, Thomas Mitchell, loses their crucial bank deposits. With his world about to fall apart, Stewart trudges out to a bridge, where he reviews his life. He has stayed in the small town to take over his father's business, sending his brother to college and into the great world where he himself had longed to go adventuring. Because of a hearing loss, he could not go to war, and had to content himself with being a good husband to his loyal wife, Donna Reed, and a good father to his loving children. He ponders the futility of selflessness and considers himself a failure. As he is about to jump into the river, he encounters an old man (the charming Henry Travers), who takes him through a mystical tour of Bedford Falls and shrewdly shows how it would have been without him. Stewart sees that Barrymore has ruined and corrupted the town, that the people look blighted and lost, that his beloved wife has become a stunted old maid, that his mother (Beulah Bondi) has become wizened and withdrawn. He realizes that the people he helped with his savings and loan business have benefitted from his existence, that he has meant a great deal to the people whose paths he crossed, that his life has been eminently worth living, both for his own sake and for others'. In a somewhat unrealistic, but heartening dénouement, the angel restores him to the present and he goes joyously home. There he finds that his grateful fellow townsmen, through a collection, have raised the missing money, and that he is on course again.

This, then, was the film. Beautifully directed by Capra, based on a 1939 story, *The Greatest Gift*, by Philip Van Doren, and scripted by Capra, Frances Goodrich and Albert Hackett, it nonetheless met with a public response that both Capra and Stewart found disappointingly inadequate.

Even so, the film, and Stewart, were not without adherents. *The New York Times* critic reported: "As the hero, Mr. Stewart does a warmly appealing job, indicating that he has grown in spiritual stature as well as in talent during the years he was in the war." *The Nation* felt that "the hero was extravagantly well-played by James Stewart."

Thomas Mitchell, in 1947, recalled the wonderful atmosphere on the set, with all the character performers perfectly cast. "Lionel, Henry Travers, Beulah, H.B. Warner, Gloria Grahame, Sam Hinds, Frank Albertson — who could ask for a better lineup!" he enthused.

"The spirit was there all along, all through the shooting, just as it was with *Mr. Smith Goes to Washington* all those years before. And Jim had matured tremendously in his four years away in the War — he had always been a wonderful, decent person, but he went away a boy and came back a man. He was somehow different to play with, more aware, more sophisticated. Oh, not sophisticated in any cynical sense, but he did seem to have acquired a new depth of spirit."

When Stewart recalled how Frank Capra came to him with just the germ of a film idea on two scraps of paper, he sparked up: "I always trusted Frank — he had done a lot for me before the War, and I considered everything about him good luck." On another occasion, he waxed enthusiastically to Victor Scherle and William Turner Levy, co-authors of *The Films of Frank Capra*: "In my opinion Capra is one of the giants of the picture business and always will be. It is amazing the contribution that he made to the industry when it was young and just getting on its feet . . . Frank has a great deal to do with the progress of my career over the years, and I will always be grateful to him."

Liberty Films, the independent producing organization that Capra had set up did not survive, and the founding directors went their separate ways. Wyler went on to win the 1946 Best Director Oscar for *The Best Years of Our Lives*, and Fredric March copped his second Academy Award for his performance in it. Capra and Stewart were both nominated, but failed to win. In 1948, Paramount bought out Liberty Films, and a disillusioned Capra's career went into sad, steady decline.

Not everyone in the cast of *It's a Wonderful Life*, however, thought of the film, or Stewart, in undilutedly affirmative terms. Donna Reed, for one, seems to have emerged from it with ambivalent reactions. Doug McClelland, in his books *StarSpeak* and *Hollywood Talks Turkey*, quoted Donna as saying: "Working with Jimmy Stewart in *It's a Wonderful Life* was very demanding. He's so natural, so realistic, that I never knew whether he was talking to me or doing a scene. He's the most demanding of all the actors I've ever worked with."

McClelland also has Donna saying: "*It's a Wonderful Life* is my favorite film, but it was a box office failure." Donna had been scheduled for the part June Allyson would play in *The Stratton Story* two years later, with Van Johnson in the lead. "But something happened with Van, and they cast Jimmy Stewart. I was thrilled, because I thought we were pretty good together. But, as it turned out, I was taken off the film and replaced by June Allyson. I was told that Stewart was fighting for his professional life, and I said, 'What do you think *I'm* fighting for?'" Donna Reed claimed, in *Hollywood Talks Turkey*, that she had four more years on her MGM contract but never worked there again.

Donna Reed was not the only actor in a Stewart picture to imply that he could be ruthless where his own best interests were concerned. Even Thomas Mitchell said that Stewart had his own way of letting everyone know who was the star. He saw to it that setups, lighting, angles, and dialogue worked primarily to *his* advantage. "A star has to have ego, of course," Mitchell laughed, "but this idea people have of Jimmy as self-effacing and deferential is bunk. He made sure his own interests were taken care of first and foremost."

Mitchell was not the first or the last to say that Stewart was "damned tight with a buck" and "chintzy." "He made some very ruthless deals, was obsessed with money and financial success, especially after he married," Mitchell told me in 1960. "The buck meant a great deal to him, and he went after it single-mindedly."

In the fall of 1946 Stewart began production on *Magic Town*. It was produced and written by Robert Riskin for RKO release, and directed by William A. Wellman. Co-starring with Stewart was Jane Wyman, whose career was on the upgrade after her Oscar-nominated triumph in *The Yearling* (1946) with Gregory Peck for MGM. Riskin had scripted *Mr. Deeds Goes to Town* (1936) and *You Can't Take It With You* (1938) for Frank Capra, and felt he could duplicate those All-American successes with Wellman. In this case, Riskin was suffering from *hubris*, as *Magic Town* lacked the populist fervor and humane spirit that distinguished Capra's films.

There is some confusion to this day about Capra's relationship to *Magic Town*. Stewart has it that Capra worked on the script, but another version has it that he thought the story too weak to bother with, and bowed out. Yet another has Riskin wanting to go it alone in a bid to prove himself, and yet one more has William A. Wellman, who had hardly been noted for such material, wanting to widen his range. Wellman later said the picture stank, but after he had reflected about it, he told me that he had given it his best efforts. There was even a story that Capra had been deliberately shut out by Riskin and Wellman, who in turn left Stewart with the impression that Capra had passed it up. Whatever the background, *Magic Town* did not do well with critics or public when it was released in 1947, a full year after it was shot.

The story has Stewart as an opinion pollster who learns that a town named Grandview exactly reflects the popular sentiment on various national issues over the past fifty years. Posing as an insurance salesman, he invades the town to do some secret checking and runs up against newspaper editor Wyman. She wants nothing more than to improve the town, thus countering Stewart's scurrilous efforts to keep it just as it is. Wyman discovers his duplicity, and exposes his methods, but he has fallen in love with her and tries to make amends. The town's special flavor disintegrates in a welter of commercialism and harebrained financial schemes, and it is only when the children goad their elders into reinvesting in civic integrity that matters improve. The misunderstandings between the leads are (inevitably) worked out, and all ends happily.

There are several problems with the film. The Stewart character, though he later recants, is really nothing but a con man, and audiences did not buy Stewart in that guise. The poll idea was too diffused to engage the audience in any personal trials and triumphs, and the human element was weakened. There was something forced about it all, and it lacked Capra's infusion of heartfelt humanism and righteous regard for the individual. Capra may well have sensed that this was what was wrong with Riskin's story concept, and hence backed out.

Photoplay magazine led the chorus of critical ambivalence: "*Magic Town* is unusual enough to rate a cheer; it's unrealistic enough to rate a brush-off. The goings-on are a bit too implausible to convince an adult audience, a bit too childish to be fantasy about Small Town, U.S.A. Mr. Stewart has something, so does the picture; but we wish both had used them a little differently to come up with a real winner."

The advertising for *Magic Town* gave everyone a wrong steer. One particularly vulgar ad appeared in a fan magazine with garish yellow lettering, neon-style, against a black background that implied, pictorially at least, that the film was about Big, Bad New York, and along the sides were vignettes of Stewart and Wyman in various undignified and pseudo-romantic attitudes, with captions such as

James Stewart, Jane Wyman, *Magic Town*, RKO, 1947

"Their meeting was saucy and flippant!" "Their romance found birth in the magic of a sudden kiss!" and "Their love jeopardized the happiness of thousands!" Beneath the blatant yellow lettering, Stewart was holding Wyman in an awkward but sexy embrace in which her upturned legs dominated the surroundings.

In 1957, I talked with Stewart about *Magic Town;* his initial disappointment and disillusionment with the film had dissipated somewhat. "We really thought we were going to duplicate the success of *It's a Wonderful Life,*" he told me. "Frank [Capra] had even helped Riskin on the script, and I had a wonderful, responsible, creative costar in Janie, and the idea seemed fresh and unique. I just don't know what kept it from ringing the bell as loudly as I had hoped. The parts just didn't add up to a compelling whole." Stewart added, "But we did give it an all-out try, and to this day I feel there were some sharp, clever things in it."

Perhaps the best analysis of *Magic Town*'s shortcomings was given by Stewart's old friend Kent Smith, who had a prominent supporting role. He told me: "Jimmy and Jane really tried; they gave it all they had. And I know Bill Wellman put maximum care into it.

The cast was fine; they all looked like born-and-bred small-towners, but I remember Donald Meek [also a supporting player] saying quietly to me that something was missing, some spark, some extra something that, regrettably, spells the difference between a smash hit, something that endures, and an also-ran entertainment, the kind of thing the critics like to label 'pleasant, escapist fare.'" Smith felt that the weakness lay in the basic story line, that it was gimmicky and weak on motivation. "It just didn't seem realistic. A film can be wacky and wild, but if there is that underpinning of realism it holds up. I never felt *Magic Town* did, really."

The film seems strained, unable to hit the essential dynamic that writing and direction have striven for. Stewart tends to overact, and Wyman tends to eloquently underact, her subdued yet striking impersonation ringing more changes. Stewart, in fact, even found himself under direct critical attack. One reviewer said that Stewart was in danger of becoming the screen's most colossal bore if he insisted on overdoing cutesy-poo characterizations. He referred to the star as "this long beanstalk, hemming and hawing all over the place."

Stewart, reading the box office returns and critical appraisals of *Magic Town*, began to do some serious thinking about his onscreen persona. Certainly it appeared that he was in imminent danger of wearing out his welcome, and that the Old Jimmy Stewart, after 12 years of filmmaking, would have to make way for Someone New. Had *Magic Town* failed precisely because it had been tailored to his measure—or had the fit been wrong? Had he gone astray trying to be villain and hero all in one characterization? Would the public recoil from the intimation of a possible darker side?

One writer pointed out that "the basic idea was the reverse of that in *Mr. Smith Goes to Washington*. In [that] a country bumpkin went to the big city; here a city-wise guy invades a small town. But the threat was the same: false urban values almost destroy the simple beliefs out in the hinterland." The writer added, "Stewart was cast, ill-fittingly, in the role of the predator, the big businessman—in fact, the heavy. Perhaps it was time for him to play a more worldly type, but this wasn't it."

Gossip columnists and fan-mag hacks, perhaps secretly egged on by the studio publicity flacks, strove to drum up interest in *Magic Town*. They tried to imply that Stewart was romantically interested in the very-much-married Jane Wyman, who was in the early stages of pregnancy by hubby Ronald Reagan when she shot *Magic Town*. Despite the efforts of both to squelch this story, it persisted, aided and abetted by rumors of trouble in the Wyman-Reagan marriage. The couple did, indeed, soon divorce, but the true reason was that Wyman had become more career-oriented and clearly overshadowed Reagan as a performer. (The next year, 1948, she would give an Oscar-winning performance as the deaf-mute rape victim in *Johnny Belinda*.) An even more absurd rumor had director Wellman romantically interested in Wyman, but this soon petered-out, having no sound basis. "Fuck nosy reporters" was Wellman's characteristically blunt reaction.

Stewart's two most recent films, *It's a Wonderful Life* and *Magic Town*, had failed to win any noticeable appreciation. With critics commenting that his drawling, folksy awkwardness was becoming repetitious, Stewart cast about in late 1947 for something grittier. The new noirish realism had taken hold, and he felt he should keep up with the changing screen mores.

After much meditation and careful perusal of a number of scripts, Stewart decided on *Call Northside 777* (1948). He plays a newspaper reporter who uncovers the truth about an old crime, and though he had played journalists before, this man had a more dogged edge. Stewart felt this would be a step in the right direction towards firming up any decisions about the future of his essential screen persona. At 39, the major shift in the nature of his roles was a couple of years down the road, but *Call Northside 777* certainly represents the advent of a different, more mature Stewart. To his delight, the fans responded warmly. *Call Northside 777* was well received and was, in actuality, the first of Stewart's post-war successes.

The New James Stewart was not completely on view in this film, but there are strong hints of him. Henry Hathaway, who made the film for 20th Century-Fox, was a brusque, pragmatic director and was just right for Stewart at this time. Hathaway aimed for gritty reality rooted in actual human experience in his movies, and, when possible, he shot in actual locations. Striving for original atmosphere, he took his troupe to Chicago, where many of the exteriors were shot. The result was a *cinema vérité* immediacy that several critics extolled upon the film's release.

The story, written by Jerome Cady and Jay Dratler, was based

Doug McClelland Collection

Helen Walker, James Stewart,
Call Northside 777, 20th Century, 1948

on some razor-sharp magazine articles by James McGuire that had made quite an impact when published. The plot deals with reporter Stewart's determined efforts to exonerate a man (Richard Conte) who has spent eleven years in prison for a crime that Stewart is convinced he did not commit. It begins when editor Lee J. Cobb spots an ad in his own paper offering $5000 for information about the possible murderer of a police officer back in the early thirties. Intrigued, Cobb orders Stewart to follow up on it.

Stewart first goes to see the prisoner's mother, a scrubwoman who scrimps and saves every penny in the hope of clearing her son. Conte himself is stoical, feeling that he will never be freed; he has even told his wife to remarry for the sake of their son. When Stewart visits Helen (Joanne de Bergh) and her new husband (E.G. Marshall), he notes that they are optimistically supportive of Conte.

Editor Cobb and his wife (Helen Walker) urge Stewart to pursue the tangled webs of the original indictment to their logical conclusion. After uncovering false witnesses and unearthing other telling evidence, he manages to get Conte freed. In an emotional scene, the ex-prisoner is met by his wife, son and her new husband, and embraced by the mother whose dogged fidelity has made his freedom possible.

Conte and his mother play Americans of Polish extraction, and this inspired Hathaway to seek authentic Polish atmophere. He shot the film in Polish neighborhoods of Chicago, and used real-life citizens of the Windy City as extras.

The film was masterfully photographed by Joe MacDonald and evocatively and fittingly scored by Alfred Newman, and the result won creditable reviews. This may not have represented the full flowering of the New Stewart but, as critical reaction attested, it helped set Stewart's film career on a new, more steady path. "Mr. Stewart has never been more in command of his medium, if his fine acting in this is any indication," one critic said. "It is one of the more solid and true performances he has essayed." And from another: "It is good to see Jimmy Stewart get down to earth and act out a solid set of realistically-drawn situations, to which he does ample justice."

Many wondered why James Stewart and his longtime friend Henry Fonda had never co-starred together in a film. Both were now of equal rank as stars, and it was well-known that they had been looking around for the right vehicle for some time.

The chance finally came in 1948 in the form of a film called *A Miracle Can Happen*. The title was later changed to *On Our Merry Way*, and filmland wags commented that the producers should have come up with yet a third title, for neither applied to a limp and forgettable film. Limp and forgettable, that is, except for Stewart and Fonda.

The picture was constructed in three segments. The first, directed by George Stevens from a story by John O'Hara, has Paulette Goddard suggesting to her reporter husband, Burgess Meredith, that he pursue her notion for a story: "How Does A Child Influence Your Life?" The first people Meredith encounters on his quest are Stewart and Fonda, a pair of itinerant musicians appropriately named Slim and Lank. Down on their luck, they are attempting to rig a phony music contest so that the son of the local mayor will win. However, a six-foot-tall girl saxophone prodigy named Babe (Dorothy Ford) wins the hearts of the band and the contest into the bargain. The whole episode lasted a mere thirty-five minutes!

The actors in the two other episodes are Dorothy Lamour and Victor Moore, in a segment dealing with movie extras, and Fred MacMurray and William Demarest as drifters who are baited by a practical-joking little boy.

More than one critic commented that the first third with Stewart and Fonda should have been expanded for a feature-length effort. The other two episodes, despite their good acting, shape up as tame, forgettable stuff, despite hefty efforts applied by directors King Vidor and Leslie Fenton. The picture had been written by

Lawrence Stallings, based on stories by O'Hara, Lou Breslow and Arch Oboler. Everything in the picture seemed to come in threes, in fact, with the exception of the music by Heinz Roemheld, what with photographers John Seitz, Ernest Laszlo and Joseph Biroc assigned respectively to each segment.

When they did *On Our Merry Way*, Fonda was 43 and Stewart was 40. There is a winning warmth and ease in their onscreen interplay. In 1957, on the set of *Stage Struck* in New York, I asked Fonda why he and Stewart had not held out for a full-length co-starring picture for their first effort. He replied, "Well, it seemed like a fun project, and one that would not take up too much time, given our respective picture schedules at that time. I think if we could have done it over we would have held out for something more substantial, but then we did make up for it later and some of the situations as written by John O'Hara were amusing and bright—and, well, I have no fundamental regrets, not at all."

Given the rumors about Stewart and Fonda, there is a certain irony in their having appeared together for the first time in 1948. In the same year, Stewart had tackled a role in a film, *Rope*, that had an implicit homosexual subtext and ambience.

After completing his performance in *On Our Merry Way*, and before starting *Call Northside 777* (both films would be released almost simultaneously in early 1948), Stewart returned to the stage for the first time since 1935. Substituting for Frank Fay in *Harvey* on Broadway, his engagement began in early July 1947 and extended until late August.

Harvey had brought Frank Fay a renewed fame after some years in relative obscurity. A vaudevillian and former husband of Barbara Stanwyck, Frank had known some bad years since a brief, unsuccessful stint of filmmaking in the early 1930s. As the eccentric alcoholic who has taken as his best friend a large white rabbit named Harvey, visible only to himself, he won a whole new audience. The play had opened in November 1944 and was to run for years. Stewart was the second actor to sub for Fay while he was either on vacation or with the play elsewhere. (Bert Wheeler had been the first, in 1946.)

There were many rumors that Stewart wanted to do the film version of *Harvey*, and that his seven week stint was regarded as a warm-up. The consensus of critical opinion was that Stewart lacked

Fay's feel for the part, that he had missed the nuances and wistful lovability of the character. Brooks Atkinson of *The New York Times* observed that, generally speaking, Stewart was a better actor than Fay, with a wider range, but only Fay could convey Elwood P. Dowd's elfin poignancy. Other critics observed that at age 39, he was not yet old enough to do justice to the role, and that his movie mannerisms obscured the reality of the character.

Stewart later conceded that there was some justification for the criticism he had sustained in 1947, but added: "I got better. And I must have done the job reasonably well because I was asked to do it again the following summer [1948], which I did."

From March 29 to April 24, 1948, Stewart had another Broadway session in *Harvey* while Fay did it in Philadelphia with a second troupe. Before Fay came back, Joe E. Brown, Jimmy Dunn and Jack Buchanan had each had a go at the role.

Rope was James Stewart's first experience with Alfred Hitchcock —and a peculiar pairing they made. Stewart almost didn't get cast. Hitchcock, newly liberated from a Selznick contract in 1948, was producing as well as directing *Rope* for Warners, and wanted Cary Grant for the lead, but he was not available. Stewart was awarded the role of Rupert Cadell, a professor who believes in the Nietzschean philosophy of the Übermensch, a superior man beside whom inferior specimens are expendable. He has influenced—or infected, depending on the viewpoint—two of his former students, John Dall and Farley Granger, with his views, and therein lies the plot origin.

Dall and Granger are homosexuals and super-intellectuals who consider themselves above the common law. For kicks, they devise an objective experiment: they kill a school friend (Dick Hogan) by strangling him with a rope, then hide his body in a chest on which they serve food to their cocktail party guests. These latter include the victim's father (Sir Cedric Hardwicke), his aunt (Constance Collier), his fiancee (Joan Chandler) and his rejected love rival (Douglas Dick). Cadell is also a guest, and he gradually begins to pick up on the hosts' hints and eventually comes to realize the truth. Coming back later under the pretext of recovering his misplaced cigarette case, Cadell nails Dall and Granger down. He opens the chest and to his horror discovers the body. He narrowly escapes being mur-

Farley Granger, James Stewart, John Dall, *Rope*, WB, 1948

dered himself, fires some shots in the air to attract the police, and waits for justice to overtake the murderers.

Under Hitchcock's guidance Stewart gives one of his more interesting and complex performances. He is not quite convincing in the impassioned final confrontation scene in which he accuses the boys of pathological insanity and deplores the effect on them of his superman teachings. But he blends in surprisingly well with these two sociopathic gay characters, realistically limned by Dall and Granger. Had the film been made twenty years later, they might have been held up as distortions of certain gay stereotypes.

Dall is most effective, partly because his screen persona had always emitted a smarmy aura. (In his debut film, *The Corn Is Green* [1946], in which he essayed the role of a decidedly hetero coal miner, director Irving Rapper and Bette Davis, the star, had had to keep him from swishing instead of striding.) Offscreen, he was a voracious homosexual who lived with his mother and took her to openings (they were unkindly referred to as "The Dalls"). He had a rather unhappy and promiscuous life until he died at 53, in 1971, his screen career long in the past. Dall was, however, a very fine actor who, in 1948, seemed to have unlimited promise. He is far and away the most at ease and natural (if that is the word) in *Rope*, playing with a poise and authority that are impressive. But the unwholesome atavism of his personality, ideal for *Rope*, tended to limit Dall in other roles, which accounts for the brevity of his Hollywood career.

Playing a character who obviously is the homosexual lover of Farley Granger, Dall makes absolutely believable the master-slave implications of their onscreen relationship. Their scenes together were given extra bite because it was whispered around that Dall, then 29, was genuinely in love with Granger, then 23. Granger was probably not aware of this, but his rabbit-versus-cobra reactions to Dall play extremely well, and produce an authentic onscreen intimacy between them which adds greatly to the film's darker aspects.

More than one critic has commented that Stewart seemed surprisingly at ease in his long scenes alone with this unpleasant pair. Many have since wondered why he wanted the role; at 40 he was still a bachelor and the subject of many rumors regarding his sexuality. Certainly, appearing in a picture in which two homosexuals murder another young man (the graphic scene has Dick Hogan screaming and gasping before finally going limp in his murderers' arms) seemed to be validating the rumors about Stewart. Some have theorized that he had a masochistic attraction to the morbid, indeed rather necrophilic material, which motivated him to go after the role when Cary Grant passed on it. It is interesting to speculate on how the bisexual Grant would have handled the role, but he doubtless thought that in his case it would be cutting too close to the bone.

Stewart has always reacted ambivalently and strangely to questions about *Rope*. I had several conversations with him on it over the years, and he seemed surprised, even alarmed, when I told him how at home he had seemed in the role. Since his professor's sexuality is not defined (he arrives at the party alone), there is no reason not to believe that the character is also gay.

When the picture came out in the fall of 1948, many in Hollywood and in the national audience were asking: "What is wholesome Jimmy Stewart doing in *this* gloomy thing?" He has told different reporters varying stories: that he needed material that was different and fresh, that he wanted to broaden and deepen his screen image, that he had long wanted to work with Hitchcock, and so on.

Hume Cronyn adapted the 1929 Patrick Hamilton play with Arthur Laurents doing the screenplay, and Joseph Valentine photographed in color. With the exception of the ice-skating sequences in *Ice Follies of 1939*, this was Stewart's (and Hitchcock's) first film in color, another element which might have drawn him to the material. Hitchcock certainly was attracted one hundred percent to the story. It contained a number of the elements that he had already exploited so successfully and famously prior to *Rope*: fear of discovery; psychological undercurrents disrupting surface placidities; ominous psychopathologies ready to leap out from deceptively normal circumstances. Hitchcock sacrificed one characteristic element for *Rope:* his fascinating cinematic interplay of character with camera angles and lighting. With *Rope* Hitchcock was determined to make a startling experiment: He would film the 80-minute film in ten-minute continuous takes (the length of a reel) in the manner of a stage play. Instead of cutting, he would focus on a back or an object while the reel shifted. (Actually there is one cut midway through the film, from Granger to Stewart, that is rarely remarked upon.)

Hitchcock was determined to shoot in eight days, but there were so many fluffs, camera problems, and blowups by actors in their lines, that the total shooting time ran almost three times as long. There was tremendous tension on the set, not only because some of the supporting actors were uneasy with the meloncholic ambience, but because Hitchcock, Stewart, Dall and Granger took out their inner frustrations on each other. All were reported to be relieved when the film was finally in the can.

Jack Warner had brought Hitchcock to his studio for *Rope* because he admired such prior Hitchcock blockbusters as *Rebecca* (1940) and *Shadow of a Doubt* (1943). Later, he expressed his regret that he had ever gotten involved with this "queer mess" and when the previews indicated that audiences were either embarrassed, nonplussed, or snickeringly derisive, he rushed *Rope* out to exhibitors in the precipitate hope of redeeming his costs. The film eventually made a small profit, but it has a cult following today, not only among Hitchcock aficionados but among gays, who enjoy some of the innuendoes and in-jokes. Examples: the murdered man is *Dick* Hogan; Douglas *Dick* (a handsome, baby-faced actor of the time) is Hogan's love rival for Joan Chandler; Constance Collier comes on like a fag-hag; Sir Cedric Hardwicke acts like an auntie at a gay function; Edith Evanson, the fussy servant, has a dyke aura, and so forth.

Asked later how Hitchcock directed actors, Stewart said to a London reporter: "He expected us to have worked out the characters and how they should be played, and he went along with it. If he didn't like it he would come up afterwards and suggest trying it another way for comparison. But he didn't say 'my way's right and your way's wrong.'"

In his three subsequent films with Stewart, Hitchcock was to apply the same *laissez-faire* principle: the actors had to come fully prepared, their lines learned, and their characterizations firmly in mind. This was the exact opposite of William Wyler's meticulous, detailed technique in which he forced the effects he wanted out of nerve-racked actors in take after take. Yet for Hitchcock it worked. Hitchcock felt that "my actors are experienced and know what they're doing; I want to see for myself what comes out of them when they approach a character; I may modify later or suggest changes but I want to encourage actors' inner processes." Stewart was fascinated by Hitchcock, however uneasy the director may have made him. At one time Stewart even defended Hitchcock's alleged aphorism that all actors were cattle, by insisting that what Hitch *really* said was that some actors occasionally *behaved* like cattle and had to be treated accordingly.

The reviewers did comment on the fact that all the actors seemed to be externalizing their inner processes, for better or worse. Dall certainly exposed his true mystique; and Granger's hesitant persona in *Rope* prefigured his later Hitchcock performance opposite Robert Walker in the homoerotic *Strangers on a Train* (1951), though he was to be somewhat more forthright and feisty in that depiction. One critic, speaking more truly than he knew, observed that "Stewart seems thoroughly at home amidst the morbid doings, shuffling off his boy scout image for something interestingly darker in hue."

Rope is significant in the Stewart career. It galvanized him into drastically changing his personal and professional image. 1949 found him playing Monty Stratton, an unmistakably hetero ball player, and, at 41, finally getting married. 1950 found him toughing it up even more emphatically under Anthony "Macho" Mann in a series of muscular Westerns.

William Schoell, one of the leading Alfred Hitchcock authorities and author of the acclaimed *Stay Out of the Shower: 25 Years of Shocker Films Beginning With Psycho*, has written of *Rope*:

"Hitchcock's 'ten-minute takes' approach works, but the film would have been more effective had it been done in his usual style. There *is* one actual 'cut'—from Granger to Stewart midway through the film, although the rest of the time the camera moves up to someone's back so that the photographer can change the reel. The picture is suspenseful and entertaining, with great dialogue and excellent performance, but it's never particularly moving, and it should have been."

In Schoell's view, James Stewart "is outclassed by the rest of the cast. He's okay, fits well into the morbid, sophisticated ambience through most of the picture, but he really falters at the conclusion. His climactic speech is delivered with too much surface intensity and loudness instead of the more restrained kind of hysterical numbness the sequence requires. He isn't giving a speech to Congress, after all, but supposedly reacting to a horrible discovery he in part feels responsible for."

In a *Quirk's Reviews* article Schoell elaborates: "He pulls out all the standard Stewart techniques from his proficient bag of tricks, but this time they aren't enough. He reminds one of that strident murderer he played at 28 in *Another Thin Man* (1936) and for this picture that's just, well, murder!"

Farley Granger, when I interviewed him in 1955, said that *Rope* had stretched his abilities as an actor and it was a pleasure to appear with so many good performers—he especially singled out Constance Collier and Sir Cedric Hardwicke. But I got the distinct impression that he thought he had done better, three years later, in *Strangers on a Train*. He had kind words for Stewart and John Dall, but had reservations about *Rope* itself.

Still concerned over his involvement with *Rope*, and its reception, and nervous about its possible consequences, Stewart decided that a light romantic comedy with screwball overtones would be the ticket. Joan Fontaine and her husband, William Dozier, then a top man in production at Universal, obligingly provided him with it.

You Gotta Stay Happy (1949) has something of a desperate ring in the title, as if it were designed to make up for any deficiencies the picture may be saddled with. The film harks back, after a fashion, to the screwball comedies of the Thirties, but by skeptical 1948 standards (when it was shot) the premise was outdated. Stewart seemed a shade too old for the role of a freight air service entrepreneur, with two battered planes to his credit, who takes on somewhat unorthodox cargoes. For instance, on the flight he is about to embark upon, he will carry some dangerously perishable seafood, a corpse (hopefully embalmed), a chimpanzee who smokes cigars, an eloping young couple, and, for good measure, an escaping embezzler (Porter Hall).

As the disparate cargo items indicate, Stewart's Marvin Payne is not only impecunious; he has yet to establish himself in the business. (The latter is a point which added to the film's unlikelihoods, given Stewart's age. It sounded more like something a 22-year-old, rather than a 40-year-old, would undertake.)

Also, while Stewart could hold his own in comedy if he put his mind to it, the story really called for the efforts of accomplished super-farceur Cary Grant. Nor was his co-star a comedienne in the tradition of Arthur (Jean) or Lombard (Carole) or Dunne (Irene), all of whom could have run rings around Fontaine. She flounders in the role of a discontented, disoriented heiress who deserts her stuffy husband (Willard Parker) on his wedding night to take off into the wild blue yonder with Stewart and his partner, Eddie Albert.

En route, the dizzy heiress, having already forgotten her marital obligation, decides she is in love with Stewart, but it takes him a while to come around to her way of thinking — and feeling. Forced to put down at a Midwestern farm owned by — who else? — the always reliable Percy Kilbride, their romance develops. When they finally arrive in California, Stewart is temporarily discombobulated by his new love's wealth and social position, to say nothing of her legal marriage to Parker. But all ends well with the implicit plot assumption that with his entrepreneurial brains and her capitalist money, they will do just fine.

Karl Tunberg produced, from his own screenplay. Director H. C. Potter did his best to inject the requisite life and pacing into the proceedings, but Stewart was no Grant and Fontaine was no Lombard, so Potter proved, at least this time out, he was no Leo

Joan Fontaine, James Stewart, *You Gotta Stay Happy*, UA, 1948

McCarey or Gregory LaCava. On hand with talent to spare, but with little opportunity to prove it were such dependables as Roland Young and Halliwell Hobbes.

Looking back on *You Gotta Stay Happy*, Fontaine later admitted that she and Dozier had thought they were varying her pace after the heavier *Kiss the Blood Off My Hands* (1948) and *Letter From an Unknown Woman* (1948). She expressed disappointment that the final result did not measure up to initial expectations, as did Stewart, telling me in 1964: "It could have been a lot better; I'm not sure what went wrong."

Fontaine's references to Stewart in her autobiography and elsewhere in print have always been sparse and perfunctory. He had been her sister Olivia de Havilland's boyfriend at one time, and some friends felt that Joan believed he had sided with Olivia against her on various occasions. Another story, often repeated, had it that she had carried a secret crush for Stewart herself, but Olivia had beaten her to him. While she was gracious enough to refer to Stewart as "a good actor; professional to work with," there has always been a certain coolness between them that neither has seen fit to publicly explain. "Cherchez Olivia!" one mutual friend insists to this day.

Nonetheless, when Doug McClelland interviewed Joan Fontaine for *American Classic Screen Magazine* in 1978, she must have been feeling expansive, for she told him:

"You Gotta Stay Happy was made right after *Kiss the Blood Off My Hands*, and I was pregnant with my daughter in both of them. I almost lost her on *You Gotta Stay Happy*. The director, H.C. Potter, made me jump off a hay wagon, and in ten minutes I was in the hospital!"

She described James Stewart as "a dream to work with! After I went to the hospital, Jimmy came to visit me that very night, which I thought was awfully dear of him. Jean Louis, who did the costumes for the picture, designed some lovely camouflage for me."

What Joan might not have known at the time, but Jerry Asher did, was that Bill Dozier had worked up an unaccountable jealousy and insecurity about Jimmy. "Bill never considered himself a good-looking man, Jerry remembered, "though he was actually quite sexy and jaunty, with a line of fast gab that probably got him into more beds in town than even Joan realized."

According to Jerry: "Bill kept skulking onto the set, hiding behind flats, and watching intently. As Jimmy and Joan filmed their love scenes he'd stalk off with a mean scowl on his face. 'Bill, this is ridiculous!' I told him, 'You know Jimmy can always be relied on to have total respect for the wives of other guys; he's the farthest thing from a home-wrecker!'"

"I don't know," Dozier contradicted Jerry. "He has always had a weird reputation as a scavenger of women. What about Norma Shearer?"

"Norma was a *widow* at the time, in case you've forgotten," Jerry told him. "And if anyone was on a romantic scavenger hunt, *she* was the one! Jimmy acted like a frightened rabbit around her most of the time!" "Rabbits can be the horniest of animals," Bill insisted. Jerry finally made him see that any romance between Joan and Jimmy existed solely in his imagination.

The Stratton Story, Stewart's first film for MGM since *Ziegfeld Girl*, in 1941, is often hailed as his finest post-war film after *It's a Wonderful Life*. To a modern audience, however, it seems rather pedestrian and redolent of many films of its kind, to wit: top athletic star is riding high, meets a reverse, goes into a funk, gradually rouses himself from the depths, and comes back fighting.

In this case, Stewart is Monty Stratton (the real-life Monty was signed as technical advisor and coach), a professional ball player who scales the heights, before losing a leg in a hunting accident. He sinks into the depths of despond, but with the help of his ever-faithful wife June Allyson, and his mentor discoverer Frank Norman, he makes a smash comeback. With an artificial limb (he's a pitcher, yet he often manages to run around) and an optimistic outlook, he finds himself physically and spiritually whole again. In 1949 audiences were far more gullible, and this kind of schmaltz went over big. *The Stratton Story* was ranked (along with *The Pride of the Yankees*, Gary Cooper's 1942 gem) as one of the two best baseball films ever made.

Despite the sincerity of the acting (Stewart underplays beautifully, though in this case a few more of his famous mannerisms might have sparked things up a bit) and the fine direction of no-nonsense Sam Wood, who also did the Cooper film, *The Stratton Story* today seems rather cloyingly superficial. Much is made of Stratton's triumph over his loss of self-esteem as a one-legged man, and his advent to humility as he matches his baby son's first steps with his own on his artificial leg. There is some merit in watching him under the tutelage of Morgan and even his wife (who plays ball with him in the back yard until she falls down and then announces another baby is coming, so no more ballplaying for *her*) as he recovers his sense of purpose and self-respect. But a modern viewer is conditioned to more subtle forms of triumph over less clear-cut adversity. The film, though nicely handled by all, seems sentimental and contrived. To its credit, it does succeed in making baseball suspenseful and entertaining — no small feat considering the boredom it inspires in many film and theatre audiences.

As various reporters on Stewart have commented, Louis B. Mayer did not think *The Stratton Story* was the appropriate MGM comeback film for Stewart; in fact, he didn't want him back at all. Billy Grady told me that Mayer had reversed his earlier position and was seething that Stewart had not signed on again with MGM after the war. Mayer was in no mood to advance his wandering star's fortunes, nor did he particularly care for movies about sports figures. "They rank as box office attractions around the level of Civil War

James Stewart, June Allyson, *The Stratton Story*, MGM, 1949

movies," he often said, ignoring the success of *Gone With the Wind* and *Pride of the Yankees*, both made by other producers. But by 1949 there was a new regime at MGM under Dore Schary (Mayer was to leave outright in 1951) and Dore had no ancient axes to grind with Stewart; indeed, he roundly admired him.

Van Johnson was to have originally starred with June Allyson, now in her ascendancy with MGM, and he had the advantage of being eight years Stewart's junior. Arguments raged in the front office as to whether Stewart, under Monty Stratton's tutelage, could convincingly muster the necessary diamond skills — but Stewart's supporters prevailed. Stratton coached him assiduously, the film was shot on authentic baseball-field locations, and when it was released it was hailed as a much-needed Stewart hit.

June Allyson told me during her 1957 visit to New York: "Jimmy was wonderful to play with; he underplayed with such sincerity and tact and sweetness, and he was so supportive toward me. I had admired him years before when I was unknown in New York, and it was a big thrill to play with him that year. I know some people thought Van Johnson should have had it, but he and I were wearing out our welcome as a team, and much as I loved — and love — Van, I felt in retrospect that Jimmy was more right for it. And he looked so young in it — I know he was in his early 40s but he made those scenes where he was supposed to be just a green kid totally convincing!"

Many years after she had co-starred with him in three films, June Allyson's memories of Jimmy Stewart would always be fond and loving. "He was absolutely adorable," she told me some years ago. "So boyish and so honest; no matter how old he got he never lost that boyishness!" In her autobiography, she wrote that her then-husband Dick Powell loved to kid her and Jimmy about being "the reigning romantic team in Hollywood." Gloria Stewart, she remembered, would say, "June is Jimmy's perfect wife in movies — and I'm his imperfect wife." Referring humorously to her and Jimmy's "husband-and-wife relationship" Dick Powell once got up at a banquet and hailed an embarrassed, but somewhat blushingly pleased Stewart with the words, "And now, let me introduce my wife's husband — Jimmy Stewart!" Referring to the films they had made together, Powell added: "June here must have been a good wife. Jimmy Stewart has married her three times." Ruefully, Allyson rejoindered, "But he couldn't make it stick!" She remembered husband Powell lamenting that neither she nor Gloria could fix things around the house, but June always had the standard answer for that: Weren't men supposed to fix things? Hadn't Powell been paid by the chore as a kid, and didn't Jimmy study engineering and architecture in college? That ought to qualify them to fix leaky faucets!

Recalling the Stewart she knew before he married Gloria, June Allyson commented on his "scary thinness" and how her "lousy cooking," which, she said, had never been among her skills, would only have made him thinner. She remembered the bachelor Stewart days: "Jimmy hated being photographed with a girl when he was out and he seldom took his dates to nightclubs. Instead he fed them steak that he grilled himself in his own backyard. If they didn't like that and wanted the limelight then they were not for him." Of his marital alliance with Gloria, June said: "Gloria was the perfect choice for him. They were so suited to each other — both tall and slim and dignified, and both with the same wry sense of humor." She remembered that in his bachelor days Stewart had a unique way of letting his dates know that it was time to leave. He alerted his housekeeper to make a sudden appearance with wraps or stoles or whatever, at which time the hapless lady knew that the jig was up, at least for that night.

Stewart loved to joke about that housekeeper, June said. He laughingly put the blame for his late marriage squarely on her. She read all his mail before he did, he claimed, and anything romantic or pushy never reached the Master's eyes. Asked why he hadn't fired the housekeeper for overstretching her function, so to speak, Stewart quipped that she was too good a judge of scripts to be dispensed with. "You just didn't fire a person like that," he continued, "as she kept me from bothering with bad scripts."

Allyson recalled to me Stewart's utter relaxation between scenes: "I wouldn't know if he was asleep or awake. But when you needed him, he'd jump right up and be all ready to go right through the scene. I never knew anyone like him."

Stewart loved to keep Allyson off-balance with his wit. He came to the set one morning and told her, "You know, June, I never do my exercises at home. I wait till I get to the studio. You don't mind if I do them now, do you?" Allyson, mischievously hoping that he would stand on his head, or something equally outlandish, told him she'd love to see what kind of exercises he had up his sleeve. Thereupon, Stewart started energetically wiggling his fingers. Nonplussed, Allyson asked if that was all he did. He told her that was it; if he did any more than that "I wouldn't weigh as much as I do now." Stewart, she said, found her extraordinarily gullible, hence a perfect mark for whimsy of all kinds.

Frank Morgan, who ably supported Stewart and Allyson in *The Stratton Story*, and who died shortly after it was finished, was not one of her favorite people. Frank had always been a heavy drinker. Barbara Barondess MacLean, who had acted with him on Broadway in the 1920s, had many a tale to tell of his frequent inebriations. He would show up for a play totally soused, then go out on the stage acting as cold-sober as you please straight through to the Act III curtain. But Barbara "was never sure *what* the evening would bring!"

Allyson remembered Frank, who played the over-the-hill manager who discovered Stratton, coming onset noisily drunk. When the director tried to quiet him down, telling him that Allyson was in the middle of a scene, Morgan would rudely opine that "Allyson can't act anyway." She remembered that Frank Morgan often loudly voiced his total contempt for actors since "it was an actor who shot Lincoln!"

Allyson recalled that Stewart hated to look at rushes, could not stand to see his face onscreen, and even avoided the finished picture. "He said he'd just embarrass himself by going to our gala premieres."

In 1957, I asked Allyson if, in her view, Stewart was simply a natural talent or had acquired a professional technique through sheer hard work and concentration. She said, "It's both! He must have been a natural, to have walked on the stage way back when he was only 24 without a single acting lesson! Later, certainly by the time I got him, he had layered that wonderful instinct and that natural talent over with lots of applied concentration and carefully thought-through technique, but it never destroyed his naturalness. He knew when to highlight and when to underplay; he had an instinct that was unfailing."

Asked if she had ever felt a personal attraction to him, Allyson laughed and merrily replied, "Everyone who ever acted with him — I mean the women of course — fell in love with him and never fell out of love. Had he gotten me between marriages and I had felt he was serious about his proposal, I'd have married him on the spot! But the timing just didn't favor me — or a lot of other people I can think of." Informed that Stewart said he fell in love, however briefly, with all his leading ladies, June fervently whispered, "*Oh, I hope so!*"

Stewart about this time moved out of Hank's and Frances' playhouse and back into his own quarters. He elected to live alone except for occasional interruptions by old pals from New York, or wherever, "who stayed — but not too long." He later recalled: "I sort of liked living alone by that time. I was getting on to forty; no kid stuff anymore. And in the back of my mind, I knew I was wife-hunting, though I didn't always admit it consciously." One of his dates was fan magazine writer Florence Pritchett, a pert, attractive scribe who got to know a lot about Jimmy if her *Silver Screen* reports on him are accurate — and they sure ring true. "He was living," she told her readers, "alone, with a couple to take care of him. His house is decorated by his own thin hands in a collection of modern paintings with Currier and Ives prints alongside. His father gave him the

James Stewart and parents, Elizabeth and Alexander

Currier and Ives, but it wasn't until last year [1947], when he found out their value, that he took them off the shelf and hung them. He still doesn't think they're anything to rave about."

Florence obviously knew her way around the Jimmy Stewart menage, and reported that the furniture was a combination of Modern and Early American, mostly in shades of brown. "He eats at home a lot when he works," she added. Waxing, if not purplish, at least muted shades of violet in her prose, Florence told the readers that, though pushing 40, Jimmy appreciated marriage and what it stood for. He was "Scared! Yes, Scared! . . . . that somehow, some day, somewhere, some girl is going to marry him. He's as scared as any man who has waited forty years to take the horrible step. . . . however, there is hope for you eager females! [And at the moment for Florence herself, one assumes]. Several weeks before his 40th birthday Jimmy was heard to say, in a loose moment, that as soon as he was 40 he would *get married!*" Florence Pritchett's prose took an oddly culinary turn as she enthused: "Jimmy has made his little frying pan as cozy as can be, and there he lies, filled with trepidation, peering timidly over the edge into the fire!"

The doubtless eager distaff readers of *Silver Screen* gleaned other facts from Florence's article: Jimmy thought one of the advantages of having a wife was she could arrange his social life; he rarely saw his men friends, for they were all wrapped up in the wives and kiddies; going out on endless dates with a series of women was lonely; he could never marry a dumb girl; he liked women to be alert and attractive in their own right. On the previous Thanksgiving, Florence mourned, Stewart had sat alone in his house, having sent the servants home for the day, and ate a cold chicken sandwich. No one invited him for dinner that day. Moral: a bachelor may have his cake and eat it, too, but cake can taste sour when eaten alone. Florence portrayed him as skittish and unreliable with women. One young lady confided: "[Jimmy] is sure a queer one [sic]. Why, do you know, he took me out every night for three weeks and then practically disappeared for six months! Now I ask you!"

Florence went into Jimmy's weight problems in the intimate manner of a fan-mag femme who came for an interview and stayed for, well, dinner. "Even with the fifteen pounds movies add onto a person's weight, if [Jimmy] turned sideways they'd mark him absent. Weight is one of Jimmy's biggest worries. Though he really dislikes food and can't seem to eat it, he tries hard. Every meal will find him downing a glass of half milk, half cream. Baked potatoes come next, but always mixed with sour cream and chives."

The besmitten Florence went on: "Knowing Jimmy, you realize his extraordinary love for music is a strong manifestation of his finely tuned perceptions. He loves Fred Waring and will talk for hours about a certain chord hit during a number. Three notes in the middle of a song that strikes him as particularly well done will really give him pleasure. Whenever he sees a piano or an organ he just plays the chords he likes, over and over." Florence breathlessly babbled that she was sure, "having watched the faraway expression on his face when music is played, that when Jimmy was flying during the War, he heard a symphony at ten thousand feet!"

After telling how Jimmy thought of nothing but work, how parties and dates couldn't tempt him from hitting the sack early to be fresh for the next morning's work, and how (contrary to June Allyson's claim) he looked at rushes so long and so intently that "not one line or one nuance misses a study on his part," Florence suddenly transported her readers to New York. There she had double-dated with Stewart and the Hank Fondas. They ate peanuts and laughed at the clowns at the circus, then gawked at the freaks in the sideshow. It all wound up with Fonda and Stewart getting sudden attention from the circus fans, especially the women, with Frances and Florence relegated to the edge of the crowd. On that date, and on others, Florence continued to learn more about Jimmy; that he was observant about women's clothes, liked them chic with beautiful taste, yet he still wore rags from the Princeton days. While in New York, completely unconscious of his appearance, he bought a new topcoat because she and others pointed out how worn his old coat looked. Ensconced on that trip in the Waldorf Astoria, Florence remembered that he blew up when they moved his room three times; once they forgot to tell him he was moved, so a very frightened young woman found him banging impatiently on her door. Year by year he shifted his car makes: in 1947 a Chevrolet, in 1948 a Ford.

Florence inevitably joined the other ladies in Stewart's past, though one would think that with her command of language she might have talked him into a longer involvement. Soon he was on a dizzy round of:

Mitzi Green: "A great guy, Jimmy, kind, understanding, a great listener. A wonderful shoulder to cry on."

"Lana Turner: "A marvelous man, always so good for laughs, so companionable and consoling." (Lana at the time was between husbands.)

Rita Hayworth: "Jimmy is so tender and sweet, and so kind. He really understands women; he is sensitive as few men are. He is always there when needed."

(Rita was also between husbands at that time, being en route from Orson Welles to Prince Aly Khan. She had dated Stewart before the War, but that had obviously been only a trial run. For a while, their renewed romance, if the fan mags were to be believed, was "hot and heavy." But that, too, passed.)

Soon, another smitten fan-mag maven, Alyce Canfield, in *Screenland*, was rhapsodizing: "There's a loneliness about Jimmy that perhaps he, himself, doesn't see. Somehow Jimmy and a Right Girl seem to go together like pie à la mode. There is no sense in his traveling alone. But you know that Jimmy will never settle for anything less than a stars-in-your-eyes kind of feeling. About love, he is idealistic." Alyce worked herself up to an indignant lather at this point, and wailed: "How can such an appealing guy as Jimmy Stewart not have found his girl?" As aggressive as Florence Pritchett had been in getting into Jimmy's, well, confidence, Alyce told her readers that Jimmy lived in a really plain little home; didn't read anything but the newspapers; that his favorite meal was fried chicken, mashed potatoes, apple pie and milk; that on dates he likes to go to a movie; that he likes to dance, but made a face when rhumba music started; that his favorite Sunday recreation was playing golf; that he loved to fiddle with car engines, loved to make model airplanes, loved to tinker in a workshop. Alyce really topped Florence's ace with her summation: "Like a psychiatrist, you have to be aware of all the little things he does or does not do in order to discover what he really is like!"

Next, a *guy* took on Jimmy's private life. Jack Wade in *Modern Screen* (issue of January, 1949) listed Myrna Dell, Anita Colby and about fifteen other ladies as keeping Jimmy mighty busy. "He is everybody's Romeo — and nobody's," Jack decided, with a twinge of envy. He then proceeded to voice his deep, dark suspicions (soon to be proved wrong) that there would never be any Really Right Girl for Jimmy.

Of the many women Stewart dated between 1946 and 1949, sexy, perky, talented Myrna Dell was the most typical. Pretty, blonde, witty, intelligent, the kind the guys call "a good companion", Myrna found Jimmy "like a big, transplanted country boy — and very, very sweet!" In a 1990 interview, she reflected on that distant romance: "I wasn't in love with him; looking back I know that now, but oh, I liked him, really did! He was the most gentlemanly and courteous man I ever went out with — he was charmingly old-fashioned that way." Myrna admits she heard that he could be quite the Lothario, "but with me he was adorable, always." (In 1990, Myrna had been directed by her own daughter, Laura Patterson, on a segment of the *Unsolved Mysteries* TV series for NBC.)

"I did a number of pictures even before getting signed by RKO for a 1944–49 sojourn," Myrna remembered. "I was in *A Night at Earl Carroll's* and *Ziegfeld Girl* with Lana Turner over at MGM. That was 1941. Jimmy was in that, too, but he didn't notice me then; later, after he came back from the War, was when we really connected!" From 1946 on, Myrna got some meaty supporting parts, with Dorothy McGuire in *The Spiral Staircase* (1946), in *Nocturne* (1946) with George Raft, in *Fighting Father Dunne* (1948), with Pat O'Brien. As late as 1950, as Wendell Corey's dance-hall girl liaison, she was exchanging sharp dialogue in *The Furies* with Barbara Stanwyck. She always remembered one particularly snappy exchange: Myrna (jealous and catty): "I never knew what men see in the thin ones." Stanwyck (brittle and contemptuous): "It's not what they can see." She recalls as her "biggest disappointment" not landing the role that zoomed Gloria Grahame to stardom, in *Crossfire* (1947).

"Jimmy was always a good listener, helpful with career tips," she recalled. "We went to movies, held hands, talked, cooked dinner. It was nice, but no big deal for either of us." According to Adela St. Johns: "By 1949 Jim was tired of actresses. He'd been around the track with them too often, didn't think of them as wife material. I was not at all surprised when he wound up with a non-professional."

Chapter Ten

A Bridegroom — At 41

It was in 1947, when he turned 39, that Stewart finally met the girl who would become the one and only Mrs. James Stewart. There are two versions concerning their first meeting. One is Billy Grady's:

"One Christmas eve, Jim and I, as was our habit, hired three broken-down musicians, loaded them in the car, and stopped at homes in Beverly Hills to sing Christmas carols. At one, we found Keenan Wynn pouring for his guests. As we entered, I noted a beautiful young lady seated on a staircase. She seemed a bit on the down side. I recognized her. It was Gloria Hatrick . . . Jim stopped to talk with Gloria. That was the beginning. They saw much of each other in the ensuing two years."

Gloria Hatrick MacLean Stewart's lengthier version was somewhat different: "Gary and Rocky Cooper were giving a dinner party. It was in 1947. Rocky told me that Ann Sothern was coming, and Ronnie Reagan, and Slim and Leland Hayward — he was Jimmy's agent — and Jimmy. Rocky was always trying to get me to meet Jimmy."

Gloria continued: "And it wasn't that hard. Jimmy Stewart was always my favorite actor. Anyway, after dinner, we went to Ciro's. Nat 'King' Cole was playing, and we danced. I saw Jimmy making hand signals to Leland not to cut in. But I pretended not to notice. The first real date we had was to play golf, and I beat him, which was dumb. But he didn't mind, so I guess it wasn't so dumb after all — it showed me right away what kind of man he was."

She had been born Gloria Hatrick, some ten years after Jimmy, the daughter of Edgar Hatrick, a Hearst executive who had been a pioneer in the movie newsreels and documentary movies. Starting as a publicity man, Hatrick went to work for Hearst in 1908, and served as head of Hearst Metrotone News (later News of the Day). He had also worked in the United States Information Service and had, at one time, been General Manager of Cosmopolitan Pictures. Comfortably fixed financially, the Hatricks had given Gloria the best of educations. Billy Grady held the Hatricks in the highest regard, and often bragged to Stewart about them. "Ed Hatrick was a great friend of mine," Billy told me. "We had had adjoining offices in the old days in New York, and he was loved by all with whom he came in contact. He had personality to spare and he did all right by his daughter — she inherited it!"

In her early 20s, the socially active Gloria was a slim and svelte model. Beautiful, with a warm, outgoing personality, "full of sparkle and fire," as Billy described it, she won the attention of Edwin "Ned" MacLean. He was the spoiled playboy son of super-rich Evelyn Walsh MacLean, fabled owner of the legendary Hope Diamond. A "Trust Fund Pet" of the first order, Ned was shallow and weak, and as Billy put it, "married Gloria for all the wrong reasons. She was pretty and sexy and vital, and that was all that noodlehead spoiled-brat saw — the sexy surface!" Emotionally immature in his mid-20s, and sexually insatiable, he kept Gloria busy bearing two sons in the first years of her marriage. Meanwhile, he cheated on her and drank to excess, "the very model of a rich boy gone wrong," as Helen Ferguson described him. Gloria gave birth to Ronald on June 19, 1944, and his brother Michael followed him on February 5, 1946. By 1947, with Ronald three and Michael one, Gloria had had her fill, and got herself a prompt divorce.

"Ned MacLean went on with his profligate ways," Billy told me, "and everyone knew he would come to a bad end. Too much money, spoiled rotten, no firm goals in life, he was not much of a character. Gloria was thoroughly disgusted and disillusioned with him, but being the lady she is, she would never discuss him at all. But hell, everyone knew what she had been through! She carried her heartbreak and hurt with her head held high. Valiant was the term for Gloria!"

According to Barbara Barondess MacLean and others, Ned MacLean was going rapidly downhill all the time. He wound up marrying a hat-check girl from Sherman Billingsley's Stork Club, who later evolved into a top society beauty in Palm Beach. She stayed married to him, friends said, "so she could come into the fortune once his liver gave out." It finally obliged her, as Ned MacLean literally drank himself to death, some twenty years after Gloria had taken herself and her sons (she won absolute custody) out of his life forever.

James Stewart, Gloria MacLean at Mocambo, 1949

The Gloria whom Jimmy Stewart met and courted in 1947 was a survivor. Hurt by love, betrayed by hopes, she was game for more. But *this* time she would not make a mistake; *this* time, she told friends, she would marry for character and decency in a man. Above all, he would be the proper father and role model for her two young sons.

"It was the boys who won him for her as much as her own wonderful self," Ruth Waterbury later said. "Jimmy *felt* for those little kids; they were in a single-parent household, however affluent. They had no father worthy of the name, no role-model. His heart went out to them. And to Gloria."

Jimmy and Gloria were married on August 9, 1949, at the Brentwood Presbyterian Church. Billy Grady was the best man. "I still carry his gift," Billy said in 1964 (he died in 1973 of emphysema at the Motion Picture Country Home), and he pulled it out and showed it to me. It was a money clip, with an inscription: "You are the best man of all time—your friend, Slats. August 9, 1949." "Slats," he said, "was my nickname for the slim guy I first saw at Princeton twenty years before." Gregg Draddy, the bride's sister ("another stunning Hatrick blonde," as Billy remembered her), was the matron of honor. The church was packed with celebrities, including Spencer Tracy and Gary Cooper. On hand from Indiana, Pennsylvania, were the Stewart family members, including Alexander and Elizabeth, the parents who had waited, as they bluntly told reporters outside the church, "longer than we ever expected it would be" for their son's wedding day. After a reception at their friends', the Jack Boltons', the couple shortly took off for Honolulu, where they enjoyed an extended honeymoon. There was one sadness: Gloria's father, Ed Hatrick, was too ill to attend the ceremony; he died only a month later.

Stewart told a reporter that year: "Writers keep asking me why I was getting married at forty-one. They seemed to resent it." Upon reflection, he continued: "My bachelor years, let me tell you, were just wonderful . . . just wonderful! Boy, did I have some good times! But when you're forty-one, life means more than just a bookful of phone numbers. I needed the security of a permanent relationship with a woman I loved. I needed a family and I needed to put down roots. I can say all the usual things about meeting the right girl and falling in love. But it was also the right time."

Some gossips, in and out of the press, noted that it was Billy Grady, the solid, married, unassailably-heterosexual older pal, who made Best Man. Not Henry Fonda, to whom he had been so close; not Josh Logan, who had influenced him so greatly in emotional terms; and certainly not Guthrie McClintic the man who had loved him so passionately. Nor was it Johnny Swope, with whom Stewart had lived for years. These men represented Stewart's bachelor past; and though they would remain friends with him (and he with them) all their lives, they were, in certain respects, a closed chapter in his book. Now those rumors would be stilled, those rumors fueled by national attention to his fortieth birthday, unmarried, on May 20, 1948; fueled by that homoerotic picture *Rope*, which he now regretted making. All would be different now. The All-American, Boy Scout, Rock of Gibraltar, Unassailably Heterosexual, Home-and-Fireside-and-Little-Ones image would be secured, for all time. In Honolulu, his emotionally and sexually sated bride still asleep in their suite, Jimmy Stewart went out in the Hawaiian sun and contemplated his new life with contentment.

Once back in Hollywood, after putting up at a temporary residence that Gloria finally vetoed because it was in a bad location for growing children, they settled in a solid Tudor-style house in Brentwood. There they were to remain throughout their marriage. "Once Jimmy stays put — oh, he stays put!" Josh Logan later commented. "One house — one marriage — decades of it now! Hank's had five marriages; I've had two. Only Johnny Swope stayed with the one woman over the years. Not that it's any surprise. After all, we who were his intimates know that for all his youthful cuttings-up and didoes, Jimmy always held in his heart this rock-solid craving for respectability! Oh, did he!"

Stewart worked tirelessly to keep his straight-arrow, husband-and-daddy image untarnished. Clive Hirschhorn in 1977, twenty-eight years into their marriage, got some personal reminiscences from Gloria. She was then pushing 60, her husband seventy. Talking about her doubts in their earlier years together (and who could blame her, after her roller-coaster ride with Ned MacLean?) she told Hirschhorn: "It gave me a lot of cause for anxiety, because during this period Jimmy was working with some of the most glamorous women in the world — women such as Kim Novak, Joan Fontaine, Marlene Dietrich, and Grace Kelly. And, of course, my constant fear was that he would find them more attractive than me and have an affair with one of them. A lot of men in Hollywood constantly became involved with their leading ladies — and as Jimmy was a red-blooded American male, naturally I thought it could happen to him, too."

She continued: "I was convinced initially that it would only be a matter of time before the phone would ring and it would be James telling me he had to work hard at the studio, or that he would be out playing poker with the boys. Well, no such phone call ever came! And I can honestly say that, in all the years we've been married Jimmy never once gave me cause for anxiety or jealousy. The more glamorous the leading lady he was starring opposite, the more attentive he'd be to me! He knew the insecurities I was going through, and made quite sure that they were totally unfounded. His consideration was incredible and one of the reasons why our marriage has lasted so long and is still so good!"

In 1973, Gloria was telling Cleveland Amory: "Jimmy's a wonderful father. My sons just became *our* sons so naturally. And when the twins, Judy and Kelly came [they were born on May 7, 1951], well, to this day, they just worship him, and so do the grandchildren."

Once, in 1965, I asked Ruth Waterbury if, in her opinion, Stewart was the exceptionally faithful and steadfast husband Gloria consistently claimed he was. "The flesh is weak — that's a universal," she commented crisply. "And whatever he was up to, *if* he was up to it, he certainly kept it from her!"

Ruth felt that one salient reason Stewart was anxious that his wife not be distressed in any respect was because the birth of their twins had almost cost Gloria her life. The surgical aspects had gone awry and for some weeks she hovered between life and death. "She was really sick," Ruth said, "and I'm sure the doctors told her there could be no more children. She was close to death for some days. This got Jimmy in a very guilty state — he sort of blamed himself for what had gone wrong, as new fathers will — thought it was something in his genes or in his blood or something. After nearly losing her, that way, and they not even married two years, he went out of his way to keep her happy."

Jerry Asher felt that Gloria got a little uneasy over Jimmy's constant attentions to director Anthony Mann. "That's why she went out on location with him when she could," Jerry said. "She knew — what wife with any intuition and intelligence wouldn't — that Jimmy had a complicated makeup — and I'm sure the Mann thing made her nervous. But she probably reasoned that it would have been worse had it been another woman. That would have *really* devastated her!"

Asked by a reporter how good — or bad — a disciplinarian with his two stepsons and natural twin daughters Stewart was, Gloria replied: "The funny thing is, he thinks he was strict. I'm sure he'll tell you that. Because his father really was strict, and that's what he's always wanted to be. Actually he was anything but!"

Gloria Stewart then recounted an incident when the family were having dinner in the main dining room of the New Stanley Hotel in Nairobi, during one of their African trips. "One of the girls dropped something under the table and couldn't find it, and suddenly all three of us were under the table, looking for it. And then we heard Jimmy, speaking in a voice we had never heard before. 'All right, all of you,' he barked. 'Come right up here this instant!' Then he started on us in that same voice. 'I never, ever,' he said, 'want to see such behavior in a public place again!' We just sat absolutely still, looking down at our plates. I was as bad as the girls. We almost died trying so hard not to giggle or look at each other, or worse still, at him. The only thing we could do was keep on looking down. I felt about twelve. The whole thing just surprised us so much, because really, he had never done a thing like that before."

Gloria said that Jimmy's humor was what she liked best about him. She recalled a time when she was trying to explain to someone "for the umpteenth time" the difference between identical and fraternal twins. "Anyway, whoever it was didn't get it very well, and Jimmy, as he always does, broke the ice. 'Golly,' he said, 'I always thought they were *nocturnal!*'"

Johnny Swope later claimed that, after Gloria almost lost her life with the twins, Jimmy was secretly glad that she could never have any more kids. "Four were enough for him," he told me. "Four were all the handful he needed."

Swope felt that Jimmy's attitude toward the boys, as they grew through childhood and into adolescence, was "anxious, strict, harried. Ron was four when his mother married, Mike three or so. He told me they were going to be brought up right, by the golden rule, by all the old verities. 'I'm not ever gonna let them go their father's way!' he almost shouted one night at my house over a beer. 'There'll be no drunks or parasites or bums in *my* family!'" He said he agreed with the Catholics (he was, of course, a Presbyterian) in their statement about the need to bring up a child in the way he should go on, so that in adulthood he would not depart from it. "I think he was afraid of Ned MacLean's blood in them," mused Johnny. "He was afraid one of them would go wrong like his father."

"He loved those boys deeply, devotedly," Henry Fonda said. "They weren't his natural children, Mike and Ron, and yet he was a helluva better father to them than I was to mine. And he worried over them; the twins too. Oh, how he worried! 'What kind of world are we bringing them up in, now?' he declared. 'They've gotta be steered right.'"

Spencer Tracy, at 49, was tired. His drinking was growing more pronounced when he made *Malaya* with Stewart in 1949. This was Stewart's second post-War MGM picture. Directed by Richard Thorpe, it was written by Frank Fenton and based on a true story by Manchester Boddy, about the efforts to smuggle much-needed rubber out of Malaya to the Allies during World War II. Tracy is a smuggler released from prison because of his certain expertise, who teams up with Far East reporter Stewart to get the rubber out. Aided by publisher Lionel Barrymore and a foxy dealer, Sydney Greenstreet, they infiltrate the rubber fields right under the noses of the Japanese occupying forces. They get two shipments out, but almost lose the third when they skirmish with the Japanese. Stewart forfeits his life but a wounded Tracy, accompanied by Italian refugee Valentina Cortese (a romantic subplot), makes it through.

The unprepossessing plot is dressed up with some fast pacing by Thorpe, and some good acting by Tracy, Stewart, Greenstreet and Barrymore. Despite his personal problems, Tracy is a magician before the cameras, as always, and Stewart matches, though never outplays, him.

The project had an interesting history. Manchester Boddy, who had been involved in a real-life smuggling plan in Malaya, had sold the story originally to RKO when Dore Schary was in charge of production there. Schary took it on to MGM when he transferred there as head of the studio. Spencer Tracy came upon the story and was immediately enthused about doing it. Stewart asked for, and got, his role because he had long been looking around for a chance to co-star on equal terms with Tracy.

Critics and observers have commented that the picture is chiefly interesting because it affords an opportunity to contrast two highly individual acting styles. For all the work that went into it, however, *Malaya* is no classic, and over its 98-minute running time even commits the sin of dullness occasionally. But the chance to see two first-rate actors at their peak almost redeems all.

Tracy always liked and respected Stewart, and during the shooting they had many extended conversations. It is in their scenes together, where they are relaxed, yet alert, that the picture comes most alive. Stewart relished his role as the newspaperman, John Royer, because it gave him a chance to play a cynical realist. Disenchanted by life and essentially detached, he retains underlying hints of basic humanity. Tracy, as the hard-bitten ex-convict who is forced to take positive actions for a change, and secretly enjoys it, is his usual understated, unassuming self.

John Hodiak, one of the supporting actors, later stated that watching Stewart and Tracy play off each other was one of the ex-

Jane Wyman and James Stewart receiving *Photoplay* Gold Medals

citements of his time on the picture, a sentiment echoed by experienced character actors Sydney Greenstreet and Lester Matthews.

The critics, for the most part, charitably glossed-off the script's deficiencies by commenting on the lavish MGM production qualities, Bronislau Kaper's rousing score, and the excellent acting of all the principals. One reviewer noted that "*Malaya* is not really any great shakes as an action epic, being rather terse, and redolent of many films of its type that have gone before, but the pairing of Spencer Tracy and James Stewart in co-starring roles of equal depth and range is something that had to be done sooner or later, and MGM has done it here, for which we should all be grateful, as they are always exciting together on screen."

Valentina Cortese, whose role was strictly subordinate to the men, told me years later: "You could tell Spencer and Jimmy liked and respected each other; they cooperated wonderfully before the camera and held many cordial sessions off-camera. I saw no trace of professional jealousy, only of cooperation and mutual esteem. But then neither man was a prima donna type, was he?"

Obviously Valentina wasn't present during all the Tracy-Stewart offscreen sessions, for Tracy's less affable side did emerge on occasion. Stewart told Tracy biographer Bill Davidson: "Spence was more cantankerous than usual because the film was a real potboiler. We knew that was a dangerous situation for Spence. He could walk out and pull one of his famous disappearances at any time. So I decided on a strategy to keep him interested in something other than the picture."

Stewart proposed to Tracy a post-production jaunt to Europe and Asia. "We'd talk about what countries we were going to visit and I kept collecting brochures to show to him. He'd pore ever the brochures and talk with great excitement about Greece and Rome and the Taj Mahal." According to Stewart, "the strategy seemed to work, and Spence showed up every day and did his usual fine job. When it was over, I said to him, 'Well, have you gotten your passport yet?' He said, 'What passport?' 'For our trip to Europe and Asia.'"

"Europe and Asia!" Tracy exploded. "Why, I wouldn't go across the *street* with you, you son of a bitch!"

Stewart took the outburst in good part, as he had already figured out that Tracy was nipping more than usual, and trying (unsuccessfully, as always) to keep it a secret from everybody. Doubtless Stewart felt, and indicated to friends, that a jaunt around the world with Tracy and his stash would have been hazardous to life and limb, so he was just as well out of it.

John Hodiak told me in 1951 that he felt Kate Hepburn had her work cut out for her keeping Tracy on course, professionally and personally. "What I couldn't understand about Kate," Hodiak said, "was that she had never put herself out for any man before Tracy, indeed seemed to scorn them on a personal level. And here she was, worrying over him like a mother hen, and waiting on him hand and foot. And he a married man, too!"

Chapter Eleven
Going West with Macho Mann

Winchester '73 (1950) is one of the great watershed films in the Stewart career. As one commentator put it, he was referred to, more often than not, as Jimmy Stewart before 1950: after *Winchester '73* he was referred to far more often as James Stewart. For in this first of his *real* Westerns (*Destry Rides Again* does not really qualify, despite its setting), Stewart reveals his darker side. He summoned all the reserves of anger, inner ambivalence, and emotional complexity in his nature that his audiences had hitherto failed to catch.

The background of how he came to do *Winchester '73* is interesting. In 1950, with his box office somewhat reestablished by his success in *The Stratton Story* the year before, Stewart made a deal, with the aid of his astute agent Lew Wasserman, for two films with Universal. The terms accorded him a relatively unimpressive upfront financial remuneration, but guaranteed him a percentage of the profits. This was not exactly unprecedented, but in Stewart's case it was implemented full-force, and became an ongoing policy that blazed a new trail in actors' dealings with the studios. Eventually it was to become the rule rather than the exception among major stars. Stewart's advent into the Big Movie Money can be dated from *Winchester '73*.

Ever since *Rope*, Stewart had been making, consciously and unconsciously, a series of personal and professional decisions calculated to refurbish his image in the public mind. The shy, awkward, befuddled, soft-spoken, almost femininely diffident character would be seen in *some* films; but with the series of Westerns and other super-macho films he made in the 1950s and 1960s, starting with *Winchester '73*, public perceptions of James Stewart: man and artist would forever change. Those audiences that had once considered him a charming and lovable, but indefinably weak buffoon, fit only to be patronized for his boyish ungainliness, would discover that, after 1950, James Stewart was no one to tangle with.

Aiding and abetting him was a director he had never worked

with before, but who, starting with this film, was to be inextricably associated with the New James Stewart, and who worked with him through a total of eight films, five of them Westerns, in a manner that put a whole new stamp on both men.

Anthony Mann was born Emil Anton Bundmann in San Diego on June 30, 1906. Stage-struck from youth, Mann had gotten involved with New York theater in 1925 at 19, as both actor and stage manager. By the early 1930s he was making a name as a stage director, and in 1938 he went to Hollywood, where David O. Selznick hired him as a test supervisor, talent scout and casting director. Soon he was an assistant director for Preston Sturges. With the outbreak of World War II, he changed his too-obvious German name and became Anthony Mann. From 1942 on, he directed forgettable low-budgeters for studios like Republic and RKO, among them also-rans like *Two O'Clock Courage* (1945), *Sing Your Way Home* (1945), and *Border Incident* (1949).

When he and Stewart found each other for *Winchester '73*, Mann was 44, Stewart 42. An intense male bonding set in, as they found that they complemented each other's needs, personal as well as professional. Mann, intensely masculine, obsessed with machismo, was compensating to an extreme for early identity problems. He was, in his way, a genius, with what one film commentator called "meticulous craftsmanship, a keen eye for spectacular outdoor cinematography, and an instinctive sense for the visual expression of inner conflicts." He was the perfect director for the newly rugged James Stewart. They rubbed off on each other. Stewart's sensitivity refined Mann's technique; Mann's intense awareness of his masculinity reinforced Stewart's own emergent macho self-image. "It was like a homoerotic love affair without the sex," as one actor on *Winchester '73* described it. "They fed off each other, on and off the set. One got the feeling Jimmy was playing to Tony alone, and that Tony was taking a deep subconscious joy from the blending of their creative macho inspirations." They were together constantly.

The James Stewart who stormed across the screens of America in *Winchester '73* was a far more tormented, more dimensional, and, oddly, more sexually and emotionally ambivalent figure than had been hitherto displayed. He plumbed dark reserves of desolation and revenge with an inner ferocity that, critics and audiences now realized, had always been a part of him but had never before emerged full-force.

Stewart himself has said of this period, "I knew I just had to get tougher on the screen; I knew I had to get taken seriously as an actor in certain ways that I never had before. I wanted to be completely myself, but a more dimensional self, with all my inner facets on view, *or at least as many as I cared to show.*"

Many film observers, to say nothing of his Hollywood friends and associates, were to conjecture, from 1950 on, that Stewart had proceeded to show far more than he realized, or bargained for.

No longer was Stewart passive in the face of older men's manipulations as a pliable young actor in early 1930s New York theatre. No longer was he content to tag along with Henry Fonda out of an agreeable helplessness. No longer would the almost feminine, whispery voice murmur ambivalently-flavored sweet nothings to the likes of Jean Arthur. Nor was this the awestruck and self-abnegating Stewart, who had hopelessly mooned over Margaret Sullavan, or who had played puerile, but super-sexy real-life swain to Norma Shearer or Olivia DeHavilland. That creature was nowhere to be found, once his new partnership with Anthony Mann was established.

George Cukor, always so direct and witty, had guided Stewart through his Oscar-winning role in *The Philadelphia Story* and at that time thought him "boyish, sweet, a little — or more than a little — passive." He once speculated that Jimmy's macho-buddy interplay with Tony Mann was "undoubtedly one of the great romances of his life, regardless of whether it was platonic or not."

Anthony Mann certainly felt the same way; this was a requited bonding, perhaps the most important of *his* life. When I interviewed Mann in connection with one of his more trivial later films, *Serenade* (1956), he extolled Stewart as one of the great male stars. He indicated, in rather extravagant terms for a man so essentially laconic, his deep respect for Stewart as both artist and man. He used terms on that occasion that were frankly hero-worshipping, and, oddly, those same terms were played back to me in Mann's direction when Stewart spoke of him to me a year later, in 1957.

Winchester '73 had been a low-priority script in the Universal stockpile for years. For some reason major male stars shied away from it, probably because its lead character was forced to express, in an unusual manner for a Western, complexities and contradictions that set up an alarm in their respective subconscious lives. Stewart and Mann saw it differently; it offered a chance for deepened characterization for Stewart, and a more probing and incisive directorial delineation for Mann. They snapped it up.

James Stewart, Shelley Winters, *Winchester '73*, UA, 1950

John Cocchi Collection

Stewart, significantly, has described his first meeting with Anthony Mann: "I felt here was a take-charge guy who knew what he was about; I felt here was a guy who would probe and push and force the kind of performance out of me I knew I was capable of—something new and fresh, something deep and probing."

Meanwhile, back in the year-old Stewart marital ménâge, Gloria, already pregnant, was giving such comments to the fan magazine *Movie Life* as: "I have never seen Jim so absorbed in his work. He brings it home with him from the studio; he has lost himself in his character...."

Winchester '73's script had already gone through several incarnations when the Robert Richards-Borden Chase screenplay finally made it before the cameras. Both gentlemen were later to concede that Mann's directorial highlightings and Stewart's interpolations of telling bits of business had given their work added depth and excitement. Always watchful on his friend and client Stewart's behalf, Lew Wasserman, who later became President of Universal Pictures, saw to it that the best of everything was provided, including the great William Daniels to photograph and Joseph Gershenson to provide the correct musical leitmotifs. A carefully chosen cast, featuring Shelley Winters at her saucy best, Dan Duryea at his nastiest, Stephen McNally, Millard Mitchell, John McIntire, Will Geer, Jay C. Flippen, Charles Drake, and a very young and untried Rock Hudson, at 25 attempting the role of an Indian chief, augmented the proceedings in fine style.

These handpicked people ably complemented the front-and-center Stewart and Mann, working so closely together that they were "almost making love to each other in a creative sense," as one of the actors put it.

The Mann-Stewart symbiosis was certainly not lost on a number of commentators, most notably Tony Thomas, who in *The Films of James Stewart*, remarked that in *Winchester '73* Stewart stood revealed as "an actor capable of displaying anger, neurosis and ferocity." Thomas described Mann as "a director of tough authority, and he seemed fascinated with the ambivalent nature of the human animal." According to Tony Thomas, Mann saw in Stewart "qualities that no other director had spotted — the ability to reveal the anger beneath the surface of even the most docile man, the containment of anger and temper, and the occasional bursting of that containment."

Winchester '73 is the story of a perfectly crafted, and highly prized, rifle in the Dodge City of 1873. Stewart and his estranged brother, who bears another name (Stephen McNally), compete fiercely for possession of it, and though Stewart wins, McNally steals it and sets off cross-country with Stewart in pursuit. What gives the pursuit an element of the demonic, is Stewart's determination to revenge his father's death at the hands of that same renegade brother — a revenge fed by long-standing fratricidal hatred.

McNally, adventuring hither and thither, manages to lose the precious weapon to John McIntire, an unscrupulous character who trades in guns with the Indians. Indian chief Rock Hudson kills McIntire and inherits the weapon, then after a massacre Charles Drake gets it. Shelley Winters enters the action here as Drake's girlfriend. Dan Duryea then kills Drake and gets a hold of the rifle. Stewart, in hot pursuit throughout these successive killings, dispatches Duryea, but not before he has choked from Duryea the whereabouts of the hated brother.

After all this phallic imagery gone berserk, Stewart and McNally engage in a macho mountaintop *Götterdämmerung*, and Stewart finally dispatches the parricidal brother. He also gets back the rifle, and even inherits Shelley Winters. One would think, from the plot, that Winters would get lost in all this darkly homoerotic chaos. (Mann treats each of the numerous shootings and killings as if they were successful orgasmic penetrations.) Instead she injects her insouciant self into the proceedings with a sardonic offhandedness that tells the audience: "These little boys are having a hard old time for themselves and I'm not here to *soften* it, but to *spice* it up."

One critic praised *Winchester '73* in the following terms:

"It is splendidly crafted, as is the rifle that is the centerpiece of its story. In essence the film is rather like a parable, with the rifle a mystical symbol of perfection for which men must strive, and in so doing reveal their character."

Seen today, *Winchester '73* comes on as powerful and arresting, acted with deep feeling and intense concentration, not only by Stewart but by all the supporting characters. It also comes across as a trenchant jamboree of sado-masochism, with the sought-after, fought-over rifle of the title a thinly disguised phallic symbol.

Broken Arrow was made before the epic *Winchester '73*, but was released two months after it, in 1950. Stewart plays a scout who seeks to heal the divisions between the Apaches and white men, in tandem with the Apache chief Cochise, played by Jeff Chandler. He does not even begin to reveal the force, tension and ferocity he managed under the direction of his alter-ego Anthony Mann in the later film.

In fact, critics commented — ironically enough, in view of later developments — that Stewart fell back too much on his well-known mannerisms. He seemed too detached and citified for Westerns — one critic even went so far as to call him "soft!"

While *Broken Arrow* is a perfectly acceptable depiction of frontier struggles, it does not display Stewart to the best advantage. Delmer Daves was a competent enough megaphoner, but he lacked the ultimate virility and intensity of Mann.

Darryl F. Zanuck, for whose 20th Century-Fox the film was made, had already become noted for his filmic attacks against racial prejudice and other forms of bigotry. *Broken Arrow*, shot in 1949, examines, rather intensely and pointedly, the mistreatment and crass exploitation of the Indians by whites in the early West. To Zanuck, this film was a pioneering concept in the name of tolerance. The theme had been touched on before, as far back as 1925 when Richard Dix starred in *The Vanishing American*, but the late 1940s and early 1950s were a particularly fertile time for such films. James Stewart, who had often made known his hatred of discrimination, was, in Zanuck's view, the perfect star for the occasion.

Though not of Indian blood, Jeff Chandler (born Ira Grossel) was quite apt and professional. He was so believable in the role of the Apache chief Cochise that he was to essay it again in *The Battle at Apache Pass* (1952). Chandler's facial bone structure lent itself to noble, incisive Indian profiles, and unlike other Caucasian actors he did not look out of place. He was even nominated for Best Supporting Actor at that year's Oscars.

The story of *Broken Arrow* is relatively simple and far less complicated than the more famous *Winchester '73*. Stewart wants to see justice for the Indians, even marries Indian Debra Paget (who is almost comically ill-suited to her role, looking unmistakably Caucasian, and comporting herself like a swimsuit model). Paget is killed in a skirmish, and an enraged Stewart is ready to lead the Apaches against his own people. The ever-wise Chandler counsels him that he must learn to live with his whiteness just as his new friends must contend with their own place in the cosmic scheme of things. Cochise has words of stark consolation for Stewart: "As I bear the murder of my people, so you will bear the murder of your wife."

The most interesting aspect of *Broken Arrow* is not the phony interracial romance between Stewart and Paget, but Stewart's relationship with Chandler's Cochise. There is intra-character complexity here, as Chandler struggles to overcome his distrust of all whites, and Stewart attempts to comprehend the different philosophy and cultural stance of the Indians.

While not particularly kind to the pre-Mann Western posturings of Stewart, the critics opined, as a whole, that *Broken Arrow* was a well-paced, creditably-intentioned film, and that it offered some interesting insights into the Apache culture. Stewart might have winced if he saw the Los Angeles review that stated:

"Despite a weak and wavering performance by Mr. Stewart, replete with his usual splutterings and shamblings that might have been cute in the man of 27 he once was but now seem backward in a man past 40, *Broken Arrow* reflects clearly the fine intentions of its makers and Darryl Zanuck's ongoing filmic pleas for tolerance."

Broken Arrow had been written by Michael Blankfort, based on a novel called *Blood Brother*, by Elliott Arnold. Some critics noted that the book had been stronger than the resultant movie, despite its handsome color by Ernest Palmer and restlessly insistent music by Hugo Friedhofer. Miss Paget was justly dismissed with terms like "tepid," "anemic," and "woefully miscast."

The Jackpot was well received when it premiered late in 1950, because it highlighted the comfortably beloved (and widely-expected) Stewart turn as the well-meaning little fellow who finds redemption by surviving assorted trials and tribulations. Stewart's timing, as always, was on target, but Walter Lang, clever as he could be, did not seem to be the director to nurse Stewart into a top-grade performance. The Phoebe Ephron-Henry Ephron screenplay, based on a John McNulty magazine article, was timely enough, considering that radio quiz shows and big winnings were constantly in the 1950 public's mind. It was surely intended to cash in on trends of that year, yet the result seems dated today. It is simply not the kind of picture that has a lasting appeal.

The plot has Stewart as a department store manager who wins $24,000 on a radio quiz program. This brings annoying, indeed exasperating, changes into his homelife with wife Barbara Hale and children Natalie Wood and Tommy Rettig. Inappropriate prizes flood in, obviously geared solely to merchandising whims; taxes come due with alarming persistence; Stewart is suspected of infidelity by his wife when a beautiful artist wants to paint his portrait; he gets involved with a fence when he tries to sell off his prizes, and temporarily winds up in jail; and his boss, Fred Clark, fires him due to one of those usual plot misunderstandings. After an hour of onscreen chaos, Hale realizes the artist was not after her husband, Clark realizes Stewart is an honest fellow after all, the fence bails him out of financial difficulties with a $5000 windfall (a highly unlikely plot turn), and things get back to what passes for normal in Hollywood contrivances like this.

Barbara Hale always had a healthy respect for Stewart, and she made the interesting point, in an interview in 1960, that Stewart's professionalism was often underrated because he ran the range of characters that only he could play, and was so often associated with the good guy at the mercy of fickle Fate. Hale must have been an avid Stewart film-watcher as well as admirer, for she noted: "There were numerous small variations in his portrayals even when he seemed to be ringing the same change on the same theme. Jimmy had a great respect for the acting craft, and I know he was always seeking out new nuances and emphases." She added: "As a co-worker he was warm, down-to-earth and delightful, always looking for ways to make the other actor in the scene look good along with him."

Natalie Wood, who had played child parts with the best, including Bette Davis and Claudette Colbert, told me that she was 12 years old when she did *The Jackpot*, and that Stewart couldn't have been nicer. In 1960 Natalie said, "He was only recently married then, and I don't think he had had his own children as yet, but in later years I was not at all surprised at reports that he had been a wonderful father to his daughters and to his stepsons because he made me as feel like I was really his daughter all through shooting of *The Jackpot*. I know Tommy [Rettig] who played my brother, felt the same way, because he told me."

As an adult star shooting what was to be her big breakthrough film, *Splendor in the Grass* (1961), Natalie, in our New York interview where *Splendor* was on location, said that Stewart would always be among the great, legendary stars because he was natural, honest and sincere in all his work, and was like that offscreen, too. "They talk a lot about 'the art that conceals art,'" Natalie said, "but Stewart was simply a natural talent — it all came spontaneously from instinct, as Garbo's did — pure instinct. It's there or it isn't there — with him it was there!"

Alan Mowbray, who played an eccentric interior decorator trying to redo the hapless leads' abode, against their protestations, commented interestingly about Stewart:" He never loses his natural poise even when up against actors whose style and approach are in striking variance with his own. They never outplay him; they have to settle for co-existence status." The critical verdict on *The Jackpot*: Amusing, but a trifle.

In 1950, with the termination of the long-running play's contract, *Harvey* was finally brought to the screen, with Stewart in the role of Elwood P. Dowd. A pixillated gentleman in his forties who has an inherited income, Elwood just wants to be helpful to others and to enjoy life. But he turns strangers, and his forebearing sister Veta (Josephine Hull), off when they discover that he has, as his great and good friend, a 6-foot-tall rabbit called Harvey. They consider his pooka to be a product of his mildly deranged imagination, and he almost gets committed to a mental hospital. But when his sister and his doctor start imagining that they, too, see Harvey, things turn around. Veta is advised by a sympathetic taxi driver that Elwood might lose his sweetness if cured, and might turn into just another neurotic, "normal" character.

The plot was not new to Stewart, as he had replaced Frank Fay in it several times on Broadway when Fay was either on vacation or doing the play elsewhere. Many felt that Fay should have been allowed to do the film version, but Fay had been proven "not cinematic" in the 1930s. The part called for a man with a command of film technique and a screen presence — namely Stewart.

Nonetheless, when the reviews of *Harvey* came out at the Christmas 1950 release (it had been made in the spring, before *The Jackpot*, but released after it), Stewart suffered in contrast with the Fay concept of the role among some key critics. In spite of kind voices, like the *Library Journal* pundit who declared "as the generous and pleasant Elwood [Stewart] gives one of his finest performances," *Newsweek* drove in the shaft with: "Although Stewart lacks the precision, timing and the delicately deranged humor that Frank Fay brought to the original Elwood, his amiable, gregarious [impersonation] is a very satisfactory substitute." The *Saturday Review* put it even more pointedly, declaring, "[Stewart's] Elwood does lack something of the magic of Frank Fay's wizened creation, perhaps because Mr. Stewart just doesn't look like the kind of man who ever spent much time in a barroom." And *Time* declared Stewart's Elwood to be "an able actor's performance, but one that subtly dilutes the quality of the whole play. Dowd takes on the coloration of Stewart's movie personality, the gangling awkwardnesses, the fumbling, apologetic gestures, the verbal false starts."

Stewart reportedly studied these reviews and conceded to friends that they had some validity. Luckily for his histrionic self-esteem, he was to get other chances at *Harvey* on TV, and on the stage in 1972, that satisfied both him and his critics. He was, in time, to get a solid grasp of the role, especially with Helen Hayes opposite him as his sister, and he kept his Hollywood mannerisms to a minimum.

Among those who, in 1950, congratulated Stewart on his filmic interpretation of Dowd was Barbara Stanwyck, an actress he always regretted not working with in any medium. "We've just *got* to do a movie or something together some day!" Missy, as Stanwyck was affectionately known to all, would tell him when they met at parties. Wife of his onetime MGM colleague Robert Taylor and a great star in her own right, Stanwyck had also been the wife of Frank Fay. There had been no love lost between them; Fay's drinking and insecurity about her success in films made their parting a bitter and unfriendly one. When Fay made his original hit in *Harvey* on Broadway in 1944, Stanwyck had been scheduled to visit New York from Hollywood. A friend told her to go see her ex-husband's startling renaissance in a role that afforded him stardom after years of relative obscurity. Stanwyck's tart reply was, "No thanks! I saw all the rabbits Fay had in his hat years ago!" Stanwyck told Stewart in 1950 that Fay, fine as she had heard he was on the stage, could not have brought Dowd alive onscreen as Stewart had done. Biased as she may have been, Stanwyck had a point.

Stewart was to get an Academy Award nomination for *Harvey*, but lost the 1950 Oscar to Jose Ferrer's Cyrano de Bergerac. Josephine Hull, reprising the sister role she had played with Fay on the stage, did win a Best Supporting Actress Oscar. Repeating their Broadway roles were other supports Jesse White and Victoria Horne, with Hollywood regulars Charles Drake, Peggy Dow, and Cecil Kellaway lending able support.

In 1953, I interviewed Frank Fay at the Lambs Club. He had had a few drinks that day, but was in a fairly genial mood until I brought up *Harvey*. It was obvious he was disappointed that he hadn't played it on film. "I knew enough about movies from those early talkies I did to have brought it off," he said. "I think this business of creating a role on Broadway, putting your heart and guts into it, and then having some other actor cash in on it and become more identified with it, just because he is 'cinematic' or whatever-the-fuck it is, is stinking lousy!"

Produced by John Beck and directed by Henry Koster, the movie *Harvey* was written by Mary Chase and Oscar Brodney based on Chase's play, which had gone on to win a Pulitzer Prize. It was

James Stewart, Josephine Hull, *Harvey*, UA, 1950

ably photographed by William Daniels and the music by Frank Skinner was not unduly intrusive.

Harvey's enduring appeal is based on the notion that illusion, even an illusion that borders on the pathological can, if it is comforting and promotes peace and well-being, be infinitely preferable to the harshness of bleak reality, with its assorted painful compromises. Of course, one has to win others over to this way of thinking, but, since everybody is a little crazy in one way or another, the 6-foot rabbit is to be seen as a palliative being. If Dowd's sister and his doctor imagine that they, too, have seen and talked with the beneficent bunny, it is because they suffer unfulfilling illusions that Harvey satisfies.

Harvey did well at the 1950 box office, and was one of Stewart's great personal favorites among his performances. He has called it "sweet and good and well-meaning."

No Highway in the Sky was produced in England, Stewart's first film shot outside of his native land. He had the Hollywood expertise of director Henry Koster, some good fellow actors, and a fairly well-paced script based on a Nevil Shute novel, but the result does not deserve a high listing in the Stewart film pantheon.

Stewart portrays an eccentric, constantly bemused aviation scientist who is an expert in metal fatigue. He alarms everyone on a trans-Atlantic plane by predicting that the tail will fall off after a flying time of 1440 hours, which the plane is imminently approaching. Among his fellow passengers are movie star Marlene Dietrich and stewardess Glynis Johns. The pilot, and later the authorities, dismiss him as a nut, especially after he pulls a lever on a stopover in Newfoundland that releases the undercarriage and wrecks the plane.

Back in England, he is in for big, predictable trouble but later tests prove his calculations correct. Meanwhile, Johns moves in with him to help take care of his somewhat neglected daughter (Stewart is a widower) and Dietrich waxes more maternal than romantic, looking in on him and Johns and taking his side against the authorities. A promise of amour between Stewart and Dietrich is never fulfilled, as they talk about their lives on the plane and she goes to sleep on his shoulder. It is Johns who gets him, and presumably his daughter, and so she must be considered the co-star of the film. Dietrich's footage is limited to what is essentially a supporting role, though it looks like it was deliberately fattened to give the flacks an opportunity to herald a screen reunion of Stewart and Dietrich after twelve years and their 1939 success, *Destry Rides Again*. In no respect is *No Highway in the Sky* to be considered a successful Stewart-Dietrich reprise, and Stewart, though expert as always, seems slightly ill at ease among the accents and disparate styles of such British actors as Jack Hawkins and Maurice Denham. Despite its Hollywood-wise director, *No Highway in the Sky* seems more British than American in overall style and feel, and one gets the feeling that any number of British actors could have done as well as Stewart.

Stewart was initially attracted to the movie because it seemed an interesting variation on his audience-pleasing turn as the misunderstood loner who triumphs over adversity. But the theatrical potential, despite his slouching, detailed characterization of a work-obsessed drone, is somewhat dimmed and perfunctory.

As her autobiography makes only too abundantly clear, Marlene Dietrich was no Stewart fan, though she was enough of a professional to recognize his skills. Considering what she had said of him during and after the *Destry Rides Again* shooting, it is surpising that she agreed to work with him again, even after a dozen years. Reportedly, she needed the money, and objectively realized that Stewart's name would carry the picture. Even so, it must have been humiliating to her to realize that hers was a character role. Though approaching fifty when she made the film, Dietrich looks young and glamorous and is superbly coutured. As movie luminary Monica Teasdale, her performance, what there is of it, is warm and animated. She is forced, by the script, to make a rather perfunctory speech to Johns to the effect that the latter is better suited to domesticity than a careerist like herself. Dietrich admirers were left wishing that the women's roles had been combined and that Marlene had gotten her man.

One critic reported: "Stewart and Dietrich are reunited on the marquee, to be sure, but it is the younger Glynis Johns who lands him. The plot is okay but there is a *déja vu* feeling about it all, and 43-year-old Stewart and almost-fifty Marlene generate no sparks despite the fact she looks sensational throughout. Blame the scriptwriters."

The Greatest Show on Earth was an opulent Cecil B. DeMille circus extravagana, one of the big filmic outings of 1952, and much publicized. Though ridiculed by some critics, the film surprised one and all by winning the Oscar for Best Picture and Best Story, proving as always that he (DeMille) who laughs last, laughs best.

In an all-star story that included the likes of Charlton Heston (who had the nominal starring part if screen time is any indication), Betty Hutton, Cornel Wilde, Dorothy Lamour, and Gloria Grahame, James Stewart, surprisingly, accepted and shone in, a role as a clown called Buttons who never removes his makeup throughout. The reason emerges at the climax when he saves Heston's life in a train wreck by applying his surgeon's skills. It turns out that he is a doctor wanted for the mercy killing of his wife. He is then arrested by the detective (Henry Wilcoxon) who has been long on his trail.

In the midst of all the three-ring hoopla, elaborately tricked up by super-showman DeMille, it is impressive that Stewart manages, despite limited footage, to deliver a believable and human performance. His heavy makeup, with its chalk-white pastiness, enlarged mouth and soaring eyebrows, to say nothing of outlandish costumes, would have distracted from the impact of a lesser actor. In the climactic scene, when his life-saving ethic as a doctor triumphs over his self-preservation, he is indeed admirable, and almost steals the picture.

In one interview, Stewart said he had conceived his role as a sort of *hommage* to the late great silent star Lon Chaney, who had essayed similarly tragic figures hiding beneath disguises. Each was an actor of highly individual mystique and histrionic aplomb; each brought an integrity and dedication to such a role as this, which the critics did not fail to note, with Stewart winning deserved kudos.

"The man can do anything!" Cecil DeMille told me excitedly when I interviewed him in New York in 1956 (he was there for the opening of *The Ten Commandments*). "Jimmy Stewart is one of the most versatile of actors, and people just don't seem to realize it as they should! They still think him the shy, gangling, awkward but endearing buffoon of his earlier pictures, but this man is a fine artist who can do anything he sets out to!"

Also in Stewart's corner was Charlton Heston, who told me that same year that Stewart's wise performance had vastly enhanced *The*

Charlton Heston, James Stewart, *The Greatest Show on Earth*, Paramount, 1952

Greatest Show on Earth. "I had admired his work long before I myself entered movies," Heston said, "and it was a privilege to appear with him in that film. And he accomplished, for my money, a real miracle in getting across his emotions so strongly and so poignantly while covered with all that outlandish clown makeup. It takes a *real* actor to bring *that* off!"

The Greatest Show on Earth, of course, is ridden with a tangle of romantic subplots: aerialist Betty Hutton carrys a secret torch for oblivious Heston, while The Great Sebastian (Cornel Wilde) is in love with *her*. Elephant performer Gloria Grahame, in turn, has the hots for Wilde, which drives elephant trainer Lyle Bettger, who is in love with Grahame, to such anguish that he cuts out from the circus and brings about the climactic train wreck.

Stewart himself has said of his clown-surgeon role in *The Greatest Show on Earth*, "I'd rather have a role that is brief in running-time terms but that has some substance and depth, and I took that part because it presented a challenge and one I felt compelled to meet. At the end of shooting, I felt inwardly that I had accomplished what I set out to do, which is what every actor hopes for." The critics agreed with Stewart. "Honest, poignant, sensibly underplayed, deeply felt" were among the encomiums they lavished on him.

Two years after their initial felicitous pairing, Stewart and Anthony Mann were reunited for yet another Western, *Bend of the River* (1952). Again their work together turned highly rewarding, reviews hailing the fine blend of fierce action and profound, depthful characterization that had become the masterful Mann's specialty.

And yet again the star and director got wrapped up in an intense creative absorption. On the location shooting they spent sixteen hours a day together, analyzing the character of Stewart's Glyn McLyntock and all the other interrelationships in the story. In an interview that same year, in describing male-male friendship at its best, Mann remarked that "a true friend becomes like one's other self — or part of one." Stewart, as usual, seemed to take on an extra glow in Mann's company. They counted themselves lucky to have a taut, well-written script by the same Borden Chase who had collaborated in their *Winchester '73* opus. Irving Glassberg photographed in handsome color, and Hans Salter's music highlighted the action. More than one critic noted that in some scenes Stewart looked a good ten years younger than his admitted 44 years. Cast members also noted that he hugely enjoyed his work on *Bend of the River*, was the first one on location, and couldn't wait to begin each day.

Stewart had the advantage of a worthy co-star in *Bend of the River*. The admirable Arthur Kennedy, then about 38, had been brought to Hollywood by James Cagney, who had admired him in a play. He was immediately off to the races as Cagney's younger brother in his first film, the Anatole Litvak-directed *City for Conquest* in 1940. Kennedy, while never achieving major star status, proceeded over the twelve years between *City* and *Bend*, to develop an estimable career as a highly respected character actor in roles that ranged from the tormented Branwell Brontë in *Devotion* (1946) to Tom in *The Glass Menagerie* (1950). When I interviewed Arthur Kennedy in 1953, a year after the release of *Bend of the River*, he expressed fervent admiration for the skills of Anthony Mann and James Stewart. His references to Stewart were particularly warm, calling him "versatile" and "hardworking."

Stewart, Mann, and the other cast members, who included such character stalwarts as Jay C. Flippen, Harry Morgan and Royal Dano, spent weeks on location. Kennedy, always loquacious, made some shrewd observations about his co-star. He felt that Stewart, who, in 1951, found himself with new twin daughters in addition to two stepsons, relished the time away from home. Domesticity, children, and even the devoted ministrations of a loving wife, got on his nerves after a while, hence his joy in male company and the wilderness. "He did get hitched rather late in life," Kennedy said, "and while a wonderful husband and father, I think he missed the freedom he had had before. He seemed to me often tense, ready to cut loose, and his role in *Bend of the River* certainly gave him the range for that!"

Kennedy, described by one critic as "a highly subtle actor whose surface friendliness and affability usually concealed either weakness or malice or both," is in his element in *Bend of the River*. Stewart matches him all the way as a former outlaw who guides a wagon train of settlers to Oregon. There he gets double-crossed by associates who try to divert essential supplies to gold-rush activities. Kennedy is Stewart's *bête noire*, a former companion-in-crime whom Stewart saves from hanging, and who helps him fight the Indians on the way to Oregon. Tricky and unreliable, Kennedy turns on him and is later killed for his pains by an exasperated and enraged Stewart. Julie Adams is along for the ride as a love interest of sorts, but she gets short shrift in all the macho interplay. Stewart, under Mann's intense guidance, is once more startlingly vivid as a laconic, quiet man driven by betrayal to demoniacal fury. "Mr. Stewart continues to develop interestingly as a delineator of complex characters who seethe and churn beneath deceptive exteriors," one critic noted.

In 1952, Stewart went back to MGM for his first picture there in three years, *Carbine Williams*, under the uninspired direction of workmanlike Richard Thorpe. Art Cohn wrote the screenplay, based on a true story, with fine photography by William Mellor.

Carbine Williams is a creditable but scarcely top-grade Stewart vehicle, and when it was released many of his fans wondered why he had accepted the uncharacteristic role. Williams was a convict who invented a short-stroke piston which became the key element in the M-1 carbine. When developed by Winchester, it revolutionized U.S. Army tactics and was credited by General MacArthur as a deciding factor in the World War II Pacific victory.

David Marshall "Carbine" Williams is certainly not a character in the sympathetic league of such other Stewart onscreen biographical subjects as Monty Stratton, Glenn Miller, and Charles Lindbergh. In the early 1920s, Williams is a metalworker in North Carolina who gets involved in bootlegging on the side. He is accused of killing a revenue agent, though he was one of many present at the time. When a protracted court trial results in a hung jury, he is forced to plead guilty of Second Degree murder to avoid a risky retrial. Sentenced to thirty years, he is a prison rebel and is punished with chain-gang work. The prison warden (Wendell Corey) comes upon him, after he has served a month in solitary confinement for one of his stunts, and rehabilitates him with machine shop work. Here he begins to reveal mechanical aptitude, and with a pipe, wire, and scraps of metal, develops the new carbine mechanism. Corey fights the prison authorities to allow him to test it. The test is a success. The governor then pardons Williams, who has served an eight-year stretch, and goes on to develop numerous patents.

The original Carbine Williams was on hand throughout the shooting to give both writer Cohn and director Thorpe sharp, telling insights which assured the authenticity of the proceedings.

He was often on the set with Stewart and Bobby Hyatt, the young actor who played his own son David.

Jean Hagen has a nice little part as the loving wife and mother who loyally stands by Carbine, and she and Stewart have some affecting scenes together. But despite the authentic background, the steady direction of Thorpe ("Steady, but never particularly inspired," as the blunt Wendell Corey once described him) and the solid efforts of his fellow actors, Stewart was hard put to make the complex character of Carbine Williams believable.

Part of the problem lay in the ambivalence of the original character. It was never established if Williams had indeed shot the revenue agent, and he wasn't about to enlighten anyone. The man had been a tough convict, difficult and intractable, and his earlier activities in bootlegging and the shifty quality of his life somehow did not compensate for his inventive skills. What Stewart had to contend with here was an ill-defined, unsympathetic character who appeared opportunistic and self-seeking. Had his genius for invention not reshaped the quality of his life, there is little question as to how Williams would have turned out. Stewart did the best he could to make sense of an essentially enigmatic man, but this is not one of his fans' or critics' favorites. Even Stewart's own attitude toward it was contradictory, as he told me in 1964: "The role was challenging and I did the best I could with it. Some liked me in it. Others didn't. Everyone has a right to his or her opinion." (Which, at the time, struck me as damning with faint praise.)

Certainly the man on whom the film was based was highly pleased with it, and after its release Williams went around telling the press in city after city that it was as authentic a depiction of his life as any man could desire. That writer, director, and star had caught the man's essential trickiness and instability, along with his great mechanical talent, did not seem to occur to him. Possibly he saw himself objectively and was simply flattered, in any event, to be a movie subject.

Having weathered the mixed critical reaction to *Carbine Williams*, and the competent but impersonal ministrations of Dick Thorpe, Stewart made it plain to MGM that for the second of his two-picture independent deal, *The Naked Spur* (1953), no one else in the world but Anthony Mann would do for director. Mann was signed up for the film, their third Western together. And once again the strange Stewart-Mann *simpatico* wrought its telling magic: *The Naked Spur* is regarded as one of the best Westerns ever made, and the duo had the satisfaction of topping even themselves this time around.

In *The Naked Spur* (as phallic a title as one could wish) Stewart, at 45, gives a performance so intense and taut as to border, in the words of one critic, on the hysterical. It was shot for many weeks on location in the Rockies, thus giving the star and director a lengthy period to commune creatively and personally.

Considerable critical interest was again stirred up by the fact that, when directed by Mann, Stewart took on a fierce, almost pathological aspect never before associated with him, a sort of diabolical aura. Whatever it was, it played most effectively. It was once more apparent to his fellow actors that Stewart relished mightily being away from hearth and home. Even Henry Fonda, who greatly admired *The Naked Spur*, later made the irreverent observation that the Mann westerns, and his other action pix of the Fifties and Sixties, probably saved Stewart's marriage. They at least gave him a semblance of footloose freedom, reminiscent of his bachelor days. Even more bluntly, and possibly with a hint of jealousy, because he had never aroused such personal devotion from Stewart, Fonda called Mann "the nearest thing to a Svengali that Jimmy ever had."

As in the first two Mann-Stewart films, it is the atmosphere, the subtle emotional colorations, the psychological underpinnings, and above all, the intensity which count. The plot, which, in this case is not particularly original, doesn't matter much at all.

Written by Sam Rolfe and Harold Jack Bloom and beautifully photographed in stern, sharp color by William Nellor, *The Naked Spur* tells the story of Stewart, once a landowner cheated out of his property, who has taken to bounty hunting as the quickest way to regain a measure of respectability. He is hot on the trail of murderer Robert Ryan, who has a $5000 reward on his head, dead or alive. Janet Leigh, the token woman in the cast, seems incongruous, though she does her earnest best to temper the intensities of the men, who include rascally Ralph Meeker and sly Millard Mitchell. Once captured, the saturnine, wily Ryan turns the men against each other, and almost escapes. But he is finally killed by Stewart after a multiplicity of the usual vicissitudes, during which Stewart gets his life saved by Leigh. She had originally been drawn to Meeker, but was finally won over to the bounty-hunter's side.

Ostensibly, Stewart finds his renewed decency thanks to Leigh, who persuades him to bury Ryan's dead body rather than cart it back for the reward. Allowing for decomposition problems, this seems like a judicious decision. In a final scene that is widely admired by critics for its purgative éclat, but which, to even an elementary Freudian, smacks of a homoeroticism thoroughly out of control, Stewart breaks down and weeps. He finally grasps the inhumanity of his bounty-hunting obsession, and is shriven for his preoccupation with the roped body as a merely commercial property. There is a fallacious note to the dénouement, when Stewart asks Leigh to go on to California now that he is allegedly purged. One gets the feeling he would still prefer to be bounty-hunting and killing other men rather than settling down with Leigh; women simply don't register in his scheme of things.

Ralph Meeker matches Stewart in his tense, hostile projections, and Ryan is in his Faustian element as the evildoer who finally falls victim to the driven Stewart. Janet Leigh, when I asked her about the film in 1957, was terse and to the point. "It was a man's picture, all the way," she said.

Janet Leigh, in her autobiography, recounts pleasant memories of shooting *The Naked Spur*. She mentions that, in this picture anyway, Gloria Stewart joined them for a time on location. "We were housed," Leigh recalled, "about twenty-five miles from the town of Durango, in a complex of cabins on the perimeter of the main building, where we ate and played when we had the energy. [Jimmy and Gloria] occupied the same quarters Clark Gable and Lady [Sylvia] Ashley lived in when Gable shot *Lone Star* (1952) in this area a year or so before."

Leigh recalled that Ashley (Gable's third wife) must have done some remodeling, as their cabin boasted the most modern décor. "But although they were primitive, the cabins were comfortable and clean," Leigh remembered. "It was a congenial, pleasant, cheerful group, and I believe everyone thoroughly enjoyed themselves." Leigh wrote that she and husband Tony Curtis celebrated their first anniversary on that location "and Gloria and the major domo put together a bash." She remembered Tony haunting the fishing streams and doing some painting. "Certainly," Janet loyally added,

"[Tony] was surrounded by a gorgeous palette of natural colors. He also had an inborn flair with a paintbrush."

Leigh never forgot Stewart's consummate professionalism. She, Robert Ryan and Stewart were doing an emotional scene, and "Mother Nature was not fully cooperating. The wind was strong, and the sun capriciously played peekaboo with the clouds.

"Jimmy was propped against a tree trunk, and Bob and I faced him. We were able to shoot the master and Jimmy's closeup without too much interference. But the reverse angle on Bob and me presented a dilemma." Leigh recounted that the background showed the sky and the landscape, and the light changes were a source of much bafflement and frustration among the crew. The assistant director told Stewart that he was free to leave, but as Leigh recalled it, Stewart replied: "Well, I can't do that, you see, because, well, that wouldn't be right, now, would it? I think I'll just — hang around — and be off camera — for my friends there."

Stewart remained for the entire tedious afternoon, and wound up playing the scene behind the camera while it was focused on Ryan and Leigh. To Leigh, "*That* is a pro! It makes my blood boil when I hear instances of recent 'stars' insisting their closeups and shots be done first so they can leave, thus forcing their fellow actors to emote with a detached script supervisor. You'll never have it reported that a real star was guilty of such egregious behavior!"

To Janet Leigh, Stewart was that "real star."

"One picture I *did* want a part of was *The Naked Spur*," wrote Leigh. I tested with a giant — the man and his talent — James Stewart. Anthony Mann, the director (fittingly named, for he was a real man's man), and producer William Wright had to determine if we sparked the proper chemistry. I guess we did, because I won the coveted role. Oh glory, was I happy!"

Leigh recalled that "My hair was chopped short as if I had done it myself. I wore old pants and a shirt, hardly any makeup, and I played a tough, spirited, uneducated daughter of a dead outlaw. Lissy Anne was a mountain lass, but this firecracker was altogether different. Challenging, evocative, almost an anti-heroine." Leigh remembered the location, near Durango, Mexico, as beautiful country, "in the rugged Rocky Mountains," where "wild rivers raged," "with terrifying boulders jutting high above the whipped waters."

She and the cool, collected Stewart and Ryan, had their cresting sequence on a plateau of one of the dizzying cliffs. They filmed the climb up, and she found it petrifying, while the men were exhilarated. She remembered the panic she felt up on top, looking down at the angry water. "With no guard rails, with no nothin'! As in any self-respecting climax, there was a fight-to-the-finish encounter. Up there! Dramatic, to be sure! The fear we registered was *genuine*!" Stewart, however, was totally unperturbable and restrainedly businesslike. "His self-containment was a real wonder!" Leigh marvelled.

Feeling that they might have run the Western genre into the ground, Stewart and Mann, now regarded by Hollywood executives as regular partners, struck out for what they thought were fresh pastures. *Thunder Bay* (1953), an action-filled, testosterone-emphatic story about the rivalry between wildcat oil drillers and shrimp fishermen on the Gulf coast, was the first of two films they contracted for, on profitable freelance terms, with Universal.

A strong cast was marshaled for this, including such old standbys as Harry Morgan, Dan Duryea and Jay C. Flippen. Joanne Dru and Marcia Henderson were forgettably, and rather peripherally, in attendance as the women who added plot complications. But again this was strictly a man's picture, with Joanne Dru later echoing the sentiments of Janet Leigh.

The New York Times put it this way when it came review-time: "James Stewart is properly tough, harried, begrimed and laconic as the indomitable wildcatter whose dream finally comes true." It seems that Stewart and partner Duryea have come up with a drilling platform that resists the encroachments of even the worst storms. Away they go to find offshore oil, with the blessing of business magnate Jay C. Flippen. The drilling conflicts with the plans of shrimp fishermen who are trying to locate new beds. Duryea introduces complications by falling in love with the girlfriend of one of the fishermen, whose sister, Joanne Dru, sets her cap for Stewart. But the machinations of the girls seem like tired, tepid stuff measured against the conflicts between the guys, which is actually the main thrust of the picture. After numerous obstacles, fierce storms, romantic distrust (Stewart suspects Dru for a while, of being on the fishermen's side), and the withdrawal of backer Flippen, who has lost faith in the project, all ends well when Stewart (improbably) discovers not only oil but a plentiful source of shrimp. Almost as a plot afterthought, Stewart and Dru pair off, and the former enemies become allies as they ply their fruitful trades.

Stewart and Mann went off once more on a lengthy location trek, this time to the Gulf Coast off Louisiana. They took along famous photographer William Daniels, who outdid himself with the color photography here. Once again it was noted in the columns that Stewart seemed to enjoy lengthy location treks, with Gloria home raising the two-year-old twins, and her boys. "Do they miss each other during these long location sojourns that Hubby must of necessity undergo?" cooed a *Movie Life* writer. "No, this is a marriage based on mutual understanding [sic] and Gloria knows that she is mistress of the home while Jimmy goes out earning the bread." Be that as it may, some gossip started up about the frequent marital separations. In a more sophisticated time, jokes might have been cracked about the fact that Stewart spent far more time with Mann than he did with his wife. It also might have been noted that after the birth of the twins in 1951, Jimmy and Gloria had no further children. Asked by Louella Parsons in 1953 if he hoped for a larger family, Stewart, just before leaving with Mann for location on *Thunder Bay*, harrumphed, "I have four now — the two boys, and the twins. Gloria and I have, already, a big family!" To another interviewer, for *Modern Screen*, a dour and reticent Stewart (as described by the writer) said that he had first become a father at age 43 (not counting the stepsons) and that he wanted to live to see his kids grow up. Children, he pontificated, after a certain age were an unfair risk to both parent and child, given too great an age difference — one excuse, as a wag of the time put it, being as good as another....

Thunder Bay was fairly well received by critics and public, and made a nice profit for Universal. Asked if he and Mann felt they functioned better together in Westerns, Stewart huffed that *Thunder Bay was* a Western, with boats and oil substituting for horses and guns.

Perhaps to demonstrate that they could, in fact, make a movie with a theme that was not Western, the Stewart-Mann combine decided, in 1953, to do the life of Glenn Miller. This was their second picture under their current arrangement with Universal. Written by Valentine Davies and Oscar Brodney, *The Glenn Miller Story* (1953) was based on the famous trombonist and bandsman, whose death in 1944 saddened America. It was photographed by the always reliable

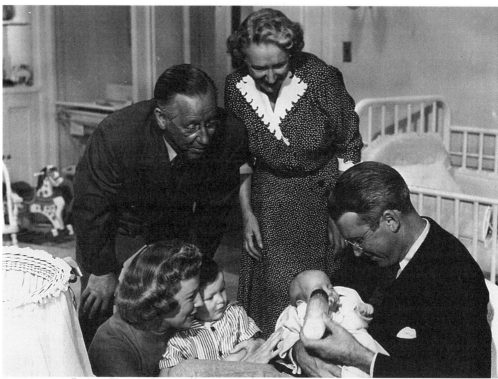

Irving Bacon, June Allyson, Katherine Warren, James Stewart,
The Glenn Miller Story, UA, 1953

William Daniels, with Joseph Gershenson providing apropos musical direction that ably captured the Miller spirit.

There was some opposition at Universal to the idea of Anthony Mann directing a film that was heavy on the music and light on the drama. Stewart's insistence that his friend be assigned may be seen, in retrospect, as one of his career's *faux pas*. There was criticism around the lot that Stewart's desire to work with Mann, regardless of the subject, had clouded his judgment. The director's aptitude for such material was severely limited, but Stewart insisted, and Mann proceeded to turn in a workmanlike but uninspired job.

In Mann's defense, there was very little for him to do. The musical interludes and famous Miller songs and routines take up most of the film's rather protracted 116 minutes. The actual story, what there is of it, was stinted, perhaps of necessity, because Miller's private life seems to have been spectacularly pedestrian and dull. Drafted for yet another wifely incarnation was June Allyson, who practically reprised wholesale her work in *The Stratton Story*. Again she is the gal in the background who, once married, is supportive and inspirational. She bails him out of a tough spot when he needs money, having saved (conveniently) in her kitty the exact amount he needs to start his own band. There's a smidgen of the usual Hollywood pathos thrown in: When it turns out Allyson can't have children, the script solves the problem forthwith by letting them adopt two little ones. And so forth and so on. Though the film follows the Miller life story with reasonable fidelity, it was a tedious and predictable story to begin with. Allyson tries her darndest to inject warmth and humor into it, but with only partial success. She was hardly to blame: the deadly, sentimental situations defeated her.

When I asked June Allyson about *The Glenn Miller Story* during a 1957 interview, she said, "I always hugely enjoyed working with Jimmy; I knew I was there as a back-up more than anything else but that was okay. I was honored to be working with such a fine actor, and it was pleasant going from start to finish." Asked if she didn't think the plots of both pictures were banal, she rejoindered: "Well, they were biographical films, weren't they, and we had to stay faithful to the actualities — and life often *is* banal, isn't it?"

The story traces Miller's progress from trombonist to band leader and, finally, to organizer of musical entertainment for World War II American troops. In the course of his duties he disappears in a plane flight over the English Channel. His body was never found. At the time, the actual Glenn Miller was only forty, and for years his death was widely mourned by the many fans he had made with the new sound he had introduced into dance music. Much footage is taken up with his popular hit numbers, well performed by guest stars like Frances Langford, Gene Krupa, the Modernaires and Louis Armstrong. Henry Mancini, later to be famous, did much of the arranging of such Miller standards as "Little Brown Jug," "Moonlight Serenade" (composed by Miller himself), and "In the Mood."

Stewart applied his natural musical expertise to faithfully approximating Miller's playing style on the trombone, with trombonist Joe Yuki hired to record the actual sounds. In "juxtaposition pix" sent out by the Universal publicity department, Stewart, in glasses and winning grin, replete with trombone, bore only a passing resemblance to Miller, but nobody minded. One critic yawned at "Jimmy Stewart in yet another of his biographical treatises. It's 90 percent music, eight percent plot, and two percent Stewart mugging." Most critics were similarly lukewarm.

Grace Kelly, James Stewart, *Rear Window*, Paramount, 1954

Chapter Twelve

Life on Hitchcock Heights

Despite his rather macabre and psychologically risky experience with Hitchcock in *Rope*, a picture he was to privately regret ever having made, Stewart continued to be fascinated by Hitchcock's artistry. Six years later, he made the second of his four films with him. The three films that paired Stewart with Hitchcock in the 1950s were among the best Stewart ever made, and they stand high in the Hitchcock creative pantheon also.

Rear Window (1954) (doubtless to Stewart's inner sigh of relief) had nothing to do with homoeroticism or superman theories or master-and-slave relationships. Produced and directed by Hitchcock for Paramount, and written by John Michael Hayes from the Cornell Woolrich novelette, *Rear Window* follows a linear plot-line of accumulating horror and suspense. It deals with one of Hitchcock's favorite leitmotifs — the gradual emergence of sinister events from an ostensibly placid existence.

Stewart plays L.B. "Jeff" Jeffries, a successful photographer who has sustained a broken leg in the course of his work. Confined to a wheelchair, he amuses himself with voyeuristic observations of his neighbors across the courtyard in a New York apartment complex. Bored and distressed by the unaccustomed physical inactivity, he gradually acquaints himself, almost out of necessity, with their daily routines; among them are a Miss Lonely Hearts who has problems with male visitors, and a sexy, busty type whom he dubs Miss Torso. And then there is dour, heavyset Raymond Burr. He is always having quarrels with his wife, and he attracts Stewart's special interest.

After he has acquired high-powered binoculars, Stewart turns more and more into a Peeping Tom. He elicits the scorn of his nurse-therapist Thelma Ritter, who tells him he ought to be thoroughly disgusted with himself. He finds himself discussing his neighbors with his fashion-model girlfriend, Grace Kelly, and his cop pal, Wendell Corey, who at first laugh off his harmless, but mildy perverse "hobby."

But Ritter and Kelly, and finally Corey, come to think he has something worth investigating when he notes that Burr's invalid wife seems to have disappeared. Burr makes surreptitious dead-of-night trips in and out of his apartment, smuggling a saw and carving knives wrapped in newspapers.

Kelly enters Burr's apartment and is trapped by him. He realizes he is being stalked by Stewart and that the latter knows he has murdered his wife. Burr tries to kill Stewart, who blinds him temporarily with flashlight explosions from his professional equipment. Corey finally saves Stewart as he hangs from a window ledge with Burr pounding on his hands. In a comic twist, Stewart falls three stories to the courtyard, breaks the other leg, and is doubtless doomed to lots more window-watching.

In an interview on *Rear Window*, Hitchcock, in answer to some critics' comments on the blatant voyeurism, stated that movies are inherently a voyeuristic medium, eliciting more vicarious intimacy from the audience than any art form before or since. The film was praised for its multi slices of life, tragic, comic, humdrum, all of them recognizable aspects of the human condition.

Grace Kelly's relationship with her wheelchair-bound lover is slyly depicted by Hitchcock. It is more erotic than it appears, with the implication that Stewart's enforced passivity does not preclude Kelly's aggressive come-ons. There were many stories that Grace Kelly, still single and playing the field (the film was made two years before she married Prince Rainier), had developed a woman-size crush on Stewart. Stewart did nothing to encourage (or discourage) her, but Thelma Ritter told me she felt he enjoyed Grace's attraction to him. "I think it took him back to his fancy-free, footloose bachelor days; I don't say he flirted, but he didn't seem to mind it either," she laughed.

Stewart, as he usually did in such cases, made extra daily phone calls to wife Gloria at home, especially as she had told several fan-magazine writers that his romantic onscreen dalliances with various screen lovelies made her nervous. Sensing her insecurity, he gave her little extra attentions to reassure her that she was very much permanent head woman.

Grace Kelly made all parties a bit anxious by declaring to Louella Parsons and Hedda Hopper that she found Stewart to be one of the most masculinely attractive men she had ever known.

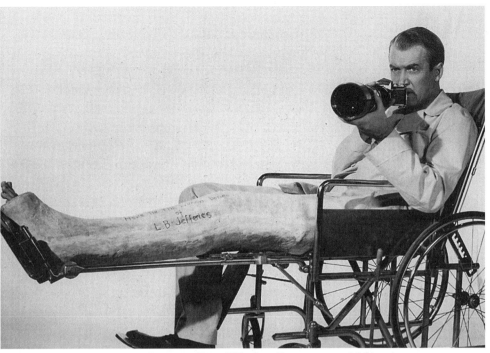

James Stewart, *Rear Window*, Paramount, 1954

The Paramount flacks made of this what they would, until they were reined in. Stewart undoubtedly felt this kind of rumor, however baseless, was infinitely to be preferred to the innuendos that had gone around when he did his first picture with Hitchcock.

Critics greatly admired the steady accumulation of highly sinister tension that Hitchcock had developed, climaxing in Stewart's frighteningly graphic fall from the window ledge. There was praise all around: "There is a nervous, amiable vitality in Stewart's performance of the photographer," the *New York Herald-Tribune* critic wrote, and *Variety*, picking up on the romantic element, said, "There's a very earthy quality to the relationship between Stewart and Kelly." Another critic commented with wry amusement on Kelly's take-charge relationship with the crippled Stewart. She brings in gourmet meals and tries to seduce him into adopting high-style fashion photography instead of his adventurous globe-hopping. She bossily tries to keep her swain grounded and acting his age.

Stewart spoke highly of Kelly, as actress and as woman. He was most disappointed, he said, when he didn't get to do *Designing*

Woman with her a year or so later at MGM. The script, settings and casting had all been arranged, but Kelly announced her marriage to Rainier, and the picture was called off. (It became a 1957 release with Lauren Bacall and Gregory Peck.) The Stewarts' friends joked that "Kelly is now off the list Gloria has to worry herself about!"

In the years that followed, Stewart was never at a loss for words of praise for Grace Kelly. He told one of her biographers, James Spada: "She was completely cooperative. There was no selfishness connected with her. She was there to do a job, and she depended on her director as much as she depended on her own ability, which she didn't force on her director or on the other players. I think she was, in this respect, an ideal actress . . . she seemed to have a complete understanding of the way motion picture acting is carried out. And she was so pleasant on the set; she was really in a class by herself as far as cooperation and friendliness are concerned."

He also told Donald Spoto: "The publicity people don't know what to write about her so they hang this tag 'aloof' on her for lack of anything else!"

When he was asked if Grace was a cold fish, Stewart got his dander up for real: "Grace *cold*? She's anything *but* cold! She has those big warm eyes — and, well, if you ever have played a love scene with her, you'd *know* she's not cold . . . besides, Grace has that twinkle, and a touch of larceny in her eyes."

Another interviewer cornered Stewart on the subject of Grace's bosom. It seems that Hitchcock didn't think she was busty enough and told Edith Head to do something about it. According to Stewart, "There was nothing wrong with Grace in that department. Hitchcock was just splitting hairs. I told her not to let him fuss like that; she just made a few adjustments and stood straighter and she looked just fine in that negligee."

Wendell Corey, who appeared with Stewart in several films, including *Rear Window*, told me that "There was a whopping big ego underneath that allegedly shy, stuttering, bumbling persona. When Jimmy Stewart didn't like the way a scene was going, he could yell with the best of them — you could hear him over to the next sound stage! He was plenty fussy about the right shots, the right lighting, and he could out-argue and out-shout Hitchcock — I even think Hitch got a little afraid of him at times. There was steel under all that mush, believe me!"

In *The Far Country* (1955), their fourth Western together, James Stewart and Anthony Mann were off on yet another manly jag. The conventional plot, situation, and dialogue were counterbalanced somewhat by the spectacular settings of the Canadian Northwest, evocatively captured by William Daniels' camera. Borden Chase was again hired for the screenplay, and Joseph Gershenson dreamed up more of his familiar Western musical motifs. The usual members of Stewart's Western stock company (Jay C. Flippen, Harry Morgan) were in situ, with the welcome addition of veteran character actor and three-time Oscar winner, Walter Brennan, who contributed his usual powerhouse portrayal as an old, eccentric sidekick of Stewart's.

Stewart is a Wyoming cattleman who wants to make enough money to buy a ranch, so he drives his livestock herd clear to Alaska and on to Dawson, in Canadian territory, where he sells them. Along the trail he runs afoul of villainous sheriff John McIntire who attempts, unsuccessfully, to rob him of his cattle in Skagway. Later, in Dawson, McIntire and his posse reappear, this time interfering with Stewart's gold claim. Inevitably, McIntire must bite the dust, for Stewart is a coldly self-centered fellow with respect for neither man nor beast "until softened by a woman's love" (how many times have we heard *that* phrase?) and been (relatively) enlightened by the civilized townsfolk of Dawson.

In this one, Stewart has two leading ladies to contend with. There is flamboyant barroom gambler and sucker-roller Ruth Roman, a lady as self-sufficiently self-protective as Stewart; and the more gentle, nurturing and man-dependent French-Canadian girl, Corinne Calvet. In conventional fashion, Stewart is torn between the racy titillations of hard-as-nails Roman and the wife-candidate sweetnesses of Calvet. Calvet wins out by default as, in a plot twist reminiscent of *Destry Rides Again*, Roman is killed trying to warn Stewart of the confrontation with McIntire. The further sorrow of having lost sidekick Brennan in one of the assorted shooting melées, cannot prevent the predictable: Stewart and Calvet will eventually settle down on that ranch that he now has the wherewithal to buy.

Despite Macho Mann's obvious efforts to stress the inner demons of his latest Stewart creation, the picture reeks from start to finish of a deadly *déjà vu*. Not one confrontation, situation, or plot

Skitch Henderson, James Stewart, Henry Fonda, *On Our Merry Way*, 1948

point has any originality, either in Chase's dialogue or in Mann's overemphatic staging.

Walter Brennan, a distant relative of mine, reminisced about *The Far Country* with me a few years after it was made. "I had a nice part, so I have no right to kick," he said. "I played a grizzled old eccentric and I had some good laugh-lines and some nice situations, but I have to confess it all turned out so predictably, and it followed the well-worn Western path. The best thing about it was that wonderful location shooting, those spectacular mountains, and that clean, sweet air!"

Of working with Jimmy Stewart, Walter related: "He was a wonderful companion after shooting was done; very down-to-earth, full of good stories, fine sense of humor. He had a great talent for concentrating when the camera started going — he was on top of his part every second, even kept going after Tony Mann called 'cut!'"

The critics dutifully gave *The Far Country* its kudos, citing the spectacular scenery and the professional acting and direction, but more than one of them emphasized the almost stifling familiarity of the film. "You know what these guys are gonna do and say long before they do or say 'em," one Pittsburgh critic groaned. "And that doesn't exactly make for suspense nor does it really rivet the attention." Another critic remarked, not without sarcasm, "I know how Mr. Stewart and Mr. Mann enjoy working at these Westerns — this is, if I am correct, their fourth Western go-round, but their intense interest in making such fare is not, I fear, matched by audiences' interest in seeing it...."

Strategic Air Command (1955) the Paramount film that Stewart practically barnstormed into being, has a distinctly dated look today. It is so full of clichés and stock situations that it borders on the laughable: indeed, it must have seemed so even in 1955. There is some good aviation stuff (one critic opined that the film only got off the ground when Stewart did) and Stewart brought to it all the concentrated knowledge and enthusiasm of his U.S. Air Force service and his lifelong avocation for aviation. It is just the kind of film that a man who wound up a Brigadier-General in the Air Force Reserve would feel compelled to make.

Feeling that the Strategic Air Command constituted a vital first line of defense, Stewart wanted to apprise the public of its purpose and exploits (he didn't spoon-feed it to his public, as another critic put it, he rammed it down their throats). Stewart talked Paramount producer Sam Briskin into giving the subject the all-out treatment.

And *Strategic Air Command* does well enough when it stays aloft. Filmed at such bases as MacDill in Tampa, Florida, and Carswell at Fort Worth, Texas, the B-36 and B-47 aircraft look positively antiquated, but given the VistaVision technicolor work of old standby Bill Daniels (Thomas Tutweiler's aerial footage is thrown in for good measure), and Paul Manta's aviation expertise, the action is fairly exciting. Tony Mann, required to participate in another non-Western, at pal Stewart's earnest insistence, tries his darndest. He is unable to find character nuances in the stalwart, monumental figures of Frank Lovejoy's General Ennis C. Hawkes (modeled on Stewart's real-life hero, SAC chief General Curtis LeMay), Barry Sullivan's Lt. Col. Rocky Samford, or others of their ilk.

Stewart is said to have had a pervasive (some thought interfering) hand in a subject inextricably linked to his wartime memories. Where he and screenwriters Valentine Davies and Beirne Lay went way off the track was in introducing a plotline that threatened to reprise *The Stratton Story*. Stewart is a successful third baseman with the St. Louis Cardinals, married (yes, again) to cheerful, sacrificing June Allyson. Stewart and company probably felt they were warming audiences' hearts with this third re-teaming, but the ploy boomeranged. Some critics declared that enough was enough was enough, and they weren't quoting Gertrude Stein either!

As this tired plot reworking has it, Stewart had done his duty in wartime service, but now wants to play ball, and only ball: playing war has long since lost its enthrallments for him. But the Air Force commands otherwise, recalling him because of the shortage of trained men. Stewart is initially exasperated, having been torn out of his job and forced to leave his perpetually perky wife, but of course, war games shortly regain their charms for him, and he delivers with a vengeance. His pregnant wife must cope in the end with his desire to remain permanently at the behest of the Strategic Air Command.

Recalling this woefully dated film, June Allyson repeated what she always said about being Stewart's cinematic wife — that he was wonderful to play with, that their onscreen chemistries were just right for each other. But the more interesting observation on *Strategic Air Command* was given me by Barry Sullivan in 1965. He told me that when Stewart was engaged on a subject close to his heart, his dedication assumed "subjectively manic" proportions — a double-edged statement if ever there was one!

The Man From Laramie, released in 1955, was to be the last of the Mann-Stewart Westerns. Many critics, and not a few industry insiders, felt relieved that the duo had finally run their course with this subject. Mann had completed his Universal contract and had gone over to Columbia on a two-picture deal. As usual, he decided the two films would be Westerns, and, again as usual, persuaded Stewart to appear for him in the first. The second Mann Western for Columbia was *The Last Frontier* (1956) with Victor Mature. It was duly noted that Mann failed to elicit the effects from Mature that he had with Stewart, not only because Stewart was a better actor, but because Mature rebelled (some said recoiled) against Mann's sado-masochistic inspirations.

Mann told the press that in *The Man From Laramie* he was after a Western variation on *King Lear*, but the result turned out less Shakespearean than "Macho Mannic." Stewart was 47 in 1955, and many wondered why he had allowed Mann to cajole him into performing such risky stunts in what was probably the most brutal western of the 1950s. The more sinister aspects of Mann's psyche are on stark display, and Stewart's character is disturbingly simplistic, though Mann (erroneously) gave out with a lot of psychobabble about the Hero-as-Avenger role being Stewart's most fully developed yet.

The ubiquitous scriptwriter Borden Chase was dumped for this outing, with Frank Burt and Philip Yordan taking over. They based their script roughly on a mediocre story by Thomas T. Flynn, and were as obviously under the spell of Svengali Mann as Stewart. One critic put his finger on the difference between this Mann-Stewart collaboration and the others: "It is as if Mr. Mann has decided that this time around he is going to dredge his own darker self, expressing it as director, leaving Mr. Stewart to be yanked by his contrary, often perverse puppet-strings."

Stewart poses as a wagon handler from Laramie, Wyoming, but is, in actuality, an army officer out to avenge the death of his younger brother, also an army man, slain at the hands of Indians who were sold guns by persons unknown. It is these persons that Stewart pursues.

Soon he is in an area of New Mexico which is feudally ruled by the iron hand of Donald Crisp (as authoritarian and strong as ever at 75). Crisp's one weakness is his love for his spoiled son, Alex Nicol. Weak yet vicious, Nicol accosts Stewart in several fights in which (among other indignities) Stewart is dragged through fire by horses, and has his hand held tight while a Nicol henchman puts a bullet through it. Mann continues in this vein throughout the film, growing ever more sadistic. Stewart proves his fealty, or professionalism, or possibly just bad judgment, by enduring even the more hazardous and dangerous stunts and fights himself. As one critic put it, "It's as if Mr. Stewart [at 47] is out to prove to Mr. Mann that he is as tough as they come, hence worthy of buddy-style partnership, or maybe it goes deeper than that, and he is out to prove something to himself."

Practically everybody in the picture winds up getting killed; even the elderly Crisp dies by violence. Arthur Kennedy plays an adopted son of Crisp's, who is jealous of Nicol, and who kills him after the old man's death. He, in turn, is later killed by Stewart. Only the fragile beauty Cathy O'Donnell is allowed to live, but in the Mann scheme of things a mere girl doesn't deserve a gruesome fate. A lot of good character actors are squandered, including Wallace Ford and Aline MacMahon (who are also allowed to live, presumably because they are not that important to the action.) Of course, Nicol and his men were the miscreants who sold those guns to the Indians, and at the end Stewart stands tall, purged by his revenge of his brother's death. Mann, it is assumed, is similarly purged by the bloody catharsis he has achieved — and to the death. Either because of his age, or possibly because his subconscious wisely told him to back off, Stewart never did another Western with Mann, though he still remained attached to him.

Having greatly savored his experience in *Rear Window*, Stewart arranged to star for Hitchcock in *The Man Who Knew Too Much* (1956), a remake of Hitch's own 1934 thriller from his early English period. Doris Day was (somewhat surprisingly) cast as Stewart's leading lady. Both parties were thoroughly married, so there were no romantic rumors of any kind, much to their mutual relief. The columnists and fan magazine writers were left to comment on the pair's "solid partnership" and "steady work together," making them, as Doris Day later wryly commented "seem more like a couple of lumberjacks pulling in the logs than a man and woman starring in a movie!"

Doris Day, by 1956, had won increasing esteem as an actress as well as a singer. She had been particularly strong opposite James Cagney in the Ruth Etting biopic, *Love Me or Leave Me* (1955), but she was still unsure of her basic thespian talents. She much preferred a director who contributed to the scene with her and guided her according to his individual lights, so she was baffled when Hitchcock told her to use her own judgment and instincts. As Stewart told Day's biographer, A.E. Hotchner, Hitchcock actually held her abilities in high regard, having seen several of her recent films. Stewart passed on the good word to Doris, explaining what he told her as follows: "Hitchcock didn't believe in rehearsals. He preferred to let the actor figure things out for himself. He refers to this method as 'planned spontaneity.' Of course this is confusing to an actor who is accustomed to a director who 'participates' in a scene. In the beginning, it certainly threw Doris for a loop!" Stewart added that Hitchcock believed that "if you sit down with an actor and an-

James Stewart, *The Man Who Knew Too Much*, Paramount, 1956

alyze a scene you run the danger that the actor will act that scene with his head rather than his heart, or guts."

Reassured by Stewart's wise advice on the Hitchcock directorial method, Day went on to give a fine performance as the ex-singer wife of a surgeon (Stewart) who is on holiday in Morocco with her and their son, (Christopher Olsen). Soon they are caught up in an assassination intrigue: a tip is given to Stewart by a dying man that a certain diplomat will be assassinated during a concert at London's Royal Albert Hall. Their son is kidnapped, to Day's extreme distress, by the conspirators who want to prevent Stewart from informing the authorities about the plan. The trail, after many complicated plot twists, leads to London, where Stewart learns that the diplomat will be shot just as a cymbal crashes at the climax of a composition called "Storm Clouds Cantata." Day manages to get to the Hall and, spotting a pistol emerging from a curtain, distracts the would-be murderer's attention. He is pursued by police and later plummets to his death from a balcony. The couple's son is saved by a rather awkward device: Day loudly sings a piece he is familiar with, "Que Sera Sera," which aids him in eluding his captors and making his way to her.

Critics were mixed in their views on *The Man Who Knew Too Much*. Some called it too convoluted and far-fetched, and praised the 75-minute economy of the 1934 original as against the two-hour ramblings of the 1956 version.

Stewart pointed out that in the climactic scene, while the music of the cantata mounted, he and Day were gushing a lot of explanatory dialogue. Hitchcock impatiently told them to just shut up and let the music take over, which proved to be a highly effective tension-inducing gimmick. "Hitch is a very visual person," Stewart later said of this scene. "He feels, basically, that if you can't tell a story visually without a lot of dialogue, you are not using the medium properly."

There was some amused critical comment on the fact that two songs had been worked into the plot for Day to belt out, but composers Jay Livingston and Ray Evans had the last laugh: they won the Best Song Oscar for "Que Sera Sera." Hitchcock injected an added note of interest when score composer Bernard Herrmann led the on-screen orchestra at the Royal Albert Hall. Robert Burks' color photography was handsome, and the John Michael Hayes-Angus MacPhail screenplay was workmanlike if not overly distinguished.

James Stewart reluctantly admitted that *The Spirit of St. Louis* (1957), the story of Charles A. Lindbergh's famous 33$\frac{1}{2}$-hour flight to Paris, was not a felicitous assignment. His main reason for embarrassment was that he was simply too old to play a 25-year-old.

Stewart was 47 when the film began shooting in the summer of 1955, and he was pushing 49 when it was released in early 1957 after a complicated and painstaking eight-month shooting schedule. Despite meticulous makeup methods and his inspired attempts to recapture the spiritual mystique and intelligence of the cerebral Lindbergh, he failed to give the role the requisite believability. This was a severe disappointment to Stewart, who had wanted to play Lindbergh since age 19. The historic flight, a solo pioneering feat, actually occurred on Stewart's 19th birthday, May 20, 1927, and he had followed via radio the world-shaking events of that day. He recalled it in later years as one of the inspirational high points of his youth.

James Stewart, *The Spirit of St. Louis*, WB, 1957

Stewart was in New York in early 1957 for press interviews connected with the film's opening, and as a *Motion Picture Herald* critic-reporter, I found him sanguine and optimistic about the result. "They said I was too old," he told me, "but age is not the point here. Many men in their forties still have an adventurous, probing spirit. Some men retain a youthful idealism all their lives — I've known them and I can testify to the truth of that." Rumors abounded that Billy Wilder, who directed the film, had wanted a young actor for the part (Tony Perkins, John Kerr, and Marty Milner had all been mentioned). But he reluctantly went with Stewart in the knowledge that such an expensive production required a major name to keep it from going deeply into the red — as it turned out, the picture was far from a financial smash. Wilder blamed a number of factors for the film's meagre returns, but one of them, unmentioned by him, was doubtless his own quirky, ironic approach. He was a poor choice to direct a film that cried out for a Sam Wood, a John Ford, or even a Raoul Walsh, all of whom had a facility for finding a vigorous pace in even a pedestrian script.

Another problem which hindered box office success was the one-dimensional writing. Wilder himself, with Wendell Mayes, had written the sycophantic script, based on a Charles Lederer book. Lindbergh, who wrote the original account, had sold the rights to Warners for one million dollars, a phenomenal amount at the time. But the Wilder-Mayes treatment was overly noble and cloyingly heroic. Lindbergh, admirable and courageous as his achievement was, emerges as a rather stuffy young man with a one-track mind. Many in 1927 had felt that Lindbergh's pronounced physical attractiveness and the novelty of the flight had disguised his essentially pedestrian personality. By 1957, however, Lindbergh's dabblings in unpopular politics, coupled with the sinister circumstances of his son's 1932 kidnapping, had tended to fog the previously sympathetic public's perception of his life.

There was also much criticism of the simplistic approach to what could have been a far more interesting picture. But *Time*, trying to look on the bright side, ticklishly approached the final result with an equivocating review that has often been quoted. In typically Eisenhower-conservative language they wrote: "Stewart, for all his professional, 48-year-old [sic] boyishness, succeeds almost continually in suggesting what all the world sensed at the time: that Lindbergh's flight was not the mere physical adventure of a rash young 'flying fool,' but rather a journey of the spirit, in which, as in the pattern of all progress, one brave man proved himself, for all mankind, as the Paraclete of a new possibility."

Despite these lofty words, this is only mildly suspenseful fare. A lone flier who loses his compass, flies by the stars, fears ice on the wings, and indulges in barnstorming reveries should have been the subject of an exalted film. Instead, the final result was hollow and grandiose.

From 1957 to 1959 Stewart was subjected to one of the more embarrassing episodes of his life when the U.S. Senate wrangled publicly over his projected promotion to the rank of Brigadier-General in the Air Force Reserve.

On September 2, 1957, Lt. General Emmett (Rosy) O'Donnell went before the Senate Armed Services Committee to set forth what, he felt, were Stewart's "splendid" credentials. Trouble broke out immediately, with arguments raging pro and con. On November 2 of the same year Senator Margaret Chase Smith of Maine succeeded in preventing the action. She claimed that the administrative assistant representing her had not been treated with what she considered the requisite respect.

Smith charged that the Air Force, in this matter of reserve-officer advancement, was putting "success in big business and the movies" above actual military qualifications. The publicity was awkward in the extreme as Stewart partisans, for the next two years, argued that his superior war record deserved the honor. His detractors in the Senate loudly insisted that he was a movie star whose image and popularity far outweighed the necessary attributes for a Brigadier-Generalship. They conceded the value of his World War II service, but did not consider there was sufficient merit for the promotion.

Helen Ferguson recalled that, during this period, whenever the controversial subject came up, Stewart looked very sad and mightily disconcerted. Not one of the top Hollywood columnists or correspondents could get a word out of him on the issue. "That is a matter for others to discuss, not myself," was about the most he would concede.

Finally, a combination of popular outrage and senatorial pres-

James Stewart, James Cagney, and Orson Welles on the set of
The Man of a Thousand Faces, 1957

sure brought about his promotion. In 1959 he became a Brigadier-General in the Air Force Reserve, a post from which he was to retire, with honors, at the mandatory age of sixty in 1968.

There are conflicting stories about the 1957 Stewart Western, *Night Passage*. One report had it that Stewart offered it to Anthony Mann, but the director didn't think the character played by Stewart was sufficiently malevolently intricate, and refused. The other has it that Stewart wanted more control of the project and made a show of offering it to Mann knowing it would be refused. Stewart then handed the directorial reins to the relatively inexperienced James Neilson, who hero-worshipped Stewart and proceeded to slavishly follow Stewart's own concept. I incline toward the second story: Stewart's experience with Mann on what turned out to be their final Western, *The Man From Laramie*, had left him alarmed. He still continued to cherish his friend, but after getting thrown under horses' hooves, being shot in the hand, and dragged through fire, Stewart doubtless felt he had had enough of the Mann style.

Whatever the reason, there was a temporary cooling in their hitherto intense personal relationship. Matters were not helped when super-egotist Mann promptly undertook *The Tin Star* (1957) with Henry Fonda and Anthony Perkins, a Western full of complexities and ambiguities dear to the heart of Mann.

With Neilson doing as he was told, and a "soft" cast, including boyish Brandon De Wilde and mild-mannered Herbert Anderson, Stewart felt himself very much in command during *Night Passage*. He even indulged himself by playing the accordion, and singing two Dimitri Tiomkin-Ned Washington songs. "Follow the River" and "You Can't Get Far Without a Railroad" were show-stoppers, or rather show-slowers. One couldn't imagine Mann holding still for such dreary fare.

The character Stewart portrayed in *Night Passage* is, understandably enough, the kind Mann found anathema: a good guy who covers younger brother Audie Murphy's robbery by assuming the blame for it himself. After this, he becomes a sort of troubadour, and wins a chance at a railroad job. Jay C. Flippen (yet another of Stewart's stalwart supports), egged on by daughter Elaine Stewart, who has a yen for Jimmy's character, sends him on a mission: to pay off the field workers.

In a concession to Western rough-stuff, Dan Duryea assumes the role of a railroad raider whose gang includes Stewart's wayward brother Murphy, tabbed with the moniker of the Utica Kid. Gentle Brandon de Wilde is a teenager in whom Stewart takes a filial interest. There is the requisite shootout, with Duryea and his miscreants all being killed, and Murphy dying in his brother's arms. On hand is yet another young woman, an admirer of the Utica Kid, but who, it is implied, will now be big brother's consolation prize.

The differences between Mann's Western concepts and Stewart's are on dramatic display in *Night Passage*. The screenplay, by henchman Borden Chase, is tailored much more to Stewart's style, displaying a more benign humane quality. While Neilson was no action director, he did passably well with the gunfights and chase scenes; but the picture lacks the hard edge and sadistic severity that Mann would have given it. On the other hand, the restrained characters would have undoubtedly sent Mann stalking off the set in disgust on the first day.

It is very likely that Stewart, fond as he continued to be of Mann, realized that some unhealthy element had entered into their relationship. It was increasingly difficult to separate the professional from the personal. As for Mann, he failed to extract the proper homoerotic results out of Tony Perkins and Hank Fonda in *The Tin Star* (the two mixed like oil and water). He directed *Man of the West* (1958) with Gary Cooper (who controlled Mann strictly), and a second-rate *Cimarron* (1960) remake with a wooden Glenn Ford, before attempting epics like *El Cid* (1961) and *Fall of the Roman Empire* (1964). He died of a heart attack in 1967 while filming *A Dandy in Aspic*. When informed of Mann's death, Jimmy was reported "very sad."

Vertigo (1958) is widely considered to be Stewart's best picture. This psychological suspense masterpiece—which many have repeatedly viewed to decipher its strange charm and haunting mystery—certainly passes a hallmark requirement of true art: It reveals something new with each viewing. This doubtless accounts for the fact it is one of the most-watched films of all time.

Hitchcock produced and directed for Paramount, and surpassed even himself: many Hitchcock aficionados consider *Vertigo* his best picture as well as Stewart's. Written by Alex Coppel and Samuel Taylor, and based on a novel by Pierre Boileau and Thomas Narcejac called *D'Entre Les Morts* (Between the Dead) the film was originally titled *From Amongst the Dead*. *Vertigo* is vastly enhanced by one of Bernard Herrmann's most evocative and hypnotic scores, one that lingers long with the viewer, even after one showing.

Stewart had contracted for his fourth and final Hitchcock film a full year before it was shot, but script problems intervened, and production did not begin until late 1957. Vera Miles had originally been slotted to co-star with Stewart, but she became pregnant by actor/husband Gordon Scott (Tarzan!). Kim Novak, then on the ascendant as a Columbia star, was substituted. In order to coax her away from Columbia Stewart offered a two-picture deal with Harry Cohn, at his usual ten-percent of the gross. Stewart was not immediately impressed with Novak, who, he felt, had distinct limitations as an actress. His first reported statement on her was far from flattering: "I was alarmed when I saw her first — this great big busty blonde, twice the weight I was." Later he backtracked, declaring, "We worked together well — it really worked. The chemistry was there."

For yet another time, Stewart had to advise a female co-star on Hitchcock's directorial method. Uncertain of her acting talents, Kim Novak, at 25, was very nervous. "Here she was, the most beautiful woman in Hollywood at the time, and she was very shy and self-effacing — very unsure of herself," Stewart later recalled. At one point she went to Hitchcock asking what her motivation ought to be for a difficult scene she was about to play. Hitchcock had little patience with Actors Studio psychobabble, and curtly informed her, "It's only a movie, Kim!" Stewart later apprised her of what was required, and after that she was fine.

The story of *Vertigo* is a fascinating one. Stewart is Scottie Ferguson, an aging police detective in San Francisco who has been retired from the force because of acute acrophobia, or vertigo. He had barely survived when a policeman trying to rescue him from a roof gutter fell eight stories to his death, but he was left with a mortal fear of heights.

An old schoolmate, Tom Helmore, hires Stewart to follow the latter's wife (Novak), a beautiful blonde woman with enormous charm. He fears she is possessed by the ghost of her ancestor, a woman named Carlotta who died 100 years before. Stewart follows Novak to the ancestor's old Nob Hill mansion, where he observes her sitting in a bedroom window. Later he watches her at an art gallery contemplating a painting of Carlotta, who at 26 had committed suicide. Shortly after that, he rescues Novak when she tries to drown herself in San Francisco Bay.

Obsessed with her beauty, Stewart takes her home rather than to a hospital, and tenderly nurses her. They become better acquainted, and he falls deeply in love. In a redwood forest he assures her he will protect her always, that he is responsible for her. She in turn tells him about her fear of death and they make love. She brings him downcoast to an old Spanish mission which has figured in her dreams of her ghostly ancestor; he goes with her, feeling it may free her of her obsession. At the mission she rushes to the top of a bell-tower, but he cannot follow her because of his vertigo. He can only watch in horror as he sees what he thinks is her body plummeting from the tower to her death.

Shattered by the death of his beloved, Stewart spends months in a sanitarium, filled with self-reproach for not having been able to save her. He can find no comfort from the devoted loyalty of a young woman (Barbara Bel Geddes) to whom he had once been engaged. She notes with alarm his increasing descent into total psychic withdrawal.

One year later, sufficiently recovered, he encounters a young woman (also played by Novak) who, though brunette, is the image of his blonde love. She is common and unlettered while the other woman was reserved and ethereal, yet Stewart and she get to know each other. She appears to be somewhat afraid of him, but finally accedes to his obsession to see her with blonde hair. Gradually Novak comes to pity, then love Stewart, but a shocking revelation comes: she really is the woman he knew before. She was actually Helmore's mistress pretending to be his wife so that the real wife could be thrown from the tower. Of course, Stewart's vertigo would have prevented him from saving her, a factor the murderous plotters had taken into account.

Stewart learns the truth and, disillusioned, he forces Novak to repeat the episode at the mission bell tower so that he can conquer his demons and go on with his life. Angry over the deception, he overcomes his vertigo long enough to make it to the top of the tower with her. While Novak confesses her crime, Hitchcock keeps the suspense high as we wonder if Stewart, still romantically obsessed with her, will forgive her. Panicking at the sight of a shadowy figure (later to be revealed to be a nun) Novak falls to her death. As the nun mutters a prayer, the famous final shot has, at its center, Stewart standing atop the tower, arms outstretched, an agonized expression on his face. Looking down, he realizes he has lost his beloved twice.

Stewart gives a masterly interpretation of a man destined to lose in life's game, hobbled by his fear of heights, humiliated by his early retirement. When the assignment to trail Novak comes, his drab pedestrian life takes on new meaning. He is drawn into her romantic obsession with the past, with the poetic necrophilia of the atmosphere that encloses them both. This is something totally new to his experience: a lovely, mysterious woman takes him into a haunting dream world that obliterates an existence he can no longer countenance. When he loses the woman, and the escapist catharsis she so gorgeously represents, his return to the real world is so shattering that he retreats into temporary psychosis.

When the first stirrings of renewed hope are snuffed out by the revelation of her perfidy, he is still reluctant to part with the fantasy elements that have transformed his life. Yet his attempts to make a fullsome whole of the parts of his dream bring him yet another catastrophic loss. Hitchcock leaves us to decide whether Stewart will become irretrievably insane, or if he will jump to his own death after her.

Stewart gives a wonderfully multifaceted, complex tincture to Scottie Ferguson. He runs the gamut from romantic obsession to abstract necrophilia to a complex delineation of shattered self-esteem. He is a plain, pragmatic man who deals in facts and certainties; he is given a taste of Heaven and is twice cast down into Hell. Stewart conveys all this with consummate sensitivity and iron control.

Novak is so fine in *Vertigo* that for thirty-odd years there has been a spirited debate as to how such a limited actress so surpassed herself in a performance that was haunting and believable. It is hard to imagine another actress playing the role so perfectly. She is not so much required to act as to be, and her very remoteness and inscrutability give a perfect dimension to her dual roles.

Possibly Novak's fine performance is the result of Stewart's advice, echoing Hitchcock's, to just be herself and let her native instincts guide her. Actually, the character echoes many aspects of Novak's own life at that time: a beautiful woman, manipulated by the men around her; timid and withdrawn, yet not without a consciousness of her charm and magnetism; unsure of how to use her gifts; but finally guided by the instinct that Tennessee Williams has so eloquently referred to in his famous apothegm: "The beautiful make their own laws."

Stewart has always referred with a kind of awe to the success of *Vertigo*. "It got a decent audience attendance when it came out in 1958," he has said, "and it was regarded as one of Hitch's more professional and expert outings. Kim and I both got off with decent notices, and then everyone concerned with it was prepared to forget about it and move on. And now, over the years, its legend has grown among critics and the public, and that is a very wonderful thing, and for it I am grateful."

Stewart added: "It means a lot to an actor, or anyone who tries to do something creative, to know that something done long ago has reverberated and is still moving and exciting people who weren't even born when it was made."

Bernard Herrmann, the score's composer, reported that the plot and general mood of *Vertigo* inspired him beyond the ordinary: "The story was so original, so haunting, that I knew pretty much what was called for, and I dredged it from my subconscious. As I scored it throughout, I found myself entirely in sympathy with what was going on on the screen, and it is good to know that what I did musically with it is admired by so many." *TV Movie and Video Guide* ably encapsulates current critical and audience regard for *Vertigo*: "(A) haunting, dream-like thriller, with riveting Bernard Herrmann score to match: a genuinely great motion picture that demands multiple viewings." Or, by definition, a true work of filmic art.

In a retrospective piece on Hitchcock's films, William Schoell wrote in *Quirk's Reviews*: "As much as I admire *Psycho* (1960) and *The Birds* (1963) (to put it mildly), I must admit that *Vertigo* is probably Hitchcock's masterpiece. The entire picture has the quality of a hypnotic dream, while the second half in particular weaves a haunting spell of loneliness and isolation. Kim Novak is much stronger than usual, and Stewart, in one of his best performances, offers a very sympathetic portrait of the tormented Scottie. The

James Stewart, *Thunder Bay*, 1953

lush Herrmann score is the perfect undertone for a completely absorbing and fascinating picture."

Hitchcock was always to take a special pride in *Vertigo*, though he was on record as being more complimentary about pictures like *Shadow of a Doubt* (1943) and *Rebecca* (1940) and even *Suspicion* (1941). "Everything came together in that film extremely well," he said years later in an interview on *Vertigo*. "There were things I would have done differently, I think, with Kim Novak, for instance, but on the whole I was pleased with the result. There was a rhythm to the film that was like no other I did, and the music and photography were all I could have desired. It pleases me greatly that *Vertigo* has picked up such a following; I was a little concerned about it when it first came out, but now I realize my fears were unfounded; it seems to stand the test of time very well, and that is what counts."

Of Stewart, Hitchcock said, "He was a very responsive actor, with a fine intuitive grasp of what I was after, what was required of a scene. He has a great natural gift. He was about fifty when he made *Vertigo*, yet he suggested the bemused ardor and haunted romantic nature of a man twenty-or-more-years younger. I have always been surprised by what Jim Stewart can dredge up out of his own inner feelings for a scene. He always came in fully prepared. I gave him little or no guidance and that is how I have always preferred it, for I try not to get in the way of any actor's basic conception of his role. If they have any talent or intelligence (and we mustn't underrate the seasoning of experience; that is *most* important) they usually know right away what they want to do with a role."

Producer Julian Blaustein and director Richard Quine, ensconced in 1958 over at Columbia Pictures, took note of the popularity of the Stewart-Novak teaming in *Vertigo*. They decided that since Novak was basically a Columbia star, they should cast her with Stewart again, with Columbia Pictures reaping the box office bonanza this time around. Stewart at first was doubtful of the project. He turned 50 that year, and had come to feel that romancing women on screen who were half his age was no longer attractive or dignified. Some critics and commentators have stressed that after Stewart made *Bell, Book and Candle* (1958) with Novak, he eschewed romance on screen. They overlook the fact that even in his tough, gritty Westerns of the 1960s he did his share of womanizing. Stewart in a 1967 interview, spoke of this: "Yes, it is true that I did some courting and marrying and what-not after I turned 50 (on the screen, that is); I think I shifted the emphasis away from that more often than not."

Still, *Bell, Book and Candle* continued to be hailed in the Stewart pantheon as his last romantic leading man role. Certainly it was a weak followup film to *Vertigo*, which had contained one of Stewart's stronger, more complex performances, but the critics, while not taking it seriously, commented favorably on the Stewart-Novak chemistry. The light and amusing Daniel Taradash script, based on the John Van Druten play, and Quine's deft directorial guidance, had resulted in a pleasant, albeit forgettable product.

Stewart is a publisher who is about to marry Janice Rule but instead gets involved with a beautiful and mysterious art dealer (Novak) who turns out to be a witch; she longs for love, but is unable to feel it. Stewart gradually becomes enamored of her, and casts about for a means to free her from her witch-spell. He has his work cut out for him, because Novak resents his well-intentioned meddling, as does her Siamese cat, Pyewacket. Still, Stewart persists in his attempts to metamorphose her into a loving, feeling woman for he wants to marry her. Also standing in his way are such disparate characters as Novak's brother (Jack Lemmon) a fey, inventive warlock who can sashay through walls; a mischievous (non-warlock) author who is writing a book about witchcraft; and the Head of the Association of Manhattan Witches (our term), none other than the perfectly cast Hermione Gingold. Novak's Aunt Queenie (Elsa Lanchester), unlike her other relatives, is a sentimental witch who believes that nothing should block the course of true love. She aids and abets them in turning Novak into the girl of Stewart's dreams, for a happy ending.

"Charming fluff" was the consensus of critical opinion, with one reviewer stating, "While it is delightful to see Mr. Stewart and Miss Novak reunited on the screen, and while it is evident that he manages to make his beautiful co-star look like more of an actress than she in actuality is, we only wish they had been accorded a sturdier vehicle from which to purvey their evident charisma."

Kim Novak has often praised Stewart, commenting on how wonderful he was to play off. There was some resentment on both their parts when the overzealous flacks of Columbia's publicity department made a lame attempt to titillate columnists Parsons and Hopper with sly innuendoes about the "warming up" of the Stewart-Novak love scenes beyond the requirements of the script. When the importunate Hedda Hopper dared to ask about this, Novak loftily informed the inventively-hatted hack that Mr. Stewart was a happily married husband and father, and that he had always been the acme of respectability in all their dealings. Moreover, she sniffed, her romantic interests were distinctly elsewhere. Hopper, who always respected Stewart and in many areas shared his conservative politics, would not take the bait. "I have the profoundest respect for Jimmy Stewart" was her usual verdict on him. Occasionally even Stewart found himself in a misunderstanding with the touchy Hedda, but it would blow over in short order. John Wayne's attitude on Hopper was: "One of these days I'm going to give her a kick in the ass she won't forget!"

In the opinion of many film commentators and ordinary fans of Stewart, *Anatomy of a Murder* (1959) is his finest performance. For his outstanding effort Stewart received the New York Film Critics' Award and was nominated for an Oscar. The film itself received a total of seven Oscars in various categories, but was overtaken by *Ben-Hur*, the blockbuster of the year, whose star, Charlton Heston, beat out Stewart for best actor. Many found this outrageous, with one observer commenting, after the winners were announced in the spring of 1960: "Mr. Heston is a proficient, capable, seasoned actor but in winning his Academy Award he was greatly aided by the variegated cinematic skills put on lavish and stately display in a mammoth costume epic, while Mr. Stewart practically carries *his* picture [*Anatomy of a Murder*] with a cunning, amusing and psychologically dimensional performance. The Oscar, by all rights, should have been his for 1959."

Stewart, always a gracious winner and magnanimous loser told reporters that: "I have my Oscar — have had it twenty years. Charlton Heston has never had one before, and I know what a lift that can give a man, broadening his creative horizons, and I wish him all the best."

Certainly *Anatomy of a Murder*, all 160 minutes of it, is one of the best courtroom dramas ever put on the screen. Masterfully produced and directed by Otto Preminger, and tautly written by Wendell Mayes, it was based on the novel by "Robert Traver," a pseudonym for Michigan Supreme Court Justice John D. Voelker. (Voelker possessed an invaluable expertise on the crime of rape, on which the story focused.) The film boasts a variety of unique qualities, among them the score written by the great Duke Ellington, who makes a brief appearance, and a surprisingly authoritative performance by the famed Joseph Welch, the lawyer who cut Joe McCarthy down to size in the 1954 HUAC hearings. Welch later became a judge, and in this, his one and only film, he rang true on all counts. Later he said of Stewart, "He was wonderfully believable as that defense lawyer, more believable than I was as the Judge, and I'm the professional in that field!" Stewart rejoindered that Welch was much too modest, for his forthright performance, making use of his true personality, is one of the ornaments of the film. Asked later how he did it so truthfully, Welch said that Preminger had given him a priceless piece of advice: "'Just be yourself, as you are in your day-to-day life, and forget there's even a camera there!' That carried me through splendidly." Audiences agreed with him one hundred percent.

Ben Gazzara and Lee Remick also appear to good advantage as, respectively, the army lieutenant with the trigger temper and his footloose wife. He is on trial for having murdered a man who, his wife claims, raped her. Stewart, a small-town lawyer, masterfully guides his defendant through all the twists and turns of the court-room action. He is aided by his loyal assistant Eve Arden and his al-coholic associate Arthur O'Connell, who gives a gem of a portrayal as a man who can rise to the occasion when Stewart needs him. George C. Scott is the big-city prosecutor, who ably counters but never overwhelms Stewart, and is eventually defeated by the latter's canny shrewdness and thorough research. Sam Leavitt's black-and-white photography is particularly impressive, setting as it does the stark mood of the authentic Michigan locations. The studio offered to lay out more money to shoot the film in color, but Preminger wisely decided that the overall sleazy mood called for monochrome.

The courtroom fencing between Stewart and Scott is particu-larly compelling, with Judge Welch (in the film, Judge Weaver) forced to pull the two overzealous men into line when tempers and expletives flare. The film is unusually frank and graphic in its dis-cussion of sperm tracings, and women's panties, and the niceties of rape. Today it seems par for the course, but in 1959 Preminger was blazing new and daring trails, and the censors of the time had to be consulted almost daily when matters got too racy. Convinced that the film was a work of integrity with a necessarily documentary-style realism and meticulousness as to legal details, the censors ap-proved much "in the interests of legitimate depiction."

Lee Remick gives one of her very best performances as the amoral wife, in a role originally destined for Lana Turner. But Turner, then pushing 40 was insecure about her looks and de-manded extra considerations for makeup, lighting, and costuming. Preminger decided that she wasn't worth the trouble and let her go. Remick, then 24, seemed more authentic as the charmer who drove her angry husband to murder. The trial poses several difficult ques-tions: Was the Remick character unduly provocative in dress and manner during her peregrinations at the neighborhood bar? Did her bruises come from the man whom she claimed raped her, or from her jealous husband? The statutory definitions of rape and carnal knowledge are thoroughly explored. There is the crucial matter of Remick's missing panties. At the denouement, Kathryn Grant, who, it turns out, is the victim's illegitimate daughter, finally overcomes her reluctance to expose her father. She tells how she re-covered the torn panties from a laundry hamper after he had thrown them in there as he passed her room on the night of the rape. A not-guilty-by-reason-of-insanity verdict eventually gets Gazzara off, as he profits (thanks to Stewart's research) by an old "irresistible impulse" decision.

While Remick's and Gazzara's characters are thoroughly explored (he is shown to be a far from admirable person and she has the instincts of a trollop) *Anatomy of a Murder* refrains from springing the usual trap-ending. The only surprise is that after Gazzara goes free, he and Remick skip town without paying Stewart his fee.

Preminger was well-known to be a martinet on his sets, with a caustic temper which made him particularly authentic, in his earlier career as an actor, when he portrayed nasty Nazis. Many wondered, as shooting began, how he and Stewart would get on, as both men were accustomed to getting their own way.

Arthur O'Connell later told me, "I think there was a lot of mutual respect between Jim and Otto. Both were seasoned at what they did, and they had the good sense to let the other do his thing in his own way. So far as Jim was concerned, it was, I suppose, a 'happy' set, though he couldn't have helped taking note of how Otto badgered the other actors, though he let *me* alone!"

Stewart is in full command throughout: coping ably with Remick's flirtatious overtures; studying with a cynical eye the quirks in Gazzara's character; tolerating with amused resignation O'Connell's drunken lapses; joshing with Eve Arden; sparring ably with judge, jury, and Scott.

When the film was released, *The New York Times* gave the film all-out praise, citing it as a superior courtroom drama. Of Stewart, the review said: "Slowly and subtly he presents us a warm, clever, adroit and complex man, and, most particularly, a portrait of a trial lawyer in action which will be difficult for anyone to surpass."

Another reviewer commented on "Stewart's wonderful, easeful presence, his masterful addressal. 'The art that conceals art' is, it is true, an overworn cliché, but it can be drafted yet again to convey Stewart's wonderful dimensionalism, the complex dynamics over which he has total control. Here is one of our finest American actors in full-throttle."

Stewart always referred to his work in *Anatomy of a Murder* with genuine pride, and has delighted in the compliments his fellow actors in the film have bestowed in various interviews. George C. Scott: "Masterful." Lee Remick: "Seasoned and sure." Ben Gazzara: "A great actor at the height of his form."

Chapter Thirteen

Settling In

It was no surprise to any of the close Stewart watchers that in 1959, at age 51 (admittedly long in the tooth for such a subject), Stewart expressed a strong desire to do a film about the Federal Bureau of Investigation. Warners acceded to his wish, and Mervyn LeRoy (not the ideal director for such material, excellent though he was in different fare) was assigned to direct. The screenplay was by John Twist and Richard L. Breen, based on Don Whitehead's earlier, and well-received book. The result was *The FBI Story* (1959).

The story was numbingly reminiscent of numerous previous Stewart plots. He is an agent who starts right off as one of new Bureau director J. Edgar Hoover's men, and from 1924 to 1959 engages in exploits that reconstruct many of the more heroic episodes in the FBI saga. Of course, he marries a nice girl (Vera Miles), who bears him three children but is distressed by his dangerous work. For a time she leaves him, but eventually returns.

The Stewart character is a composite of many agents who figured in that 35-year period. He combats Ku Klux Klan mischief in Louisiana, chases after Dillinger, Baby Face Nelson, Pretty Boy Floyd, and other naughty boys in the Midwest, and, come World War II, rounds up enemy aliens and nabs German agents. His one son becomes an FBI man, he loses another son in action. Finally, he prepares to take on the new enemy: International Communism.

Critics were somewhat reserved in their reaction to *The FBI Story*. One compared it to an expanded and barely dramatized March of Time treatise, another citing its odd lack of pace, spirit, and excitement. Jumping as it did from one perfunctorily-handled situation to another, linear progression was certainly not one of *The FBI Story's* merits, though it deserves some credit for documenting, sometimes in tedious detail, the multifarious functions of the Agency and its men.

Among the film's few positive aftermaths: it inspired Warners, its producer, to further explore the subject in a long-running FBI

TV series starring Efrem Zimbalist, Jr. This wound up being better received by the public than Stewart's feature film.

Joseph Biroc photographed *The FBI Story* in color, though many considered it was really a black-and-white subject. The great Max Steiner, by then in his "later period" at Warners, gave it a lush, variegated score that some critics thought was better than the story, and its handling, deserved.

Years later, Vera Miles complained that she had been haunted by the ghost of June Allyson in her portrayal of the loving wife and mother. True, she reneges on her devotion at least once, but redeems herself by returning for more punishment. (At the end of the film, Miles' character's deep relief is almost audible when her aging husband is finally assigned to indoctrinating new FBI recruits.) "There really wasn't that much I could do with the role," Vera Miles told me. "She was a compendium of all the most deadly and repetitious clichés, and everything she did you expected reels before it happened." The forthright Miles was of the mind that such roles merely kept actresses "dancing attendance in second-fiddle style." She wasn't the first "loyal little wife" to express the opinion that since the boys so much enjoyed being boys in plots like this, they should simply leave the women to the scenes best suited to them. Miles never disguised her disappointment that, after a promising start, she seemed to be second-fiddling it to one actor after another.

Once, when I interviewed Mervyn LeRoy about his career, he sloughed off *The FBI Story* with a few lukewarm words of praise about Jimmy being so nice to work with, while the picture was a "neat, professional job." *The FBI Story* will never make the list of Stewart's Top Ten Films, and certainly it is not one of the talented LeRoy's best. For some inexplicable reason, however, when he wrote his autobiography some years after I had talked to him, Mervyn LeRoy had done quite an about-face on *The FBI Story*, stating that he was "extremely proud" of it and that it was one of his own favorites. He wrote: "It was all authentic, down to the smallest detail. It had to be. In the first place, J. Edgar Hoover was a personal friend and I didn't want to jeopardize that friendship by doing anything that wasn't accurate — and anyway, he wouldn't let me. He assigned two agents to be with us at all times, to make sure of the technical details."

LeRoy went on to tell of the five weeks of shooting in the FBI

Building in Washington. The book was written two years after Hoover's death, and LeRoy seems to be eulogizing and sentimentalizing him and his work. Of the shooting in Washington he wrote: "It was an education for all of us; we learned the amazing things the Bureau's laboratory technicians are capable of doing. Given the smallest, most insignificant clues, they can build an airtight case. I think that, in the FBI, we have the finest law enforcement agency in the world. Too many of us don't appreciate what we have." He rhapsodizes, in his 1974 opus: "Hoover, who built the Bureau almost singlehandedly, was one of our greatest men. If the real history of the FBI is ever written, it will show that J. Edgar Hoover did much to save the things about America we all hold most dear."

Shortly before he died, LeRoy was asked about the posthumous downgrading of Hoover's reputation. There were charges that he was homosexual, engaged in refined blackmailing, authorized wiretapping, and so on. LeRoy brushed the allegations aside as a political ploy to denigrate the memory of "a great man." In his book he attests to what he considers to be Hoover's honest nature. When LeRoy urged him to consider running for the Presidency, Hoover replied, "Mervyn, I'll run for nothing where you have to make a deal."

Unwittingly casting light on the more pedestrian aspects of *The FBI Story*, LeRoy told of how Hoover had insisted on okaying the film before it was released. LeRoy sat as tensely and nervously as any FBI neophyte agent as he watched the faces of Hoover and his lieutenants viewing the flick in the Bureau's own little theatre. He remembered that they were grim and unsmiling and didn't even laugh during the lightly humorous passages of an otherwise heavy and hagiographic movie. When the movie ended, LeRoy recalls, he was sure he read all-out condemnation on the "tough and unsmiling faces." To his vast relief, the great man approached, smiled, and told him that they were all proud of him and that it was a fine film. Later, the FBI gave LeRoy a Distinguished Service Award plaque. The author of the original book, Don Whitehead, LeRoy recalled, told him the picture was "magnificent" and cited his "honesty, imagination and humor."

Yet the FBI seemed tyrannical, as LeRoy recounts it, in insisting on constant changes in the script during the shooting "for security reasons. Everybody on the set, down to and including the carpen-

James Stewart and Henry Fonda making a commercial for
The Cheyenne Social Club, 1970

ters, had to be passed-on by the Bureau." It was doubtless for reasons like this, with Hoover and company diluting much of the film
into a "docudrama," that some critics demurred on the result.

Shortly after the film's completion, as LeRoy has recalled, Stewart, his wife, and their four children went on a European trip.
Hoover told them that his agents overseas would keep a careful eye
on them. At first pleased and grateful, Stewart and his wife soon
found the constant FBI surveillance to be a nerve-racking experience, though the agents were always helpful. On the way back to
Los Angeles, Stewart felt that he should tell one FBI agent that,
much as they appreciated the courtesies, he and his family could
take care of themselves. The agent surprised and amused him by
telling him they were on the last lap of the journey in order to keep
an eye on a jewel thief, whom the agent invited Stewart to identify
by the oversized diamond stick-pin he was wearing. Stewart remembered that the man in question looked very meek and mild;
nonetheless, he was arrested and carted off when the plane reached
Los Angeles. Gloria laughed that it had been quite a conclusion to
what the Stewarts had originally projected as a low-key, fun European vacation!

The Mountain Road (1960) must be counted among James Stewart's weaker films, not because the subject — the 1944 operations of the U.S. Army in China — was not a rousing one, but because the treatment was flat and the handling uninspired. The director, Daniel Mann (no relation to Anthony), was a product of the theatre, though he had worked in films for eight years. When he undertook *The Mountain Road* he was more noted for his direction of high-powered actresses like Shirley Booth and Anna Magnani (who had both won Best Actress Oscars for *Come Back, Little Sheba* [1952] and *The Rose Tattoo* [1955], respectively) and, even as late as the Stewart film, was bound by the conventions of his earlier stage career. In short, when it came to action films, Anthony Mann he was not, lacking that director's forceful, masculine, and psychologically-complex approach.

Nor is Stewart at his best as one Major Baldwin, whose duty it is to destroy any aspects of the Chinese landscape that might facilitate the Japanese army invasion. Leading an eight-man demolition team, anxious to test himself to his personal limits, he is guilty of an excess of zeal that borders on sadism. He blows up bridges, knocks out roads, sets bomb traps with military precision. As he continues his destructive course through the Chinese countryside, he comes in contact with an American-educated, and cultured Chinese lady, played by Lisa Lu. To some extent he is influenced by her humanistic qualities. With Lu and Chinese general Frank Silvera, who offers aid when he is cut off from his own command, Stewart is faced with the disastrous effect on the Chinese populace of his scorched-earth policy. When renegade Chinese murder several of his men, Stewart becomes hardened and all the more disillusioned, and begins to question who are his allies and who his enemies. At the end, realizing that he has compromised Lu's love and vitiated his own capacity for compassion and human flexibility, Stewart ponders his own character and his suitability for command.

The script was written by Alfred Hayes, based on the novel by Theodore White. The photography by Burnett Guffey was not particularly outstanding, and the barely adequate score was composed by Jerome Moross. Daniel Mann displayed a lack of experience with, and a lack of feel for, an action epic that required shrewd editing and authoritative directorial command to succeed. Most of the reviewers considered *The Mountain Road* a perfunctory and even tedious exercise — all the more regrettable because some of its situations could have been milked for top action values.

Another problem with the film was that it sacrificed action at the expense of psychological musings. Stewart's fans did not want to see him in an action film in which he uncovered his own self-doubts and questioned his methods. "The American public likes their heroes with his convictions and aims undiluted," as one critic put it, "and the inner ruminations and doubts and evolvements of the character of Mr. Stewart's Major Baldwin unfortunately do not translate into exciting linear-progression cinematics of the kind they are accustomed to when it comes to this category of action fare."

Henry (Harry) Morgan, long a Stewart standby, told me in an interview some years later that he did not feel Stewart and Daniel Mann had a good rapport. He felt the screenplay was overwritten and could have used less psychologizing and more physicality. Morgan agreed with the critics who called the film oddly flat. "Jimmy was not happy with the film, even during its making or afterward," Morgan told me. "In fact none of us were. The plot didn't seem to be going anywhere and we all sensed it, and Daniel Mann was obviously unfamiliar with action stuff." When I remarked that the psychological changes in Stewart were supposed to be part of the theme, he replied, "Fine, but not for that kind of film. The audience came to see action, decisiveness. They just didn't associate Jimmy Stewart with that kind of thing — they wanted to see him forge ahead, and win out."

Many film authorities have expressed keen regret that by the time John Ford did his first film with James Stewart, in 1961, he had lost most of his idealism about the West, his nostalgia for its past, and his stately yet moving depictions of the frontier spirit. Described by one critic as "a folk artist, a master storyteller and a poet of the moving image," Ford, in his film portraits of men, their women, and their horses and wagons, has never been surpassed for stoical lyricism. In his early years, he had evinced a moving compassion for his characters' fates, and his camera had caught them in evocative long shots that powerfully juxtaposed the human condition with the forces of Nature.

Sadly, by the time of *Two Rode Together* (1961), Ford was burning out, and his approach, especially to his male protagonists, had turned increasingly bleak and cynical. Whereas many of his charac-

Nicholas Ray visited by James Stewart and his sons
Ronald and Michael on the set of *King of Kings*, 1960

ters had earlier evinced a rough-hewn idealism and almost naïve simplicity of spirit, his Guthrie McCabe, as delineated by Stewart in *Two Rode Together*, is a venal, self-seeking figure. He sets out to rescue white women and their children from Indian captivity, not for reasons of humanity, but because he is able to command $500 per head for their safe return to the authorities.

Stewart is rather unrelentingly grim as he goes about his mission. He is accompanied by army lieutenant Richard Widmark, a more likeable character, who is initially disgusted by Stewart's cynicism, but later comes to understand (though not admire) him. Among the disparate people Stewart rescues are a wild white boy grown too accustomed to his Indian life-style to comfortably accept his liberation, and a Spanish woman (Linda Cristal) who has been forced into concubinage by the Indians. Stewart later falls in love with her, if such a man can be described as softening to that extent. Shirley Jones is along for the ride as a woman who deplores her brother's "savaging" by the Indians, and she and Widmark pair off for a romance.

By the time Stewart has set out for California with Cristal, his character has been forced to move in five directions at once. Ford is credited with prying more characterizational nuance out of Stewart than any other director, but the Stewart character here, as he limns him, smacks more of a man who lives by instinct and the primal laws of self-preservation. When he reveals passing glints of humor and tolerance, they seem fleetingly inappropriate in a character so essentially unsympathetic. *Two Rode Together*, along with *The Mountain Road*, must be counted among the films Stewart's fans least admired. In both he is a disorganized, instinctual man who, animal-like, reacts to the experiences of the moment.

"Mr. Stewart should remember," one critic wrote, "that audiences expect a certain persona from an actor they have lifted to star status; he can delineate many aspects of character while remaining essentially himself, but in *Two Rode Together* the inner truths of Stewart's character seem obscure and it is difficult to get a handle on him."

Richard Widmark told me in 1980: "I wasn't too keen on *Two Rode Together*; I didn't think either Jim's or my characterizations were well-developed by the screenwriter, and Jack Ford didn't seem, in this instance, to know quite what to do with them. Everything tended to come out confused, and the ending trailed off. My romance with the character played by Shirley Jones, and Jim's with Linda Cristal, seemed sort of dragged in by the ear, and while the characters of the whites we 'rescued' from the Indians had some variety, they were meshed together confusingly."

Widmark added, however, "that it was a privilege to play with Jim, whom I always admired greatly. Ford thought the script was bad; he told me so, but he said he would patch it up and liven it and open up the action as we went along—I don't think he accomplished these things successfully."

Columbia and Stewart had struck a deal for *Two Rode Together* before a director was chosen, and after considering a number of them, Columbia's head selected John Ford because "he owed me a film." More than a few people in Hollywood wished later that Ford had recompensed Columbia with something more upbeat and suitable.

The Man Who Shot Liberty Valance (1962) was Stewart's second film with John Ford, and his first with John Wayne. By 1962, Wayne had become one of the screen's—and America's—great legends, the embodiment of the American spirit, whether in cowboy or military garb. As one critic put it, "He came to project the essence of strength and confidence in his many bigger-than-life roles as a crusader for just causes and a leader of men." In later years, after he had made the Vietnam War his own personal pet project, Wayne ran up against much political criticism from those of a more liberal persuasion, but stuck to his guns to the end, once stating, "They'll take me as I am and like it!"

The first Stewart-Wayne pairing under the Ford aegis is interesting on a number of counts. Stewart ceded first billing to Wayne, an act of courtesy the other man greatly appreciated. Their acting styles were quite different. Stewart, the more talented of the two, had developed a standard repertoire of mannerisms that his public had come to cherish, and that even his tough Western roles of the 1950s had only partially adulterated. Wayne's style was spare, clean and unadorned; he stood tall, very much himself. Wayne's detractors were always to claim that he had no other choice but to play extensions and variations of his own personality. But, as John Ford, who with *Stagecoach* (1939) had transformed Wayne from a faceless sagebrush hero of numerous B "oaters" into a top male star, put it: "What you saw you got. It was because the man was so much himself that he had such impact." Wayne was to win an Oscar for a fine Western characterization in *True Grit* (1969), and he and Stewart would co-star in 1976 in Wayne's final film, *The Shootist*. But in 1962, Wayne was 55 and at the top of his form, giving his fans what John Wayne gave best.

John Ford mitigated and diluted the cynicism of *Two Rode Together* somewhat for *The Man Who Shot Liberty Valance*. Thanks primarily to the fine screenplay provided by James Warner Bellah and Willis Goldbeck, based on a Dorothy Johnson short story, Ford blended his rough idealism with his appreciation of the pragmatic and expedient, an approach that came all the more easily since it was intrinsic to the plot. Certainly this film exemplifies a wonderful blending of three great talents, Ford's, Stewart's, and Wayne's, and their seamless mutual chemistry is one of the more salient aspects of it.

Since both men were of a conservative political bent, Stewart and Wayne hit it off wonderfully during the shooting, and enjoyed many discussions on politics, filmmaking and other matters. The picture was shot mostly in the studio this time around, with occasional location work, and lensed by William Clothier in the only photography possible: black and white. (Had it been done in color it would have prettified and neutralized a somber and ironic theme.)

Vera Miles is once more the lady who is first drawn to Wayne, but finally marries Stewart. Of this film she would later say only, "I did my usual thing. . . ."

The plot has Stewart, a famous elderly senator, and his wife, Miles, returning to the little Western town of Shinbone to attend the funeral of an old derelict, John Wayne. When asked by the town reporter why he would deign to pay such a humble character honor, Stewart tells the story of how he had come to Shinbone as an idealistic young lawyer decades before. He had been rescued by Wayne from the bullying Liberty Valance (Lee Marvin), a tool of the ranchers who opposed statehood. Stewart stands up to Valance and finally they square off for a duel, which the contemptuous Valance expects to win easily, but a shot rings out and the bully falls dead. Later it turns out that Wayne, at Miles's urging, has actually shot him, but Stewart gets the credit and it leads to a great political career for the Man Who Shot Liberty Valance. The reporter later refuses to use the story Stewart gives him with the words, "It ain't news. This is the West. When the legend becomes fact, print the legend!"

The Man Who Shot Liberty Valance originally opened to patronizing and disdainful reviews, though a few critics perceived its merit. It has acquired a large cult following in the decades since its release, and is now regarded as a mature and acerbic commentary on the blending of Western fact and fiction. Since the Stewart character is a fundamentally decent man who made a fine lawyer and later an honest and admirable senator, the initial deception does not assume the negative proportions that it might have in a less subtle and intrepid film. Ford, for one, found it appealing because it enabled him to set forth much of his original epic sense of history and idealism, while demonstrating that even men of the purest intentions and the noblest spirits need not shun a sensible approach in order to achieve fundamental ends. Critics of a later period came to understand this approach.

Stewart himself greatly admired this film, and said later that working with Wayne and Ford on a movie that gave out "a good, positive feeling" (in Stewart's words) had been profoundly heartening for him. During the making of the film he made no bones about wanting to work with both men again, which he did, but for all three, this was to be the highpoint of their professional association.

Edmond O'Brien, who played a crusty newspaper editor who supports Stewart in his bid to clean up the town and rescue it from Valance and his scoundrels, later said of *The Man Who Shot Liberty Valance*: "Everyone seemed to enjoy making it — Andy Devine, Ken Murray, Jeanette Nolan, Lee Marvin, Strother Martin — fine actors all, giving all they had, in a worthy enterprise. I have never seen John Ford happier than he was in making this; he came on the set positively beaming every morning — and that was not the usual thing with him. And Jim Stewart and Duke Wayne gave, for me, topnotch performances in a picture ideally suited to them." O'Brien added: "And it didn't do *me* any harm, either!"

Doug McClelland Collection

James Stewart, Audrey Meadows, *Take Her, She's Mine*, 1963

Chapter Fourteen

Holding His Own

At age 54, with energies soundly intact, Stewart embarked on a series of light domestic comedies for 20th Century-Fox, the first of which was *Mr. Hobbs Takes a Vacation* (1962), from Edward Streeter's novel, *Hobbs Takes a Vacation.* Years later, Stewart confessed that the insertion of the "Mr." in the title for the screen transcription puzzled him for some time: "I don't know to this day if they were trying to show respect for me or my character, or underline the ironies in the script." He added: "I know it's a minor point, but I have discovered through life that minor points are often highly indicative of what is going on in a picture as a whole.

Contracted to lend his usual comedy touches was writer Nunnally Johnson, who told me: "I felt Jimmy needed something light and amusing after the heavy stuff they had been saddling him with, and he was kind enough to tell me later that psychologically he felt he *was* vacationing when he made this film, and that he found himself chuckling at some of my lines."

Henry Koster was signed to direct, while gifted cinematographer William Mellor and composer Henry Mancini lent it their best creative inspirations. Koster said of this film: "Jimmy Stewart was a more adept comedian than he was ever credited as being, and in his mid-fifties his timing was never better. He had toned his famous mannerisms down somewhat by this picture, and underplaying brought out all the funny aspects much more than if they had been played broadly."

Also singing Stewart's praises was co-star Maureen O'Hara, who said she felt Stewart "was one of the most relaxing people to play with that I had ever known. And he had the delightful trick of living his role and the little things he was required to survive and triumph-over as the standard put-upon head of household were delightfully gotten across. And he was one of the more natural players, as if people didn't know that by 1962! And totally without vanity or pretentiousness."

O'Hara, who was in her forties by that time but looked years younger, later told Marie Wilson, one of the supporting players, that Mellor's color camera made her a little nervous, and she hoped he would get his lighting and his angles right. Marie remembered, "But Jimmy couldn't have cared less. I think he was less conscious of his looks than any man I had ever known, on or off camera. He told me during shooting, 'I'm several years past the half-century mark now, and if the camera shows up my character lines and a few bulges it will only make me look more real and increase audience empathy.'" Marie added: "Since Jimmy was a pretty trim and taut man for his age, I felt this showed wonderful humility."

Stewart plays a hard working banker who wants a nice, quiet, tension-free vacation away from it all with lovely wife O'Hara. But O'Hara is a family type, obsessed with her kids and grandkids; she can't relax on a sabbatical when she is wondering what they are up to. She and hubby get more than they bargain for when their off-spring show up at the quaint but ramshackle home O'Hara chooses

John Cocchi Collection

James Stewart, Chad Everett on the floor of the Republican National Convention, 1972

for them at the beach. The children (Natalie Trundy and Laura Peters) arrive replete with husbands, kids and assorted family problems: one girl has marital miseries; a grandchild tells Stewart he hates him; a cook loathes her surroundings; a bored son-in-law sullenly watches television; a second son-in-law develops an interest in a sexy, bikini-clad vixen on the beach. Then there is the daughter, self-conscious about her braces who finds love in the form of Fabian; the son-in-laws' straitlaced new employers, Marie Wilson and John McGiver, turn out to be secret drinkers; and so on and so on. Stewart gamely tries to cope with his wife's child-obsession, the odd quirks of the tumbledown house, and the constant barrage of emergencies.

Stewart displays in his performance a low-key humanity that reaches a high audience identification level; he makes the film endearingly tolerable, a triumph of performance over material. O'Hara is charming as the harried mother and wife, and the younger set have Fabian to admire. (Fabian even throws in a song for good measure.) One critical verdict: "Pleasant, at times amusing, otherwise forgettable."

Stewart next found himself back at MGM in a mammoth project that, in final cut, ran some 155 minutes. It was called *How the West Was Won* (1962), and it involved a host of top stars, a welter of extras, and the vaunted services of three top directors—Henry Hathaway, John Ford and George Marshall. It boasted revolutionary Cinerama photography from William Daniels, and eventually marched off with Oscars for writer James R. Webb and editor Harold F. Kress.

Several stories are told during the course of the action, which spans the fifty years from 1840 to 1890. Stewart appears in the first half hour as a trapper named Linus Rawlings, who marries the daughter (Carroll Baker) of a family migrating West. He runs afoul of a river pirate named Hawkins (Walter Brennan in an uncharacteristic rascally role) who almost kills him and steals his furs. Stewart prevails, marries the girl after her parents drown in rapids, and settles down on a farm with her where their sons, George Peppard and Claude Johnson, grow to manhood. Later, Stewart leaves for the Civil War and never comes back. Baker must also see Peppard off to war, but by the time he returns, she has died.

The rest of this Western epic largely concerns the fortunes of

Peppard, and Baker's sister, Debbie Reynolds, who marries gambler Gregory Peck. Narrated by Spencer Tracy, *How the West Was Won* enlists the services of such top stars as Henry Fonda and John Wayne, and colorful individuals such as Karl Malden and Agnes Moorehead as Baker's parents. Harry Morgan plays General Ulysses Grant, Raymond Massey (who else?) is Abraham Lincoln, and Robert Preston, Lee J. Cobb, Eli Wallach and Thelma Ritter, among many others, give excellent accounts of themselves.

The critics, were lost in admiration for the superb color photography, which has to be seen on a large screen to be fully appreciated. The actors all got solid pats on the back for their efforts in a sprawling story, based on a *Life* magazine series, that touched all the bases: rafts tossing around on the Ohio River, a buffalo stampede, a runaway train, pitched battles, and some thrilling hand-to-hand fighting. The pace and suspense are tiptop. The film is widely regarded as one of the best Westerns ever made, with directors Hathaway, Ford and Marshall justifiably dividing the credit.

Stewart also came in for his full share of admiration. Though a ripe 54 when he made it, he manages to suggest the passing of some twenty years from youth to middle age with remarkable veracity. As Tony Thomas wrote of him in the role: "Decked out in buckskins, [Stewart] had to play a man twenty years younger. With expert makeup and his own quirky kind of energy, he brought the part off with conviction. His Linus Rawlings is a feisty frontiersman. He looks very much like the kind of man who helped win the West."

Nor did other critics ignore Stewart when the congratulations were dished out. Typical of his reviews was that of a Washington, D.C., critic, who stated: "Mr. Stewart, last seen in a light domestic comedy (*Mr. Hobbs Takes a Vacation*), demonstrates his impressive versatility; there is a strength to his characterization, a resource, a variety, that marks him as one of our all-time major actors, something beyond the 'personality star'—a designation for too long misapplied to him."

While *How the West Was Won* has to be numbered among the films in which James Stewart and Henry Fonda co-starred, they went their separate ways in the script. Their performances were equally robust, but were not written by Webb to play off each other. Fonda told a reporter he felt "lost in such an overwhelming epic—it's like I wasn't there." But Stewart took the opposite tack, saying that he'd rather have a strong, well-directed, well-written half-hour than two hours of slipshod tedium, and in this film he got what he wanted.

Carroll Baker told me, "It meant a lot to me to appear with Jimmy in this. The great thing about him is that he considers the other actors — he's an ensemble player, yet never loses his essential dominance; it was real joy to play with such a professional!"

With *How the West Was Won* under his belt, Stewart went back to 20th Century-Fox and Henry Koster (producing as well as directing) for the second of the three comedies for which he had contracted. Again he had the writing services of Nunnally Johnson, whose sharp wit and comic ripostes kept the plot bubbling along merrily. Based on a play by Phoebe and Henry Ephron, and decked out in lush color by ace cameraman Lucien Ballard, *Take Her She's Mine* (1963) had Audrey Meadows (of *Honeymooners* fame) as the current Missus, and Sandra Dee and Charla Doherty as the daughters. Dressing things up were such stalwart character actors as Robert Morley and John McGiver, and dashing Philippe Forquet put in an appearance to romance Dee.

Art Carney (another 'Honeymooner') had played Stewart's role on Broadway, and Stewart, who greatly admired Art, was determined to put his individual stamp on the role. Once again he was the hapless husband and father (this time an attorney) who must keep fun-loving, adventurous daughter Dee out of trouble. In college, the intrepid miss gets herself into Ban-the-Bomb demonstrations and the beatnik lifestyle. When Stewart visits to check up on her, he ends up in trouble with the police himself, with the consequent embarrassment of unwanted publicity.

Having flunked out, Dee jets off to Paris, where Daddy must go a-hunting again to keep his darling daughter out of Gallic galavanting. Dee has taken up with avant-garde painter Philippe Fouquet, who is as eccentric as he is handsome. Stewart winds up in an outlandish costume at a bohemian ball, falls into the Seine, and gets arrested by the Paris police. Finally, a promise of relative stability is presaged when Dee and Fouquet head to the altar. Back home (and greatly relieved to be there), Stewart realizes that his middle-aged domesticity with Meadows will be short-lived: their second daughter has reached an age to emulate, and possibly surpass, her older sister's propensity for unpredictable mischief-making.

Stewart pulls out his usual bag of tricks for *Take Her, She's Mine*. "He's been this way before," one critic groaned, "and oh, hasn't he! But Mr. Stewart's strange, guileful, honest art is such that he gives a new twist to standard material. Without him, this film wouldn't amount to much — indeed it seems a tired re-treading of material long worked-out to a frazzle. But *with* him, it has zest, excitement and *joie de vivre*!"

A running gag through the film has Stewart's relatively staid lawyer being constantly mistaken for movie star James Stewart; the changes are rung on this perhaps a bit repetitively by writer Johnson.

Audrey Meadows is just the woman to complement Stewart's hijinks; she is poised and self-contained in a somewhat underwritten role. Morley and McGiver contribute lively elements. Robert Morley, who was not given to praise of other actors, or even his own abilities, went out of his way to pay tribute to the art of James Stewart, calling it "a natural gift, expertly honed and projected."

Sandra Dee told me in 1965 that playing with Stewart was one of the high points of her life: "He was wonderful as a husband and father because he fit the part naturally, and he always brought so much of his own wonderful self to it! By the time I made *Take Her, She's Mine*, I had been around for some years, and thought I knew all the tricks, but believe me, I learned quite a few new ones, just from watching him. He seemed never to run out of inspiration!"

Interviewing Stewart on the set that year, I noted that at 55 he took very good care of himself. I asked him his secret. "I balance my life," he confided, "and I don't overdo. I eat right, exercise as much as I feel necessary, and try to keep a good, positive, relaxed mental attitude." He added: "A lot of it is in the head, you know. The body follows the mind. If you're thinking right, you feel right, in all departments."

Sonia Wolfson, then a 20th-Fox studio publicist and a good friend, endorsed Stewart's self-assessment: "It's his positive attitude; he's spiritually at peace with himself. He likes himself. So he finds it easy to like others."

Sandwiched between Stewart's 20th Century-Fox comedies was *Cheyenne Autumn* (1964), the last Western John Ford was to make. It met with a mixed critical reaction after its 1964 premiere. Stew-

James Stewart, *Cheyenne Autumn,*
WB, 1964

art had a mere cameo in which, showcased in Panama hat and spiffy clothes, he portrayed Wyatt Earp. It was a relaxed and, indeed, comic turn. Presiding over a poker game in a saloon, he almost stole the show from a cast forced to labor through a rather dull and lengthy film (164 minutes) about the forced migration of the Cheyenne Indians from their native Wyoming to a bleak reservation in Oklahoma.

Ford was reported in the press to be expiating some of the guilt he felt for not highlighting the Indian plight more vividly in his earlier films, in which they were usually depicted as the savage enemy. Here they are portrayed as the victims of insensitive herding. The picture was handsome, shot in Monument Valley and Moab, Utah, but considering its genre it was slow, even tedious. The comical Stewart interlude was later cut, because the studio deemed it out of kilter with the serious subject matter of the movie. When the picture went on videocassette, however, the Stewart scenes were restored, which is all to the good.

Ford vividly depicted the starvation and disease plaguing the Cheyenne trek. Carroll Baker appears as a Quaker teacher who tries in vain to help the unfortunate migrants. Richard Widmark is the army captain who has to herd in the Indians, and Arthur Kennedy is razor-sharp in his impersonation of Doc Holliday, who, with Stewart's Earp, is drafted into leading a posse against the Indians. Stewart deliberately re-routes them and the Indians get away. Edward G. Robinson plays a humane and kindly Secretary of the Interior who helps bail out the hapless Cheyenne.

One critic said of this oddly unbalanced film: "It gives the impression that Mr. Ford is caught between a guilty need to showcase the plight of the Indians and still give us lots of action and excitement. The blend is not fortuitous. But James Stewart, in a rowdily comic spoof of Wyatt Earp, gives the picture some needed adrenaline. Too bad he wasn't kept in there as a character running straight through the picture; it would have helped — lots!"

Rumor had it that the Warner front office had originally insisted on the rowdy poker game in order to relieve the tedium of the rest of the film. They later reneged. But some of the sequences would have warmed the heart of Indian-cause-activist Marlon Brando: the white man's barbaric treatment of the Native Americans is shown in grimly realistic terms.

Arthur Kennedy credits Stewart with providing the tone for the notorious card game: "He had wonderful humor, and I always felt Jim would have made a great writer-director. In fact he practically directed our sequences himself. Part of it was sympathy for John Ford; Jim instinctively sensed that the picture was not turning out well. I thought what he did to hype up our scenes was pure miracle. I know the Wyatt Earp sequences were regarded as throwing the picture off, which is why they were cut from the original print, but some of Jim's best work and, largely thanks to him, some of mine, is in there."

Stewart himself has said of *Cheyenne Autumn*:

"It set out to be an honest, realistic, truthful picture, and I think it largely succeeded. Sure, in my sequences they were trying to apply some escapist counterbalance, some humor and fun, and maybe the picture doesn't have the pace it should have — Jack Ford was not at his best, admittedly — but in its honesty, in its hands-on approach, it was a film with the best of intentions, and I'm not sorry I made it."

Nonetheless the film was the object of some harsh criticism. One critic, obviously determined to keep the Western myth alive and well, noted: "We go to films for honest escape — not for factual realism carried too far. Of course the Indians were often mistreated by the Whites, but there's a way of getting across both viewpoints, and the point is not sufficiently stressed that the Whites went through many vicissitudes and lost many people to disease and violence while on their push to the Pacific. There was attrition on both sides."

For his third and final Fox comedy, Stewart found himself again under the directorial aegis of Henry Koster. The script was written by Hal Kanter based on John Hasse's novel, *Erasmus with Freckles*, but retitled *Dear Brigitte*. Why? Because the film's main gimmick has professor Stewart granting his mathematical-genius eight-year-old's fervent wish to meet Brigitte Bardot (then at the height of her sex appeal). The two go to Paris, and Erasmus (Billy Mumy) is kissed by Bardot and given a puppy.

Prior to this, the boy's mathematical skills have been misappropriated by everyone, from his sister's boyfriend (Fabian), who needs help with homework, to a British con man (John Williams), who illegally wins gambling bets to allegedly finance a humanitarian arts foundation. Fabian also comes up with another idea: for Erasmus to pick racetrack horses.

Stewart is a poetic, whimsical college professor who wants the simple life with wife Glynis Johns on a rather primitive, if quaint boathouse. Stewart's accordion skills are resuscitated, albeit briefly, as he insists that the entire family take up musical instruments. But Erasmus is tone-deaf, and when he takes up painting he turns out to have no eye for color either. The belated discovery that he is a mathematical genius brings more trouble than satisfaction, as the baffled Stewart dolefully discovers.

There was some silly publicity at the time as to exactly what Stewart's reaction to the womanly charms of Brigitte Bardot was. Since he had been married sixteen years by 1965, was the father of fourteen-year-old twins and two older stepsons, and since there had never been a hint of scandal about him ("No extramarital dalliances for Jimmy," Perry Lieber, 20th-Fox publicity head told me. "I don't know how he does it — or rather does without it — but he does"), it all came to nothing. Stewart later told the press that in the one scene they did together he found Bardot kindly and cooperative — no wild copy was to be gotten from him on the matter.

Bardot provided some diversion for the French press when she pronounced Stewart, then 57, "a gentleman with ageless sex appeal, enormous charm. But then age has never meant anything to me. It's the person himself. I have known old men who were experts in the art of *amour* and handsome young muscular boys who were totally inept." Translated from the French, these comments made amusing copy in the American papers, but an unfazed Gloria Stewart told a fan magazine writer: "None of it keeps me up nights. I know all

Double Family Portrait – on the right, gun "genius" David Marshall Williams, his wife Maggie and their son David; on the left, their screen portrayers James Stewart, Jean Hagen, and Bobby Hyatt, *Carbine Williams*, MGM, 1952

about her — and I know even more about Jim, and it's just silly publicity."

Fabian, aided by Fox's publicity experts Perry Lieber and Sonia Wolfson, let it be known that Stewart had taught him some new dance steps and had advised him on women. Stewart's rejoinder was that "the kid knows more than I do about romance; he doesn't need any lessons from me."

On the 20th Century-Fox lot in 1965, on one of my annual Hollywood jaunts (I was editing six movie magazines at the time) I lunched with Lieber and Wolfson, and the stars of *Dear Brigitte*. Stewart was warm, amusing, quizzical, kidding with Fabian, and keeping young Billy Mumy in stitches with his wisecracks. I ventured to ask Mumy his eight-year-old's impression of Bardot, and his four-letter rejoinder was "keen!" "Starting young!" Perry Lieber laughed. "But not *too* young, hopefully," Stewart quipped. "He should slow down a bit for a few years and give the older guys their chance." "Amen," Fabian chimed in. "That's *my* territory just now, Billy." In a snappy riposte that had everyone laughing, young Mumy glared at Fabian and piped, "*I* met her — *you* didn't!"

Glynis Johns, who had been on the point of marrying Stewart in *No Highway in the Sky* back in 1951, was at last his wife, and mother of his progeny, in *Dear Brigitte*. "It was long a dream of mine to be with him again," Glynis said, adding hastily: "Professionally, I mean." "She's a proper British lady," Stewart chided, good-naturedly. "She wants to be quoted accurately!"

When Billy Grady and I had one of our annual reunions in Hollywood in 1965, he took me to dinner and spoke for hours about Jimmy Stewart. "I am worried about his boys, Ron and Mike. They are his stepsons, of course, but always he calls them *his* boys. They are Ned MacLean's kids, but to Jim they're *his*, always *his*," Billy said, with sadness in his tones. "Jim always says, '*I* raised them; *I'm* the one who ushered them into manhood; *I* am their father!'"

Ron was then 20, and Mike 19. "He worries about them too much," Billy said. "He wants them to be the most conventional of solid citizens. He has been obsessed with raising them the way his own father would have wanted them (and for that matter, him) to be. Somehow I don't think he's letting them be themselves. They adore him, they look up to him, they are going to emulate Jim every way they can, but what do they want for *themselves*? What are they possibly sacrificing in order to live up to these rigid standards of his?"

"Jim's father, Alex, died a year or two back" (he died, actually, in 1961), Billy continued. "His mother died back in '53 — such a nice woman she was, too — very gentle, but quietly forceful, too. Jim told me how he went back to Indiana, got his dad buried, closed the hardware store. His father stayed with that store until his late 80s; he died at 89. After Jim sold the property, it was torn down; there's something else going up there now."

Billy remembered that Stewart had been very sad on those visits to bury his father and settle his estate. "I always tried to be the son, and the man, Dad wanted," Jim said to Billy. "But I was always afraid I had disappointed him by going into acting. I don't think my dad ever thought of that as a real man's profession."

Billy told him: "But you are an artist. You owed yourself fulfillment along the lines that were right for you, Slats. You spent too many years living for your parents' opinions, worrying about what those people in Indiana, Pennsylvania thought. Not to care what other people think is a great psychological strength! You had to live

Billy Mumy, James Stewart,
Dear Brigitte, 20th Century-Fox, 1965

by your own rules!" Billy continued that he had known many creative and talented people over the years in his profession, "and they still worried about what the neighbors in their old home towns thought. But they had moved on to a different world, with its own rules. They had to live for themselves, sooner or later."

And then Billy added: "The trouble with Jim is, he is caught between two worlds; that conventional, wife-and-kiddies, conformist, bourgeois world that he thinks is safe and secure, that world represented by his father. And the world of the artist, who has to live sufficient unto himself and his own instincts and rules."

Billy Grady was right. Stewart was torn between the desire to be a conventional, All-American icon, and the need to express his creative individuality. He had paid tribute to the bourgeois world over and over: Work hard, be a solid citizen, get (and stay) married for a lifetime. Have the regulation number of kids. Be financially successful. Boast of a good war record. Be a good Republican, stalwart and sensible. He was expected to thwart those instincts that evoked that other Jimmy Stewart, the boy who had sacrificed provincial predictability for the uncertainties of the acting profession.

But that inner Jimmy Stewart was still there, closer to the surface than he might have wanted. That was the Stewart that Logan, Fonda, McClintic and Mann had known so intimately; the Stewart who had fallen so in love with bohemian Margaret Sullavan, rather than with the non-existent "nice girl" from Indiana, Pennsylvania that his parents hoped for.

And now, as Billy indicated, Stewart was looking for signs of free-wheeling behavior in Ron and Mike, dreading to find the undesirable aspects that their real father had demonstrated so painfully. He catalogued any deviations from the norm that he had, by age 57 in 1965, come to approve of as safe and respectable. Since his marriage to Gloria, he had kept himself remarkably scandal-free. There were those impressionable kids to think of, and the public demanded of James Maitland Stewart all the virtues that made up the archetypal American male. But these were impossible standards that only a paragon or a saint could have attained.

Stewart, despite himself, had departed from the straight and narrow. He had hurt and confused his father by becoming an actor. He had been a romantic free spirit, scattering his oats where it pleased him, and sometimes those oats had fallen in strange places. He had waited until age 41 to marry, perhaps too late to reassure his father. Then he had given that convention-ridden parent an added jolt by marrying a divorced woman with two young sons. Nor were his wife and children conventional churchgoers as he had tried to be at the Brentwood Presbyterian Church. They went at times to please him, but he knew their hearts and spirits were not in it. Gloria had been a good wife to him. Lively, individualistic, extroverted, sophisticated: She had been the perfect foil for him.

But, Billy told me, Stewart always felt that he hadn't completely fulfilled his father's expectations, namely, that he should be as perfectly similar to Alexander Stewart as human imperfection allowed.

"The town back there was so empty without my father," Stewart mournfully told Billy. "Not to have him there any more. Like the Rock of Gibraltar suddenly torn away, with only waves left in a bottomless sea. The store sold, the building torn down, and him and my Mother up in the cemetery, gone from sight or sound, forever."

In 1965, Stewart agonized over how Ron and Mike would turn out. He wondered to Billy if his discipline and care could counteract their dad's bad blood. Would they be okay? Billy told him: "The important thing is that they should be themselves. People get along, in their own way. Once they're men their lives are their own. You will have done your part." But Stewart, he said, felt concerned about them and, "unaccountably guilty in some way I couldn't decipher."

As the years went on, Billy was struck by the fact that it was *the boys* he worried about, not his twin girls. "Girls are not the problem," Stewart told him. "They don't have the pressures boys do, and their mother has raised Judy and Kelly so wonderfully! If they turn out like *her*, they'll do just fine!"

When Billy asked Stewart what he would have done if the girls had wanted to be actresses, he said he would have preferred they didn't. "It's tougher for girls than boys — they get exploited more, they are more victimized by fate. One wrong guy, and that's it." Whereas, Stewart added, "an actor — a guy — can meet a lot of wrong guys — and women — and survive." "A lot of them didn't," Billy told him. "What about Ross Alexander?" "Well, I survived," Jimmy rejoindered heatedly. "I rooted out of myself anything that was negative or harmful, or would hurt my family or disillusion my fans. I grew up, I got sensible. I settled down." In a 1967 interview Jimmy Stewart had said more or less the same thing to me: "By the time middle age comes, you learn from your mistakes, you grow up, you go straight and sensible."

But at what price, I had been tempted to ask him. Did it have to be at the expense of the other selves within you? True, he had sublimated his demons in his personal life, but they came out clearly enough in his interpretation of his roles: the iconoclastic ferocity of the Mann westerns; the tormented incongruencies in Hitchcock's *Vertigo*; the fragile other-worldliness of Elwood Dowd of *Harvey*.

Professionally, that rabbit Harvey had been given his head by Stewart. But personally, he had been banished to the outer darkness. Had that been all to the good? In that same 1967 interview, Stewart seemed to think so: "One has to be a role model to one's children; one has to stick by his marriage vows, and to one woman only. One has to work hard, love community, country and God." These were the values Alexander Stewart had lived by. But after all, Alexander Stewart, had been only a small-town merchant with limited goals and opportunities. James Maitland Stewart was a world-famous artist. Could he, I asked Billy Grady, combine both aspects successfully in one person? "Slats seems to think he can," he replied, sadly and thoughtfully.

The girls were not to disappoint Stewart in at least one respect: they had no interest in acting, despite the fact that both were pretty and had personality to spare. Both married: as of that time, Kelly had become a zoologist and married a man of the same profession, and Judy had given him grandsons.

Kelly's and Judy's attitude toward their father was always respectful. They admired him, but were somewhat disinterested in his creative accomplishments. They had enjoyed his movies, but had not been enthralled by the life of Hollywood. Thanks to their careful upbringing, they had not "gone Hollywood" in any way: no drugs or alcoholism, no wild romantic adventures, no multiple marriages.

"I think this was a great consolation to Jimmy," John Swope said. "These girls were steady and sensible. Not a smidgin of creative talent in them; but lots of common sense and character."

"None of Jimmy Stewart's kids will ever write a *Daddy Dearest* book about him," Henry Fonda said once. "They have no gripes and no beefs; they were never a problem to Jimmy so they have no guilts to rationalize. They were not at all interested in being actors or hogging his spotlight [Was this a subconscious dig at his own Jane and Peter?] and I don't think they ever gave him a moment's worry in all their lives."

Michael MacLean certainly trod the straight and narrow: he became an investment banker, married, and gave Jimmy and Gloria the joy of grandchildren. Mike, according to Stewart, never gave his parents a moment's worry.

A few years before he died, Stewart summarized his four kids for me, during a rather conventional interview in Hollywood. Kelly and Judy were sensible down-to-earth kids, in love with their husbands, totally satisfied with their lives. Ronald had "fulfilled his destiny," said Stewart, and he was deeply proud of his son's war hero status. I was tempted to suggest that, having been killed in Vietnam at 24, Ron had hardly had the chance to fulfill his destiny, and indeed had probably never even discovered his true self. (I thought it ill-advised to suggest this to Stewart; he would have been horrified.) As for Michael, everything pointed to one thing: he had lived to please and, so far as was humanly possible, emulate the loving but strict stepfather to whom convention was all.

Shenandoah, released in 1965 when Stewart was 57, exhibits him in full maturity, as actor and man. Anyone who wishes to grasp the essence of one of America's great national ornaments, need only see this film.

A handsome picture with a Civil War background, *Shenandoah* is not the most profound of Stewart's films, nor is it the greatest. But it is a deeply human work suffused with that current of emotion that is often sought by directors and actors, but rarely found. It is old-fashioned in the sense that it deals with love of family and friends in an unapologetically sentimental manner. For this, and many other reasons, it lingers in the heart and mind.

Stewart has never been in better form than in *Shenandoah*. He is the archetypal paterfamilias, a widower, deeply concerned for his six sons and one daughter on their farm in a remote section of Virginia, while the Civil War rages around them. A pacifist and a man who scorns slavery, he holds himself and his sons aloof from both the Confederate and Union causes. But, for all his hatred of war, the rush of events finally draws him into that tumultuous and heart-breaking clash. When he loses his 16-year-old youngest boy to the Union soldiers as a prisoner, he is compelled into action. He presides with gruff affection over his daughter's marriage to a young Confederate officer. He visits his wife's grave (she had died giving birth to the son who is now a prisoner) and in simple and sincere words movingly talks with her. Stewart underplays so convincingly that all trace of the maudlin is absent.

The tragedy of war strikes even more deeply when he loses one son to a Confederate sentry's bullet and another son and his wife to renegades who invade their farm while Stewart and his remaining sons are foraging for their youngest. By the end of the film he is a chastened and deepened spirit, his hatred of war still intact, but his faith in family stronger than ever. In a tearful final scene, Stewart's 16-year-old, who has escaped his Union captors, comes down the church aisle on crutches while the remainder of his family are worshipping. He is embraced joyfully, and joins his father and family in their pew, along with the orphaned baby granddaughter.

The film is alive with sterling performances by such up-and-coming young actors as Glenn Corbett, Tim McIntire, Patrick Wayne, Charles Robinson, and James McMullan. Philip Alford is most touching as the beloved youngest son, and Katharine Ross, in her first film role, is moving as the daughter-in-law who dies with her husband when the farm is invaded. Rosemary Forsyth is strong and stately as Stewart's only daughter, who dresses in male clothes and joins her brothers in their search for their captured sibling. Many other fine actors make a noteworthy appearance: George

Philli Alford, James McMillan, Glen Corbett, Tim McIntire, Patrick Wayne, Charles Robinson, Rosemary Forsyth, James Stewart, Katharine Ross, *Shenandoah*, 1965

Kennedy is effective as a Union officer who helps Stewart with a pass to obtain his son, and who fervently relates that his own 16-year-old is in school in Boston — "thank God!" Paul Fix is affecting as the solicitous and concerned family doctor, and Kelly Thordsen, Strother Martin, James Best and Denver Pyle round out a superb cast.

Shenandoah was Stewart's first film with director Andrew V. McLaglen, the 45-year-old son of the famous Victor, who had won a Best Actor Oscar in John Ford's *The Informer* (1935). Young McLaglen had been raised in a show business atmosphere, and had learned his craft in industrial productions. He had established himself as a director in 1956 with two creditable films: *Gun the Man Down* and *The Man in the Vault*. McLaglen had been an assistant director to John Ford, Budd Boetticher, and others, and had absorbed much from them, before emerging with his own individual directing style. He was to do other films with Stewart, but he informed me in later years that *Shenandoah* was the closest to his heart.

"Jim Stewart had already become a national icon by the time he made this film," McLaglen told me, "and all the personality-force, the rough-hewn integrity, the deep feeling concealed beneath a gruff exterior, was on total display in *Shenandoah*. I was deeply honored to be associated with him on this, and I tried to do justice to him by giving of my very best."

I had interviewed McLaglen briefly while he was directing the film in 1965 on Universal City's back lot, and I had also come to know several of the cast, including Jim McMullan, Patrick Wayne and Charles Robinson. Robinson, who played one of the sons, told me how deeply impressed he was with Stewart; he couldn't get over his luck in playing with a man who had been one of his childhood idols. Robinson felt Stewart had attained "a kind of majesty in *Shenandoah*, and that was how he was in person — majestic. What character and what strength!" In Robinson's opinion, "he could have had a great career in politics, had he chosen to go that way."

When I visited the set of *Shenandoah*, I sensed at once the unique spirit surrounding it; everyone seemed to be caught up in the spell of its theme, approaching it with a kind of reverent determination to give their very best. And there at the center, the figure of Stewart, just as Robinson had described him, pulling it all together with his intense force of spirit, his unceasing positivism.

I talked to Stewart several times between set-ups and he said that *Shenandoah* was the kind of film he had always sought to make, that its heart was in the right place. He told me: "We must never lose certain values in the American spirit. And this picture has them; it makes the point, among others, that there comes a time when one must fight for one's beliefs — to the finish."

Shenandoah exudes a quality that seems to have partially disappeared from American life. The picture represents a time of virtuous sentiment and unflinching devotion to certain established ideals. *Newsweek*, in its respectful review of the film, said it best about Stewart: "What [he] achieves must be a source of some discouragement as well as instruction for the young, unskilled actors working with him. He is far from young. His role of paterfamilias is more tired than his eyes. Yet Stewart compels belief with his strength and his simplicity."

Two of Stewart's greatest admirers among the supporting cast of *Shenandoah* were the actors George Kennedy and Kelly Thordsen, both solid performers who, over the years, worked with the best.

Here is what George Kennedy told me:

"Jim Stewart dominated his surroundings. Not because he was authoritative or up-front in the way Duke Wayne was — he didn't come on like that. He was just quietly there. One felt he put the good of a picture above any of its components, including himself. He was good to play with because he played things back to you, kept the ball going back and forth. And one felt he was rooting for one. And he listened — oh, how he listened! As any good actor does, he listened and he reacted! I've played with some star actors who gave the impression they couldn't wait for you to finish speaking so they could jump in with their main-line act, as if you were there to feed cues to them, and nothing more. Jim was never like that. He made you feel like an equal in the scene."

And from Kelly Thordsen:

"I didn't have as many scenes with him as I would have liked in *Shenandoah*, but he was the smoothest act I ever encountered when it came to confrontational give-and-take. He made you want to give your best. And he *shared* his scene with you...."

Considering that he celebrated his 57th birthday while making *The Flight of the Phoenix* (1965), a film heavy on action in a scorching desert location, James Stewart's enduring stamina testified to a sound constitution and a good genetic inheritance.

Ostensibly set in the Sahara, the film was actually shot on location in a much-used area outside Yuma, Arizona. Stewart is a grizzled old pilot, tired and cynical but still feisty, who carries a group of oil company people to a Saharan outpost. On board is the usual variety of types: simple crewmen, intellectual experts, sophisticated advisors, all limned with individuality and solid impact by the most expert group of fellow-actors any James Stewart film has ever boasted. Consider the likes of Richard Attenborough, Peter Finch, Hardy Kruger, Ernest Borgnine, George Kennedy, Christian Marquand, and Ronald Fraser.

Due to the alcoholic indulgence of navigator Attenborough, the plane is forced down in the middle of the desert, and then, as is standard in such films, the true characters of the men emerge under the blistering heat and the threat of starvation.

Based on a novel by Elleston Trevor, scripted by Lukas Heller, and photographed in striking color by Joseph Biroc, this 20th Century-Fox production was ably directed by Robert Aldrich who, when he wanted to, could summon considerable visceral force in his depiction of human frailty.

The Flight of the Phoenix is rather unusual in its plot: several of the marooned aeronautic engineers manage to construct, from the wreckage of the old plane, a single-engine remnant, a "phoenix," that eventually transports the survivors to safety. The depiction of the construction is fascinating, with much of the suspense, tautly orchestrated by Aldrich, predicated on whether the plane will get successfully airborne. Aldrich lets loose his talent for compressing violent action and explosive personal tension, and the audience is cheering along with the survivors when the phoenix rises from the ashes.

The film did not do well with the public, possibly because the advertising failed to underline the uniqueness of the phoenix angle, or to promote the clever suspense elements. Some critics opined that Stewart was too old for these kinds of heroics, and there was some discussion as to why he didn't look for more solid dramatic roles in more traditional settings.

Certainly there is a sense of despair in watching the immeasurably seasoned Stewart persona being wasted on vehicles which, however professionally wrought, emphasize physical action. It was abundantly apparent that, by 1966, Stewart had much more to offer in character work in a greater variety of fare.

I interviewed, in following years, several actors who worked with Stewart in *The Flight of the Phoenix*.

Peter Finch played an intrepid British Army captain, who, with his sergeant, Ronald Fraser, reconnoitered valiantly but unsuccessfully for a way out of their desert position. Finch thought Stewart "a wonderfully resourceful actor who in my view has been scandalously wasted in all the action and western material he has chosen to undertake. Possibly he felt it was 'safer' to do outdoor stuff with a minimum of 'romance,' due to the age he had arrived at, but I, for one, cannot believe that Hollywood could not have come up with more solid fare for him. He should be playing presidents, captains-of-industry, supreme court justices — why isn't he?"

Richard Attenborough told me that Stewart was "an actor of infinite resource, and he should have left the movies permanently for the stage. In London and New York he could have climbed to the peak of his profession. I know he went to the stage in both cities once or twice but he should have gone back permanently; the stage would have given him a far greater range of solid characterizations."

Stewart's *The Rare Breed* (1966) is a Western of consummate integrity: it does not sentimentalize its characters and keeps to the main business. Under the direction of Andrew V. McLaglen, who understood the John Ford mystique, *The Rare Breed* is a solid, gritty example of its genre, with Stewart again playing a cynical, hard-bitten man who has become disillusioned with human nature. He is not however devoid of glints of understanding and spiritual insight.

Maureen O'Hara, who has always played well with Stewart, is the distaff co-star. The title refers to a certain breed of cattle, and *not* to men, rare, courageous, or otherwise. Described by one writer as "a slightly mangy drifter-cowpoke, not above a little cheating, but, of course, a man who has a residual sense of decency," Stewart gives a performance of thoroughgoing integrity in a role that does not particularly elicit audience sympathy.

O'Hara is an Englishwoman who comes to America with her daughter, Juliet Mills, bringing a prize Hereford bull named Vindicator. Her husband has died enroute, and O'Hara is delivering the bull to Brian Keith in Dodge City. Her late spouse has always maintained that the Hereford could be successfully interbred with the indigenous American Longhorns. This notion is met with ridicule by Keith and Stewart, who has been put in charge of delivering the bull. Originally Stewart had planned to kidnap the bull and hand it over to a rival dealer, but he falls under the spell of O'Hara's womanly integrity, and becomes her ally. Soon a triangle is set up between Stewart, O'Hara and Keith, with predictable results: Keith has also been spiritually rejuvenated by O'Hara and proceeds to clean up his act. O'Hara's daughter and Keith's son (naturally) pair off romantically, and Stewart, after overcoming assorted obstacles, successfully breeds the Hereford and Longhorn.

Critics commented again on the raw strength and integrity that Stewart brought to his Western characterizations. "The force of the man is one of his salient characteristics," one reviewer noted. "Force — and adaptability. He can suggest human sidelights, poignant underpinnings, even in an unlikeable character, and can bring that character to thrilling and strengthful life."

Brian Keith said of working with Stewart in *The Rare Breed*: "There is so much more to the man than appears on the surface. People have wondered why he can shine with equal effectiveness in pictures by directors whose styles and approaches differ, often so radically, but the answer is in the complex nature of his character, and his creative instinct, which is more wide-ranging and deep than I think he has ever been credited with."

More than one commentator has praised the scene, toward the end of the picture, when Stewart comes upon the calf which is the offspring of the unlikely bovine union. "His satisfaction in the success of the cross-breeding is so apparent on his face, and he gets across the excitement of a cattleman's vocation, his deep fulfillment from tasks well performed and events that transpire positively," a Washington reviewer commented.

Nor are the dramatic elements neglected in *The Rare Breed*. The rivalry between the men, the poignant situation of the young lovers, O'Hara's attempts to adjust to an environment that she, a new widow, finds inescapably alien, are all set forth eloquently and powerfully by McLaglen's directorial hand. The color photography by William Clothier, the music by John Williams, and the tautly written screenplay of Ric Hardman are all pronounced assets to the proceedings.

A Boston reviewer complimented: "This is one of the more admirable Westerns of 1966 or any year. There is an integrity to its unsparing bleakness, an honesty to its pointed depictions of reality."

Some 33 years after they had both begun making movies, Jimmy Stewart, 60, and Henry Fonda, 63, finally got to star together in a full-length film. *Firecreek* (1968) is a somber, downbeat Western directed by Vincent McEveety, written by Calvin Clements and photographed by William Clothier in bleak, striking colors. It also had the benefit of Alfred Newman's musical inspiration. The film started off well, but went steadily downhill in a welter of unrelieved negativism.

The public was indifferent to it the year of its release, and it has subsequently failed to pick up any kind of following. One obvious reason for public antipathy, was the disappointment that the two legendary friends and intimates had not been afforded something more affirmative. "Even a light comedy would have suited their pairing better," their mutual pal Johnny Swope declared later.

Fonda himself in his book as told to Howard Teichmann (*Fonda: My Life*) felt compelled to point out the glaring incongruity of his casting, saying: "Jim Stewart and I played together in a thing [sic] called *Firecreek*. You know, someone had the bright idea of making me the villain. I played a bad guy who tried to kill Jim Stewart. Now, any man who tries to kill Jim Stewart has to be marked as a man who's plain rotten! You can't get much worse than that!"

And Fonda was just that: plain rotten. He was grim, sadistic, and unrepentantly villainous from start to finish. He and his gang descend on a small Arizona town (shot in authentic locations) and make nuisances of themselves. Farmer-turned-sheriff Stewart straps on his guns and goes out to do battle with them, especially after they lynch a boy who had caught one of the Fonda gang in mid-rape and killed him. Stewart, an uncomplicated good-guy and family-man, decides enough is enough: In a no-holds-barred shooting spree he kills all the gang except Fonda. As Fonda takes aim at Stewart he is shot down by young Inger Stevens. She had nursed him from earlier wounds in her boarding house, and had even started to fall in love with him. But she realized that he was no good, beyond redemption, and hence deserved to die.

Such is the plot, and a monotonously driven business it is. Stewart seems not to have held it in high esteem, and faulted it on the grounds that the Cal Clements screenplay made him too transparently one-dimensional. He also implied that the director (McEveety) had not summoned up the effects that his close pal Anthony Mann (who had died the previous year) would have achieved. But the truth was that, without extensive rewriting, Mann in his prime could not have done much with so simplistically upbeat a guy as Stewart's Johnny Cobb in *Firecreek*. While regretting, in more than one interview, that he and Stewart had not been handed a more cohesive screenplay to do together in their vintage years, Fonda reluctantly conceded that his villainous character had given him a good chance to project undiluted evil, a quality not usually associated with Fonda. But, as he later put it, "I could get away with being an all-out villain because my persona had never been deified in the way Jim's was. Had *he* played *my* role, the public would have boycotted the theatres; they could never see Jim as all-out bad."

The tormented and unhappy actress Inger Stevens, who committed suicide two years after *Firecreek* at the early age of 36, managed to suggest sincere evocations of underlying neurosis in her role. Stevens had debuted in 1957 in *Man on Fire* opposite Bing Crosby, with whom she was to have a doomed offscreen romance. She had also loved, and been spurned by, Fonda, off screen as well as on. In 1961, she secretly married black musician Ike Jones. Her real-life torments, sadly, gave her role more dimension than either the all-good Stewart or all-bad Fonda were able to achieve in *Firecreek*.

Bandolero! featured Stewart in yet another Western. As directed by Andrew V. McLaglen and written by James Lee Barrett from a Stanley Hough story, Stewart's character is given more to action than to psychological musings. The entire tone of the picture, which co-stars Dean Martin as his outlaw younger brother and Raquel Welch, singularly out of place in a Western setting, is decidedly superficial. Stewart probably didn't expect McLaglen, whom he greatly liked, to inspire him to complex character histri-

Dean Martin, Raquel Welch, James Stewart, *Bandolero!*, 1968

onics; McLaglen's forte was action, and this he delivered in a professional, if hardly spectacular style. *Bandolero!* has gone down in filmic history as an also-ran.

Raquel Welch seems painfully ill at ease as the widow of a man killed by brothers Martin and Stewart in a holdup. She comes across more as a tartish camp-follower than as an outraged widow, who gradually falls in love with Martin. Her suit is aided by Stewart, who would like his younger brother to leave his life of crime and settle down to something more respectable. (Stewart later remembered that Welch had a great deal of trouble with her characterization, such as it was. He had to tell her there wasn't much in the script to begin with, and she should just get in there and say the lines. A puzzled but compliant Welch obeyed.)

The plot piles on the Western clichés. It is the post-Civil War west; older brother Stewart fought in the Union Army, younger brother Martin in the Confederate ranks. Pretending to be a hangman (he has stolen the guy's getup on the road) Stewart rescues Martin from the scaffold. After they've held up a bank, intrepid sheriff George Kennedy chases Stewart and Martin (with hostage Welch in tow) to Mexico. In a peculiar plot twist, the outlaws find themselves temporary allies with the sheriff when they are set upon by Mexican bandits. Stewart and Martin lose their lives, and back to the U.S. go Kennedy and Welch. It is indicated that, for differing reasons, they will not forget the dead they have left behind.

Stewart told Tony Thomas about his beloved horse Pie, described by him as "a light reddish brown sorrel stallion, part Arabian and part quarter-horse." *Firecreek* was the last picture in which Pie would appear with Stewart; they had worked together for eighteen years, since *Winchester '73* in 1950. Stewart loved the horse but its owner, one Stevie Myers (a lady), would never let him, for unexplained reasons, buy it. Stewart described Pie to Thomas as "a ham of a horse. There was a scene in *The Far Country* in which Pie had to walk down a street at night by himself. I told him what I wanted and set him off, and he did the shot in one take!" Two years after *Firecreek*, Stewart wanted to use Pie for *The Cheyenne Social Club*, but the mile-high altitude of the Sante Fe location was too much for the animal's breathing. He died shortly thereafter. Stewart informed Thomas that Fonda, who had a talent for painting, did a rendition

James Stewart, Fred MacMurray, Bob Hope, President Richard Nixon, 1970

of Pie as a gift for Stewart. It hung, for years, on a favored wall in the Stewart living room.

The critics did not throw up their hats over *Bandolero!* which they found flimsy, perfunctory, and "redolent of two thousand Westerns that have gone that away before." McLaglen does keep the action moving, to be sure, and Welch tried to be super-sexy in the style audiences had come to expect of her, but she was suffocated under the placidities of her wistful widow character. Fan magazines and columnists, doubtless in a lean season, tried to work up a love triangle between Stewart, Martin, and Welch, all of whom were very much married. Welch denied the reports as "outrageous and totally untrue," but the publicity men got a laugh out of it anyway. They sobered up later under Stewart's stern injunction "never to embarrass me or my family in that way again, ever!" Sex Goddess Welch always referred to Stewart and Martin as "gentlemanly."

Stewart sank into profound grief when he heard of the death of his elder stepson, Ronald McLean, on June 11, 1969, eight days before his 25th birthday. Ronald, a first lieutenant in the Marine Corps, had been killed while leading a reconnaissance patrol in

South Vietnam. Two years before, when he was sworn in as a USMC second lieutenant, his stepfather, one year before retiring as a Brigadier-General in the Air Force Reserve, had participated in the ceremony, pinning on his bars. The accompanying photographs, widely distributed in the press, had demonstrated, for the entire nation to see, the enormous pride father and son took in each other.

In 1968, Stewart, then 60, and his wife had gone on a tour of Vietnam, visiting hospitals, encouraging the soldiers, signing autographs. He had also gone on an inspection tour, and had accompanied the crew on a B-52 mission from Guam to near the Cambodian border, close to Saigon. He had observed action in Quang Tri, just south of the Demilitarized Zone, and had spent some time with Ronald, who, he later told reporters, "was performing ably and manfully as a U.S. Marine officer."

He would later reminisce at length about Ronald, whom he clearly loved as his own son, and greatly doted on. He told reporters on several occasions that Ronald had always wanted to please him and make him and his mother proud, even when it went against his own inclinations: "He was never a good student, either at Colorado State or elsewhere, but he stuck in there and graduated with creditable grades because he didn't want to disappoint us." Another time, with tears coming down his cheeks, he told a reporter: "People say what a terrible tragedy that he had to die. We never look on it as a tragedy. It's a loss, no tragedy. He had a useful life. He graduated from college, and his country was at war. He became a Marine and when he got on the battlefield he conducted himself with gallantry. What's tragic about that? What's tragic is boys losing their lives without a unified country behind them. *That's* what's tragic!" Stewart always maintained that the only thing wrong with the Vietnam conflict was that "we didn't fight to win! The war was justified, but some of us failed to measure up as patriots!" John Wayne once blasted a throng waving a Vietcong banner in front of Stewart at an anti-war demonstration, telling them that Stewart had lost a son, and they should be more respectful.

Many friends and numerous fans had been pressing Stewart and Henry Fonda to co-star in a picture that would stress their longtime deep affection for each other. Stewart did a lot of cogitating about this, and, in 1970, called in his friend and associate James Lee Barrett to work up a concept. Stewart raised his eyebrows more than an inch when Barrett proposed that Stewart and Fonda play two cowpokes, getting on in years but still feisty and adventurous, who learn that Stewart's brother has died and left him a whorehouse. The establishment gave the film its title: *The Cheyenne Social Club* (1970).

Stewart was hesitant for a time. He didn't know how his fans would take to whorehouse jokes and he almost refused the picture, but Fonda, who had a more earthy approach, felt it would be fun and different, and demanded they go ahead.

After an interminable journey across the plains, for which Barrett devised the ploy that laconic and straitlaced Stewart found the incessant gab of easygoing Fonda a crashing bore and repeatedly told him to shut up, the two pals reach Cheyenne and the bordello, which is well-managed by pretty Shirley Jones. They run into assorted problems with the townspeople, and when Stewart kills a guy who has beaten Jones, the murdered man's family becomes an implacable enemy. Stewart toys with turning the bordello into a saloon, but Fonda is having a high old time with the girls. After numerous plot complications, many of them artificially devised by the over-eager Barrett, Stewart and Fonda decide that to close the bordello would be to put the girls out of work. They hand it over to Jones, and set off on their travels again.

Shot on location near Santa Fe, New Mexico, by old standby William Clothier, who gave the film a handsome appearance, *The Cheyenne Social Club* is mediocre cinema fare, qualifying neither as farce nor Western. Some of the jokes about the bordello are labored and repetitious, and there was some fuss over Jimmy compromising his clean cut image when he confronts one of the prostitutes in a see-through negligee. Stewart wanted the scene cut out, but the company overruled him.

The film's director was a surprising choice: Gene Kelly, a good friend of both Stewart and Fonda. Stewart's reasons for wanting to use Kelly, whose reputation was hardly associated with Westerns, remain obscure. Perhaps he felt Kelly would slyly inject more tongue-in-cheek elements, given the bordello angle, than an action-oriented director like Andrew McLaglen would have. In any event, Kelly liked the project and took it on as both producer and director, while Barrett wore both the writer and executive-producer hats.

Henry Fonda seems to have had a solid affection for *The*

James Stewart, *Fools Parade*,
Columbia, 1971

Cheyenne Social Club, especially as it gave him and Stewart a chance to *really* co-star in a film with some human dimensions. In *Fonda: My Life*, Hank dwells on the film at some length, citing just the one sad event connected with it: Stewart's learning of the death of his stepson Ronald in Vietnam. As Fonda recalled it: "Here we were making this comedy [sic] when the Defense Department notified [him.] Jim tried hard not to spread his grief through the company. He and I avoided discussing the war before the tragedy. Now I did everything I could to take his mind off it. We chawed about old times at the Madison Square Hotel in New York, and our early bachelor days living together in Brentwood."

Fonda recalled Stewart slipping food to his adored stallion, Pie, "an apple or a piece of watermelon or a carrot. That was when I began to realize what Pie meant to him. His boy was gone, and I couldn't do anything about that, but now, seeing the expression on Jim's face when he reached for something to take to his horse, I had an idea . . . ."

"On Sundays, when we weren't working, I'd trek over and have the wrangler bring Pie out and stand him in front of the barn. And then I made sketches of the horse, the barn, a carriage, and the gate. I planned it to be a surprise for Jim. I finished the watercolor after I got home, I had it framed and gave it to Jim. He was surprised all right. He just dissolved when he saw the painting. He's got a light over it now, like it's a shrine. Ole Pie died about ten days later." Gene Kelly was later to remember that losing his son and his horse within such a short time of each other really bothered Stewart. "He started talking about how he was 60 years old and more, and nothing lasted, and life flew by so swiftly the older you got. He was very meditative and very sad. Then, with his usual resiliency, he snapped right out of it. 'Life goes on; we have to take our hurts in stride.'"

Fonda recalled that it was about this time that his daughter Jane's politics proved an unwelcome intrusion into *The Cheyenne Social Club's* publicity campaign. The story goes that, although he was a liberal Democrat, Fonda felt Jane had gone too far in her anti-war protests (her visit to Hanoi was to cause an anti-Jane Fonda protest that rankles veterans organizations to this day). As Stewart recalled it: "We were in Salt Lake City to do a television promotion on the picture. The man who was going to interview us said, 'Is there anything you'd rather not talk about?' And Hank said, 'Well, I'd just as soon not get into a discussion about Jane and her politics. I'd just as soon stick to what we're here for, the picture.'" As Stewart related it, the first thing the interviewer brought up as they went on the air was Jane: "Mr. Fonda, I understand your daughter Jane sort of looks upon herself as an American Joan of Arc. Is that true?" Fonda testily replied that it was true, and that he didn't think Jane would be satisfied until they burned her at the stake.

Fonda and Stewart consciously avoided any political talk, as they knew that, with their opposite views, they might well jeopardize their friendship if they waxed too passionate. But Fonda sensed Stewart's deep disapproval of Jane's activities in the anti-war movement and the lengths to which she went to favor Hanoi — a stance she later regretted and recanted. It was well known that Stewart took deep satisfaction in Fonda's stern public statement that if he ever thought Jane was a Communist he would disown her on the spot.

Stewart was later to express privately, and only to close friends, his honest astonishment that Jane Fonda went on to Oscar recognition and smash hit movies, considering the disgraceful way she had behaved during the Vietnam War. One actor, who wishes to remain anonymous, and who acted with Stewart in his next picture, *Fools' Parade* (a title he jokingly applied to Fonda and her politics), maintained that on the set of that picture Stewart opined that Jane Fonda had been no better then a traitor. In later years, Stewart remarked ruefully that the anti-capitalist, anti-U.S. Jane of the Sixties and early Seventies had since profited brazenly from capitalism, becoming a millionairess several times over from her fitness videos and other commercial gimmicks. She eventually bagged super-rich Ted Turner as a husband. "And that they should reward her with an Oscar!" Stewart scoffed. "It's like that Leftist bunch in Hollywood wants to heap orchids on her for the damage she did this country." Determined, however, not to undermine his many years of friendship with her father, Stewart never brought it up to Henry personally. In *The Cheyenne Social Club*, as an inside joke, they had played a scene walking along a street in which Stewart in character refers to himself as a solid Republican and Fonda's character asserts he is a true Democrat. But Stewart told interviewer after interviewer, at that time and later, that "Hank and I never, ever discuss politics!"

The story goes that Fonda, deeply upset that Stewart's Marine stepson should have given up his life for a cause that his own daughter was busily tearing down, much to the contempt of many Americans, tried to convey his shame over Jane and his sorrow over Ronald. Stewart abruptly cut him off with the words, "If we dwell on it, it will only lead to arguments, Hank! We've been too close to let anything come up now between us after all these years."

Stewart always maintained a certain coolness and reserve toward Jane Fonda, as did his wife, Gloria, who had lost her firstborn child in that tragic war. One friend of Stewart's added to the controversy over Jane, by declaring: "Instead of shooting her as a traitor, they give her awards and set her up in the very capitalistic big business she affected to scorn! What a hypocrite!" But on the subject of Jane Fonda, her father and Stewart maintained a mutual silence to the end.

Fools' Parade (1971), when the 63-year-old Stewart got around to it, turned out to be a mistake, and he was not to show up in another theatrical film for five years. Though not technically a Western, the picture, with an early-Thirties West Virginia setting, had all of a Western's action and plot situations. Once more, the journeyman, but earnestly efficient Andrew V. McLaglen directed Stewart in an ambivalent, morally reprehensible characterization that cried out for the ministrations of Anthony Mann.

There was real affection between Stewart and Andrew McLaglen, but Stewart was never blind to the younger man's limitations. He told a fellow actor during the shooting of *Fools' Parade*, "Andy's great on action stuff but this time around I wish I had had Tony to call upon." Stewart had grieved mightily when Tony Mann died suddenly in 1967, and often referred to him during conversations on set: "Tony would have done this; Tony would have changed this." McLaglen, who understood the closeness of the two men over a number of pictures, was always tolerant. "What I do, I feel I do well," McLaglen once told an interviewer. "I have never pretended to have more scope or depth than I have. I know my limitations and I'm satisfied to stay within them...."

Unfortunately, both McLaglen's limitations and those of screenwriter and Stewart sycophant James Lee Barrett are very much on display in *Fools' Parade*. The script was based on a forgettable novel by one David Grubb, and though Harry Stradling was on hand with the color camera, and Henry Vars injected what musical inspirations he could, the result was strictly second-rate. It was even, on occasion, unintentionally funny, with the audience, as a chagrined Anne Baxter commented, "laughing in all the wrong places." Baxter said that she wished she had never been associated with the film. Among Anne's many frank utterances for public consumption over the years, this observation went relatively unnoticed at the time, much to the relief of the film's publicist.

In an uneasy blend of melodramatic themes, Stewart is a convict who squirrels away $25,000. A murderer, he has done all the hard prison jobs and has been a model prisoner. He gets out of prison with bankrobber Strother Martin and rapist Kurt Russell, and having paid their collective debt to society, they set out to make their fortune as civilians once more. But corrupt cop George Kennedy and banker David Huddleston are out to relieve Stewart of his nest egg. After fending off would-be murderers on a train, Stewart meets up with Baxter, whose houseboat is doing part-time bordello duty. Baxter wants Stewart's money, too, but gets blown up by dynamite (in)conveniently left behind by Stewart.

At the bank, Stewart fends off his enemies by claiming he is wired with explosives and if he doesn't get his dough they'll all be blasted to bits along with him. Finally, he triumphs over any and all obstacles, and is ready to begin his new life, complete with the $25,000.

The critics complained that no one in *Fools' Parade* was very admirable, and that the lack of any positive elements gave the picture a grimness that did not make for audience approval. Their predic-

tions were amply confirmed when the film did poorly at the box office. The adverse critical reaction and the popular distaste gave
Stewart some pause, and he drew in his horns for a while, cogitating on the future. "I really think that in 1971, at 63, Jimmy almost
decided to retire for good," Anne Baxter said later. "Also, while not
a vain man about his looks, I don't think he relished his image aging
before the cameras, at least at that point." Stewart sported an oversized glass eye in the film, which critics claimed looked grotesque
and almost lent a comic rather than dramatic touch. In a later comment about *Fools' Parade*, Stewart would only say, "I'm afraid that
big black-pupiled glass eye was a mistake...."

Strother Martin, James Stewart, "Hawkins on Murder," CBS-TV, 1973

Chapter Fifteen

Tackling TV

In the five-year period between his two theatrical films *Fools' Parade* (1971) and *The Shootist* (1976), Stewart kept busy in other media. He narrated two Peter Bogdanovich documentaries about John Ford in 1971, and *Pat Nixon; Portrait of a First Lady*, in 1972. The President and Mrs. Nixon personally thanked him for "lending great dignity and professionalism" to the tribute, and Nixon wrote him that no other actor could have done justice to it as he had done. Bogdanovich called Stewart's contribution to the John Ford documentaries "priceless." There was much critical admiration also, with one reviewer stating that he "brought solidity and stature to everything with which he cared to involve himself."

Asked in 1972 why he had temporarily put feature films to the side, and if he planned to make his decision a permanent one, Stewart replied: "I am 64 years old, one year short of the official retirement age, and, no, I do *not* feel like retiring; let's just say I'm regathering and reallocating my forces." The year before, he had embarked on a television series called *The Jimmy Stewart Show*. It ran for 24 weekly half-hour episodes in 1971 before the network killed it. The chief reason seems to have been, according to the press, that Stewart had reverted to his youthful, bumblingly lovable incarnation rather than explore the mature, authoritative persona of his later years. As one Professor James K. Howard he seemed to be giving Robert Young and his *Father Knows Best* series competition, but many of the situations were too depressingly familiar for comfort. As in his 1960's domestic comedies, he was the confused, but well-intentioned father of an unpredictably wacky family.

Reviews of *The Jimmy Stewart Show* started off charitably enough: "It is always good to see Jimmy Stewart, and he will doubtlessly enhance the television medium as he has the film," one stated. As the series progressed, however, reviews ran more along these lines: "In films like *Mr. Hobbs Takes a Vacation*, *Take Her, She's Mine* and *Dear Brigitte* (all between 1962 and 1965) Mr. Stewart gave us Daddy Bumbler to a fare-thee-well, and he is still ringing changes on it in *The Jimmy Stewart Show*, and frankly the changes are ringing worn and hollow these days."

The Jimmy Stewart Show went off the air in early 1972. Stewart told interviewers that he agreed with what the critics had said, but he recovered all his lost ground on television in one grand swoop. He appeared for Hallmark Hall of Fame on NBC in *Harvey*, with Fielder Cook directing, and Helen Hayes, scintillatingly humorous, in the role of his sister. Reviews for this were among the best he and Hayes had ever received in any medium. "Mr. Stewart, who has been playing *Harvey* for years, has acquired an extra dimension of comic nuance and fey understanding with this portrayal, and Miss Hayes is right there with him. Here are two seasoned actors at the top of their form, playing off each other for exciting results!" one reviewer wrote. The television version had followed upon the Broadway success Stewart and Hayes had made with a 1972 revival, with *The New York Times* saying of him: "This production of *Harvey* restores James Stewart and a sense of innocence to the American theatre." Another critic said of his Broadway version: "Mr. Stewart is such a commanding presence on the stage that it seems a shame he has left us for the films for so many years. The film's gain was the theatre's loss, assuredly."

Stewart told reviewers that he had never been completely satisfied with the 1950 movie of *Harvey*, and now that he was of an age to grow into the role, he felt he had to have another crack at it. To another interviewer he indicated that he had needed a sabbatical from Hollywood in order to "recharge my batteries. I was getting stale out there." Asked if he didn't miss the comforts of Beverly Hills [sic] and a temperate climate while taking his chances with the harsh New York winter, he said that he found seasonal changes bracing. Cold weather, Stewart said, revitalized him; there was a certain monotony to consistently sunny climes. He hastily added that California would always be his base and his permanent home.

When I interviewed him in 1972 during his Broadway sojourn, he looked hale and hearty. He told me, "I wish I had come back to the Broadway theater more frequently, and if I had it to do over again, I would have! Of course, there was always the problem of finding a vehicle that was exactly right." He reminisced about the Broadway theatre of four decades before, when he had been a wide-eyed neophyte actor. "I sort of fell into the theatre," he said. "I was very lucky; the parts sort of came to me rather than my having to go out and scrounge them up. I feel lucky when I look back, and profoundly grateful."

Always generous in his remarks about *Harvey's* original interpreter, Frank Fay, Stewart told me on that occasion "that I had some big footsteps to follow in, and I tried to measure up." Told that the role was now associated more with him than with Frank Fay, he said to me: "Whoever originates a role and makes the success with it that Fay did, always has his own niche of honor. I never pre-empted a role from any colleague; I simply did a variation on it. Whatever I have done with the role of Elwood in *Harvey* takes nothing from Fay's excellent work. In fact, I am sorry that he didn't get it on record, on tape or film. That's the one problem with the theater — unless you tape it (and the results are often static and stagey) it's written on water. Look at all the splendid work on stage of Katharine Cornell, which will always go unrecorded. A great loss!"

Of the play's popularity he said: "Wherever I go I'm always asked about *Harvey*, about how he is and where he is. At first I thought it was a joke but then I could see people were serious. So I just say that he's home with a cold and that I'll pass along the regards." Three years later, in 1975, age 67, Stewart went to London with *Harvey*, and made a smash hit with it at the Prince of Wales Theatre. Anthony Quayle directed, and Mona Washbourne, the distinguished British actress, took over the Helen Hayes role of Veta. (Hayes had been asked to go to London with Stewart and the company, but had demurred, reportedly for health reasons.) The West End critics were as enthusiastic as those on Broadway had been, with the *London Times* reviewer writing, "It is a tribute to Mr. Stewart's timing that even the most predictable lines exert a comic shock." *Variety's* reviewer in London waxed equally enthusiastic: "Stewart is superb as Elwood P. Dowd, and his reading of the second act finale is one for the textbooks." Other reviewers added their voices to the chorus of praise, with one saying, "Mr. Stewart is already a legend in London and throughout our land as one of the most durable and accomplished of film actors. What a joy to see him here, in the flesh, sending his charismatic personality so forcefully across the footlights." Mona Washbourne and Anthony Quayle both gave interviews to the British press lauding their American associate. Miss Washbourne said: "It is amazing to contemplate that this fine, seasoned, highly sophisticated actor should have spent the bulk of his career in the film; yet he demonstrates that he was born for the stage, is in thorough command of it, and the London and New York theatres are all the poorer for his long preoccupation with Hollywood. Indeed, Hollywood's gain was our loss." Quayle was even more laudatory, saying, "I felt I was at the feet of a master."

Back in Hollywood again, fresh from his television triumph with *Harvey* in 1972, Stewart took a few months off to rest and contemplate his future. On May 20, 1973, he turned 65. "It's retirement time for most other citizens but not for me. I haven't run out of mileage yet. I'll know when I do," he told me that year. Later in 1973 he was approached by a television producer who had greatly admired his performance fourteen years earlier in the film *Anatomy of a Murder*. The producer felt that the compelling character of lawyer Paul Biegler could be given an interesting variation in a sort of spinoff—namely, eight episodes, each about 90 minutes in length, on television. Stewart pondered this, and when he liked the initial scripts CBS sent him, he signed up. All eight episodes were completed between March 1973 and March of 1974.

Again Stewart was a small town lawyer, this time named Billy Joe Hawkins, and he resolved, with folksy yet shrewd ingenuity, a variety of crimes, beginning with "Hawkins on Murder" and ending with "Hawkins — Candidate for Murder." Other titles were "Hawkins — Murder in Movieland"; "Hawkins — Die, Darling, Die"; "Hawkins — A Life for a Life"; "Hawkins — Blood Feud"; "Hawkins — Murder in the Slave Trade"; "Hawkins — Murder on the 13th Floor." All of these productions were well received by the television critics, with one reviewer commenting: "The seasoned authority of James Stewart lends a real distinction to these tellingly-ingenious tales. Age has not withered nor custom staled the infinite varieties of his technique."

All the "Hawkins" films were done on the old MGM lot, and his memories were poignant, for this was the studio of his Hollywood beginnings. In a 1974 interview, he told me that ghosts from the past haunted him when he went amid the old sound stages: "But they are pleasant ghosts — happy ghosts, wishing me well . . . ." He was to win a Golden Globe Award for Best TV Actor in a Dramatic

Doug McClelland Collection

James Stewart, *That's Entertainment,* MGM, 1974

Series for his "Hawkins" portrayals.

He admitted to a number of interviewers that he felt the strain of "so much work" now that he was pushing 67, "but the enjoyment counters the fatigue; I still feel much exhilaration coming on the set each morning; I think it keeps me alert. It is important to live in the present, and to look forward to tomorrow, as if one is going to be around forever. Of course we know we are not, but some illusions are dynamic in their effects. They have been so, for me." He admitted that his hearing was deteriorating and that learning lines was even more of a chore for him than in the past. Laughingly, he remarked that his verbal mannerisms, the trademark hesitancies in his youthful prime, made useful tools for him circa 1974 "because they cover up my problems with learning lines."

Yet William Windom, who appeared with him in one of the "Hawkins" telefilms, has called Stewart "one of the sharpest of studies," and even recalled some points when Stewart had cued *him* when he forgot lines, and even covered up for him. "I don't care how old he gets or how old and tired he sometimes says he is; I have never been up against such controlled energy, such disciplined precision. He makes it all seem effortless." Windom added: "This man is going to be around for a long haul. For him, there'll not only be a second, but a third and a fourth wind!"

While engaged on the MGM lot in 1974 with the "Hawkins" films, Stewart, to his delight, found himself drafted for *That's Entertainment*, a retrospective MGM extravaganza featuring stars from the Glory Days recalling favorite roles and amusing situations. Tours of the lot were thrown in for good measure, with the stars as conductors and the nostalgia was "served in big, fat gobs" as one critic put it. Stewart had a field day in one sequence recalling his singing and dancing in the 1936 Eleanor Powell co-starrer, *Born to Dance*.

I was on the MGM lot when *That's Entertainment* was being shot. After an enjoyable lunch with Stewart and a publicist, we walked about the great lot where he and so many other stars of the Golden Era of the Thirties and Forties had held forth. During the walk, he waxed gently nostalgic, saying, "We had such fun in those days — it was all part of a family, the work we did, and we got a family feeling out of it. What wonderful training we had, going from film to film!" We passed one sound stage where Stewart had done some of his best MGM films. He was reminded of stars he had appeared with and who had passed on, including Margaret Sullavan and Jean Harlow. Of Louis B. Mayer, Jimmy said: "He was a great orchestrator. He understood talent and he knew how to handle it. He has never been credited with the expertise and shrewdness he showed in handling so many creative talents and getting them to do things his way." I informed Stewart that Robert Taylor had told me much the same thing in 1965, joking that he (Taylor) had once asked Mayer for a raise but instead got fatherly advice. Later, when a friend asked Taylor if he got the raise, he said, "No, but I did get a father!" Stewart and the publicist laughed heartily at that.

For five years before his 1976 appearance in *The Shootist*, Stewart had been turning down role after role. To one interviewer in 1975 he had said, "I am 67 years old, and I just don't feel I look right any more for those heavy action things. I have all the money I want, and I can afford to be picky." Asked if he were contemplating all-out retirement, Stewart shook his head vigorously and declared, "Oh, no! It's a matter of the right role, one I know I can do, one that is suitable to my age. It'll come along."

Within a year the right role did come along, but it was not a starring one. John Wayne was the star and the film was Warners' *The Shootist*. Don Siegel directed, and screenwriters Miles Hood Swarthout and Scott Hale adapted it from a novel by Glendon Swarthout. Handsomely photographed in color by Bruce Surtees, it benefited from highly evocative music by Elmer Bernstein.

In *The Shootist*, Stewart plays a role with limited footage but considerable impact. One step above a cameo part, it displays him as a doctor in Carson City, Nevada, in 1901 — a time when the tradition of Western loner-heroes is giving way to modern conditions. It is his duty to tell an old gunfighter, John Wayne, that he is dying of cancer and has only about six weeks to live. There was enormous poignancy in this onscreen situation, since Wayne was himself dying at the time. Wayne is surrounded by old enemies who would like to have the credit of dispatching him. He puts up at a boardinghouse run by a widow, Lauren Bacall, who at first distrusts him but finally feels compassion for his mortal illness. Her son, Ron Howard, hero-worships the once-celebrated gunman, much to the distress of his mother.

While giving Wayne a painkilling medicine for the increasing discomfort in his groin and lower back, Stewart, in an affecting and trenchant scene, warns him that the pain will eventually increase to an unbearable extent. If he has the courage, Stewart says, he can avoid so humiliating a death. Taking the cue, the old gunfighter sells all his belongings. He tries to make the admiring Howard understand the hollow fame of being a gunfighter, before he goes to meet his adversaries (among them Richard Boone, Hugh O'Brien and Bill McKinley) in a saloon. He knows that going out the way he has lived, by the gun, is the most honorable and dignified way for a man of his ilk to make the Grand Exit. In the fight, he kills his rivals but is shot in the back by the cowardly bartender. Ron Howard, who has followed his hero, shoots the bartender and throws away the gun in disgust, much to the satisfaction of the old gunman, who then dies.

Many critics were moved by the poignancy of an actor, himself a cancer victim, playing a man devastated by the same disease and who chooses his own time to depart this life. There was much praise for Stewart's solid delineation of the doctor, and indeed, despite his limited screen time, Stewart makes every line and situation count. Looking every bit of his 68 years, Stewart seems perfectly in character, old and wise, a man who has seen it all; he mixes equal doses of human compassion and stern realism in what he projects.

Stewart was deeply moved by Wayne's quiet heroism during the making of *The Shootist*; he knew Wayne was in discomfort at times, despite the medication he was taking. Stewart tried to cheer him up by any means that came to mind, including sudden forays with the accordion, and his ready fund of jokes. Richard Boone remembered Stewart clowning on location, keeping everyone keyed up with laughter. "I know that Jim was trying to create a light atmosphere for Big John," Boone recalled. "It was touching to see the concern and interest he showed in making the shooting as easy for his great colleague as possible."

Stewart himself said: "John Wayne was a fine, good man. He stood for the hardiness, the persistence, the valor, and essential integrity of the American spirit — not just in the period he was most notable for portraying, the era of the West in its newness and ascendancy, but all the decades since. To me he was the personification of the American Spirit at its best, and his faithfulness to his ideals has been most lamentably misunderstood by some. His detractors should pray to develop just one percent of this man's guts and integrity."

As he approached 70, Stewart made some poor judgments, notably in his acceptance of what amounted to a cameo role in yet another of those popular disaster productions, in this case an item called *Airport 77*.

Universal released this 114-minute opus in — when else? — 1977. Directed by Jerry Jameson, and with a perfunctory script by Michael Schoff and David Spector, based on a story by H.A.L. Craig and Charles Kuanstle, inspired by the film *Airport* and the Arthur Hailey novel (are you still with us? The many cooks who stirred up this broth are a clue to its muddled progression) *Airport 77* serves up the same tired brew in what one critic called a "Grand-Hotel-in-the-Air danger yarn."

In this effort, photographed in color by Philip Lathrop (its one real merit), Stewart plays a wealthy collector of art. His enormous wealth permits him to have a 747 for his very own, and it is customized and lavishly appurtenanced.

On the trip in question, he is transferring some of his possessions, including valuable art work, some guests, and relatives, from New York to his Florida estate. Some miscreants, hell-bent on getting their hands on Stewart's art, hijack the plane. The airliner crash lands in 50 feet of ocean water, but remains in one piece (the logistics of this complicated happenstance are never sufficiently explained); it then becomes a matter of gaining enough time to refloat the plane before the air runs out and the water seeps in. Navy frogmen eventually get into the act and coax the plane to the surface, but not before much handwringing and noble self-sacrifice under adverse circumstances has prevailed.

Pamela Bellwood plays Stewart's estranged daughter, and there is the stock winsome grandson on hand. Brenda Vaccaro is Stewart's husky secretary. To add to the plot complications, if hardly to the film's depth, Stewart is suffering from a terminal illness. Great is his joy when his loved ones are rescued, and it is only in this scene that Stewart is allowed to do anything approximating true acting. He brings it off well enough, all things considered.

The critics seemed in general agreement that *Airport* 77 was one airport too many; the 1970 and 1975 editions had said and done all that could be said and done on such a plot premise. "Mr. Hailey's novel has been given yet another go-round, and we hope this is the last one — the very last," a Philadelphia reviewer pronounced. "And wouldn't it be wiser of Mr. Stewart to retire altogether from films rather than submit himself and his still estimable talents to such cheap melodrama and such cardboard (as written) characterization."

And this from another reviewer: "Mr. Stewart is one year short of the Biblical three-score-and-ten and he frankly looks it with his deepening lines, his white hair, his doddering, and the standard mannerisms held over from his middle and youthful years which now seem more influenced by age than acting artifice. He is not being fair to himself or us getting involved in such childish melodrama, nor were the producer powers-that-be fair in proposing to him that he should waste his time in such a way. Surely there are roles fit for older people that Mr. Stewart could essay admirably, along the lines that Lionel Barrymore and Lewis Stone made capital with when they, in their time, were around the age Mr. Stewart is now."

Stewart, in his interviews that year, tended to be relaxed and philosophical. "I've had a good run of it," he told me. "Some physical disabilities are catching up with me; my hearing isn't what it once was, and I get pains here and there, but then what do I expect at 69? I have lived to see my wonderful children grow up, though sadly I did outlive one fine son [his stepson who died in Vietnam], and on the whole I have no complaints."

In a 1977 issue of *Quirk's Reviews*, I wrote: "There should be a Society for the Preservation and Protection of Mr. James Stewart founded by someone, and maybe we will do it. Surely there are good and worthy parts, well-written and well-characterized, that this sterling veteran could play the pants off. So where are they? And why aren't they being ferreted out by producers?"

Many wondered why, in the year he turned 70, James Stewart elected to take what can only be described as a walk-on role in the Robert Mitchum starrer, *The Big Sleep* (1978), a reprise of the Bogart-Bacall smash of 1946. Mitchum, a bit old himself at 62, was detective Philip Marlowe, a role he had essayed in *Farewell, My Lovely* (1975), another film in which more than one critic remarked that the part called for a man fifteen or twenty years younger.

The 1978 version more or less follows the plot of the 1946 original, which had been a smash hit due to the Bogart-Bacall chemistry, the Howard Hawks direction, the Sid Hickox black-and-white photography, and the rousingly atmospheric Max Steiner score. Of course, the plot of the original had made no sense, but no one cared, for this was authentically a triumph of style over content.

This time around, with Elliott Kastner and Michael Winner producing in England (many critics complained that the location was unsuitable), the film was directed by Michael Winner from his own screenplay, based on the Raymond Chandler novel. With color photography that many thought ill-advised for such a theme, the familiar plot was given yet another working-over — if plot is the term for the confusing series of events. Mitchum-as-Marlowe is taken on by a retired millionaire, an invalid, who had once been a general. The millionaire, old and in a wheelchair, wants to find out why he is being blackmailed, but can make no headway. Neither can Marlowe — at first.

It later turns out that the millionaire, played by Stewart with feisty dispatch, has two daughters who are attractive and charming, but big trouble in all other areas. Sarah Miles has a husband with criminal connections. Candy Clark is a man-hungry slut who moves in the London underworld and has connections with a pornographer. The necessary excursions and alarums of the plot consume the next 90 minutes before Mitchum-Marlowe brings matters to a resolution that is, in its way, almost as murky as the preceding convolutions.

Stewart plays Guy de Brissac Sternwood with as much vitality as he can summon, considering the physical restrictions of his wheelchair and the necessity throughout his one scene (it took only two days of shooting) of appearing bewildered and helpless. Stewart labors mightily to overcome the essential passivities of the role, but one is given reason to wonder why he ever bothered with it.

In 1978, for his 70th birthday, he gave a series of interviews, in one of which he claimed that he did *The Big Sleep* "only to keep my hand in." The interviewer asked him if such a small and passive role, hardly central to the main action, had been worth the trouble, and why did he bother when he didn't need the money? He replied: "Well, I like to keep people reminded that I'm still alive, I guess." The interviewer did not pursue the question.

Many top talents were on hand, including James Donald, John Mills, Oliver Reed, and Edward Fox. Some critics asked in print why any of these luminaries had bothered either, as the net result was pretty poor goods by any standard.

One critic, describing Stewart, wrote of "his valiant attempts to suggest movement and vitality while confined to his chair. His dialogue does not support his efforts, nor does director Winner. It is a mystery why such a sterling actor, with one of the most prestigious careers in filmdom history, should want such a throwaway, worthless, peripheral role, moreover a role in a film that has been remade once too often."

Nor did Robert Mitchum, the nominal star, fare any better. His role dominated the picture, so he garnered the lion's share of the inevitable critical abuse, with acid remarks about his sleepiness, age, weight and general immobility. "To follow an electric actor like Humphrey Bogart, who could flash lightning with a glance, with such a somnolent, sleepy-eyed, shambling performer like Mitchum only invites those inevitable odious comparisons," one British paper lamented, and even the British press considered that the goings-on were inappropriate in an English setting.

Lassie, James Stewart, *The Magic of Lassie*, Int'l Picture Show, 1978

Chapter Sixteen

Grand Old Man

The Magic of Lassie (1978) was the last official *theatrical* film of Jimmy Stewart. As Clovis Mitchell, a Californian of the best kind, he is a vineyard owner proud of his acres and his product. He even sings one of the numerous songs — courtesy of Richard M. and Robert Sherman — with musical director Irwin Kostal superintending in fine professional style. Stewart has two grandchildren, Stephanie Zimbalist and Michael Sharrett, and a dog — Lassie. Of course, the famed canine dominates the action. After the first successful *Lassie Come Home* (1943), Lassie starred in a half-dozen other films, followed by a nineteen-year run as a television series, beginning in 1954.

Bonita Granville and her husband Jack Wrather decided that Lassie deserved a reprise, because wholesome entertainment, in 1978, was becoming a rarity. They had no trouble in persuading Stewart, then 70, to star in the picture they produced. That it turned out to be the weakest incarnation of the Lassie legend was regrettable, for everyone concerned got an "A" for good intentions. The plot is disarmingly simple: Villain Pernell Roberts wants Stewart's land; when he doesn't get it, he kidnaps Lassie to Colorado. Stewart's son sets out after the dog; then the dog escapes; dog and son meet up and make their way back to Stewart's vineyard.

Stewart has always defended the picture, and he didn't mince words. At the time of its release, he said: "Look at the theatre advertisements and what have you got? You've got violence and films of an explosive nature, and films of a depressing nature. You haven't got a choice."

Unfortunately, the public of 1978 did not choose Lassie; it was a subject whose time had long gone. Supplying some human interest was Alice Faye, then 63, as a waitress who helps out the boy and dog along their way home. She even sings one of the many musical offerings in the film. Time had played, inescapably, some tricks with the famous Faye voice, but she proved that she could still deliver a song with all the old zing.

In another cameo role is Mickey Rooney, aged 58, and then in one of his professional slumps. He contributes some amusing footage as a wrestling manager Lassie encounters. The rest of the actors, including Pernell Roberts, Gene Evans, and Mike Mazurki, give only standard performances, but Stephanie Zimbalist as Stewart's grandchild, acquits herself well.

One Cleveland critic said of *The Magic of Lassie*, "James Stewart at 70 is a doughty old veteran of the filmic wars with all his charisma and quiet force of personality consummately — and beautifully — intact. He says he wants to make wholesome pictures, and of course he has to be given points for excellent intentions; the problem is that the sentimental Lassie is hopelessly out-of-date by now, and the direction of Don Chaffey tends to be slow and dawdling. But very possibly he was discouraged by the limp script provided by Jean Holloway. Certainly a theme so dated by 1978 standards would have defied the efforts any of the more celebrated directors. But then they wouldn't have bothered with *this* picture in the first place!"

Bonita Granville, an actress of no mean attainments, had hounded, as a child star, Miriam Hopkins and Merle Oberon is *These Three* (1936), and mercilessly ragged, as a teenager, Bette Davis in *Now, Voyager* (1942). She had later matured into a charming young romantic lead, but her acting days by 1978 were far behind her, nor did she care. She told me in 1979, "Jack and I wanted to do wholesome pictures that had some values to them, and we don't regret the Lassie picture, not at all. Twenty years earlier it would have been regarded as a perfectly acceptable picture on its own terms, but the climate of 1978 was just not hospitable. But not for a moment do Jack and I regret having done it, and Jimmy Stewart was a tower of strength all the way!"

Castigated by reviewers as old-fashioned and saccharine, the film landed first on cable TV, then finally in the video stores, where it continues to languish.

There has been much discussion of, and curiosity concerning, the last *feature* film James Stewart ever did. Surprisingly, considering his war service against the Axis, Stewart made it for a Japanese firm. Originally carrying the title *Afurika Monogatari (A Tale of*

Africa), it was shot in Kenya in late 1979 and early 1980. While shown in limited release abroad, most notably in Japan and Africa, it has never had a formal American or British Commonwealth debut, reportedly because it was so bad.

A Tale of Africa finally made it to Showtime Cable (TV) in the fall of 1981, and got an indifferent reception. *Variety* later reviewed it, calling it "the slowest moving picture this side of a Cezanne still life." Writer Tony Thomas called it "the least successful movie in which Stewart has ever been involved and the only one that deserves to be forgotten." According to Thomas: "It apparently came about because [Stewart] was visiting a game preserve in Kenya, which he and his wife had visited several times before." Stewart, for some inexplicable reason, had considered it a good idea at the time to appear in a Japanese picture being shot in Kenya, though the logic of his thinking escapes this writer."

Variety reviewed the film's 1981 premiere in Tokyo. It seems to have dealt, according to the print the *Variety* critic saw, with — what else? — the activities in a Kenya game preserve.

In *A Tale of Africa*, Stewart is listed as "Old Man" (which he was indeed, looking every bit of his 71 years). He appears very fleetingly ("Now you see him, now you don't," one Japanese reviewer noted,) looking like he'd rather be somewhere else. He was saddled (or lightly caparisoned, rather) with only a few snippets of dialogue. The *Variety* review had stated that the other players in the movie were more wooden than the animals. It was an inauspicious finale to his feature-film career.

Stewart and Bette Davis had always enjoyed a friendly, if distant, relationship over the years, having known each other through such mutual friends as Henry Fonda. Only six weeks apart in age (she was born on April 5, he on May 20, 1908) they were both seventy-four years of age when they finally did a movie together in 1982. "Right of Way" was released exclusively to cable television in 1983.

Davis had always been highly complimentary in her references to Stewart. Professionally, she had termed him "a really wonderful actor with a magical blending of naturalness and technique." And personally, Davis had told a reporter, when both she and Stewart were in their 70s, "If I had met him way, way back, he would never have escaped me, but it's too late now!" When an interviewer

Bet te, Davis, James Stewart, *Right of Way*, HBO, 1973

wanted to know why they had never acted together, Davis stressed that she had been under contract to Warners while Stewart had been an MGM man, at least in their younger years. "And later," she added, "well, the right opportunity never arose."

"Right of Way" finally brought them together before the cameras, but it proved to be an ill-chosen project. It was done for Home Box Office television because the regular commercial networks considered the theme too downbeat for their audience. It dealt with an elderly couple who decide on a joint suicide when they discover that the wife has terminal cancer. As the Stewart character tells their grief-stricken daughter (Melinda Dillon), "Your mother and I have lived as one and we'll die as one." The first Hollywood film made expressly for cable, "Right of Way" enlisted Davis' undiluted enthusiasm, especially when she learned that the writer, Richard Lees, had had Davis and Stewart in mind when he created the characters and plot.

Davis was irritated when told by producer-director George Schaefer the reasons why it had been rejected by the networks. "I've seen far more downbeat subject matter on regular TV," she snapped. "They'll clout and clobber the audience with sex and violence and killings and all sorts of morbidities, so why can't they cotton to something as intelligent and thoughtful as *this*!" She was somewhat mollified when Schaefer assured her that Home Box Office was ideal for the production: it would get careful treatment because the HBO people aimed at more adult and provocative fare.

Henry Fonda and Katharine Hepburn had co-starred the year before, 1981, in *On Golden Pond*, which won them both Oscars. It had been *their* first outing together, too, and Davis over-optimistically referred to their new film as hers and Stewart's answer to the Hepburn-Fonda success. Fonda died in 1982, the year "Right of Way" was being shot, and Davis and Stewart were both greatly saddened by this. They consoled each other by reminiscing about Fonda between takes, sitting quietly on the set. Davis talked of having known Hank as a teenager and of their great triumph together in *Jezebel*, her second Oscar-winner in 1938. Stewart talked of their long personal association. When work went particularly well on a scene, thanks to the thought and care Davis and Stewart both put into it, Stewart would whisper, "This was for you, Hank!" bringing tears to Davis' eyes. Unfortunately, there were more tears off screen than on. It was the precise, ordered, matter-of-fact objectivity displayed by the couple that vitiates this film's impact. It lacks the emotion and poignancy that, properly orchestrated, make for a moving and cathartic experience.

Lee's script and Schaefer's direction were, in part, to blame for the cold, uninvolving result. Davis' performance, especially, was too icily detached and *grande-dame*, in her usual later manner. Stewart, despite the many deficiencies, was the best thing in the picture, triumphing over all with a humane and understandable persona. His Teddy Dwyer is determined that the wife he loves will not go to her fate alone, and they overrule the wishes of their heartbroken family and a concerned social worker. They go to the garage, seal it, and die together in their car of carbon monoxide poisoning. Typical of reviewers' reactions was one that said in part: "This pedestrian tale has the dubious distinction of making two Hollywood legends (in their first co-starring effort) seem dreary."

After doing "Right of Way," Stewart slowed down considerably. He visited the hospital a few times, once for an irregular heart beat, and for general testing on several occasions. On his 75th birthday, May 20, 1983, he had visited his home town in Pennsylvania, where they dedicated a statue in his honor, followed by a party. Several times in the years that followed, he went to England for reunions with the surviving members of his bomber squad. "They're thinning out," he noted sadly after one of these trips abroad. In 1985, he was honored with a special Lifetime Achievement Oscar from the Academy and received it from Cary Grant. There had been many such awards in the 1980s, including the American Film Institute's Life Achievement Award, held in Beverly Hills. On that occasion, in 1980, Henry Fonda and Grace Kelly had sat with him. Now both were gone. 1983 found him as one of the honorees at the Kennedy Center in Washington.

1987 was to bring a PBS documentary, *James Stewart — A Wonderful Life*.

· Of the many tributes paid him during the middle and late 1980s, he said he particularly treasured the simple words of an actor of another generation, Dustin Hoffman. At the American Film Institute Awards, Dustin had turned to him and said: "Mr. Stewart, you made my parents happy. You've made me happy. I'm making sure you make my children happy. And if this world has any kind of luck, you're going to make my grandchildren happy."

Gloria and Jimmy took comfort in their three surviving children. Judy married a banker, Steven Merrill, and lived in San Francisco with two sons. Kelly, a zoologist along with her husband, Dr. Alexander Harcourt, lived in London and visited Africa often. Michael MacLean, for years an investment banker in Phoenix, has two sons with his wife Barbara. Stewart chuckled that his four grandsons "have a pretty good idea of what I did for a living. They've made faces at some of my movies. Is that a good or a bad sign?" Stewart and his wife frequently socialized during the 1980s, going to galas and show business events in New York, Hollywood, and "wherever the best action is," as he laughed. His favorite actress was Stephanie Zimbalist ("She's wonderful, really!"), but he decried modern movies as "All sex and violence. No humanity. No sensitivity...."

In September 1989, Jimmy Stewart was running around the country promoting a project that many felt ill-advised, to say the least, and that held him up to public ridicule. Crown had put out a tiny book (31 pages, at an outrageous $9.95) called JIMMY STEWART AND HIS POEMS: BY JIMMY STEWART. An unattractive white jacket with pale red lettering, sporting a rendition of Stewart, sitting in an armchair mulling over a manuscript page, a brown dog asleep at his feet, did not help matters. The face didn't even look like his.

It was popularly believed that Crown had cynically exploited an old man of 81 whose vision and hearing were failing, and who "must indeed have been in his dotage to countenance anything so vulgar and pathetic," as a lady just ahead of me in the line at Doubleday Book Store on New York's Fifth Avenue sniffed. That was on the afternoon of September 23, 1989, and Stewart was busily writing his name on one volume after another. "I'm sorry I can't write inscriptions," he called from his desk, "but just the name's all I can manage." As it was, he looked exhausted and frail, his eyes dimming, his face mottled. But if it was attention he craved, he must have been mighty satisfied, for the line of his admirers was long, long, long.

It was merciful for him that his hearing was no longer up to snuff, for there were as many scornful comments as there were admiring ones. While I waited for my own autographed copy, I took some of them down in my notebook: "That money-grubbing pub-lisher is using that poor old fellow — and his own vanity is working overtime to put him on the sucker list!" "No wonder our literary standards have gone to pot; it's all sexy novels, scandalous biogra-phies and worthless silliness that gets sold because the writer is famous."

Countering these acerbic observations were such fan effusions as: "I saw him in *It's a Wonderful Life* when I was just a girl and I've always longed to meet him in person!" and "The poems are *ridicu-lous* but *he* is a darling!" "He's been my hero since I saw him in *Mr. Smith Goes to Washington;* now at last I'll press the flesh with him!" "Poor old fellow — he's so darling and sweet and good — his little book is *pathetic* but his autograph on it is *worth* it!"

Stewart continued signing away, and as I got to him I was struck by the energy he was summoning, given the constant scribbling and his obvious age. He had a pleasant smile for everyone: when given a compliment on some old movie, he beamed and expressed his grat-itude for being remembered, said he was glad he had given pleasure. It was obvious that all this peregrination from city to city and from bookstore to bookstore was, in some way, a substitute for the movies and plays that he no longer had the energy or inclination to per-form. Luckily, I was almost at the end of the line, and after he had signed his last book, we renewed acquaintance from many years of casual encounters, interviews, and socializing.

Jimmy said that the tour energized him; that it was so wonder-ful to meet nice, devoted people to whom he had given such happi-ness with his movies. "It has been a real experience — something I will never forget!" he chuckled. I asked him about the toll on his en-ergies given his years. "It's worth it — to get so much love and at-tention! I realize how much I miss the spotlight — I'm just an old ham, after all!" Laughing, he said he realized at last why he hadn't gone back to his dad's hardware store after college. "I wanted to be noticed — I wanted the attention. I was a showoff! I couldn't admit it to myself then, but I can now!" he chuckled. "When you get over eighty, you can admit to yourself anything — for that matter, you can *do* anything!"

What did he consider the plusses of aging? "Oh, you separate the essential from the inessential. You just narrow down the list of things that bother you. When you're thirty or forty or fifty, you tend to make unimportant things important! Later, you just relax, and you are glad to be alive!"

I asked him if he planned an autobiography. "Everybody asks me that," he rejoindered, making a slight, tremorous adjustment to his hearing aid. "The answer is no. Let others tell my life — they have already, in articles, books that weren't too bad. So many people of my time are dead now. It would sadden me to rehash my doings with them. And I am no tell-all type; wouldn't want to hurt the memory of the dead, or the feelings of what few are still around!"

I told him I had always wanted to do a good, solid biography of him; after all, I had known him, written so much about him in articles over the years, and interviewed so many people who knew him. He asked me how old I was. I said 66, and he mumbled "almost young enough to be my son — I *could* have had a kid at 15, at least *physically*. So you want to write a book on me? Well, write away, son!"

I asked him about his book of poems. "I just jotted down those things," he said, "over a period of years. I don't pretend any of it is art. I'm no poet, but I found some sentences rhymed, and, well, I wanted to share my thoughts with the public, as I did with my friends."

Over the years, Stewart had read his poems publicly. On a Johnny Carson show of some time back he had read his "The Top Step in the Hotel in Junin," ("The top step in the hotel in Junin is mean; Like the Devil is Mean; And it lies at the top of the other steps; so quiet, so still, so serene! ..." continuing on to "It's a half inch higher than the other steps. A whole inch, to be more precise," to the summation: "And it uses this inch as a weapon, the guests of the place to harass; for when you reach the third floor of that hotel in Junin; the top step trips you right on your ass ... of all the degrading, inhuman mean things, that I in my life have yet seen, The grossest most despicable one of them all, is the top step in the hotel in Junin."

When Stewart had read this poem publicly to Johnny Carson's audience, he had accompanied it with scowlings and gestures. He used righteously angry mannerisms in the best Jimmy Stewart style, coming down on key words like "ass" and "Junin" to produce a hilarious effect. Certainly the Carson audience laughed, as much out of *simpatico* — or was it sympathy? — as anything. But when I read the words of the copy of his poems that I had bought the day before getting his autograph, I was horrified to note how pathetic and childishly inept it read in cold black print. (Print, incidentally, that was double-spaced, with lots of white space on all pages, accompanied by silly, pastel illustrations that a first-grader would have disdained.)

I mentioned that the cover rendition of him didn't resemble him at all. His reaction was philosophical. "Oh, people have to earn their living doing what they do," he said. "I'm always grateful, yes, even at this point, if my name gets *spelled* right!"

At this point an officious assistant cut in with: "Mr. Stewart is really very tired now — we mustn't overtax him." The second-to-last interview I was to do with James Maitland Stewart was over. "Keep in touch!" he called out cheerily, adding: "Wasn't Billy Grady a hell of a guy?"

Linda Stahl had also interviewed him, in Washington, D.C. Just as in New York, he kept a long, faithful line filing by, and I wondered what people in that Washington line had said about JIMMY STEWART AND HIS POEMS.

He told Linda Stahl, for USA TODAY: "I'll be a one-book writer. It took me more than twenty years to write this one." He added that he reads scripts "every once in a while," that acting was "behind me!" He told the lady that he took naps, wore glasses when he needed to, and used a hearing aid in one ear. "He doesn't try to hide these inevitable signs of growing old," Stahl reported. "His silvery hair is in good supply but lacks luster. His gentle face is a bit mottled. Still, he holds his tall frame erect, walks determinedly, and keeps a busy schedule."

While in Washington that fall of 1989, Stewart went about visiting U.S. Senators he knew personally, among them Paul Simon, Mark Hatfield, and Arlen Specter, to express his outrage over that "stupid, foolish colorization of films that Turner let loose." He was incensed when *It's a Wonderful Life* was colorized. I once told him that at least it was a Christmassy subject and lent itself better to color than, say, *The Maltese Falcon*; he snapped back, "I don't care what film it is — it suffers. Photographers of that time knocked themselves out to highlight faces, to carefully place light and shade. It's a disgrace!"

While in Washington he visited, as he did every time he was there, the Vietnam Veterans Memorial. "We lost a boy," he told Stahl. "I can go right to his name. I rub my hand over it."

Stahl's report on his reception in Washington: "Many came to see an actor they adore, whose wholesomeness comes through in his poem about his late dog, Beau." She quoted some lines from the poem: "There are nights, when I think, I feel that stare, and I reach out my hand to stroke his hair, but he's not there; oh, how I wish that wasn't so; I'll always love a dog named Beau." With a mixture of what appeared to be compassion and condescension, Stahl went on to report that there was a dog named Baron in his life as of 1989, that Gloria, his wife, "took in a golden retriever found roaming the streets with every rib showing." Lavin wound up her report with: "Baron sleeps by Jimmy Stewart's bed."

The New York Times ran a low-key, ironically respectful, but indulgent review of Stewart's book. Quoting some of the poems without comment, they left the readers to form whatever reaction they pleased.

The *Times* sent Mervyn Rothstein to Washington to interview Stewart concerning the book and himself. Rothstein, as awestruck as any fan mag reporter from the old *Photoplay* or *Modern Screen*, learned from his subject that "it happened almost by accident. I didn't say 'Well, I'll start writing poetry.' Something happened, and I had a feeling it was either funny or different, and I thought I'd like to get this down so I can remember it. And my wife, Gloria, encouraged me to try to make things rhyme." "Junin" turned out to be a place in central Argentina, where he had gone to fish. "He continued his rhyming ways during a visit to East Africa and a photographic safari with his twin daughters in Kenya, where a hyena mutilated a movie camera," Rothstein breathlessly recounted, "And then he decided to write about a favorite dog."

By early October, *Hollywood Reporter* colonist Robert Osborne was aghast: "Go figure: Sunday's *Los Angeles Times* listed Jimmy Stewart's new book 'Jimmy Stewart and His Poems' as No. 3 on its non-fiction best-seller list; *The New York Times*, same day, listed it as No. 4 on its best-seller list — as fiction (!!) But no matter what the book's rightful category, there's no confusion as to Stewart's triumph on the tub-thumping trail. An unqualified success, including Jimmy's personally signing (by count) 5,286 of the books!" According to Osborne, Stewart kept saying "I don't understand it" and "I don't believe it!" over what Osborne called "the immense crowds he pulled at each of his stops to promote the Crown book. Mobs everywhere, everyone hoping to get a look at — or shake the hand of — actor-author Stewart." Osborne felt that Stewart's next book ought to be called *How to Be a Movie Star*. "Stewart's credo has always been to back up whatever he's in or whatever he does. He's always beaten the tom-toms for his films; a man of his word, he's still operating on the same philosophy." But many felt that Stewart, icon or no icon, showed lamentably poor taste (senility?) in joining literary company with Margaret Truman's murder novels and Elliott Roosevelt's shameless tradings and Kirk Douglas's novels (written by someone else).

The next, and last time I saw Jimmy Stewart was in April 1990 when, a month short of 82, he showed up in New York with Gloria for the Film Society of Lincoln Center's *A Tribute to James Stewart*. It was an elaborately conceived event at Avery Fisher Hall, followed by a party at Tavern on the Green. The house, of course, was packed. The evening included a generous assortment of scenes from his many films, interspersed with observations from what few actors and co-stars remained from his past career. At the end, Stewart came out, long and thin, frail and gray-faced, looking every day of his age. He humbly informed the wildly cheering and stamping audience, all on their feet, that "This has been so much more than I ever dreamed" — complete with the famous hesitancies and an occasional stutter that his admirers were waiting to hear, and in each of which they delighted.

George C. Scott (*Anatomy of a Murder*) looking dour and glum, informed the audience that "I hate functions, I hate tuxedoes, but I'm extremely happy to be here." Then, with a charmingly self-denigrating flourish, he added: "No one could play a role like James Stewart. Can you imagine *me* with a trombone, trying to convince anyone *I* was Glenn Miller? Or Telly Savalas as Charles Lindbergh?" Dorothy Lamour sashayed out from the wings, looking somewhat the worse for wear, and made a witticism or two about Stewart expecting to become a father for the first time during the shooting of *The Greatest Show on Earth*: "He was so nervous, he even talked fast." As was duly reported in the press, Janet Leigh spoke of his kindness to newcomers, June Allyson talked of his prankish sense of humor, Jack Lemmon said "his acting never showed." Lemmon made perhaps the most solid contribution to the often banal and perfunctory tributes when he said of Stewart, "With [him] there is no 'take 15' or 'take 20' because every scene felt as if it was the very first time he had done it!" Jack had appeared with him only once, in the forgettable *Bell, Book and Candle*, which was Kim Novak's second film with Stewart. When she emerged from stage left, looking remarkably well-preserved for a woman of 57, she commented on how afraid of heights she had actually been during the celebrated *Vertigo*, and how he had helped her get through it. Maureen O'Hara, another well-preserved gal, praised him as citizen and airman, but it was left to Robert Stack, the most remarkably preserved of all at a ripe 71 (looking 48), who had been with him half a century before in *The Mortal Storm*, who gave perhaps the best tribute of all: "I have the feeling when I read in the papers about all the bad things in the world, there's nothing wrong that a group of Jimmy Stewarts couldn't go out and make right!"

The movies were all the significant ones, with a few of special interest thrown in, cumulating with a big, juicy, passionately-played love scene between Kate Hepburn and Jimmy from *The Philadelphia Story*. The audience held its collective breath when it ended, enraptured by the thought that Kate the Great might show to hold hands with Jimmy. But show she didn't. This was something of a surprise, it was mentioned later, because she had been seen hopping around town more than usual that spring.

Stewart sat in a box at stage left with Gloria and a retinue, and occasionally bowed to people he knew in the orchestra. No mention was made of the ghosts whose presence hovered over the proceedings: Hank Fonda, Johnny Swope, Billy Grady, John Wayne, Clark Gable, Robert Taylor, Margaret Sullavan.

The Guest of Honor wrapped it all up with a graceful closing speech: "I'm such a lucky man. I thank God for all of you. And when he takes our lives into the editing room, I hope he's as kind to each of you as you've been to me tonight...."

I did manage to get in a few words with Stewart before the event. "I'm the last of them," he said, "the last of those I knew and worked with so importantly and so meaningfully—Hitchcock, Ford, Tony Mann. Frank Capra is still around, thank God, but he's over 90 and so frail. Time resolves all things doesn't it. But I'm happy. I've had a bonus of twelve years over the Biblical three-score-and-ten, and for that I'm humbly grateful."

For some years after that Lincoln Center night in 1990, there was largely silence from the Stewart camp. Word came that he liked to rest and play with his dog and occasionally swim. He would read the *Hollywood Reporter* and the major newspapers until his eyes tired. He rarely visited his office to read the fan mail he so enjoyed, but an assistant sent over letters that "*had* to be answered because they were so nice."

His hearing grew worse and the aid helped only to a point. In April 1993, he underwent emergency surgery at St. John's Hospital in Santa Monica, where a new pacemaker was installed to moderate the speed of his failing heart. In May, he was forced to absent himself from an 85th birthday charity gala held in his honor. In attendance at the Beverly Hills bash were 800 close friends, including Dinah Shore, former President Reagan and Charlton Heston.

Then came a crucial blow. Jimmy's wife, Gloria, at 75 was diagnosed in late 1993 with terminal cancer. She died in his arms on February 16, 1994, with her twin daughters and son at her side. Top celebrities and Hollywood notables from all professions turned out for her memorial service at the Beverly Hills Presbyterian Church. A friend reported at the time: "Jimmy is beside himself with grief. He just doesn't know what he's going to do without her. He feels utterly lost. Gloria was his wife, mother, best friend and adviser—the love of his life." Stewart told a confidante later in 1994, "Now that Gloria has passed over, I'll be going too, soon. The old ticker is worn out, and I don't want to spend my days here without her." He added: "I've told the kids not to grieve, to be prepared for my passing, too. I love them, but I'm prepared to meet my Maker and be with Gloria again. Our love will continue in Heaven."

The final two years, 1995 to 1997, found Jimmy slipping inexorably downhill. His life grew lonelier, sadder, ever more reclusive. John Strauss, who had worked for him for nearly forty years, told the press: "He doesn't hear that well, tires easily and spends most of his time in his library."

There were a number of sudden hospital sojourns in the last

months, for blood clots on his leg, for irregular heartbeats, for adjustments to the pacemaker he no longer cared about. "Don't put in a new one," he pleaded with one doctor. "If this one runs out, let it happen to me naturally, like it should."

In early 1997 he was admitted to St. John's Hospital after he cut his head tripping over a plant in his bedroom. The gash required twelve stitches. He had earlier developed a form of skin cancer that seemed to be worsening. His weight went down to 120 pounds. Tabloid and other headlines morbidly intoned: JIMMY RUSHED TO HOSPITAL followed by JIMMY STEWART SENT HOME TO DIE.

Then, on the morning of Wednesday, July 2, 1997, a sudden blood clot caused heart failure which brought to an end the long life of James Maitland Stewart. He was 89 years old, the same as his father's span.

He would have been happy, and humbled too, could he have seen the front page headlines that followed, the myriad tributes, the outpouring of national grief and remembrance that dwarfed, by comparison, the farewells accorded most, indeed all other film stars. But then, Jimmy Stewart was no mere film star: he was a national treasure, an identifiable American icon.

Of all who had known him, Robert Stack had said it best of all, on the night of that 1990 tribute, and it is worth repeating: "I have the feeling when I read in the papers about all the bad things in the world, there's nothing wrong that a group of Jimmy Stewarts couldn't go out and make right!"

And so he has gone to Glory — and to his Gloria . . .

The Career of James Stewart

Films

1. *Murder Man* (1935)
2. *Rose Marie* (1936)
3. *Next Time We Love* (1936)
4. *Wife Versus Secretary* (1936)
5. *Small Town Girl* (1936)
6. *Speed* (1936)
7. *The Gorgeous Hussy* (1936)
8. *Born to Dance* (1936)
9. *After the Thin Man* (1936)
10. *Seventh Heaven* (1937)
11. *The Last Gangster* (1937)
12. *Navy Blue and Gold* (1937)
13. *Of Human Hearts* (1938)
14. *Vivacious Lady* (1938)
15. *The Shopworn Angel* (1938)
16. *You Can't Take It With You* (1938)
17. *Made for Each Other* (1939)
18. *Ice Follies of 1939* (1939)
19. *It's a Wonderful World* (1939)
20. *Mr. Smith Goes to Washington* (1939)
21. *Destry Rides Again* (1939)
22. *The Shop Around the Corner* (1940)
23. *The Mortal Storm* (1940)
24. *No Time for Comedy* (1940)
25. *The Philadelphia Story* (1940)
26. *Come Live With Me* (1941)
27. *Pot O' Gold* (1941)
28. *Ziegfeld Girl* (1941)
29. *It's a Wonderful Life* (1946)
30. *Magic Town* (1947)
31. *Call Northside 777* (1948)
32. *On Our Merry Way* (1948)
33. *Rope* (1948)
34. *You Gotta Stay Happy* (1949)
35. *The Stratton Story* (1949)
36. *Malaya* (1949)
37. *Winchester '73* (1950)

38. *Broken Arrow* (1950)
39. *The Jackpot* (1950)
40. *Harvey* (1950)
41. *No Highway in the Sky* (1951)
42. *The Greatest Show on Earth* (1952)
43. *Bend of the River* (1952)
44. *Carbine Williams* (1952)
45. *The Naked Spur* (1953)
46. *Thunder Bay* (1953)
47. *The Glenn Miller Story* (1953)
48. *Rear Window* (1954)
49. *The Far Country* (1955)
50. *Strategic Air Command* (1955)
51. *The Man From Laramie* (1955)
52. *The Man Who Knew Too Much* (1956)
53. *The Spirit of St. Louis* (1957)
54. *Night Passage* (1957)
55. *Vertigo* (1958)
56. *Bell, Book and Candle* (1958)
57. *Anatomy of a Murder* (1959)
58. *The FBI Story* (1959)
59. *The Mountain Road* (1960)
60. *Two Rode Together* (1961)
61. *The Man Who Shot Liberty Valance* (1962)
62. *Mr. Hobbs Takes a Vacation* (1962)
63. *How The West Was Won* (1962)
64. *Take Her She's Mine* (1963)
65. *Cheyenne Autumn* (1964)
66. *Dear Brigitte* (1965)
67. *Shenandoah* (1965)
68. *The Flight of the Phoenix* (1965)
69. *The Rare Breed* (1966)
70. *Firecreek* (1968)
71. *Bandolero!* (1968)
72. *The Cheyenne Social Club* (1970)
73. *Fools' Parade* (1971)
74. *The Shootist* (1976)
75. *Airport 77* (1977)
76. *The Big Sleep* (1978)
77. *The Magic of Lassie* (1978)
78. *A Tale of Africa* (1981)
79. *Right of Way* (1983)

Stage Plays (On Broadway)

1. *Carry* (1932)
2. *Goodbye Again* (1932)
3. *Spring In Autumn* (1933)
4. *All Good Americans* (1933)
5. *Yellow Jack* (1934)
6. *Divided by Three* (1934)
7. *Page Miss Glory* (1934)
8. *A Journey by Night* (1935)
9. *Harvey* (1947, 1948, 1972)

A Selective List of James Stewart's TV Work

1. "The Windmill" 1955 (GE Theatre series. 30 min.) CBS
2. "The Town With a Past" 1957 (GE Theatre series. 30 min.) CBS
3. "The Trail to Christmas" 1957 (GE Theater series. 30 min.) CBS
4. "Cindy's Fella" 1959 (Startime series. 53 min.) NBC
5. "Flashing Spikes" 1962 (Alcoa Premiere series. 53 min.)
6. "The Jimmy Stewart Show" Procter and Gamble 24 weekly episodes. NBC, 1971.
7. "Harvey" 1972 Hallmark Hall of Fame series. NBC
8. "Hawkins" (Detective series) 1973-1974 CBS

A Selective James Stewart Bibliography

Allyson, June (with Frances Spatz Leighton), *June Allyson*, G.P. Putnam's sons, New York, 1982.

Capra, Frank, *The Name Above the Title*, An Autobiography, MacMillan, New York, 1972.

Eells , George, *Ginger, Loretta and Irene Who?* G.P. Putnam's, New York, 1976.

Eyles, Allan, *James Stewart*, Stein & Day, New York, 1984.

Grady, Billy, *The Irish Peacock*: The Confessions of a Legendary Talent Agent, Arlington House, New Rochelle, NY, 1972.

Hayward, Brooke, *Haywire*, Alfred A. Knopf, 1977.

Hotchner, A. E., *Doris Day, Her Own Story*, William Morrow, New York, 1976.

Kobal, John, *The Art of the Great Hollywood Portrait Photographers, 1925-1940*, Alfred A. Knopf, New York, 1980.

Leigh, Janet, *There Really Was a Hollywood*, Doubleday, New York, 1984.

Logan, Joshua, *Josh: My Up and Down In and Out Life*, Delacorte, New York, 1976.

McClure, Arthur F. (with Ken D. Jones and Alfred E. Twomey), *The Films of James Stewart*, A.S. Barnes and Co., New York, 1970.

Parish, James Robert, *The RKO Gals*, Arlington House, New Rochelle, NY 1974.

——, *The All Americans*, Arlington-House, New York, 1977.

Quirk, Lawrence J. *Margaret Sullavan: Child of Fate*, St. Martin's Press, New York, 1986.

——, *Jane Wyman., The Actress & The Woman*, Dembner, New York, 1986.

——, *Claudette Colbert*, Crown, New York, 1985.

——, *The Films of Joan Crawford* , Citadel, Secaucus, N.J. , 1968

——, *The Films of Robert Taylor*, Citadel, Secaucus, N.J., 1975

——, *The Films of Myrna Loy*, Citadel, Secaucus, N.J., 1980.

——, *The Complete Films of William Powell*, Citadel, Secaucus, N.J., 1986.

———, *Fasten Your Seat Belts: The Passionate Life of Bette Davis*, William Morrow, 1990.

Schoell, William, *Stay Out of the Shower*, Dembner, New York, 1985

Stewart, James, *Jimmy Stewart and His Poems*, Crown, New York, 1989

Teichmann, Howard, *Fonda, My Life*, as told to Howard Teichmann, New American Library, New York, 1981.

Thomas, Tony, *A Wonderful Life, The Films and Career of James Stewart*, Citadel Press, Secaucus, N.J., 1988.

Thompson, Howard, *James Stewart*, Pyramid, New York, 1974.

Selected Periodicals

Quirk's Reviews, Photoplay, Modern Screen, Movie Life, Films in Review, Time, Life, McCall's, Variety, People, Vanity Fair, The New York Times, The New York Herald-Tribune, The Sun, The New York Daily News, Films and Filming, American Film, Take One, TV Times, McCall's, Esquire, TV Guide, Newsweek, Saturday Evening Post, Collier's.

Index

Adams, Julie, 213

Adams, Samuel Hopkins, 70

Adrian, Gilbert, 64

After the Thin Man, 72-73, 322

Afurika Monogatari (A Tale of Africa), 308

Air Force Reserve, 3, 102, 229, 237, 239, 288

Air Force, 3, 102, 143-144, 146, 229-230, 237, 239, 288

Airport 77, 302-303, 323

Albert, Eddie, 173

Albertson, Frank, 81, 157

Aldrich, Robert, 281

Alexander, Ben, 53

Alexander, Ross, 80, 275, 277

Alford, Philip, 277

All Good Americans, 28, 33, 324

All Paris Knows, 42

All Quiet On the Western Front, 53

Allan, Ted, 77

Allen, Gracie, 52

Allyson, June, 158-159, 176-180, 183, 220-221, 230, 252, 319, 325

Altman, Al, 40

American Classic Screen Magazine, 175

American Film Institute Awards, 312

Amory, Cleveland, 190

An Inspector Calls, 116

Anatomy of a Murder, 247-248, 250, 298, 318, 323

Anderson, Herbert, 239

Anderson, John, 40, 44

Anderson, Judith, 34, 37-39, 57, 66

Anna Karenina, 49, 71

Annapolis, 14, 81

Arden, Eve, 249-250

Armstrong, Louis, 221

Army Air Corps, 45, 143, 146-147

Arnold, Edward, 99-101, 115

Arnold, Elliott, 203

Art Trouble, 31

Arthur, Jean, 2, 96, 100-101, 113-114, 173, 198

Artist and the Lady, The, 18

Asher, Jerry, 62, 71, 80, 96, 98, 105, 109, 175, 191

Ashley, Lady [Sylvia], 216

Astaire, Fred, 53

Atkinson, Brooks, 32, 38-39, 167

Atlantic City, 9, 42

Attenborough, Richard, 280-281

Atwill, Lionel, 48

Auer, Mischa, 99-100

Avery, Stephen Morehouse, 70

Ayres, Lew, 53, 86, 108-109

Bacall, Lauren, 226, 301

Back Street, 18

Baker, Carroll, 264, 266, 268

Baker, Melville, 58

Bakewell, Billy, 53

Balalaika, 102

Ballard, Lucien, 266

Bancroft, George, 38

Bandolero!, 285-287, 323

Bardot, Brigitte, 270

Barnes, Binnie, 65

Barrett, James Lee, 285, 293

Barretts of Wimpole Street, The, 34, 94

Barrie, Wendy, 55, 68

Barry, Philip, 130, 133

Barrymore, Diana, 93

Barrymore, Lionel, 70, 72, 81, 83, 99, 101, 156, 193, 303

Battle at Apache Pass, The, 202

Baxter, Anne, 293-294

Beck, John, 206

Behrman, S. N., 126

Belasco, David, 34

Bell, Book and Candle, 246, 319, 323

Bellah, James Warner, 259

Bellwood, Pamela, 303

Belmonti, Nene, 28

Ben-Hur, 247

Bend of the River, 211-212, 323

Benefits Forgot, 83

Bennett, Joan, 136

Benny, Jack, 52

Berkeley, Busby, 140

Bernardine, 64

Bernstein, Elmer, 300

Best, James, 278

Biegler, Paul, 298

Big Sleep, The, 304-305, 323

Big Street, The, 53

Bill of Divorcement, A, 34, 58, 130

Billingsley, Sherman, 187

Biroc, Joseph, 166, 252

bisexuality, 18-19

Blankfort, Michael, 203

Blaustein, Julian, 246

Blondell, Joan, 41

Blood Brother, 203

Blood Money, 38-39

Bloom, Harold Jack, 215

Blue, Monte, 88

Boddy, Manchester, 192-193

Bogart, Humphrey, 305

Bogdanovich, Peter, 295

Bondi, Beulah, 70, 84, 86, 157

Boone, Richard, 301

Booth, Shirley, 255

Border Incident, 197

Borgnine, Ernest, 280

Born to Dance, 66, 137, 300, 322

Borzage, Frank, 74-75, 122, 124-125

Bottome, Phyllis, 124

Boyer, Charles, 134

Brand, Max, 117

Brando, Marlon, 20, 269

Breen, Richard L., 251

Brennan, Walter, 227-228, 264

Brent, George, 104

Brentwood Presbyterian Church, 188, 274

Brentwood, 49, 52, 54, 71, 188, 190, 274, 290

Breslow, Lou, 166

Bressart, Felix, 121

Brice, Monte, 138

Bringing Up Baby, 130

Briskin, Sam, 229

Broadway Melody of 1936, 67

Broadway, 2, 18, 20-23, 31-32, 34, 37-38, 41-42, 44, 49, 57-58, 60, 62, 67, 89, 91, 98-99, 126, 130, 140, 166-167, 179, 205-206, 266, 296-297, 324

Brodney, Oscar, 206, 219

Broken Arrow, 201-203, 323

Brown, Clarence, 72, 83, 85, 134-135

Brown, Joe E., 167

Brown, John Mason, 29, 41

Brown, Tom, 81

Bruce, Virginia, 46-48, 67

Buchanan, Jack, 167

Buckner, Willis, 104

Bundmann, Emil Anton, (Anthony Mann), 197

Burke, Billie, 81

Burks, Robert, 234

Burnett, Dana, 88

Burns, George, 52

Burr, Raymond, 223-224

Burt, Frank, 231

Byington, Spring, 99-100

Cady, Jerome, 163

Cagney, James, 212, 232

Call Northside 777, 163, 166, 322

Call of the Wild, 104

Calvet, Corinne, 227

Camille, 25, 50, 71

Canfield, Alyce, 184

Capra, Frank, 98-101, 113-116, 129, 132, 153-155, 157-161, 320, 325

Carbine Williams, 3, 213-214, 323

Carmichael, Hoagie, 152

Carnegie Tech, 21

Carney, Art, 266

Carradine, John, 85

Carroll, Nancy, 88

Carry Nation, 20, 22

Carson, Robert, 81

Chaffey, Don, 308

Chandler, Jeff, 201-202

Chandler, Joan, 167, 171

Chandler, Raymond, 304

Chaney, Lon, 210

Chaplin, Charles, 138, 141

Chase, Borden, 211, 227, 231, 240

Chase, Mary, 206

Cheyenne Autumn, 267, 269, 323

Cheyenne Social Club, The, 286, 289, 291-292, 323

Chicago, 49, 151, 163-164

Christians, Mady, 75

Ciannelli, Eduardo, 32

Cimarron, 240

City for Conquest, 212

Clark, Candy, 304

Clark, Fred, 203

Clayton, Ethel, 88

Clements, Cal, 284

Clements, Calvin, 283

Clothier, William, 260, 283, 289

Cobb, Lee J., 164, 265, 284

Coburn, Charles, 86, 106

Cocoanut Grove, 52, 54

Cohan, George M., 42

Cohn, Art, 213

Cohn, Harry, 51, 98, 241

Colbert, Claudette, 110-111, 204, 325

Colby, Anita, 184

Cole, Nat King, 152, 186

Collier, Constance, 167, 171-172

Collier, Sr, William, 48

Columbia, 98, 113, 117, 128, 130, 230, 241, 246-247, 258

Come Back, Little Sheba, 255

Come Live With Me, 134-136, 322

Connelly, Marc, 44-45

Conte, Richard, 164

Cook, Fielder, 296

Cooper, Gary, 45, 82, 88, 98, 116, 145, 176, 189, 240

Cooper, Gladys, 37

Cooper, Rocky, 186

Coppel, Alex, 240

Corbett, Glenn, 277

Corey, Wendell, 185, 213-214, 223, 226

Corn Is Green, The, 168

Cornell, Katharine, 31, 34-35, 126, 297

Cortese, Valentina, 193-194

Cortez, Ricardo, 104

Courtney, Inez, 121

Cousy, Bob, 80

Coward, Noël, 36

Cowboy Joe, 29

Cowl, Jane, 25-26, 34

Craig, H.A.L., 302

Crawford, Joan, 2, 69-72, 108-109, 129, 325

Crisp, Donald, 231

Cristal, Linda, 257-258

Cromwell, John, 107

Cronyn, Hume, 170

Crosby, Bing, 285

Crossfire, 185

Crowther, Bosley, 120, 127

Cukor, George, 62, 94, 130-131, 134, 141, 198

Cullinan, Frank, 32

Culver Military Academy, 15

Curtis, Alan, 102

Curtis, Tony, 216

D'Entre Les Morts, 241

Dale, Esther, 20, 22, 28-29

Dall, John, 167-172

Dandy in Aspic, A, 240

Dangerous, 9, 128, 195, 231, 251

Daniels, Bill, 229

Daniels, William, 81, 199, 207, 219-220, 227, 264

Dano, Royal, 212

Daves, Delmer, 201

Davidson, Bill, 195

Davies, Marion, 41, 94, 152

Davies, Valentine, 219, 229

Davis, Bette, 34, 128, 168, 204, 308-309, 325-326

Day, Doris, 232, 325

Dear Brigitte, 270-272, 295, 323

Dee, Frances, 38

DeHavilland, Olivia, 2, 98, 149, 198

Dell, Myrna, 184-185

Demarest, William, 48-49, 165

DeMille, Cecil B., 76, 209-210

Designing Woman, 225

Destry Rides Again, 117-118, 120, 196, 208-209, 227, 322

DeSylva, B.G., 66

Devine, Andy, 261

Devotion, 212, 215, 252, 279

De Wilde, Brandon, 239-240

Diamond, Gangster Legs, 24

Dick, Douglas, 167, 170

Dietrich, Marlene, 117-120, 129, 190, 208-209

Dillingham, Charles, 41

Dillon, Melinda, 311

Divided by Three, 37-41, 44, 66, 324

Dix, Richard, 202

Doherty, Charla, 266

Donald, James, 305

Donat, Robert, 116

Donlevy, Brian, 117

Doren, Philip Van, 154, 157

Dorn, Philip, 139

Douglas, Kirk, 35, 318

Douglas, Melvyn, 70, 76, 121

Dow, Peggy, 206

Dozier, William, 172, 175

Draddy, Gregg, 188

Drake, Charles, 200, 206

Dratler, Jay, 163

Dru, Joanne, 218

Druten, John Van, 246

Dunn, Jimmy, 167

Dunne, Irene, 62, 173

Durango, Mexico, 217

Durbin, Deanna, 125

Duryea, Dan, 200, 218, 240

Ebsen, Buddy, 66

Ecstasy, 134

Eddy, Nelson, 55-57, 102

Edmonds, Walter D., 44

Ellington, Duke, 248

Ellis, Anderson, 125

Elser, Frank B., 44

Ephron, Henry, 266

Epstein, Philip G., 126

Erasmus With Freckles, 270

Ettinger, Margaret, 105

Evans, Gene, 308

Evans, Ray, 234

Evanson, Edith, 171

Fabian, 264, 270-271

Fairbanks Jr, Douglas, 96

Far Country, The, 227-228, 286, 323

Farmer Takes a Wife, The, 44

Farrell, Charles, 74

Fasten Your Seat Belts, 326

Fay, Frank, 166, 205-206, 297

Faye, Alice, 307-308

FBI Story, The, 251-253, 323

Fellow Americans, 146

Fenton, Frank, 192

Fenton, Leslie, 165

Ferguson, Helen, 79, 98, 187, 237

Ferrer, Jose, 206

Fields, W.C., 41

Fighting Father Dunne, 185

Films of Robert Taylor, 325

Finch, Peter, 280-281

Firecreek, 283-286, 323

First Love, 22, 125

Fix, Paul, 278

Flight of the Phoenix, The, 280-281, 323

Flippen, Jay C., 200, 212, 218, 227, 239

Flynn, Thomas T., 231

Fonda, Henry, 2, 11, 18-21, 24-30, 33, 36-37, 39-40, 43-45, 49-50, 52-55, 58, 61, 80, 91, 96, 103, 106-107, 138, 141, 143, 150-153, 165-166, 183, 189, 192, 198, 215, 239-240, 265, 273, 276, 283-286, 288-292, 309, 311-312, 319, 326

Fontaine, Joan, 98, 172, 175, 190

Fools' Parade, 292-295

Ford, Dorothy, 165

Ford, Glenn, 67, 240

Ford, John, 153, 236, 256, 258-259, 261, 264, 267, 269, 278, 282, 295

Forquet, Philippe, 266

Forsyth, Rosemary, 277

"Fox Chain Gang," 47

Fox, Edward, 305

Francis, Kay, 130

Fraser, Ronald, 280-281

Free Soul, A, 108

Friedhofer, Hugo, 203

Friele, Aleta, 80

Friml, Rudolf, 56

Froeschel, George, 125

From Amongst the Dead, 241

Furies, The, 185

Gable, Clark, 62-63, 65, 76-79, 96, 104-105, 107-108, 116, 129, 135, 140, 145, 151, 216, 319

Garbo, Greta, 2, 49-51, 88, 121

Gardner, Hunter, 40

Garland, Judy, 52, 139-140

Garland, Robert, 32

Garter, Mrs. Leslie, 34

Gaynor, Janet, 45, 48, 55, 64-65, 68, 74

Gazzara, Ben, 248-250

Geddes, Barbara Bel, 242

Geer, Will, 200

George, Gladys, 76

Gershenson, Joseph, 199, 220, 227

Gershwin, George, 29

Gerstad, Merrit, 74

Gielgud, John, 38

Gilbert, John, 48

Gingold, Hermione, 247

Girls' Dormitory, 74

Glassberg, Irving, 211

Gleason, Russell, 53

Glenn Miller Story, The, 219, 221, 323

Goddard, Paulette, 137-138, 165

Goldbeck, Willis, 259

Golden Dog, The, 17

Goldwyn, Samuel, 51

Gone With the Wind, 63, 84, 97, 116, 177

Good Earth, The, 76

Good Fairy, The, 58

Good News, 76

Goodbye Again, 20, 23, 25, 33, 58, 324

Goodbye Mr. Chips, 116

Goodman, Benny, 26

Goodrich, Frances, 57, 157

Goodrich, Marcus, 97

Gordon, Mary, 138

Gorelik, Mordecai, 28

Gorgeous Hussy, The, 69, 71, 83, 109, 322

Grady, Billy, 2, 9, 25, 32, 40-41, 44-46, 57, 61, 65, 67-68, 76-77, 79, 83, 92, 96, 109, 124, 133, 143-144, 149-153, 176, 186-189, 272-273, 275, 316, 319, 325

Grahame, Gloria, 157, 185, 211

Granger, Farley, 167, 169, 172

Grant, Kathryn, 249

Granville, Bonita, 307-308

Grapes of Wrath, The, 2, 141

Greatest Gift, The, 157

Greatest Show on Earth, The, 209, 211, 319, 323

Green, Mitzi, 184

Greenstreet, Sydney, 193-194

Gribbon, Harry, 31

Grossel, Ira, 202

Grubb, David, 293

Guffey, Burnett, 255

Hackett, Albert, 57, 157

Haden, Sara, 121, 123

Hagen, Jean, 214

Haight, George, 20

Hailey, Arthur, 302

Haines, 78, 95

Haines, William, 78-79, 95

Hale, Barbara, 203

Hale, Richard, 28

Hale, Scott, 300

Hall, Porter, 173

Halliday, John, 128, 133

Hamilton, Patrick, 170

Hammerstein, Oscar, 57

Hammond, Percy, 39

Harbach, Otto, 57

Harcourt, Dr. Alexander, 313

Harding, Ann, 76

Harding, President Warren G., 10

Hardman, Ric, 283

Hardwicke, Sir Cedric, 167, 171-172

Harlow, Jean, 2, 47, 55, 63-64, 68-69, 73, 300

Harris, Jed, 19, 58

Hart, Moss, 35

Harvey, 1, 3, 166-167, 204-207, 275, 296-298, 323-324

Hasse, John, 270

Hathaway, Henry, 163, 264

Hatfield, Mark, 316

Hatrick, Edgar, 186

Hatrick, Gloria, 186

Hawkins on Murder, 298

Hawkins — Blood Feud, 298

Hawkins — Candidate for Murder, 298

Hawkins — Die, Darling, 298

Hawkins — Murder on the 13th Floor, 298

Hawkins —Murder in Movieland, 298

Hawks, Howard, 304

Hayes, Alfred, 255

Hayes, Helen, 205, 296-297

Hayes, John Michael, 223

Hayward, Brooke, 122, 144, 325

Hayward, Leland, 36, 45, 58, 90, 122, 132, 144, 149, 151, 186

Haywire, 122, 325

Hayworth, Rita, 184

Head, Edith, 226

Healy, Ted, 68-69

Hearst, William Randolph, 94, 186

Hecht, Ben, 110

Heidt, Horace, 138

Heiress, The, 150

Heller, Lukas, 280

Henderson, Marcia, 218

Henry Miller Theatre, 28

Hepburn, Katharine, 2, 34, 58, 128-134, 141, 145, 195, 311, 319

Herrmann, Bernard, 234, 241, 244

Hersholt, Jean, 75

Heston, Charlton, 209-210, 247-248, 320

Heyburn, Weldon, 68

Hickox, Sid, 304

Hinds, Sam, 157

Hinds, Samuel S., 81, 99

Hirschhorn, Clive, 190

Hitchcock, Alfred, 1, 3, 39, 155, 167-172, 223-227, 229, 231-234, 237, 239-245, 247, 249, 275, 320

Hobbes, Halliwell, 174

Hobbs Takes a Vacation, 262, 265, 295, 323

Hodiak, John, 193, 195

Hoffman, Dustin, 312

Hogan, Dick, 167, 169-170

Holiday, 130, 156, 233

Holland, Jack, 97

Hollander, Frederick, 118

Holliday, Doc, 268

Holloway, Jean, 308

Hollywood Talks Turkey, 158-159

Hollywood, 2-3, 7, 12, 18-20, 27, 29, 32, 37, 39-42, 44-47, 49, 51-55, 57, 59, 61, 63, 65, 67, 69, 71, 73, 75-77, 79, 81, 83, 85, 89, 91, 93, 96-97, 108, 113, 118-120, 122, 129-130, 133, 144-145, 148, 150-151, 153, 158-159, 169, 178, 190, 197-198, 203, 206-207, 212, 218, 221, 237, 241, 258, 271-272, 276, 281, 292, 296, 298, 311-313, 317, 320, 325

Home Box Office, 311

Hoover, J. Edgar, 251-254

Hopkins, Miriam, 308

Hopper, Hedda, 39-40, 43, 96, 224, 247

Horne, Victoria, 206

Hotchner, A.E., 232, 325

Hough, Stanley, 285

How the West Was Won, 264-266, 323

Howard, John, 128-129, 133

Howard, Ron, 301

Howard, Shemp, 31

Howard, Sidney, 31

Huddleston, David, 293

Hudson, Rock, 41, 200

Hull, Josephine, 205-206

Hunter, Ian, 134, 136, 139

Huston, Walter, 84-85

Hutton, Betty, 209, 211

Hyatt, Bobby, 213-214

I Dream Too Much, 52

Ice Follies of 1939, 108, 170, 322

Idiot's Delight, 108

Important News, 31

Indiana, Pennsylvania, 5, 8, 13-14, 17, 20, 44, 54, 150, 189, 272-273

Informer, The, 278

It Happened One Night, 98, 111, 129

It's a Wise Child, 21

It's a Wonderful Life, 2, 101, 116, 155-156, 158, 161, 175, 314, 316, 322

It's a Wonderful World, 110, 322

J. M. Stewart and Company, 5

Jackpot, The, 203-205, 323

Jackson, Elizabeth, 5, 11

Jackson, Felix, 117

Jackson, S. M., 5

James Stewart — A Wonderful Life, 312

Jameson, Jerry, 302

Jezebel, 311

Jimmy Stewart and His Poems: By Jimmy Stewart, 313

Jimmy Stewart Show, The, 295-296, 324

Johnny Belinda, 163

Johns, Adela St., 79, 104, 185

Johns, Glynis, 208-209, 270, 272

Johnson, Claude, 264

Johnson, Dorothy, 259

Johnson, Van, 41, 158, 177

Johnston, Laurence E., 21

Jolson, Al, 41

Jones, Ike, 285

Jones, Shirley, 257-258, 289

Journey by Night, A, 44, 324

June, Ray, 66, 139

Kanter, Hal, 270

Kaper, Bronislau, 194

Kastner, Elliott, 304

Katz, Sam, 102

Kaufman, George S., 35

Keighley, William, 126, 128

Keith, Brian, 282-283

Keith, Robert, 32

Kellaway, Cecil, 206

Kelly, Gene, 289-290

Kelly, Grace, 190, 223-224, 226, 312

Kelly, Paul, 81

Kennedy, Arthur, 212, 231, 268-269

Kennedy, George, 279-280, 286, 293

Kennedy, Jack, 118

Kennedy, Joe, 118

Kerr, Geoffrey, 32

Kerr, John, 236

Khan, Prince Aly, 184

Kiesler, Hedwig, (Hedy Lamarr) 134

Kilbride, Percy, 173

King, Henry, 74-75

Kirkland Field, New Mexico, 144

Kiss the Blood Off My Hands, 174-175

Knight Without Armor, 118

Kobal, John, 77, 325

Korngold, Erich Wolfgang, 139

Kostal, Irwin, 307

Koster, Henry, 206-207, 262, 266, 270

Kress, Harold F., 264

Kretzmer, Herbert, 147

Kruger, Hardy, 280

Krupa, Gene, 221

Kuanstle, Charles, 302

LaCava, Gregory, 174

Ladies in Love, 74

Ladies of Leisure, 98

LaMarr, Hedy, 2, 134, 139

Lamour, Dorothy, 165, 209, 318

Lanchester, Elsa, 247

Landi, Elissa, 73

Lane, Lola, 109

Lang, Walter, 203

Langford, Frances, 221

Lassie Come Home, 307

Lassie, 307-308, 323

Last Frontier, The, 230

Last Gangster, The, 80-81, 322

Laszlo, Ernest, 166

Lathrop, Philip, 302

Laurents, Arthur, 170

Leatherbee, Charlie, 16-17

Leavitt, Sam, 249

Lederer, Charles, 236

Lee, Rowland V., 38

Leech, Margaret, 37

Lees, Richard, 311

Leigh, Janet, 215-218, 319, 325

LeMay, General Curtis, 229

Lemmon, Jack, 247, 319

Leon, Walter De, 138

Leonard, Robert Z., 139-140

LeRoy, Mervyn, 251-254

Letter from an Unknown Woman, 174

Levene, Sam, 32-33, 90

Levy, William Turner, 158

Lewis, Diana, 64

Lewis, Tom, 104

Liberty Films, 154, 158

Library Journal, The, 205

Lieber, Perry, 270-271

Light Up the Sky, 35

Lindbergh, Charles, 3, 213, 234, 236, 318

Lindsay, Howard, 20

Little Caesar, 80

Little Man, What Now?, 58

Little Women, 129-130

Livingston, Jay, 234

Locust Valley, Long Island, 37, 42

Logan, Josh, 15-18, 20, 24, 36, 94-95, 189-190, 325

Lombard, Carole, 2, 63, 73, 96, 106, 173

Lone Star, 216

Los Angeles Examiner, 69
Lost Horizon, 98-99
Louis, Jean, 175
Lovejoy, Frank, 229
Loy, Myrna, 63-64, 72, 74, 136, 325
Lu, Lisa, 255
Lubitsch, Ernest, 121
Lunt, Alfred, 140
Lux Radio Theatre, 76
MacDonald, Jeanette, 55
MacDonald, Joe, 164
MacLean, Edwin ("Ned"), 187, 190, 192, 272,
MacLean, Barbara Barondess, 179, 187
MacLean, Evelyn Walsh, 187
MacLean, Michael, 276, 313
MacLean, Ronald, 287
MacMurray, Fred, 165
Madame X, 76
Made for Each Other, 73, 106-108, 322
Madison Square Hotel, 27, 29-30, 45, 53, 290
Magic of Lassie, The, 307-308, 323
Magic Town, 159-163, 322
Magnani, Anna, 255
Magnificent Obsession, 62
Magnolia, 21
Mahin, John Lee, 64, 80
Malaya, 192-194, 322
Malden, Karl, 265
Man from Laramie, The, 230, 239, 323
Man in the Vault, The, 278
Man of the West, 240
Man on Fire, 285
Man Who Knew Too Much, The, 232, 234, 323
Man Who Shot Liberty Valance, The, 258-261, 323
Man's Castle, A, 104
Mancini, Henry, 221, 262
Mandl, Fritz, 136

Mankiewicz, Herman J., 110
Mankiewicz, Joe, 104
Mann, Anthony, 1, 191, 197-199, 201, 211-212, 214, 217, 220, 227, 239, 255, 284, 292
Mann, Daniel, 255-256
Mannix, Eddie, 65-67, 77, 79, 92, 105-106, 124, 135
Mansfield, Louisiana, 15
Manta, Paul, 229
Mantle, Burns, 40
March, Fredric, 158
Marie Antoinette, 93-94
Marin, Edwin L., 68
Markey, Gene, 136
Marquand, Christian, 280
Marshall, Alan, 73
Marshall, E.G., 164
Marshall, George, 117-118, 138, 264
Martin Beck Theatre, 31, 33
Martin, Dean, 285
Martin, Strother, 261, 278, 293
Martin, Tony, 139
Marvin, Lee, 260-261
Massey, Ilona, 102-103
Massey, Raymond, 141, 265
Matthews, Lester, 194
Mature, Victor, 230
Maxwell House Coffee, 76
Mayer, Louis B., 41, 50, 67, 71, 88-89, 111, 130, 134, 137, 176, 300
Mayes, Wendell, 236, 248
Mazurki, Mike, 308
McCarter Theatre, 16
McClain, John, 104
McClelland, Doug, 158, 175
McClintic, Guthrie, 31-33, 35, 37, 39, 44, 140, 189
McCormick, Myron, 10, 13, 17, 20, 23-24, 32-33, 39, 44
McEveety, Vincent, 283
McGiver, John, 264, 266

McGowan, Jack, 66

McGuire, Dorothy, 90, 103, 152, 185

McGuire, William Anthony, 139

McIntire, John, 200, 227

McIntire, Tim, 277

McKinley, Bill, 301

McLaglen, Andrew V., 278, 282, 285, 292

McLeary, Janet, 29

McMullan, James, 277

McNally, Stephen, 200

McNaughton, Ken, 144

McNulty, John, 203

McNutt, Patterson, 134

Meadows, Audrey, 266-267

Meek, Donald, 99, 134, 162

Meeker, Ralph, 215-216

Mellor, William, 213, 262-263

Mencken, Helen, 34-35

Mercer, Johnny, 152

Mercersburg Academy, 12-13, 16-17, 148

Meredith, Burgess, 105, 138, 144, 165

Merkel, Una, 68, 118-119

Merrill, Steven, 313

MGM, 2, 32, 39-41, 46-48, 51, 53-56, 58-59, 61-62, 64, 66-69, 72, 74, 76-80, 83, 88, 90, 94-95, 99, 101-103, 105, 108, 110, 121, 130, 134, 139, 145, 149-151, 159, 175-177, 185, 192-194, 206, 213-214, 226, 264, 298-300, 311

Miles, Sarah, 304

Miles, Vera, 241, 251-252, 260

Milland, Ray, 59

Miller, Ann, 99

Miller, Glenn, 3, 213, 219, 221, 318, 323

Mills, John, 305

Mills, Juliet, 282

Milner, Marty, 236

"Minnie From Trinidad," 139

Miracle Can Happen, A, 165

Mitchell, Clovis, 307

Mitchell, Millard, 200, 215

Mitchell, Thomas, 115-116, 157, 159

Mitchum, Robert, 304-305

Modern Screen, 184, 219, 317, 326

Modern Virgin, A, 18

Moffet Field, Calif., 144

Montgomery, Robert, 32, 77, 143

Moon's Our Home, The, 19, 91

Moore, Victor, 165

Moorehead, Agnes, 265

Morgan, Ainsworth, 70

Morgan, Frank, 120, 123-124, 179-180

Morgan, Harry, 212, 218, 227, 256, 265

Morgan, Ralph, 68

Morley, Robert, 266-267

Morning Glory, 129

Moross, Jerome, 255

Morris, Wayne, 104

Morrow, Honore, 83

Mortal Storm, The, 123-126, 319, 322

Moscow Arts Theatre, 16

Motion Picture Country Home, 188

Motion Picture, 97, 188, 226, 236, 244

Mount Kisco Playhouse, 27

Mountain Road, The, 255, 258, 323

Mourning Becomes Electra, 38

Movie Life, 199, 219, 326

Mowbray, Alan, 204

Mr. Deeds Goes to Town, 98, 116, 159

Mr. Hobbs Takes a Vacation, 262, 265, 295, 323

Mr. Smith Goes to Washington, 2, 4, 84, 97, 113-117, 119, 121, 123, 125, 128-129, 131-133, 139, 141, 155, 158, 162, 314, 322

Mumy, Billy, 270-271

Muni, Paul, 76

Murder Man, 46-48, 58, 322

Murphy, Audie, 239

Murray, Ken, 261

My Darling Clementine, 153
My Man Godfrey, 73, 106
Myers, Henry, 117
Naked Spur, The, 214-217, 323
Nash, Mary, 128
Nation, The, 113, 157
Natwick, Mildred, 20, 22, 28-30
Naughty Marietta, 55
Navy Blue and Gold, 81, 83, 98, 322
NBC, 26, 138, 185, 296, 324
Neff, Bill, 12-13
Neilson, James, 239
Nellor, William, 215
New Statesman, The, 100
New York Daily Mirror, 91, 123
New York Daily News, 40, 326
New York Film Critics' Award, 116, 134, 247
New York Herald-Tribune, The, 49, 62, 81, 91, 123, 126, 225, 326
New York *Post*, The, 29
New York Sun, The, 23, 33, 134
New York Times, The, 32, 37-38, 91, 120, 127, 157, 167, 218, 250, 296, 317, 326
New York World-Telegram, The, 32, 134
Newman, Alfred, 164, 283
Newsweek, 113, 205, 279, 326
Next Time We Love, 52, 58-62, 68, 77, 89, 322
Nicol, Alex, 231
Night at Earl Carroll's, A, 185
Night Passage, 239-240, 323
Ninotchka, 121
Niven, David, 104
No Highway in the Sky, 207-208, 272, 323
No Time for Comedy, 126, 128, 322
Nocturne, 185
Nolan, Jeanette, 261
Norfolk, 18, 146
Norfolk, Virginia, 18

Norman, Frank, 176
Nothing Sacred, 106
Novak, Kim, 190, 241, 244-245, 247, 319
Novarro, Ramon, 78-79
Now, Voyager, 308
O'Brien, Edmond, 261
O'Brien, Hugh, 301
O'Brien, Pat, 41, 185
O'Connell, Arthur, 249-250
O'Donnell, Cathy, 231
O'Hara, John 165-166
O'Hara, Maureen, 263, 282, 319
O'Neil, Barbara, 19, 25
Oberon, Merle, 96, 308
Oboler, Arch, 166
Of Human Bondage, 128
Of Human Hearts, 83, 85, 322
Old Maid, The, 34
Olivier, Laurence, 126, 141
Olsen, Christopher, 233
Omaha Community Playhouse, 20
On Golden Pond, 311
On Our Merry Way, 165-166, 322
Only Yesterday, 18, 27, 58
Orr, Bill, 125
Osborne, Robert, 317
Oscars (Academy Awards), 2-3, 57, 74, 76, 100, 128-129, 132-134, 139-141, 145, 153, 158, 206, 209, 219, 227, 234, 247-248, 259, 278, 291-292, 312
Page Miss Glory, 41, 324
Paget, Debra, 202-203
Palmer, Ernest, 203
Pangborn, Franklin, 78
Parade Magazine, 104
Paramount, 111, 150, 158, 223, 225, 229, 240
Parfumerie, 121
Paris Interlude, 29
Parker, Eleanor, 41

Parker, Willard, 173

Parrott, Ursula, 58

Parsons, Louella, 67, 105, 140, 219, 224

Pasternak, Joe, 117-120

Patterson, Laura, 185

PBS, 312

Peck, Gregory, 159, 226, 265

Pennsylvania, 2, 5, 9-10, 14, 16, 20, 22, 25, 54-55, 57, 102, 150, 189, 272-273, 312

Peppard, George, 264-265

Perelman, S.J., 28

Perkins, Anthony, 239

Perkins, Osgood, 20, 23

Perkins, Tony, 24, 236, 240

Perry, Fred, 104

Perutz, Leo, 44

Peters, Laura, 264

Philadelphia Story, The, 2, 128-130, 132-134, 136, 140-141, 145, 198, 319, 322

Photoplay magazine, 64, 160

Pidgeon, Walter, 89-90, 135

Pons, Lily, 52

Porter, Cole, 66-68

Pot O' Gold, 136-139, 322

Potter, H.C., 89, 173, 175

Powell, Dick, 178

Powell, Eleanor, 2, 55, 66-67, 103, 300

Powell, William, 63-64, 72-73, 76, 325

Power and the Glory, The, 47

Power, Ty, 77, 93

Preminger, Otto, 248

Presbyterian Church, 6, 188, 274, 320

Pressman, Dr. Joel, 111

Preston, Robert, 265

Pride of the Yankees, The, 176

Prince of Wales Theatre, 297

Princeton Univ., 2, 5, 12, 14-15, 17-21, 25, 42, 131, 148, 183, 188

Pritchett, Florence, 180, 182, 184

Psycho, 172, 244

Pulitzer Prize, 34, 206

Purcell, Gertrude, 117

Pyle, Denver, 278

Qualen, John, 75

Quayle, Anthony, 297

Quillan, Eddie, 31

Quine, Richard, 246

Quirk's Reviews, 101, 172, 244, 303, 326

Quirk, Jimmy, 64

Radio City Music Hall, 99

Rapf, Harry, 46, 108

Raphaelson, Samson, 121

Rapper, Irving, 168

Rare Breed, The, 282-283, 323

Ratoff, Gregory, 75, 104

Rawlings, Linus, 264-265

Reagan, Ronald, 3, 163, 186, 320

Rear Window, 223-224, 226, 232, 323

Rebecca, 39, 141, 170, 245

Red Barn Theatre, 42-43

Reed, Donna, 157-159

Reed, Oliver, 305

Remarque, Erich Maria, 53, 88, 118, 138

Remick, Lee, 248-250

Rennie, James, 40

Rettig, Tommy, 203-204

Reynolds, 136, 265

Reynolds, Adeline DeWalt, 136

Reynolds, Debbie, 265

Rice, Florence, 81-83

Riff-Raff, 47

Right of Way, 309, 311-312, 323

Riskin, Robert, 99, 101, 104, 159-161

Ritter, Thelma, 223-224, 265

RKO, 53, 58, 85, 130, 139, 141, 154, 159, 185, 193, 197, 325

Roberts, Curtis, 102

Roberts, Pernell, 307-308

Robinson, Charles, 80-81, 268, 277, 279

Robinson, Edward G., 80, 268

Roemheld, Heinz, 166
Rogers, Cynthia, 22
Rogers, Ginger, 2, 52-55, 85, 88, 96, 109, 141
Roland, Gilbert, 104
Rolfe, Sam, 215
Roman, Ruth, 227
Rome Haul, 44
Romeo and Juliet, 34, 71
Rooney, Mickey, 85, 308
Roosevelt, Elliott, 318
Roosevelt, James, 136-137
Roosevelt, Teddy, 7
Rope, 166-167, 169-172, 189, 196, 223, 322
Rose Marie, 55, 57-58, 322
Rose Tattoo, The, 255
Ross, Katharine, 277
Rothstein, Mervyn, 317
Royer, John, 193
Ruggles, Charlie, 126-127
Rule, Janice, 246
Russell, Kurt, 293
Russell, Rosalind, 126
Ruth, Roy Del, 66
Rutherford, Ann, 85
Ruttenberg, Joseph, 133
Ryan, Robert, 215-218
Saint Joan, 34
Salt, Waldo, 89
Salter, Hans, 211
Santayana, George, 4
Saratoga, 63
Saturday Evening Post, 88, 326
Saturday Review, The, 205
Savalas, Telly, 318
Say Goodbye Again, 58
Schaefer, George, 311
Schary, Dore, 177, 193
Schenck, Nick, 149
Scherle, Victor, 158

Schildkraut, Joseph, 120-123
Schoell, William, 101, 172, 244, 326
Schoff, Michael, 302
Scott, Allan, 20
Scott, Douglas, 81
Scott, George C., 249-250, 318
Scott, Randolph, 133
Screenland, 184
Seitz, John, 166
Selznick, David O., 106-107, 128, 167, 197
Serenade, 198, 221
Sergeant York, 145
Seventh Heaven, 74-75, 77, 322
Shadow of a Doubt, 170, 245
Shamroy, Leon, 107
"Shanty Town," 29
Sharrett, Michael, 307
Shean, Al, 139
Shearer, Norma, 2, 93, 96, 98, 108-109, 175, 198
Shenandoah, 276-280, 323
Sherman, Robert, 307
Shootist, The, 259, 295, 300-301, 323
Shop Around the Corner, The, 18, 120-124, 322
Shopworn Angel, The, 2, 88-92, 322
Shore, Dinah, 320
Shuberts, The, 44
Shute, Nevil, 207-208
Siegel, Don, 300
Sierras, G. Martinez, 28
Sillman, Leonard, 33
Silver Theatre, The, 76
Silvera, Frank, 255
Simon, Paul, 316
Simon, Simone, 74
Sinclair, Robert, 44
Sing Your Way Home, 197
Sircom, Arthur, 28
Skelton, Red, 52

Skinner, Frank, 207
Slacker, The, 8
Small Town Girl, 64-66, 322
Smith, Charles, 121
Smith, Kent, 17, 19, 22, 106, 161
Smith, Senator Margaret Chase, 237
Somborn, Herbert, 104
Sondergaard, Gale, 75
Spada, James, 226
Spanish-American War, 5, 148
Spectator, The, 126
Specter, Arlen, 316
Spector, David, 302
Speed, 51, 53, 68-69, 139, 320, 322
Spiral Staircase, The, 185
Spirit of St. Louis, The, 234, 323
Splendor in the Grass, 204
Spoto, Donald, 226
Spring in Autumn, 28-29, 324
Stack, Robert, 125, 319, 321
Stackpole, Peter, 150-151
Stage Door, 32, 85
Stage Struck, 166
Stagecoach, 42, 117, 259
Stahl, Linda, 316-317
Stallings, Lawrence, 166
Stanislavsky, 16
Stanwyck, Barbara, 79-80, 98, 166, 185, 206
Star Is Born, A, 48
Star, The, 4, 23, 52, 72, 128, 131, 146, 159, 162, 168, 211, 215, 300
StarSpeak, 158
Steak and Beer Club, The, 27
Steiner, Max, 139, 252, 304
Sternberg, Josef Von, 118
Stevens, George, 85-86, 154, 165
Stevens, Inger, 284
Stewart, Alexander, 5-7, 9-10, 12, 14, 54, 153, 274-275
Stewart, Elaine, 239

Stewart, Elizabeth Jackson, 11
Stewart, Gloria, 178, 186, 191, 216, 270
Stone, Lewis, 32, 108-109, 303
Stothart, Herbert, 56, 139
Stradling, Harry, 293
Stradner, Rose, 81
Strangers on a Train, 171-172
Strategic Air Command, 229-230, 323
Stratton Story, The, 158, 175-176, 179, 196, 220, 229, 322
Stratton, Monty, 3, 171, 176-177, 213
Strauss, John, 320
Strickling, Howard, 53-55, 61, 78, 96
Strictly Dishonorable, 18
Sturges, Preston, 18, 197
Sullavan, Margaret, 2, 18, 27, 36, 52, 55, 58-59, 62, 88, 91-92, 106, 120, 124, 126, 132, 198, 273, 300, 319, 325
Sullivan, Barry, 229-230
Surtees, Bruce, 300
Suspicion, 83, 245
Sutherland, Eddie, 104
Swanson, Gloria, 104
Swarthout, Glendon, 300
Swarthout, Miles Hood, 300
Swerling, Jo, 107
Swet, Peter, 104
Swope, John, 11-12, 52, 54, 103, 152, 189-190, 192, 276,283, 319
Sylvia Scarlett, 130
Take Her She's Mine, 266-267, 295, 323
Tale of Africa, A, 308-309, 323
Taradash, Daniel, 246
Taylor, Robert, 62, 64, 70, 76-77, 79, 135, 140, 143, 151, 206, 300, 319, 325
Teasdale, Verree, 134
Ten Commandments, The, 210
Thalberg, Irving, 41, 93
That's Entertainment, 299-300
Thau, Benny, 41, 105

The American Academy of Dramatic Arts, 35

The Boys in the Back Room, 118

Theatre Guild, The, 130

Theatre Intime, 15, 17

These Three, 308

Thin Man, The, 46, 63, 72-73, 172, 322

Thirty-Nine Steps, The, 111

Thomas, Robin, 93

Thomas, Tony, 69, 200, 265, 286, 309, 326

Thordsen, Kelly, 278-280

Thorpe, Richard, 192, 213

Three Comrades, 18, 88, 124

Thunder Bay, 218-219, 323

Tibenham, 146

Tiger Smiles, The, 16

Tin Star, The, 239-240

Tiomkin, Dimitri, 99

To Each His Own, 98, 150

To Hell With the Kaiser, 8

Tobin, Genevieve, 126-127

Tone, Franchot, 70, 76, 109

Tracy, Spencer, 46-47, 73, 76, 119, 130, 132, 140, 189, 192-194, 265

Tracy, William, 120

Traver, Robert, 248

Travers, Henry, 157

Trevor, Elleston, 280

Triangle Club, 2, 15-18

Trocadero, 52

True Grit, 259

Truex, Ernest, 110

Truman, Margaret, 318

Trundy, Natalie, 264

Tunberg, Karl, 173

Turner, Lana, 139-140, 184-185, 249

Turner, Ted, 292

Tutweiler, Thomas, 229

TV Movie and Video Guide, 244

TV Times, 147, 326

20th Century-Fox, 45, 47, 54, 64, 74, 269, 271

Twist, John, 251

Two O'Clock Courage, 197

Two Rode Together, 256-259, 323

United Artists, 136-137

United States Naval Academy, 14

Universal, 18, 27, 58, 60-62, 68-69, 73, 75, 77, 117, 125, 128, 172, 191, 196, 198-199, 218-221, 230, 279, 302

University Players, 16, 18-22, 26, 58

Unsolved Mysteries, 185

Vaccaro, Brenda, 303

Valentine, Joseph, 170

Van Dyke, Woody, 57, 110-111

Vanishing American, The, 202

Variety, 72, 88, 225, 248, 258, 265, 280-281, 297-298, 309, 326

Vars, Henry, 293

Vassar, 21

Vertigo, 1, 155, 240-246, 275, 319, 323

Vidor, King, 165

Vitaphone, 31

Vivacious Lady, 53, 85-86, 88, 322

Voelker, John D., 248

Wade, Jack, 184

"Wait 'Til The Sun Shines, Nellie," 29

Walker, Helen, 164

Walker, Joseph, 99

Walker, June, 45

Walker, Robert, 171

Wallach, Eli, 265

Wallis, Hal, 126

Walsh, Raoul, 236

Waring, Fred, 183

Warner, H.B., 157

Warner, Jack, 126, 170

Warner Bros., 41, 80, 94, 126, 139, 149, 167, 236, 251-252, 300, 311

Warwick, Robert, 48

Washbourne, Mona, 297

Wasserman, Lew, 196, 199

Waterbury, Ruth, 62, 79, 86, 132, 188, 191

Watson, Lucile, 106

Waxman, Franz, 133

Way Down East, 52

Wayne, John, 247, 258-260, 265, 288, 300-302, 319

Wayne, Patrick, 277, 279

Webb, James R., 264

Weidler, Virginia, 128

Welch, Joseph, 248-249

Welch, Raquel, 285-286

Welles, Orson, 184

Wellman, William A., 65, 81, 159

West Falmouth, Mass, 18

West, Claudine, 125

Wheeler, Bert, 166

Whelan, Tim, 46-48

White, Jesse, 206

White, Theodore, 255

Whitehead, Don, 251, 253

Whitney, Jock, 104

Widmark, Richard, 257-258, 268

Wife Versus Secretary, 62, 64, 73, 322

Wilcoxon, Henry, 68, 209

Wilde, Cornel, 209, 211

Wilder, Billy, 236

Williams, Ben Ames, 64

Williams, Carbine, 3, 213-214, 323

Williams, John, 270, 283

Wilson, Marie, 263-264

Winchester '73, 196-202, 211, 286, 322

Windom, William, 299

Windust, Bretaigne, 28

Winner, Michael, 304

Winning Your Wings, 146

Winninger, Charles, 117, 138-139

Winters, Shelley, 200-201

Winwood, Estelle, 35

Withers, Grant, 103

Wolfson, Sonia, 267, 271

Women, The, 108, 132, 180, 183, 218, 252

Wood, Natalie, 203-204

Wood, Sam, 176, 236

Woolrich, Cornell, 223

World War I, 8, 143, 149

World War II, 53, 120, 143, 193, 197, 213, 221, 237, 251

Wrather, Jack, 307

Wright, William, 217

Wyler, William, 58, 62, 90, 171

Wylie, I.A.R., 86

Wynn, Keenan, 186

Yearling, The, 159

Yellow Jack, 31-32, 37, 39, 42, 49, 66, 324

Yordan, Philip, 231

You Can't Take It With You, 7, 98-101, 159, 322

You Gotta Stay Happy, 98, 173-175, 322

"You Stepped Out of a Dream," 140

"You've Got That Look That Leaves Me Weak," 118

Young, Loretta, 103-104

Young, Robert, 76, 81-82, 124, 295

Young, Roland, 128, 174

Yuki, Joe, 221

Yurka, Blanche, 22-23, 28

Zanuck, Darryl F., 201

Ziegfeld Girl, 139-140, 175, 185, 322

Zimbalist, Jr., Efrem 252

Zimbalist, Stephanie, 307-308, 313

Ralph Richardson
An Actor's Life
Updated, Revised and Expanded

GARRY O'CONNOR

"STUNNING . . . THE BEST BIOGRAPHY OF AN ACTOR I'VE EVER READ."
— *NEW YORK TIMES BOOK REVIEW*

"INDISPENSABLE IN ANY THEATRE COLLECTION."
— *LIBRARY JOURNAL*

"*EXEMPLARY:* carefully researched, sensitively attuned to the subject, agreeably written and well documented . . . it reads effortlessly."
— *WASHINGTON POST*

"This is a book to be grateful for, an account of art and life joined into unusual integrity."
— *SUNDAY LONDON TIMES*

"This is *THE MOST EXCITING THEATRICAL BIOGRAPHY I HAVE EVER READ. It is an astounding book, original in form and fascinating in content.*"
— SIR HAROLD HOBSON

"*Garry O'Connor's biography is as DELIGHTFUL AS ITS SUBJECT*"
— RICHARD SCHICKEL, *TIME*

CLOTH • ISBN 1-55783-300-1

APPLAUSE

An Actor and His Time

JOHN GIELGUD

"FUNNY, TOUCHING, BRILLIANT, SPECIAL, THE BEST — EXACTLY LIKE JOHN GIELGUD."
— LAUREN BACALL

"A WONDERFUL BOOK . . . THE RESULT IS MAGICAL . . . GIELGUD IS THE GREATEST ACTOR OF THIS CENTURY . . . WE HAVE NO BETTER CHRONICLER OF THE THEATRE IN HIS TIME . . . AN ASTUTE OBSERVER, A SLY HUMORIST."
— SHERIDAN MORLEY,
THE LITERARY REVIEW

"I CAN HEAR HIS SUPERB VOICE IN EVERY LINE."
— ALEC GUINNESS

"A FASCINATING ACCOUNT OF A LEGENDARY CAREER." — SUNDAY TELEGRAPH

"A RARE DELIGHT — FULL OF WIT, THEATRICAL HISTORY, ANECDOTES, AND WISDOM."
— DIANA RIGG

CLOTH• ISBN 1-55783-299-4

APPLAUSE

SLINGS AND ARROWS

THEATER IN MY LIFE

by Robert Lewis

"A decidedly good read. Breezy, intelligent, and chatty. A stylish, entertaining, and above all theatrical book."

—*The New York Times Book Review*

"He's a marvelous storyteller: gossipy, candid without being cruel, and very funny. This vivid, entertaining book is also one of the most penetrating works to be written about the theater."

—*Publishers Weekly*

"The most interesting book about the theater since Moss Hart's *Act One*."

—**Clifton Fadiman**

"A superior performance."

—*The Los Angeles Times*

paper•ISBN 1-55783-244-7

APPLAUSE

UNFINISHED BUSINESS

A Memoir: 1902–1988

by John Houseman

For over half a century, John Houseman played a commanding role on the American cultural scene. The *dramatis personae* of Houseman's chronicle represents an awesome roster of arts in twentieth century America. When he isn't conspiring with Orson Welles, Virgil Thomson, Archibald McLeish or a dozen others to launch one of five major new theatre organizations, we find him in Hollywood with David O. Selznick, Alfred Hitchcock or Herman Mankiewicz producing one of his eighteen feature films.

In *Unfinished Business,* the 1500 pages of his earlier memoirs, *Run-Through, Front and Center* and *Final Dress* have been distilled into one astonishing volume, with fresh revelations throughout and a riveting new final chapter which brings the Houseman saga to a close.

paper•ISBN 1-55783-024-X

APPLAUSE

THE LIFE AND DEATH OF PETER SELLERS

by ROGER LEWIS,

"IT IS BY FAR THE BEST–WRITTEN, MOST LITERATE CELEBRITY BIOGRAPHY OF THE YEAR ... his research here has staggering breadth and depth, as does his relentless power of insight tempered with humanity ... THIS IS A BLUE–MOON BIOGRAPHY. THEY DON'T COME OFTEN."
—THE HOLLYWOOD REPORTER

"A PROBING, UNCONVENTIONAL, INTENSELY AGILE AND ALERT BIOGRAPHY ... A VIVID PORTRAIT."
— ENTERTAINMENT WEEKLY

"AN EXTENDED MEDITATION ON WHAT MADE SELLERS AN EXTRAORDINARY PERFORMER AND TOXIC HUMAN BEING." — MARK LASWELL, PEOPLE

"EVERYTHING ONE COULD POSSIBLY WANT TO KNOW ABOUT SELLERS IS CONTAINED IN THIS BOOK ..."
— THE NEW YORK TIMES BOOK REVIEW

"UNFORGETTABLE ... AN EPIC MEDITATION ON TALENT AND RAMPANT EGOMANIA ... Lewis' analyses of the films are MASTERLY ... SHREWD, INSIGHTFUL AND FORGIVING." — PUBLISHERS WEEKLY

CLOTH • ISBN 1–55783–248–X

APPLAUSE

MICHAEL CAINE
ACTING IN FILM

An Actor's Take on Movie Making

Academy Award winning actor Michael Caine, internationally acclaimed for his talented performances in movies for over 25 years, reveals secrets for success on screen. *Acting in Film* is also available on video (the BBC Master Class).

"Michael Caine knows the territory...*Acting in Film* is wonderful reading, even for those who would not dream of playing 'Lets Pretend' in front of a camera. Caine's guidance, aimed at novices still dreaming of the big break, can also give hardened critics fresh insights to what it is they're seeing up there on the screen..."
   —Charles Champlin, LOS ANGELES TIMES

"FASCINATING! Wonderfully practical film acting wisdom–all put across in the best Caine style."
   —John Cleese

BOOK/PAPER: $14.95• ISBN: 1-55783-277-3
VIDEO: $29.95 • ISBN: 1-55783-034-7

APPLAUSE

John Gielgud • William Goldman
Michael Caine • Cicely Berry
John Cleese • Eric Bentley
Oliver Stone • John Patrick Shanley
Alan Zweibel• John Russell Brown
Paddy Chayefsky • Steve Tesich
Harold Clurman • Sonia Moore
Bruce Joel Rubin • Janet Suzman
Josef Svoboda • Jerry Sterner
Stephen Sondheim • Larry Gelbart